African American History

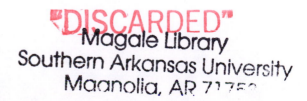

African American History

Volume 3

Editor

Kibibi V. Mack-Shelton, PhD

Claflin University

SALEM PRESS

A Division of EBSCO Information Services, Inc.

Ipswich, Massachusetts

GREY HOUSE PUBLISHING

Some of the updated and revised essays in this work originally appeared in the following titles from the *Great Lives from History series: The 17th Century* (2005), *The 18th Century* (2006), *The 19th Century* (2006), *The 20th Century* (2008), *African Americans* (2011).

Publisher's Cataloging-In-Publication Data
(Prepared by The Donohue Group, Inc.)

Names: Mack-Shelton, Kibibi, 1955- editor.
Title: Great events from history. African American history / editor, Kibibi V. Mack-Shelton, PhD, Clafin University.
Other Titles: African American history
Description: [First edition]. | Ipswich, Massachusetts : Salem Press, a division of EBSCO Information Services, Inc.; Amenia, NY : Grey House Publishing, [2017] | Includes bibliographical references and index.
Identifiers: ISBN 978-1-68217-152-3 (set) | ISBN 978-1-68217-154-7 (v.1) | ISBN 978-1-68217-155-4 (v.2) | ISBN 978-1-68217-156-1 (v.3)
Subjects: LCSH: African Americans—History.
Classification: LCC E185 .G74 2017 | DDC 973/.0496073—dc23

First Printing
Printed in the United States of America

CONTENTS

Volume 3

Appendixes

Indexes

COMPLETE LIST OF CONTENTS

MOYNIHAN REPORT

Published in 1965

This report was received negatively in African American circles.

Identification: Report issued by a social scientist that tried to explain the high levels of poverty in African American communities

One explanation for high levels of impoverishment in black communities was published in *The Negro Family* (1965), by Daniel Patrick Moynihan, a white social scientist of Irish descent who later became a U.S. senator. By postulating that "the family structure of the lower-class Negroes is highly unstable," the Moynihan Report argued that family deterioration was at the heart of high unemployment, welfare dependency, low achievement, and crime. In Moynihan's view, black communities were enmeshed in a "tangle of pathology." The report relied heavily on earlier observations by E. Franklin Frazier (1932), who conceptualized lowerclass culture as disorganized and pathological. This thesis has since been used by others who contend that disadvantaged poor and minority groups encourage cultural practices that fuel their continued poverty.

Reaction to the Moynihan Report was generally negative on the part of leaders of the Civil Rights movement—especially clear when the report's conclusions were dismissed by those participating in the November, 1965, meeting of the White House Conference on Civil Rights. The idea that poverty is caused by subcultural patterns has implications for public policy. Instead of focusing on federal efforts to ensure good jobs, housing, education, health care, and income maintenance, those who hold this view focus on improving the character of individuals and fami lies. Critics of the report said that this culture-of-poverty theory was a form of victim blaming that ignored societal and institutional structures—such as unequal access to jobs, segregated education, and unaffordable, deteriorating housing—that make groups who are discriminated against more susceptible to poverty and the problems it causes for families and communities. Poor and minority people have the same values as those in more advantaged sectors of society, but their barriers to achievement are much greater.

This culture-of-poverty perspective continues to offend and enrage many people, including African Americans, civil rights workers, and progressive community and government activists.

—Eleanor A. LaPointe

See also: Economic trends; Moynihan report, revisited; Slavery and race relations

KWANZAA CELEBRATION

Originated 1966

Dates: December 26-January 1

Maulana Karenga, Ph.D. is the organizer of the Los Angeles-based group, the US, that created the Kwanzaa celebration and holiday in 1966. Karenga is now the chair of the Africana Studies at California State University, Long Beach. The Kwanzaa holiday is an African American and Pan-African holiday, celebrated from December 26th through January 1st. It is a symbol of racial pride. The term Kwanzaa comes from the Swahili phrase, "mutanda ya kwanza" which means "first fruits." First fruits celebrations take place in the kingdoms of Ashanti, ancient Nubia, and Egypt, and amongst the empires of the Zulu and southeastern African empires.

A woman lighting kinara candles

The Kwanzaa holiday is an outgrowth of black cultural, national and liberation movements of the 1960s and 1970s where African Americans looked back to African traditions to recapture the history and culture lost through the Transatlantic Slave Trade and hundreds of years of slavery and Jim Crow. Kwanzaa follows the idea of *Kawaida*, "total way of life" through the following of African principles. Through the adoption of West African clothing, rituals, and the Swahili language, the Kwanzaa celebration emerged.

The Kwanzaa celebration, according to the official doctrine and website of the founders, is a time for celebration, renewing and reaffirming bonds between peoples, reverence for ancestors, thankfulness for the bounty of food and blessings, lessons for honor and respect, recommitment to cultural ideals and African practices, and time for the community, culture, divine, and natural. Kwanzaa holds to the Seven Principles known as *Nguzo Saba*. There are seven days of celebration. A principle in Swahili represents each day. They are Umoja (Unity), *Kujichagulia* (self-determination), *Ujima* (collective work and responsibility), *Ujamaa* (cooperative economics), *Nia* (purpose), *Kuumba* (creativity), and *Imani* (faith).

Kwanzaa celebretions and ceremonies are not afflitated with any organized religion, but are celebrated throughout the world. The ceremonies and celebrations often include the use of a kenti cloth (from Ghana culture), a candeleholder, with candles the color of the kenti cloth in Ghana culture. Black for people, green for the land, and red for the earth.

BROWN INTRODUCES FUNK MUSIC
March 15, 1966

Master rhythm-and-blues and soul singer James Brown won his first Grammy Award for his 1965 recording "Papa's Got a Brand New Bag," signaling the invention of funk.

Locale: Los Angeles, California
Category: Music

KEY FIGURES
James Brown (1933-2006), African American singer and musician
Syd Nathan (1904-1968), founder of the independent King Records in 1943, who signed James Brown to a recording contract in 1956
Ben Bart (1906-1968), Brown's agent and mentor

SUMMARY OF EVENT
On March 15, 1966, the National Academy of Recording Arts and Sciences (NARAS) awarded James Brown his first Grammy for his composition "Papa's Got a Brand New Bag" as the best rhythm-and-blues single of 1965. The recording had been a number-one soul hit and had even reached number eight on the *Billboard* pop chart. It was both a culmination of Brown's work since 1956, when he made his first recording for King Records, and a sign of a significant change in his music that would mark his work through the 1980's.

Brown performing in 1973 By Heinrich Klaffs

Brown had invented funk—a musical style that returned black music to its roots and eschewed some of the modified and more mainstream styles of the soul music of 1960's, which often dabbled in crossover styles, sweetened musical textures, and pop instrumentation. Funk music utilizes an instrumental sound based on a hypnotically riffing band working off a one-chord style. Brown himself developed his band's sound this way beginning in the mid-1960's, with reeds and horns doing staccato bursts and an electric guitar playing choked chords.

From 1965 on, Brown experimented further with this kind of backing for his voice. His raw vocal style stemmed from hard black gospel influences and from the work of earlier rhythm-and-blues shouters. His rich baritone voice could reach into falsetto, could scream and shriek in the agony of his passionate love songs, and yet could also produce warm and caressing tones; his voice was an infinitely subtle and versatile instrument for his own compositions.

By 1965, he was a major figure, live and on record, among black audiences. His kinetic live show featured large bands and many backup singers, and his continuous movement and creative dancing had become the biggest draw in black show business. A master of the one-nighter and the "chitlin' circuit" of black venues, Brown never rested on his laurels. Along with performers such as Ray Charles, Otis Redding, Wilson Pickette, and Aretha Franklin, how would epitomize soul. Fron 1965 on, he evolved his style into its funk phase, using polyrhythmic bass and chanted and semi-spoken vocals that anticipated the development of rap music.

Born in rural poverty in Barnwell, South Caroline, in 1933, Brown was the child of a broken family. Imprisoned for petty theft in 1949, he spent three years rethinking the directly of his life and decided to pursue music. After his release, he joined a gospel group that became a local success. Imitating the earlier jump-band stylings of Louis Jordan and His Tympany five and heavily influenced by such performers as Little Richard and Hank Ballard and the Midnighters, Brown and his friends sought broader exposure than they could get around August and Macon, Georgia. Their chance came in 1956 when a scout from King Records in Cincinnati listened to a demo of Brown's own "Please, Please, Please" and recommended them to label head Syd Nathan. Traveling to the Ohio studio, Brown and his vocal group, The Famous Flames, recorded the song with King studio musicians. "Please, Please, Please" made it to number five on the soul charts.

For Brown, Nathan became both a father figure and a challenge. Nathan was more comfortable with the less raw talents who were crossing over easily into the burgeoning rock-and-roll field. Nathan was an astute businessman who combined all the functions of recording and producing his records in one plant in Cincinnati. His producers scouted the South for talent and knew their market and its preferences. Yet Nathan simply seemed to think that Brown's music was not polished enough to merit much attention or publicity. Fortunately for Brown, his relentless touring and his development of a masterful stage show gave him a security and base on which to build, independent

of the whims of Nathan and his release schedule for singles—which were often issued long after they were cut in the studio.

In 1959, Brown signed a contract with Ben Bart, the agent and founder of Universal Attractions in New York. Experienced with black artists, Bart would become a more benign father figure for Brown, an astute business partner, and, later, Brown's manager. Brown and Bart wanted to capture on record the full force of Brown's live show, so his spontaneity and interaction with an audience could be conveyed to a wider home market. In 1962, they succeeded over the opposition of Nathan. *Live at the Apollo* became a huge hit album, even reaching a pop audience as number two on the *Billboard* chart. With his 1964 song "Out of Sight" he started to move his sound toward the funk style he would popularize the following year.

SIGNIFICANCE

With the recognition he received as a Grammy winner, Brown started to appear on national television and to achieve more freedom at King Records, with which he remained affiliated until 1971. More live albums followed, and more pop success. A song such as "It's a Man's Man's Man's World" was easily a number-one soul music hit, but it also managed to be a number-eight pop success. Brown, though, had never been an artist to stick to the formulas guaranteeing continued crossover acceptance. Going his own way, he began to further intensify his funk groove, changing band members and writing pieces of social commentary often called "message" songs.

As black popular music evolved in the 1960's and 1970's, Brown would be a pathfinder as well as an exemplar. Like other pioneer soul artists such as Ray Charles, Aretha Franklin, and Otis Redding, Brown helped bring the passionate singing styles of black gospel into secular music of black pride and awareness, but he differed from them in his sense of the need for a controlled and totally integral musical experience: song, backup instrumentation, dance, vocal backup, and audience interaction.

Brown's recordings continued to reflect the diversity of his repertoire. His most enterprising material, though, turned out to be the socially conscious songs he wrote in the later 1960's and into the 1970's, when African Americans became increasingly involved with civil rights and initiatives and themes of black pride. Brown spearheaded the musical involvement of African Americans in this era. Performing more as a chanting or talking preacher and testifier than as a singer, Brown created a series of classics in the funk groove: "Get It Together," "Talkin' Loud and Sayin' Nothing," "Get Up, Get into It, and Get Involved," "Soul Power," "Say It Loud—I'm Black and I'm Proud," and most remarkably, "King Heroin" and "Public Enemy #1," in which he scorned drug-taking.

In "Brother Rapp" and "Rapp Payback (Where Iz Moses)," from 1970 and 1980, respectively, Brown pioneered rap music. As early as 1966, he had put out his "Don't Be a Dropout," which addressed serious issues of black educational achievement.

While expanding soul music into funk and rap, Brown continued to sing passionate songs about the tensions in male-female relationships. Truly prodigious in the reach of his music-making and enduring exploration

of styles, Brown expanded the possibilities of black expression and gave contemporaries such as Wilson Pickett the courage to take their hard gospel-based singing styles into a broader market. Never abandoning his African American cultural and musical roots, Brown was a tradition-based "man of words" who put an indelible mark on the American scene.

—*Frederick E. Danker*

See also: Mahalia Jackson Begins Her Recording Career; Davis Develops 1950's Cool Jazz; Berry's "Maybellene" Popularizes Rock and Roll; Gordy Founds Motown Records; Hendrix Releases Acid Rock Album *Are You Experienced?*; Davis Introduces Jazz-Rock Fusion.

BROOKE BECOMES THE FIRST AFRICAN AMERICAN U.S. SENATOR SINCE RECONSTRUCTION
January 10, 1967

Edward William Brooke's popular election to the Senate made him the first black senator since Reconstruction and demonstrated that an African American could be elected to national office in a northern state that had only a small percentage of blacks in the electorate.

Locale: Washington, D.C.; Massachusetts
Categories: Government and politics; civil rights and liberties

KEY FIGURES
Edward William Brooke (b. 1919), African American, Republican U.S. senator
Hiram Rhoades Revels (1822-1901), first African American to serve as a U.S. senator, 1870-1871
Blanche Kelso Bruce (1841-1898), second African American to serve as a U.S. senator and the first to serve a full six-year term, 1875-1881
P. B. S. Pinchback (1837-1921), African American appointed to the U.S. Senate by the Louisiana legislature in 1873, whose seat was refused by the Senate

SUMMARY OF EVENT
Edward William Brooke's election to the U.S. Senate was a significant event in the history of the civil rights struggle in the 1960's. Before the passage of the

Seventeenth Amendment to the U.S. Constitution in 1913, all U.S. senators were appointed by their respective state legislatures. Brooke had been directly and popularly elected in a state in which African Americans were a small minority of the population, marking a significant point in the argument that northerners could overcome any residual racism to elect an African American to national office.

Brooke was not the first African American to sit in the Senate. Hiram Rhoades Revels was the first African American to serve as a U.S. senator. Mississippi's Reconstruction legislature appointed Revels to fill the seat vacated by Jefferson Davis, who left the Senate to become the president of the Confederacy. Revels served from February 25, 1870, to March 4, 1871. Blanche Kelso Bruce was the second African American to serve as a U.S. senator and the first to serve a full six-year term (1875-1881). Bruce was appointed by Mississippi's Reconstruction legislature in 1874. P. B. S. Pinchback was appointed to the Senate in 1873 by Louisiana's Reconstruction legislature, but the Senate challenged that election and refused to allow Pinchback to take his seat. He did, however, successfully sue for the salary he would have earned if allowed to take the Senate seat.

These elections took place during the military Reconstruction period in the South after the American

Civil War. State legislatures were effectively controlled by the northern occupying military forces. Former Confederate sympathizers were not permitted to be elected and the legislatures had overwhelming Republican majorities, including a number of African Americans. After Reconstruction, which ended in 1876 with the withdrawal of northern troops, white southerners gradually introduced legal segregation and denied African Americans the right to vote. It became impossible for an African American to hold a Senate seat from the South even into the twenty-first century.

Brooke was especially well qualified to break the race barrier, which had kept African Americans out of the Senate for more than eighty years. Born on October 26, 1919, in Washington, D.C., he graduated from Howard University in 1941. He became an officer—a rarity for African Americans—in the U.S. armed forces during World War II. After the war, Brooke earned a law degree and an additional graduate law degree from Boston University. He ran unsuccessfully as a Republican candidate for the Massachusetts legislature in 1950 and 1952. Withdrawing temporarily from politics to establish a successful legal career, he ran for Massachusetts secretary of state in 1960 but lost in a very close election.

Appointed chair of the Boston finance commission, he attracted so much positive publicity that he was elected Massachusetts state attorney general in 1962 and reelected in 1964 by the largest margin ever received by a Massachusetts Republican. In his four years as attorney general, he investigated numerous corruption cases against state politicians and was also a prosecutor of organized crime.

In 1966, Brooke was an obvious choice for the Republican nomination for the Senate. To prepare for the campaign, he wrote a well-received analysis of the Democratic domination of Congress. He then won the general election in a landslide, defeating Democrat Endicott Peabody, former governor of Massachusetts, by a vote of 58 to 42 percent. Brooke was sworn in as the first popularly elected African American senator on January 10, 1967. Compiling a moderate voting record, he won reelection easily in 1972 by an even wider margin over Democrat John Droney.

During his second term, Brooke went through a difficultu and well-publicized divorce. Among other issues, his daughter alleged that he had engaged in financial improprieties. Although a Senate ethics committee ultimately found that his violation of the Sentae's professional conduct rules was a trivial one, that judgment came too late to save his candidacy for a third term in 1978. His popularity had dropped significantly, and he faced as major challenger in Paul Tsongas. Tsongas defeated him by a margin of 55 to 41 percent.

After leaving the Senate, Brooke practiced law and was a member of a commission on low-income housing. He became a chair of the Boston Bank of Commerce in 1984 and retired to a farm in Massachusetts. President George W. Bush awarded Brooke the Presidential Medal of Freedom on June 23, 2004.

SIGNIFICANCE

Brooke's popular election to the Senate demonstrated that an African American could be elected to a major national office in Massachusetts, a northern state with a small percentage of African Americans in the electorate. His election was especially significant in the contest of the large Civil Rights movement in the United States. Most of the focus of the movement was on de jure segregation (or segregation imposed by law) in the southern states. Under this type of pressure, southerners accused northerners of hypocrisy, pointing to considerable racism and de fact segregation (segregation in fact) in northern states.

Although there had been a number of African Americans in the U.S. House of Representatives, they all had been elected from congressional districts with a a large percentage, if not a majority, of African American residents. that there were no African American senators or governors (and no state with an African American majority populate) was taken as evident that northerners were no more likely than southerners to vote for an African American for national office. Brooke's earlier election as Massachusetts attorney general helped counter this argument, but his election as a senator was far more effective because of the high visibility of the office. Many committed civil rights supporters in the North pointed to Brooke's election as evidence that racism could be overcome in the United States.

—*Richard L. Wilson*

See also: Supreme Court Rules African American Disenfranchisement Unconstitutional; Truman Orders Desegregation of U.S. Armed Forces; Council of Federated Organizations Registers African Americans to Vote; Supreme Court Prohibits Racial Discrimination in Public Accommodations; Marshall Becomes the First African American Supreme Court Justice; Chisholm Becomes the First African American Woman Elected to Congress.

HENDRIX RELEASES ACID ROCK ALBUM *ARE YOU EXPERIENCED?*

May 12, 1967

The heavy psychedelic blues and guitar virtuosity of Jimi Hendrix created a new rock genre called "acid rock" and pointed the way to the fusion and heavy metal genres.

Locale: United Kingdom
Categories: Music; cultural and intellectual history; popular culture

KEY FIGURES

Jimi Hendrix (1942-1970), guitarist and songwriter who fused blues with hard rock, surreal lyrics, and inventive, pyrotechnic sounds

Chas Chandler (1948-1996), former bassist for the Animals who became Hendrix's manager

Mitch Mitchell (b. 1946), drummer with Hendrix's first band

Noel Redding (1945-2003), guitarist turned bassist, who played with Hendrix's band

SUMMARY OF EVENT

When *Are You Experienced?* was released in the United Kingdom in May, 1967, the rock revolution of the 1960's in many respects had yet to reach its fullest flowering. Bob Dylan had recorded his classic trilogy combining visionary lyrics with folk rock; the Beatles had released *Revolver*, which fused a psychedelic pop sound with Dylan-influenced lyrics; and the Rolling Stones had recorded *Aftermath*, but nothing like the slabs of sound and feedback thrown from Jimi Hendrix's guitar had been heard.

The drug-influenced lyrics and aggressive sexuality of *Are You Experienced?* were accompanied by pounding rhythms and heavy guitar feedback, slashing power chords, and screaming guitar leads. Hendrix's manager, Chas Chandler, took advantage in his production of recent advances in recording-studio technology to create stereo effects that complemented the otherworldly textures Hendrix summoned from his guitar. On the instrumental "Third Stone from the Sun," Hendrix created science-fiction paintings in sound over Mitch Mitchell's jazzy drums; on the album's title track, Hendrix played a howling guitar lead that sounded as if it were being played backward. It was a distinctive sound that some have labeled "psychedelic blues." In the months prior to the album's release, Hendrix had become a sensation in England, guided by the careful management of

Chandler, the former bassist for the Animals, a popular British rock band. Before Chandler heard him playing in Greenwich Village, Hendrix had honed his skills for years as a sideman for the Isley Brothers, Little Richard, and many others, listening to the great blues guitarists and taking what he liked from each of their styles. By the mid-1960's, the Seattle-born Hendrix was living in New York City and playing small Greenwich Village bars. He became interested in the possibilities of guitar feedback after hearing recordings of the Who, while his discovery of Dylan influenced Hendrix's lyrics and convinced him that his voice was good enough to front a band.

When Hendrix's first band, the Jimi Hendrix Experience, played the Monterey International Pop Festival in June, 1967, Hendrix amazed an American audience only distantly familiar with his work by doing an innovative cover of Dylan's "Like a Rolling Stone," playing his guitar behind his back and with his teeth, and lighting his guitar on fire and smashing it at the end of his set. Sales of *Are You Experienced?* took off. The album stayed on the *Billboard* charts for 106 weeks and sold more than one million copies.

The rest of Hendrix's life is the archetypal story of the 1960's rock star. He toured incessantly, breaking box-office records, and continued experimenting with music. He saw the Mothers of Invention using a wah-wah pedal, a foot-controlled guitar attachment that radically changes the timbre of the instrument, and was soon using it so well that many associate the device with his music. The wah-wah and Hendrix's songwriting skills were prominently featured on his more restrained second album, *Axis: Bold as Love* (1968). On his third album, the double set *Electric Ladyland (*1968), Hendrix broke away from the formula of his first two albums. Several tracks are long jams with other musicians such as keyboard player Steve Winwood of Traffic, bassist Jack Casady of the Jefferson Airplane, and old friend Buddy Miles, a drummer. Some songs use multiple tracks of wah-wah guitar, while others display jazz and soul influences. Hendrix at this time was reportedly the highest-paid act in rock, with concerts grossing a minimum of $50,000 per show.

Hendrix's personal life, however, was falling apart. He was spending money on cars that he would quickly destroy in accidents; he often got violently drunk and was taking ever-larger amounts of drugs. Despite his artistic success, Hendrix was beginning to feel trapped in the role of guitar hero. He was tired of constant touring, of playing "Purple Haze" and his other early hits over and over again for audiences not interested in his newer material.

At the Woodstock Music and Art Fair in August, 1969, with the Vietnam protests in full swing, Hendrix gave one of his most memorable performances, one indelibly associated with the counter-culture of the 1960s. On the final day of the festival, shortly after dawn, Hendrix climaxed a brief set by playing a free-form version of "The Star-Spangled Banner." Using his trademark feedback and vibrato bar ("whammy bar") effects, Hendrix caused his guitar to howl and explode with the sounds of jets and falling bombs, turning the patriotic anthem on its head to capture the frustrations and contradictions of the 1960s generation.

On January 1, 1970, Hendrix recorded the live *Band of Gypsys* album with Cox and Miles. Chandler was worried, fearing that this all-black band would alienate Hendrix's mostly white audience. The uneven *Ban of Gypsys* included "Machine Gun," a virtuoso display in which Hendrix made his guitar sound like a machine gun and again imitated the sound of falling bombs.

After Woodstock, Hendrix worked on concert films and began recording material for a new double album. He was in bad shape as the result of his constant drug use, however, and felt more trapped than ever by his earlier image. He wanted to straighten out his life by switching to new management and taking his music in a different direction. He had been playing with diverse musicians and wanted to continue to grow as an artist. Hendrix was interested in writing for and playing with a big band, and he had arranged for rehearsals to begin with Gil Evans and his orchestra in late September of 1970.

It never happened. On September 18, 1970, at the age of twenty-seven, Hendrix choked to death after taking too many sleeping pills. Many believe that he was on the threshold of a major new direction that may have found him playing with avant-garde jazz musicians. His last true studio album, *The Cry of Love*, taken from studio material recorded in the months before his death, was released shortly thereafter; the album found Hendrix turning away from hard rock and feedback in favor of bluesy songs.

SIGNIFICANCE

Hendrix's mature period lasted only four years, but his work has had a tremendous effect on rock and jazz, and to a lesser degree, blues and soul. Many critics believe that Hendrix was the single most important instrumentalist in the history of rock and consider the scope of his influence equal to that of musicians such as Elvis Presley, Chuck Berry, and Bob Dylan.

If Muddy Waters updated Delta blues by picking up the tempo and adding electric amplification, Hendrix updated Waters's urban blues by integrating it with rock and turning the amplification into howling feedback, using a whammy bar to mimic the glissando of the slide guitar favored by many old bluesmen, and modifying the tone with wah-wah pedals, fuzz boxes, and other technological tricks. While the hardware Hendrix used is primitive by later standards, he demonstrated persuasively that technology had much to offer musicians, and his constant experimentation with guitar sound and texture was the precursor to the work of Pat Metheny, David Gilmour of Pink Floyd, and Robert Fripp and Adrian Belew of King Crimson.

An entire generation of young guitarists was influenced by Hendrix. His influence is easily discernible, for example, in the work of Robin Trower, Stevie Ray Vaughan, and Nils Lofgren, three prominent guitarists who rose to stardom after his death. Virtually anyone who modifies instruments with a wah-wah pedal is influenced by Hendrix's use of the device. Despite the excellent use of the wah-wah pedal by Eric Clapton and Frank Zappa at about the same time, the wah-wah's distinctive sound has become indelibly linked with the lead guitar style of Hendrix.

Hendrix imitators sprang up quickly. Blue Cheer, a power trio that was also fronted by overdriven guitar manipulated by a whammy bar, put out its first album about a year after Hendrix did. The vicious wah-wah guitar on the first two Stooges albums, recorded in 1969 and 1970, shows how quickly some of the more superficial elements of Hendrix's style were assimilated by other guitarists.

More than anyone else, he was the master, the standard by which other guitarists were judged. The long guitar solos of late 1960's and 1970's rock were partly an outgrowth of Hendrix's live style, as the guitar-hero image Hendrix helped create led to the glorification of guitar technique. Heavy-metal bands picked up on Hendrix's use of feedback, overdriven amplifiers, and power chords. Later guitarists such as Eddie Van Halen are flashy descendants of Hendrix.

In the early 1970's, bands with a guitar-centered sound inspired by Hendrix flourished. Frank Marino, the guitarist of the heavy-metal trio Mahogany Rush, even claimed to have been visited by Hendrix's ghost. While heavy metal evolved principally from the work of Clapton and other British blues-rock musicians, the genre's heavy guitar sound is virtually unthinkable without Hendrix. Rock guitarists as diverse as Neal Schon of Journey and Brian May of Queen owe debts to Hendrix, as do jazz guitarists Lee Ritenour and Metheny. The funkier sound Hendrix used with the Band of Gypsys was an important influence on the psychedelic soul records of the late 1960's and 1970's, including the work of Curtis Mayfield and Sly and the Family Stone. Albums by the Isley Brothers from the late 1960's on also bear Hendrix's stamp. Funkadelic's free-form music, with its numerous guitarists playing over a groove, also was affected by Hendrix's sound, as was their flamboyant dress. Prince owes a similar debt to Hendrix.

When *Are You Experienced?* was released, jazz had not assimilated the possibilities of electric guitar to anywhere near the degree that rock had. Many jazz musicians, however, took note of Hendrix's phrasings, the textures and sounds of his guitar, and the way he incorporated elements of jazz into rock. Hendrix, whose own guitar sound was influenced by the saxophone playing of John Coltrane, often played guitar in a way that made the instrument sound like a horn. This guitar/horn sound influenced a generation of jazz guitarists in the 1970's and 1980's.

By the time of Hendrix's death, jazz was beginning to explore the use of the electric guitar and other elements of rock. In the late 1960's, Miles Davis began to unite elements of rock with jazz, giving rise to the genre known as fusion. Hendrix played with many of the musicians who played on Davis's groundbreaking 1969 album, *Bitches Brew*. On *Bitches Brew* and on several albums from the 1970's, Davis is clearly influenced by Hendrix's work, even processing his trumpet and organ through a wah-wah pedal. Davis said at the time that he would have used Hendrix as the guitarist for his 1975 release *Agharta*.

According to the prestigious jazz magazine *Down Beat*, most jazz-rock fusion musicians cited Hendrix, along with Coltrane and Davis, as their major influence. Jazz guitarist Al DiMeola, who was a teenager when *Are You Experienced?* came out, has related how the sounds Hendrix wrung from his guitar were a primary influence. The funky, multitracked sound used for several pieces on *The Cry of Love* were an influence on the electric Prime Time band that Ornette Coleman formed during the 1970's. Finally, Hendrix's skill as a song interpreter sometimes influenced even those who wrote the original songs. When Dylan rerecorded his "All Along the Watchtower" in 1974, his new arrangement was clearly inspired by the powerful version of that song that Hendrix recorded on *Electric Ladyland*.

—*Scott M. Lewis*

See also: Berry's "Maybellene" Popularizes Rock and Roll; Gordy Founds Motown Records.

REITMAN V. MULKEY

May 29, 1967

The Supreme Court found a housing provision in the California state constitution to be unconstitutional because it involved the state in private racial discrimination.

The Case: U.S. Supreme Court ruling on housing
   discrimination

In 1959 and 1963, California established fair housing laws. These statutes banned racial discrimination in the sale or rental of private housing. In 1964, acting under the initiative process, the California electorate passed Proposition 14. This measure amended the state constitution so as to prohibit the state government from denying the right of any person to sell, lease, or refuse to sell or lease his or her property to another at his or her sole discretion. The fair housing laws were effectively repealed. Mr. and Mrs. Lincoln Mulkey sued Neil Reitman in a state court, claiming that he had refused to rent them an apartment because of their race. They claimed that Proposition 14 was invalid because it violated the equal protection clause of the Fourteenth Amendment. If Proposition 14 was unconstitutional, the fair housing laws would still be in force. The Mulkeys won in the California Supreme Court, and Reitman appealed to the Supreme Court of the United States.

Justice Byron White's opinion for the five-justice majority admitted that mere repeal of an antidiscrimination statute would not be unconstitutional. In this case, however, the California Supreme Court had held that the intent of Proposition 14 was to encourage and authorize private racial discrimination. This encouragement amounted to "state action" that violated the equal protection clause of the Fourteenth Amendment.

The four dissenters in the case agreed on an opinion by Justice John M. Harlan. Harlan argued that California's mere repeal of its fair housing laws did not amount to encouraging and authorizing discrimination. If the repeal were to be seen that way, then a state could never rid itself of a statute whose purpose was to protect a constitutional right, whether of racial equality or some other. Harlan also suggested that opponents of antidiscrimination laws would later be able to argue that such laws not be passed because they would be unrepealable. Indeed, several ballot measures which have reversed or repealed civil rights laws protecting gays and lesbians have been struck down on the basis of *Reitman v. Mulkey.*

Reitman v. Mulkey has not had a major effect on American civil rights law. The Supreme Court has not been disposed to expand the "authorization" and "encouragement" strands of constitutional thought. The principle of "state action"—which is all that the Fourteenth Amendment equal protection rules can reach—has not been further broadened. Nevertheless, the precedent remains, with its suggestion that there is an affirmative federal constitutional duty on state governments to prevent private racial discrimination.

—*Robert Jacobs*

See also: Fair Housing Act; Fourteenth Amendment; *Patterson v. McLean Credit Union*

LOVING V. VIRGINIA

1967

State miscegenation laws were examples of explicit racial discrimination in U.S. statutory law; they criminalized and penalized the unions of persons of differing racial heritages and denied legal legitimacy to mixed-race children born to such interracial couples.

Definition: State laws forbidding intermarriage between black and white people

Thirty-eight U.S. states at one time had miscegenation laws in force; seven of those thirty-eight repealed their laws before 1900. All southern states (not including the District of Columbia) had miscegenation statutes. Many western states (including Arizona, California, Montana, Nevada, Oregon, Utah, and Wyoming), in addition to forbidding intermarriage between black and white people, also specifically prohibited unions between whites and Native Americans or whites and Asian Americans. Penalties upon conviction varied from a maximum imprisonment of more than two years in most of the South and some other states (ten years in Florida, Indiana, Maryland, Mississippi, and North Carolina) to sentences ranging between a few months and two years in other states. Enforcement of the laws was random and irregular.

The key case in ending miscegenation laws was *Loving v. Virginia* (1967). At the time that the U.S. Supreme Court heard the *Loving* case, sixteen states still had miscegenation laws in force. Virginia's laws dealing with racial intermarriage were among the nation's oldest. They stemmed from statutes formulated in the colonial period (1691) and had been strengthened by more stringent miscegenation legislation passed in the mid-1920's in which whiteness was very narrowly defined. The codes that became law in 1924 were aimed primarily at discriminating against people of mixed African American and white heritage and/or of American Indian background.

Photograph of Mildred Jeter and Richard Loving dated June 12, 1967

In the *Loving* case, Richard Perry Loving, who was white, had married Mildred Delores Jester, who was African American, in Washington, D.C., in June, 1958. The Lovings made their home between Fredericksburg and Richmond in Caroline County, Virginia. They were issued warrants of arrest in July, 1958, and in January, 1959, they were convicted before the Caroline County court of violating Virginia's anti-miscegenation statute. Their minimum sentences (of one year imprisonment each) were suspended on agreement that they would leave the state. They moved to Washington, D.C., until 1963, when they returned to their farm in Virginia and worked with attorneys Bernard Cohen and Philip Hirschkop of the American Civil Liberties Union (ACLU), who placed their case under appeal. The miscegenation law and the Lovings' convictions were upheld by the Virginia Supreme Court of Appeals in March, 1966, but in June, 1967, the U.S. Supreme Court overruled the appellate finding. The Supreme Court ruled that use of race as a basis for prohibiting marriage rights was unconstitutional under the Fourteenth Amendment's equal protection and due process provisions. The ruling nullified all remaining laws forbidding interracial marriage. Previous to the unanimous 1967 ruling, the U.S. Supreme Court had taken a conservative approach to this civil rights issue. It had repeatedly avoided reviewing lower court convictions based on state anti-miscegenation laws (*Jackson v. Alabama*, 1954; *Naim v. Naim*, 1955; *McLaughlin v. Florida*, 1964).

—*Barbara Bair*

See also: Jim Crow laws; One-drop rule

NATIONAL ADVISORY COMMISSION ON CIVIL DISORDERS

Formed in 1967

The commission determined that the principal causes of the riots were widespread discrimination and segregation.

Identification: Commission created by executive order to study racial violence in American cities

The National Advisory Commission on Civil Disorders was created by executive order in 1967 with Governor Otto Kerner of Illinois as chairman and Mayor John V. Lindsay of New York City as vice chairman. The commission had eleven members, including four members of Congress as well as labor, civil rights, and law enforcement leaders. Other public officials and private citizens participated on advisory panels studying such things as private enterprise and insurance in riot-affected areas.

Racial violence had escalated with the Watts riot in Southern California in 1965 and, by the summer of 1967, was spreading to other American cities. After extensive study, the commission recommended new and expanded employment and educational opportunity programs, national standards for welfare programs, and increased access to housing. The commission's report stated that the United States was becoming "two societies, one black, one white—separate and unequal." It was the first major study to place the blame for creating black ghettos on white society.

The commission studied the major race riots, identified patterns in the violence, developed profiles of participants, and analyzed the conditions prior to and following the disorders. Despite concern among some officials that the violence was being encouraged by radical groups, the commission determined that the principal causes were widespread discrimination and segregation with the increasing concentration of the black population in inner-city ghettos offering little opportunity. These conditions, according to the report, led to pervasive frustration, the acceptance of violence as a means of retaliation, and growing feelings of powerlessness. A spark was all that was necessary to ignite violence, and the police often provided it.

The commission recommended new federal programs to address the problems of poverty, unemployment, education, and housing and the expansion of existing urban programs, such as the Model Cities Program, to provide economic opportunity to residents of the inner city. Guidance was also offered to state and local officials for identifying potentially violent conditions, reducing the likelihood of violence, providing training to police to lessen tensions in minority communities, and organizing emergency operations in response to escalating violence.

See also: New York riots; Newark riot; Race riots of 1967; Race riots of the twentieth century; Watts riot

RACE RIOTING ERUPTS IN DETROIT

July 23-July 30, 1967

Detroit, Michigan, saw one of the most devastating race riots in U.S. history, setting off riots in other major cities and showing that reforms of the 1960's had neglected a sizable segment of the African American population. When promised reforms, such as those of the 1960 and 1964 Civil Rights Acts, did not fully materialize, hopes were dashed and frustration led to increased anger and further impoverishment.

Locale: Detroit, Michigan

Categories: Wars, uprisings, and civil unrest; social issues and reform; sociology

KEY FIGURES

Jerome Patrick Cavanagh (1928-1979), mayor of Detroit, 1961-1968

Ramsey Clark (b. 1927), attorney general of the United States, 1967-1969

Lyndon B. Johnson (1908-1973), president of the United States, 1963-1969

George W. Romney (1907-1995), governor of Michigan, 1963-1969

Cyrus Vance (1917-2002), U.S. deputy defense secretary, 1967-1968

SUMMARY OF EVENT

On the surface, Detroit, Michigan, in 1967 was one of the success stories of President Lyndon B. Johnson's Great Society. Under the administration of Mayor Jerome Patrick Cavanagh, Detroit had prospered, and so had many of its African American residents. Many blacks commanded high wages in Detroit's factories and occupied high positions in the United Auto Workers union. Consequently, approximately 40 percent of the city's 555,000 blacks owned or were buying houses, many of which were in integrated neighborhoods. Mayor Cavanagh had also attempted to reach out to the underprivileged in his city through his federally funded antipoverty agency, Total Action Against Poverty (TAAP), which provided $200 million for jobs, job training, education, and recreation.

Blacks in Detroit had also attained a share in political power. The director of TAAP, the chief civilian assistant to the police commissioner, and two of the seven members of the board of education were black. In addition, Detroit in 1967 was the only city in the United States that had two black members of Congress.

Because of his sensitivity to the political needs of minorities, Cavanagh was popular with many blacks in Detroit. Beneath the surface, though, Detroit was a city in turmoil. The unemployment rate among blacks was 11 percent; this was double the national average. The rate of unemployment was even higher among black youth; one out of every four young black males in Detroit, most of whom were the products of broken homes and inadequate schools, ended up on the streets after high school graduation, if indeed they graduated. The best future that most of them could hope for was work at poverty wages. In an eight-block area of Twelfth Street, the west-side ghetto strip where the 1967 riot erupted, only 17 percent of the residents owned their own homes, compared to 60 percent in the city as a whole.

Like the Newark, New Jersey, insurrection a few days earlier, the Detroit riot began as the result of a minor police incident. On July 23 at 4:00 AM, plice raided a "blind pig," or after-hours bar, on Twelfth Street and arrested eighty people inside the building. Outside, a crowd gathered, cursing and throwing rocks. Instead of confronting the mob or pulling out altogether, police follow Mayor Cavanagh's "walk soft" strategy by doing nothing. As a result, violence escalated. After looking at the ruins of the city the next morning, Governor George W. Romney decided that a show of force would be more effective. However, the National Guard had little training in crowd control and tended to fire at anything and anyone that moved. As the riot raged through the rest of the day, the city lay virtually paralyzed.

On July 25, Governor Romney began at eight-hour telephone conversation with US attorney general Ramsey Clark to sort out the legalities in making a formal request for federal troops. When President Johnson finally received Romney's formal request, he ordered the Pentagon to start airlifting "Task Force Detroit," which consisted of forty-seven hundred paratroopers from Fort Bragg, North Carolina, and Fort Campbell, Kentucky, to Selfridge Air Force Base in Detroit. The troops, however, were forced to stay on the base for several hours, until an investigation of the problems was made by the president's field team, headed by Deputy Defense Secretary Cyrus Vance. Because Vance's team concluded that no troops were needed, nothing was done until one of Detroit's black congressmen, Charles Diggs, Jr., personally called the White House to demand troops. Vance finally shuttled troops to the ghetto as 1:30 AM on July 26.

During the nearly twenty-four hours that had elapsed between the time Romney requested the troops and the time the troops took up positions in the city, the riot had spread over 14 square miles of the city, reaching close to the exclusive Grosse Pointe suburbs. Instead of stopping the riot, though, the arrival of federal troops only shifted the riot back to Twelfth Street, where the violence had started. Because the west side was populated by the poorest and angriest of Detroit's citizens, the riot was transformed into guerrilla warfare. Snipers shot at firefighters and assaulted a police station. A white woman who was watching from her window was shot and killed by a sniper. Altogether, there were about one hundred snipers.

When police and the National Guard retaliated against the snipers, they also placed innocent lives in jeopardy. In midmorning, the crew of an M-48 tank pummeled a building where a sniper had been sighted, only to discover twenty-five minutes later that the sniper had vanished; the only occupants were a terrified family of four who were cowering under the front porch. Several hours later, the police strafed the Algiers Hotel, where another sniper was reputed to have been hiding. When the shooting ceased, the police found three dead African Americans but no guns. In a similar incident, a dozen National Guards and policemen shot at a white Chevrolet convertible, resulting in the death of another unarmed black man.

The rage that had fueled the violence in the early days of the riot died out by the weekend. When the authorities were finally able to assess the damage, the cost in both property and lives was found to be tragically high. Property damage exceeded that of any other riot in the United States up to that time—more than $45 million. So many people had been arrested—more than four thousand—that some had to be detained in buses. More than one thousand people were injured, and forty-three people died. The dead included looters, snipers, a police officer, and a firefighter, as well as many innocent people who had been caught in the cross fire. Only eight of the dead were white, and three of those were looters who were shot by police. Without a doubt, the African Americans of Detroit paid the highest price for the riot.

SIGNIFICANCE

Even before the Detroit riot had ended, black power advocates began to capitalize on the turmoil. Insurrections soon followed in other Michigan cities, including

Pontiac, Saginaw, Kalamazoo, and Grand Rapids. Throughout July and August, the cry "Burn, Baby, Burn" was heard in cities across the entire United States as well. By the end of the summer, more than seventy U.S. cities had experienced race riots, including Rochester, New York; Chicago; Toledo, Ohio; and South Bend, Indiana. For the bitter, downtrodden residents of the ghettos, the war cries of dissidents such as H. Rap Brown rang louder than those of the advocates of peaceful change. Indeed, Martin Luther King, Jr., recognized this point when he refused to go to Detroit during the riot. "I am not a fireman," he said. "My role is to keep fires from starting." Even President Johnson felt the fallout from the Detroit riots. Within a week after the violence in Detroit, a statement issued by the Republican Coordinating Committee blamed the president for vetoing the 1966 District of Columbia Crime Bill. The president was also criticized for waiting so long to send federal troops to Detroit.

On the positive side, the Detroit riot made many members of Congress aware of the need for legislative action to improve life in U.S. cities. Shortly before the riot, Johnson had been forced to cut expenditures for model cities, the Teacher Corps, and aid to education in order to fund the Vietnam War. After the riot, Johnson's "safe streets" bill, which provided $50 million for support for local police, had easy passage through Congress.

Advocates of gun control also received considerable support for their cause after the riot. On the other hand, the Johnson administration's view of the problem destroyed any hope that social legislation would receive a boost from the riot. Essentially, Johnson viewed the riot as a law-enforcement problem. He believed that funneling more money to the black ghettos would be construed by many people as rewarding the rioters. Consequently, little important social legislation was passed during the remainder of Johnson's term in office. The Detroit riot can also be credited with generating an atmosphere of paranoia across the nation for the rest of the year, and the prospect was raised of white backlash.

Hundreds of whites living in major cities across the United States began buying guns for protection. Even some government officials succumbed to the notion that the nation's underprivileged posed a real threat. Even though the Justice Department insisted that there was no real threat of a conspiracy, both J. Edgar Hoover of the Federal Bureau of Investigation and the Michigan Crime Commission attributed the violence to planned efforts by organized groups. Some military analysts went so far as to blame China and Cuba for the trouble in Detroit.

The most important lesson to come out of the Detroit riot, however, was the realization that the disenfranchised factions of society could disrupt any city in the United States. The revolt in Detroit, like all revolutions, was born out of hope, not despair. By taking over Detroit, the rioters demonstrated to whites and middle-class blacks that the reforms instituted by King and Johnson had not filtered down to the poorest members of society. After the riot, the nation as a whole was forced to face a startling fact: If a riot could occur in a model city like Detroit, it could happen anywhere.

—Alan Brown

See also: Civil Rights Protesters Attract International Attention; Watts Riot; Black Panther Party Is Organized; Kerner Commission Explores the Causes of Civil Disorders; Chicago Riots Mar the Democratic National Convention;

NEWARK RIOT

July 12-17, 1967

In 1967, more than one hundred U.S. cities experienced riots, mostly in ghettos, directly affecting African American communities, law enforcement officials, and the entire nation.

The Event: One of a series of major civil disorders of the 1960's
Place: Newark, New Jersey

Although riots had occurred in the Watts section of Los Angeles in 1965 and in several cities in the summer of 1967, the disturbance in Newark, New Jersey, best illustrated the "tinderbox" concept—an eruption of violence lit by a slow burning fuse. By 1967, Newark had the highest daytime population turnover, venereal disease and maternal mortality rates, and population density in the nation. It had changed from being 85 percent white in 1940 to nearly 50 percent African American by 1965. During the three years before the 1967 riot, a series of incidents of police brutality, some involving deaths of young African American men, had occurred. In July, 1967, twenty-four thousand unemployed African Americans lived within Newark's boundaries, an area of twentyfour square miles. Newark had proportionally the largest police force of any major city, yet its crime rate was among the highest.

THE RIOT

On July 12, another incident involving apparent police brutality occurred, the beating of cab driver John Smith, who had been stopped for traffic violations. Word of the incident traveled quickly through the taxi radio network and throughout the African American community, and the rumor spread that the police had killed Smith. Although this rumor was false, it was believable because of previous fatal incidents involving the police.

Soon angry crowds gathered outside the police station where the officers had taken Smith. Rocks, bottles, and Molotov cocktails were thrown at the police station. The police rushed out of the station in a show of force, setting off days of rock throwing, window smashing, looting, car burning, and firebombing of businesses. Civil rights leaders and moderate African American ministers intervened and mediated, hoping to achieve a meaningful peace. Mayor Hugh Addonizio made some concessions to the group's demands for reform. More militant elements of the community, including black nationalists and members of the Nation of Islam, denounced a commission appointed to examine what it termed "this isolated incident." City police were called in, and although they made many arrests, the situation soon was out of control.

On July 14, the mayor asked Governor Richard J. Hughes to send in state troopers and the National Guard. The 475 state troopers, 4,000 National Guardsmen, and 1,300 city police officers experienced immediate coordination and communications problems. The National Guard units had not been trained in riot control, and when sniper fire rang out, the troops, unable to pinpoint the origin of the shots, overreacted, spraying bullets throughout the congested area, hurting many innocent bystanders. At times, the three law enforcement groups mistakenly shot at each other, creating even more hysteria. During the course of three nights, law enforcement officers shot into buildings that bore signs indicating they were owned by African Americans.

On July 17, Governor Hughes ordered an end to the state of emergency and removed the National Guard from Newark. Casualties included the deaths of 1 firefighter, 1 police officer, and 23 African Americans; 145 law enforcement officers and 580 civilians had been injured. In addition, 1,465 people were arrested, including 1,394 African Americans, 50 whites, and 21 Puerto Ricans. Property damage exceeded fifteen million dollars. The major participants were predominantly somewhat educated, unemployed young African American men. Rioters directed their hostility toward property; the only people they injured were police officers.

AFTERMATH

The Newark riot was followed later that month by rioting in Detroit, Michigan, in which forty-three people died. President Lyndon B. Johnson established the National Advisory Commission on Civil Disorders, chaired by Illinois governor Otto Kerner, to determine the cause of the rioting, find ways to control it, and determine the role of law enforcement.

In 1968, the Kerner Commission, as it was commonly known, concluded that typically, a series of tension-heightening incidents over time led to one "triggering or precipitating event" that set off the riots. The nationwide study concluded that police in Newark and elsewhere were involved in more than half of the incidents that preceded riots and led to an escalation of violence. Newark's law enforcement efforts were found deficient. City police practices of over-enforcement and harassment of people on the streets negated positive initiatives (such as mandatory human relations training and police community councils) taken by Director of Police Dominick Spina. Also, National Guard troops were found to be ill prepared for crowd control, unable to contain violence in densely populated areas, and far too eager to discharge their weapons. The Newark riot nationally dramatized the severe condition of people living in the nation's ghettos.

—*G. Thomas Taylor*

FURTHER READING

Nathan Wright, Jr.'s classic *Ready to Riot* (1968) stresses the underlying causes and anatomy of the Newark riot from a community perspective, terming the disturbance a "racial rebellion."

The Kerner Commission Report (1968) presents the government commission's findings from its nationwide study on the causes of riots and its prescriptions for prevention and change.

See also: Chicago riots; Kerner Commission; New York riots; Washington, D.C., riots; Watts riot

CHICAGO RACE RIOTS OF 1967

July 25-September 24, 1967

These riots combined with more extensive riots in more than thirty other U.S. cities during the summer, reflecting serious race relations problems throughout the United States.

The Event: Racially motivated civil disturbance
Place: Chicago, Illinois

Many African Americans from the southern United States began migrating to Chicago in the early twentieth century. Racism and mostly unsuccessful competition with whites over jobs and housing persisted for decades. As the summer of 1967 began, about 800,000 African Americans, many feeling frustrated and hopeless, lived in the city's crowded black ghettos.

On Tuesday night, July 25, African American youths began looting, smashing car windows, and throwing firebombs on Chicago's West Side. During the next week, vandalism, looting, and arson occurred on the South Side and the West Side. Police attributed the riots to reports of racial conflicts in other cities, and Mayor Richard Daley announced that live ammunition would be used against rioters. Police exchanged gunfire with youths firing from a building, and five Molotov cocktails were thrown into a store. About a hundred people were arrested. On August 1, an African American man was shot by a white man, and a firebomb was thrown. Fifty-two African Americans were arrested after they did not disperse, and more firebombs were thrown.

On August 3, the Reverend Jesse Jackson requested that Chicago be declared a disaster area. The situation calmed down, but on August 26, shots were fired while a blaze was being fought in the South Side, and nine

African American youths were arrested. On September 14, an African American power rally sponsored by the Student Nonviolent Coordinating Committee (SNCC) charged police with brutality and fascism, and window smashing, rock throwing at cars, and scattered sniper fire was reported. Police, aided by leaders of African American street gangs, calmed the area. The next day, African American students boycotted classes to protest inadequate school conditions.

On September 22, in the suburb of Maywood, five hundred people pelted police cars with bottles because no African American students had been nominated for homecoming queen. Thirty people were arrested. The following day, after police shot and critically wounded a burglary suspect, about three hundred African Americans threw bricks and bottles through store windows, and police used tear gas. On September 24, ten African Americans and eleven whites were arrested in Maywood by police in an attempt to prevent a third night of violence. The Chicago riots were over for the summer of 1967.

The riots of 1967 were largely responsible for President Lyndon B. Johnson's appointing of the National Advisory Commission on Civil Disorders on July 27, 1967. The commission issued a report referred to as the Kerner Commission Report after its chairman, Governor Otto Kerner of Illinois. Although the commission did not select Chicago for one of its in-depth investigations, the conditions described in the report were also found in Chicago, and the Chicago riots were part of the unrest that led to the report.

—*Abraham D. Lavender*

See also: Chicago sit-ins; Kerner Commission; New York riots; Newark riot; Race riots of 1967; Race riots of the twentieth century; Student Nonviolent Coordinating Committee; Washington, D.C., riots; Watts riot

MARSHALL BECOMES THE FIRST AFRICAN AMERICAN SUPREME COURT JUSTICE

October 2, 1967

President Lyndon B. Johnson appointed the nation's leading civil rights lawyer, Thurgood Marshall, to become the first African American justice of the United States.

Locale: Washington, D.C.
Categories: Laws, acts, and legal history; social issues and reform

KEY FIGURES

Thurgood Marshall (1908-1993), associate justice of the United States, 1967-1991, who had been a leading civil rights lawyer

Lyndon B. Johnson (1908-1973), president of the United States, 1963-1969, who oversaw the enactment of civil rights legislation

Strom Thurmond (1902-2003), U.S. senator from South Carolina who led opposition to civil rights laws

SUMMARY OF EVENT

U.S. Supreme Court justices are responsible for defining and defending the Bill of Rights in the U.S. Constitution. The meanings of freedom of speech, freedom of the press, equal protection, and other rights are determined by the nine individuals who preside over the highest court in the United States.

The Supreme Court's decisions tend to reflect the dominant societal values of each era. While racial prejudice against African Americans was accepted in many parts of the United States, the justices declared that cities and states could segregate African Americans into separate schools, neighborhoods, and public facilities. When women were excluded from professions because of societal attitudes about their roles as wives and mothers, the Supreme Court declared that state laws could prevent women from working as lawyers or as bartenders and in other occupations. The Supreme Court determines the extent to which women, racial minorities, and others are protected by the Constitution, yet before 1967 only white males served as justices and participated in these decisions.

Because the membership of the Supreme Court has been unrepresentative of the diversity within American society, critics of the Court have argued that constitutional rights have been interpreted to favor the interests of the narrow group of individuals, namely affluent

Thurgood Marshall in 1936 at the beginning of his career with the NAACP by Livraria do Congresso

white men, who compose the Supreme Court. Critics also note that although the Fourteenth Amendment to the Constitution, added in 1868, required state governments to provide equal protection for all people, the justices of the Court did not use those words to protect African Americans from widespread discrimination until 1954, in the case of *Brown v. Board of Education.*

The Supreme Court, and American society generally, began to change during the 1950's and 1960's. The justices on the Court increasingly made decisions that struck against racial discrimination. When President John F. Kennedy was assassinated in 1963, the new president, Lyndon B. Johnson, was able to use the wave of national political sympathy to push antidiscrimination legislation through Congress. As Johnson oversaw the implementation of the most comprehensive American laws ever initiated against racial discrimination, he turned his attention to the Supreme Court.

When Justice Tom C. Clark retired, President Johnson appointed Thurgood Marshall to fill the vacancy. In

selecting Marshall to be the first black justice, Johnson chose a lawyer who had such vast experience as a litigator, government attorney, and federal judge that it was nearly impossible for civil rights opponents to claim that Marshall lacked the proper qualifications to be a justice.

Marshall's great-grandfather had been a slave. The future justice grew up in Baltimore as the son of a schoolteacher. Marshall was an honors graduate of Lincoln University, a college for African Americans in Pennsylvania. Many top law schools were closed to black students at that time. Marshall attended law school in Washington, D.C., at Howard University, an institution founded to educate black students. He graduated at the top of his law school class in 1933. After graduation from law school, Marshall embarked upon a career as a civil rights lawyer for the National Association for the Advancement of Colored People (NAACP). For more than twenty-five years, he traveled throughout the United States pursuing lawsuits on behalf of black people who wished to utilize the courts to fight against racial discrimination. He developed a reputation for thinking quickly on his feet in the courtroom because he grew accustomed to facing openly hostile judges in southern courthouses.

Marshall was the chief architect of the series of cases challenging racial segregation in education that culminated in the Supreme Court's landmark 1954 decision against school segregation in *Brown v. Board of Education.* Prior to appointment to the highest court, few justices have ever been so experienced in preparing and presenting arguments before the Supreme Court. Marshall argued thirty-two cases before the Court, and he won twenty-nine of them. In 1961, Kennedy appointed Marshall to be a judge on the U.S. Court of Appeals for the Second Circuit. He faced heated opposition from southern senators opposed to civil rights, and it took a year for him to gain confirmation from the Senate. In 1965, Johnson appointed Marshall to be solicitor general of the United States. The solicitor general represents the United States government in front of the Supreme Court. The position gave Marshall the opportunity to build his already impressive reputation and experience as an advocate before the highest court in the land.

After Johnson appointed him to serve on the Supreme Court, Marshall's confirmation by the Senate was delayed for several months. Southern opponents of civil rights attempted to prevent the nation's most famous champion of racial equality from serving. During lengthy hearings before the Senate Judiciary Committee,

Senator Strom Thurmond from South Carolina attempted to derail the nomination by asking dozens of questions about obscure aspects of legal history in the hope that Marshall would stumble in answering. Ultimately, Marshall's appointment was confirmed overwhelmingly by the Senate, with only one senator from outside the South among the eleven opposing the nomination. Marshall was sworn in as the first black justice on October 2, 1967.

SIGNIFICANCE

By becoming a Supreme Court justice, Thurgood Marshall broke the color barrier in one of the most powerful institutions in American society. Symbolically, his appointment demonstrated to American society that rigid racial discrimination was no longer socially acceptable. For black Americans, Marshall's appointment demonstrated that the old obstacles to professional advancement were being reduced.

Marshall became a powerful liberal voice on the Supreme Court, especially when cases concerning discrimination were under consideration. He was the first justice to have experienced firsthand the harassment and humiliation of racial discrimination. Because he traveled throughout the rural South as a litigator for the NAACP

during the 1930's and 1940's, he had witnessed and experienced the severest racial prejudice in American society. In fact, Marshall was once nearly murdered by a lynch mob of Tennessee police officers who opposed his advocacy of civil rights and racial equality.

Just as other justices' views are shaped by their attitudes and experiences, Marshall's experiences living with racial discrimination gave him great sensitivity to the plight of powerless people within American society. The new perspective contributed by Marshall helped generate many Court opinions during the 1960's and 1970's that demonstrated a heightened concern for protecting the constitutional rights of all Americans. Marshall's concerns for civil rights were evident beyond issues of racial discrimination, and they included attention to the constitutional rights of poor people, women, and criminal defendants. Until the addition of several new justices moved the Supreme Court's decisions in a conservative direction during the late 1980's, Marshall was a key member of a liberal Court majority that protected and expanded individuals' civil rights to unprecedented lengths. Marshall, whose health had deteriorated, announced his retirement from the Supreme Court in 1991.

Clarence Thomas, only the second African American to be named a Supreme Court justice, was nominated by President George H. W. Bush and, after contentious nomination hearings, was subsequently confirmed. Unlike Marshall, whose most effective work occurred with the NAACP during the days of struggle for the advance of civil rights, Thomas was opposed by civil rights groups who distrusted his conservative political and legal views, although he too had risen from a modest background to prominence in the American legal profession. Also unlike Marshall, Thomas's legal credentials were in question: An American Bar Association committee voted by a narrow majority to rate Thomas merely "qualified" for the bench, with a minority of the committee rating him "not qualified." Many modern nominees have received unanimous "well qualified" ratings.

—*Christopher E. Smith*

See also: Supreme Court Rules African American Disenfranchisement Unconstitutional; Supreme Court Ends Public School Segregation; Brooke Becomes the First African American U.S. Senator Since Reconstruction; Chisholm Becomes the First African American Woman Elected to Congress.

ASSASSINATION OF MARTIN LUTHER KING, JR.

April 4, 1968

The decade's greatest force for interracial peace and understanding, Dr. Martin Luther King, Jr., was shot to death while campaigning for civil rights, representing a tragedy for the United States and creating a wave of conspiracy theories about the circumstances of his murder.

Locale: Memphis, Tennessee
Categories: Terrorism; civil rights and liberties

KEY FIGURES

Martin Luther King, Jr. (1929-1968), American preacher and civil rights leader

James Earl Ray (1928-1998), American drifter and petty criminal

Ralph Abernathy (1926-1990), King's closest friend and confidant, who succeeded him as president of the Southern Christian Leadership Conference

Rosa Parks (1913-2005), African American seamstress

Bull Connor (1897-1973), Birmingham, Alabama, police chief

SUMMARY OF EVENT

The Civil Rights movement of the 1950's and 1960's proved to be one of the most consequential social and political episodes in American history. Dedicated activists effectively worked to eliminate racial barriers that had denied millions of black people basic citizenship rights in the Jim Crow South. The movement produced numerous leaders, but none was more identifiable than Martin Luther King, Jr., a highly educated and articulate Baptist minister from Atlanta, Georgia. For more than a decade, his name was synonymous with the struggle for African American civil rights in the United States.

King, a charismatic figure, encountered little difficulty in rallying support around his causes and leadership style. Influenced by the teachings of Morehouse College president Benjamin Mays, India's Mahatma Gandhi, and the German philosopher Georg Wilhelm Friedrich Hegel and by the social gospel of Walter Rauschensbusch, he developed a protest philosophy that blended religion with issues of justice, human and civil rights, and a vision of an ideal American society.

King was the Civil Rights movement's greatest exponent of nonviolent mass civil disobedience. He rose to national prominence in 1955 as the leader of the Montgomery (Alabama) Improvement Association's boycott against the city's racially segregated bus line. Black passenger Rosa Parks precipitated the boycott with her arrest for refusing to surrender her seat to a white rider. The boycott successfully desegregated the buses. It also helped initiate a period of mass protest that not only challenged Southern segregation and black disenfranchisement but also influenced human rights issues in foreign countries.

Many of the subsequent campaigns that affected Southern life were led by King through his own Southern Christian Leadership Conference (SCLC). An occasional failure, such as the SCLC's 1961-1962 Albany, Georgia, initiative to eliminate segregation ordinances and discriminatory hiring practices, did not discourage King. A foray in Birmingham, Alabama, in the spring of 1963 produced more tangible results. King, ably assisted by Ralph Abernathy, his closest friend and handpicked SCLC successor, resolved to change downtown hiring practices and to escalate the pace of court-ordered desegregation in schools and public facilities. Unlike in Albany, King employed the tactic of passive resistance with telling effect, as the demonstrators defied local law and taxed the patience of police chief Bull Connor. On national television news, Americans watched with abhorrence the acts of police brutality against the protesters, many of whom were children; they were similarly outraged over King's and Abernathy's solitary confinement in the Birmingham jail. The demonstrations eventually helped win major advances for Birmingham African Americans.

King utilized the Birmingham campaign to raise the national consciousness about the morality of civil rights causes. In the process, he enhanced his own prestige and leadership position. That stature was further strengthened by his August 28, 1963, "I Have a Dream" speech during the March on Washington campaign. Addressing 250,000 persons assembled at the Lincoln Memorial as well as a national television audience, King expressed his continuing faith in America's ideals. Speaking in his characteristic rhythmic cadence, he stirred the nation with his "dream" of an America free of racial prejudice and bigotry. The address was perhaps King's finest hour as an orator. King continued to garner national and international acclaim for his work. By the end of 1964, he had won *Time* magazine's prestigious Man of the Year award and had been honored as a Nobel Peace Prize recipient. Both recognitions further solidified his position as the United States' preeminent leader in the struggle for African American civil rights.

Sensitized national leaders reacted to King's and other black leaders' efforts with concrete legislation. The comprehensive 1964 Civil Rights Act outlawed discrimination and segregation in key aspects of American life. In the same year, King's Selma, Alabama, campaign for black voting rights provoked savage white police reaction against demonstrators similar to that in Birmingham. Congress responded to the incidents in Selma and to black voting demands with an extensive law effectively enfranchising Southern blacks, the 1965 Voting Rights Act.

Before 1965, King had confined his civil rights activities primarily to the segregated South. Such efforts, however, did not preclude a concern for oppressed people worldwide. Almost from the outset of his activism, he linked America's black struggle to human rights issues elsewhere, particularly in Africa. He spoke boldly against South African apartheid and supported the move to end colonialism across the continent. His attendance at the independence celebrations in Ghana in 1957 and Nigeria in 1960 held endear him to citizens of those emergent developing nations.

Increasingly after 19654, King's attention turned to opposing America's Vietnam involvement and to the problems of African Americans and poor urbanites in Northern cities. these initiatives produced considerably less than the desired results. His antiwar stance cost him important white Northern support, and his efforts in cities such as Chicago won for African Americans few substantive gains in better housing and employment. Nevertheless, Kings' internationalism and his inclusion of human rights and economic justice in a broadened civil rights agenda inspired plans for a major campaign to encourage massive federal spending to fight poverty rather than war. He would not, however, have the opportunity to lead this ambitious Poor People's March on Washington.

King's urban concerns took him to Memphis, Tennessee, in the early spring of 1968. His purpose there was to support striking municipal sanitation workers seeking recognition of their recently formed union. A demonstration planned on their behalf for March 28, 1968, ended violently when youthful members of a local black gang fought with police and vandalized stores along the route. Discouraged, King canceled the demonstration and promised to return to lead another march that would adhere to his nonviolent philosophy. In the late evening of April 4, 1968, several days before the scheduled second march, King was mortally wounded by a sniper while standing on the balcony near his room at Memphis's Lorraine Hotel.

King's meteoric rise to international prominence clearly had not occurred without challenges and personal dangers. A 1958 stabbing in New York by a mentally disturbed black woman had made clear the grave risks that accompanied public stature and recognition. It was the nature of his activism that provoked the greatest opposition and made him a logical target of racial extremists.

King was acutely aware of this; death threats and bomb scares constantly reminded him of it. An emotional speech to a church audience the night before his assassination was so interspersed with veiled references to dying that it makes credible his aides' suggestions that King saw his death as imminent.

If King readily envisioned his own death, it seemed not to trouble his lieutenants. They, too, fully understood the dangers inherent in his role, but they had witnessed his preoccupation with death before and were not overly concerned with his latest mood. King's assassination was certainly unexpected, and it generated a range of emotions from close associates, but few of them seemed truly surprised that such an event could happen.

After one of the nation's most intensive manhunts ever, James Earl Ray, an escaped Missouri felon with decidedly antiblack racial views, was captured, tried, convicted, and sentenced to life imprisonment for King's murder. In many black communities, however, suspicion surfaced that Ray did not act alone. Long after the trial, charges were rampant of a King conspiracy that implicated the Federal Bureau of Investigation (FBI) and the Central Intelligence Agency (CIA). No conspiracy evidence was ever substantiated in King's murder, however.

SIGNIFICANCE

The reaction to King's death was universal. The international community memorialized him and recognized his impact on human rights developments beyond the United States. American leaders praised his commitment to nonviolence and acknowledged his role in influencing many of the social and political changes affecting American life, especially in the South. Even King's militant rivals lamented his passing and predicted dire national social consequences because of it. Such predictions resulted largely from the violence that the assassination triggered in many American communities.

Rioting struck Memphis almost immediately, as black youths vented their anger and frustration over yet another fallen symbol. In Washington, leaders pleaded for calm, but the national capital and 130 other cities could not be spared from violent disturbances in the emotional wake of the assassination. The disorders caused forty-six deaths and property damage exceeding $100 million.

This violent response hardly represented the vast black majority, who memorialized King in more traditional and peaceful ways. Nevertheless, the consequences of the riots were far-reaching. King's death virtually assured congressional passage of the 1968 Civil Rights Act providing for open housing, legislation that King had long supported. That act was the last major civil rights legislation of the era. A growing conservative white backlash concerned about law and order stiffened its resolve against further minority demands.

Civil rights leaders seemed unable to reverse the trend. Before King died, the movement had already splintered badly over the issues of nonviolence and Black power. It continued to founder after his death.

Historians have debated whether King and his enlarged agenda of human rights, economic justice, and international peace could have stemmed the reversal, but his SCLC successor could not. Despite renewed fears of violence, in June, 1968, Abernathy led King's Poor People's Campaign in Washington peacefully; however, it accomplished little. Lacking both King's charisma and his leadership qualities, Abernathy soon fell from power and sank into relative obscurity.

King was not the first leader-activist felled by white racism. In the five-year period before his death, America had anguished over the loss of several others, including Medgar Evers, James Chaney, and Viola Liuzzo. To many African Americans, however, King was not merely another beloved figure victimized by racism. For most, he embodied their hopes and aspirations to enjoy the full benefits of American citizenship. He spoke for them, articulating their demands in a way that, it seemed, only he could. In life, he symbolized the black struggle, and in the years following his death no leader emerged who was capable of mobilizing the masses as he did.

In death, King's image became even more powerful, taking on new meaning and symbolism. In the nation's cumulative memory of King's work and vision, he was transformed from martyr to virtual demigod. A national holiday was declared to honor his life, and annual King celebrations were inaugurated in several West African countries. Long after his death, he continued to represent the idealism of the 1950's and 1960's civil and human rights struggle.

—*Robert L. Jenkins*

See also: King Delivers His "I Have a Dream" Speech; Assassination of Malcolm X.

CIVIL RIGHTS ACT OF 1968

April 11, 1968

The Civil Rights Act of 1968 banned racial discrimination in the sale or rental of most types of housing.

The Law: Federal legislation prohibiting housing discrimination

After 1965, the Civil Rights movement devoted increasing attention to conditions in the North. It found much segregation there, a condition that was rooted in residential patterns rather than in Jim Crow laws. The prevalence of segregated housing determined the composition of schools and other aspects of urban life. Martin Luther King, Jr.'s Chicago campaign in 1966 focused national attention on the housing issue. His lack of success showed that white resistance to opening neighborhoods to minority residents was strong and would be difficult to overcome. Urban riots in northern and western cities provoked a "white backlash," as many northern whites ceased their support for further civil rights reform. In 1966 and 1967, President Lyndon B. Johnson tried and failed to persuade Congress to pass civil rights bills outlawing discrimination in housing.

PASSING THE ACT

In 1968, liberal Democrats in the Senate brought forward a new civil rights bill containing a fair housing provision. Heavy lobbying by Clarence Mitchell, of the National Association for the Advancement of Colored People (NAACP), helped to marshal a majority of senators in support of the bill. As with earlier civil rights measures, southern senators attempted to talk the bill to death with a filibuster. However, in return for some relatively minor modifications in the bill, the leader of the Republican minority, Senator Everett Dirksen of Illinois, agreed to support an attempt to cut off the filibuster. This succeeded, and the bill passed the Senate on March 11, 1968.

In the House of Representatives, passage was far from sure. The assassination of Martin Luther King, Jr., on April 4, however, shocked the country and dramatically altered the political landscape. Support for the bill grew; it passed easily and was signed by President Johnson on April 11.

FAIR HOUSING

The main thrust of the 1968 Civil Rights Act was to outlaw discrimination on the basis of race, religion, or national origin in the sale and rental of most forms of housing in the United States, as well as in the advertising, listing, and financing of housing. Exempted from the act's coverage were single-family houses not listed with real estate agents and small apartment buildings lived in by the owner. (About a month after the act became law, the Supreme Court ruled, in the case of *Jones v. Alfred H. Mayer Company*, that the Civil Rights Act of 1866 prohibited racial discrimination in housing and other property transactions.) Two other provisions of the act also grew out of the racial turmoil of the 1960's. One enumerated specific civil rights whose violations were punishable under federal law. Another sought to make the act more acceptable to the growing number of Americans concerned about urban riots by specifying stiff penalties for inciting or engaging in riots.

As a housing measure, the act proved disappointing. Its enforcement provisions were weak. Those with complaints of discrimination were directed to file them with the Department of Housing and Urban Development (HUD), which would then attempt to negotiate a voluntary settlement. If this failed, complainants would have to file their own lawsuits; the federal government would intervene only in cases where there was a clear pattern of past discrimination. In addition, white resentment at attempts to integrate neighborhoods remained high. Banks often found ways to avoid the law's provisions, making it difficult for many African American families to secure necessary financing. By the late twentieth century, it was clear that the act had not ended the country's dominant pattern of racial segregation in housing.

THE INDIAN BILL OF RIGHTS

The Civil Rights Act of 1968 contained another provision unrelated to concerns over fair housing: the Indian Bill of Rights. This was grounded in the fact that Indians on reservations, as members of tribal communities, were not considered to be covered by the Bill of Rights. In 1896, the Supreme Court had ruled, in the case of *Talton v. Mayes*, that the Bill of Rights did not apply to Indian tribes or to their courts. In 1961, Senator Sam Ervin, a North Carolina Democrat, was surprised to discover the fact. Over the next several years, he held hearings on the subject. In 1968, he was able to amend the civil rights bill moving through the Senate to include coverage of Indian rights.

The Indian Bill of Rights extended a variety of constitutional protections to Native Americans with regard to the authority of their tribal governments. Among these were freedom of speech and religion, as well as protections for those suspected or accused of crimes. In fact, all or part of the First, Fourth, Fifth, Six, and Eighth Amendments were held to apply to reservation Indians, as was the Fourteenth Amendment's guarantee of due process. Some parts of the Bill of Rights were not included, however; the First Amendment's ban of religious establishments was not included, in deference to tribal customs, nor were the Second Amendment's right to bear arms or the Third's prohibition against the quartering of troops. Most important to most Indians was a provision that required tribal permission before states could further extend jurisdiction over tribal land.

—William C. Lowe

See also: Civil Rights Act of 1957; Civil Rights Act of 1960; Civil Rights Act of 1964; Civil Rights Act of 1991; Civil Rights Acts of 1866–1875; Civil Rights movement; *Jones v. Alfred H. Mayer Company*; *Katzenbach v. McClung*; *Shelley v. Kraemer*; United States Commission on Civil Rights

FIRST STEPS TOWARD LIMITS ON RESTRICTIVE COVENANTS

1968

Throughout the early twentieth century, restrictive covenants were major tools in the maintainance of segregated housing in American cities. However, the U.S. Supreme Court first limited, then banned, the covenants, helping reduce housing discrimination.

Definition: Private agreements or contracts meant to deny privilege, usually housing, on the basis of race, gender, or ethnicity

A common practice in northern and western cities, restrictive covenants were a prime example of de facto segregation practices. Typically the covenants required buyers not to resell their homes to African Americans, Latinos, Asians, Jews, or other ethnic/racial groups not wanted in the neighborhood or community, allowing builders to create all-white suburbs and schools. Initially, the Supreme Court permitted restrictive covenants on the grounds that the court had no jurisdiction over private property transfers.

The Supreme Court took its first step toward limiting restrictive covenants in *Shelley v. Kraemer* (1948), in which it ruled that states that enforced restrictive covenants were liable to be prosecuted for civil rights violations even if the individual homeowners were not. In *Jones v. Alfred H. Mayer Company* (1968), the Court rejected the legality of restrictive covenants under the provisions against discrimination in sale or rental of property to African Americans found in the Civil Rights Act of 1866. In banning covenants, *Mayer* also cited the enforcement clause of the Thirteenth Amendment, which gave Congress the authority to determine and eliminate the "badges and incidents of slavery." The case also legitimized the Title VIII provisions of the Civil Rights Act of 1968, which guaranteed housing rights regardless of race or ethnicity.

—*Steven J. Ramold*

See also: Jim Crow laws; *Jones v. Alfred H. Mayer Company*; Segregation; *Shelley v. Kraemer*; Thirteenth Amendment

ORANGEBURG MASSACRE

February 8, 1968

The Orangeburg massacre was the first incident of U.S. college students being killed by police because of protesting, but the killings received almost no national attention, largely because many white Americans had developed negative attitudes toward black protesters following a series of urban riots in 1967.

The Event: Killing of three African Americans by campus police at a predominantly black southern college
Place: Orangeburg, South Carolina

On Thursday night, February 8, 1968, three African Americans (two male college students and the teenage son of a college employee) were killed by police gunfire on the campus of the almost entirely black South Carolina State College in Orangeburg. Twenty-seven other students were injured. Nearly all were shot in the back or side as they attempted to flee an unannounced fusillade of police gunfire. One police officer had been seriously injured by an object thrown at the police, but despite uncorrected false reports in the media, the students were unarmed. African American students had started protesting three nights earlier because the only bowling alley in Orangeburg continued to exclude African Americans despite pleas from local white and black leaders and students.

Twenty-seven months after Orangeburg, the killing of four white students by National Guard troops at Kent State University in Ohio during a Vietnam War protest received international publicity. Jack Bass and Jack Nelson's *The Orangeburg Massacre* (1970, revised 1984) is a detailed study of the massacre. A campus monument memorializes Henry Smith, Samuel Hammond, Jr., and Delano Middleton, whose lives were taken "in pursuit of human justice."

—*Abraham D. Lavender*

See also: Civil Rights movement; Colfax massacre; Segregation

KERNER COMMISSION EXPLORES THE CAUSES OF CIVIL DISORDERS

February, 1968

The Kerner Commission's report portrayed a nation divided along racial lines and recommended measures that should be taken to cure the maladies of hatred and violence besetting American society.

Also known as: National Advisory Commission on Civil Disorders

Locale: Washington, D.C.
Categories: Government and politics; social issues and reform; wars, uprisings, and civil unrest

KEY FIGURES
Lyndon B. Johnson (1908-1973), president of the United States, 1963-1969

Otto Kerner (1908-1976), governor of Illinois, 1961-1968

John V. Lindsay (1921-2000), mayor of New York City, 1966-1973, and vice chair of the Kerner Commission

Roy Wilkins (1901-1981), executive secretary of the NAACP and a commission member

SUMMARY OF EVENT

The National Advisory Commission on Civil Disorders, also known as the Kerner Commission, was appointed by President Lyndon B. Johnson as an immediate response to race riots in American cities during the summer of 1967. The most devastating riots occurred in Newark and Detroit, within a two-week period in July. President Johnson established the commission to try to discover what had happened, why it had happened, and what could be done to prevent it from happening again.

Both President Johnson and the commission gave priority to the maintenance of law and order in the affected cities and to determining if a conspiracy had existed that created a chain reaction of riots. It was important to the president and to the members of the commission to determine the historical factors which caused the riots of 1967. It was this question that provided the commission with the opportunity to focus on systemic problems of racism in American society. The paramount observation of the commission was tersely stated: "Our nation is moving toward two societies, one white, one black—separate and unequal."

President John F. Kennedy and his brother, Robert F. Kennedy, had shown much compassion in committing the United States to eliminating segregation in schools and public facilities. The Kennedy administration was short-lived, but it did inspire a helpful political mood for government action against the more conspicuous forms of racism. President Johnson, as Kennedy's successor, pledged to continue the battle for civil rights for minorities.

In July, 1967, President Johnson appointed the commission, giving it a mandate to investigate the origins of the recent disorders in American cities. The president pledged to use national resources to remedy historical racism and social injustice. In typical folksy prose, President Johnson beseeched Americans to pray for the day when "mercy and truth are met together; righteousness and peace have kissed each other." He pledged to work for better jobs, housing, and education for African Americans.

Otto Kerner, the governor of Illinois, was selected by President Johnson to chair the National Advisory Commission on Civil Disorders. John V. Lindsay, the mayor of New York City, was appointed vice chair. The other members represented a cross-section of American politics, leaning toward moderates. Exceptions to this tendency were Roy Wilkins, executive secretary of the National Association for the Advancement of Colored People (NAACP), and Fred Harris, U.S. senator from Oklahoma, whose work on behalf of Native Americans had sensitized him to the pains of racism.

A starting point for the commission was to examine racism in its historical framework. The causes of the 1967 riots, according to the report issued by the commission in February, 1968, were inherent in the structure and dynamics of American society which established the pattern of interracial relations. African Americans had always struggled for equality in law and in social life.

Some African Americans, particularly at the end of the nineteenth century and the beginning of the twentieth, supported separatism and self-help. Black power proponents of the 1960's, such as Stokely Carmichael and H. Rap Brown, revitalized this philosophy, originally championed by Booker T. Washington. Black power supporters were actually promoting many of the objectives of white racism through their emphasis on black history, separatism, and racial solidarity, the commission noted.

Some African Americans, in the early years of the twentieth century, had organized to challenge Booker T. Washington's program of political accommodation to white racism. Washington was convinced that blacks could earn the respect of white society through hard work. Political rights, such as the franchise, could wait for an undetermined future date. W. E. B. Du Bois and Monroe Trotter began and led the Niagara Movement which rejected separatism, condemned Jim Crow laws, and took up protest and agitation for racial equality in law and in social life. The Niagara group placed the responsibility for African American poverty and violence on white racism and demanded the abolition of all distinctions based on race and color.

Booker T. Washington fought back. He had the support of southern whites and many conservative northern philanthropists who wanted to preserve the racial status quo. Nevertheless, Washington failed to subdue Du Bois and his followers. In 1909 and 1910, Du Bois was able to enlist a small group of white liberals, some of whom could trace their ancestry back to the abolition movement of the nineteenth century, and socialists to form the National Association for the Advancement of Colored People. Du Bois became the editor of *The Crisis*, a semiofficial journal of the NAACP which was adamant in its condemnation of white racism and in its demand for full equality for African Americans.

The NAACP aimed its protest against the whole nation, insisting on the right to vote, equal protection under the law, equal pay for equal work, and the dismantling of segregation in public accommodations, in schools, and in the armed forces. A variety of tactics was used by the NAACP, including boycotts, publicizing lynching (while pressing for antilynching legislation) and other atrocities against African Americans, and bringing lawsuits.

It was in these early years that the NAACP prepared the groundwork for *Brown v. Board of Education* (1954), with cases pertaining to white colleges and universities and their refusal to admit African Americans to their graduate and professional schools. In 1936, Thurgood Marshall, counsel for the NAACP, successfully contested before the courts the exclusion of African Americans from the law school at the University of Maryland. Two years later, the Supreme Court declared unconstitutional a Missouri plan that banned African Americans from the University of Missouri law school as violating the "separate but equal" doctrine.

The federal government ignored the plight of African Americans in northern cities and in the countryside of the southern states. Southern congress people, in fact, were able to expand de facto segregation in the District of Columbia, although they failed to enact Jim Crow laws. The nation's capital became another bastion and an important symbol of Jim Crowism and the subordination and segregation of African Americans in virtually every segment of society.

White prejudice and the frequent use of extralegal violence, violence often sanctioned by the larger community, by whites against African Americans who broke social or political norms were principally responsible for black riots in the twentieth century. White racism, according to the commission's report, created a pattern of failures among African Americans. The commission referred to pervasive racism and segregation, black migration from the South to the North, and the black ghettos, implicating white institutions for creating the ghettos.

The commission urged the American people to commit themselves to the elimination of the ghettos

through massive and sustained action, backed by the will and resources of the richest nation on earth.

The goals of society, according to the commission, needed to focus on creating a single American identity, a single society in which race and color would not determine a person's dignity or limit the choice of job, residence, or even partner in marriage. To reach these goals, the commission recommended the elimination of all forms of racial segregation in the United States by giving to African Americans the right to choose their jobs, where they would live, and what schools they would attend.

The commission proposed the formation of grassroots institutions based in the ghettos and in rural areas, thereby making government more responsive to citizens on the local level. The commission insisted on destroying not merely the legal status of racism but also the legacy of racism by devising an array of programs to integrate American society.

SIGNIFICANCE

The assault by the National Advisory Commission on Civil Disorders on institutionalized racism was a comprehensive proclamation which indicted white racism while condemning black violence and committing the nation to build a single, nonracial society. The impact of the commission's report was felt by African Americans and other minorities in many ways. Black Americans in general, but especially the young, began to see the federal government as compassionate and committed to eradicating legal and de facto racism throughout America.

In the area of employment, the commission proposed a comprehensive program to meet the needs of the unemployed and the underemployed through active recruitment, job training, affirmative action in the public and private sectors, and stimulation of public and private investment in poverty-stricken areas, both in the cities and in rural communities. The commission recommended the creation of two million jobs through a combination of government and private efforts over a three-year period.

Education in a democratic society is necessary to provide citizens with the capacity to participate in the political process and to enjoy fully the fruits of their collective endeavors. Schools in the northern ghettos and segregated schools in the South and West had failed to discharge their obligations to educate African Americans adequately. The commission recommended scores of reforms to remedy this failure. Many of the rioters in

1967, the commission observed, were high school dropouts. It also cited the disparity in educational achievement between African Americans and whites in the same grades.

Public schools were not teaching African Americans basic verbal skills. The commission cited results of the Selective Service Mental Test showing that during the period between June, 1964, and December, 1965, 67 percent of black candidates but only 19 percent of whites failed the examination.

To rectify the failure to educate African Americans and other minorities, the commission supported the elimination of de facto school segregation, which was connected with residential segregation in the North. It recommended increasing the funding for schools in the inner cities, improving community-school relations, spending more money on early childhood education, and enforcing Title VI of the 1964 Civil Rights Act, which prohibited giving federal financial aid to any program that discriminated against African Americans. The commission also supported year-round education for disadvantaged students and expanded opportunities for higher education and vocational training for African Americans and other disadvantaged groups.

The commission made other comprehensive proposals, addressing almost every conceivable segment of social life. It recommended a national system of income supplements, eliminating discrimination in housing, the construction of smaller housing projects (that is, "scattering") to break down racial isolation, an expansion of the rent supplement program and an ownership supplement program, and the opening up of areas outside ghetto neighborhoods to black occupancy. Many of the commission's recommendations became law. Its greatest impact, however, was perhaps in beginning the process of attaining racial equality.

—Claude Hargrove

See also: Race Riots Erupt in Detroit and Harlem; Watts Riot; Chicago Riots Mar the Democratic National Convention

FAIR HOUSING ACT OUTLAWS DISCRIMINATION IN HOUSING

April 11, 1968

The Civil Rights Act of 1968 was designed to reduce discrimination against racial and ethnic minorities in the purchasing, renting, and leasing of housing. It also prohibited discriminatory lending practices by financial institutions. The fair housing law, however, did little to alleviate the problem of housing discrimination, as its enforcement provisions were weak.

Also known as: Title VIII of the Civil Rights Act of 1968
Locale: Washington, D.C.
Categories: Laws, acts, and legal history; civil rights and liberties; social issues and reform

KEY FIGURES

Lyndon B. Johnson (1908-1973), president of the United States, 1963-1969, who was a major supporter of civil rights legislation
Martin Luther King, Jr. (1929-1968), civil rights leader

Everett Dirksen (1896-1969), U.S. Senate minority leader, who initially opposed the Civil Rights Act of 1968

SUMMARY OF EVENT

Residential segregation became a staple of American society in the late nineteenth century and continued into the twentieth. It began in southern cities, in compliance with the "Jim Crow" principle of the inappropriateness of close social contact between races. Residential segregation became the vehicle to separate African Americans from whites. It was accomplished through a combination of real estate practices, intimidation, and legal regulations.

As African Americans migrated to the North and West, residential segregation spread to those areas as well. In the North, the real estate industry led in the drive to create segregated housing. Real estate boards adopted regulations prohibiting their members from renting or selling property in predominantly white areas to nonwhites.

Members usually complied with the rules, since they could be expelled for noncompliance. Agents steered Asian and African Americans and other racial minorities away from white areas. Violence and harassment were frequently aimed against minorities brave enough to venture into white neighborhoods.

Residential segregation was also institutionalized by law. States, beginning with Virginia in 1912, authorized cities and towns to designate neighborhoods as either black or white. Urban localities enacted ordinances that designated individual blocks as available to only whites or African Americans. Many southern urban areas were already racially integrated, and problems developed in drawing up the necessary laws. Some cities defined the right to a block on the basis of which race constituted the majority. Members of a minority group did not have to move, but no more of its members could move into the block.

In 1917, in *Buchanan v. Warley*, the U.S. Supreme Court prohibited government-mandated residential segregation. It is noteworthy that the Court based its decision in property rights, not civil rights—that is, on the grounds that such ordinances denied owners the prerogative of disposing of their property as they wished. Even after the *Buchanan* decision, restrictive racial covenants, policies, and practices of real estate organizations perpetuated residential apartheid. Racially restrictive covenants, which were more prevalent in the North than in the South, bound property owners in a particular neighborhood to sell only to other "members of the Caucasian race." In *Corrigan v. Buckly* (1926), the Supreme Court ruled that such covenants constituted private agreements and therefore were not prohibited by the Fourteenth Amendment to the U.S. Constitution.

Two decades later, in *Shelley v. Kraemer* (1948), the Court, in a unanimous opinion, ruled that even though restrictive covenants were private agreements, enforcement of them through the use of state courts constituted state action and therefore violated the Fourteenth Amendment. In a companion decision, *Hurd v. Hodge* (1948), the Court held that judicial enforcement of restrictive covenants in the District of Columbia violated the Civil Rights Act of 1866 and was also inconsistent with the public policy of the United States.

Actions by the real estate industry after those decisions illustrated the entrenched nature of racial exclusion in housing. In 1924, the National Association of Real Estate Boards (NAREB) revised article 34 of its official code of ethics to forbid Realtors from assisting sales to members of any race or nationality or to any individual "whose presence will be detrimental to property values" of a given neighborhood. Shortly after the *Kraemer* and *Hurd* decisions, a NAREB leader expressed doubt whether those Supreme Court decisions would "mitigate in any way against the efficacy of Article 34." Although NAREB and most local real estate organizations eliminated mention of race from their codes during the 1960's, Realtors resorted to the clandestine exclusion of cultural and racial minorities.

During President John F. Kennedy's administration, those regulations that authorized residential segregation in federally funded housing were removed, and many municipalities adopted open housing laws. Even then, there was very little movement toward housing desegregation.

Real estate agents continued to steer whites to predominantly white neighborhoods and African Americans to black neighborhoods. Financial institutions continued to discriminate in providing mortgages to minorities. Because residential segregation contributed to school segregation and kept African Americans and Latinos in economically depressed neighborhoods, a strong federal fair housing law became an urgent priority for civil rights leaders. In 1966, as Martin Luther King, Jr., campaigned against segregation in the Chicago area, President Lyndon B. Johnson proposed a fair housing law. It presented a dilemma for liberals. The coalition that had successfully steered major civil rights legislation through Congress in 1964 and 1965 fractured. Fearful of "white backlash," northern liberals were unwilling to act against discriminatory practices. A badly divided House of Representatives passed an open housing bill in 1966. Support by some Republicans ensured its passage, even though the House Republican leadership, including minority leader Gerald R. Ford, opposed it. The bill died in the Senate.

The next year, the House passed the Civil Rights Bill of 1967, proposed by Johnson largely to protect civil rights workers and to reduce discrimination in jury selection. This bill became the Civil Rights Act of 1968. The Senate's push for a strong open housing statute was led by Democratic senators Philip Hart of Michigan and Walter Mondale of Minnesota and Republicans Edward William Brooke of Massachusetts and Jacob K. Javits of New York. Until the final days of the debate on the bill, Senate Republican leaders opposed any open housing legislation, ostensibly because federal action would usurp prerogatives of the states. Explaining his conversion, Senate minority leader Everett Dirksen of Illinois told the Senate that only twenty-one states had open housing laws. He expressed a fear that it might take fifteen or twenty years for the other twenty-nine states to enact similar laws. In reality, he and other conservative opponents of open housing were won over by a compromise that added what they claimed were "tough sanctions against rioters and provocateurs of racial violence." The Senate approved the bill on March 11.

Immediate consideration of the bill in the House was blocked by opponents of fair housing laws. Many opponents wanted to delay consideration of the bill until after the "poor people's march," which King had planned to begin in Washington on April 22. They reasoned that the march would annoy enough members to doom the bill.

King's assassination, however, created a groundswell of support for the bill. The House adopted the Senate's version without amendment on April 10, one week after King's assassination. Reminding the nation that he had waited three years for the bill, Johnson signed it the next day—April 11. The Civil Rights Act of 1968 applied to about 80 percent of the nation's housing. It reduced racial barriers, in three stages, in about 52.6 million single-family dwellings.

When it became fully operational on January 1, 1970, the law prohibited discrimination on the basis of color, race, religion, or national origin in the sale or rental of most apartments and homes. The only dwellings exempted were single-family homes sold or rented without the assistance of a Realtor and small apartment buildings with resident owners. The law also prohibited discriminatory lending practices by financial institutions.

The law also provided severe federal penalties for persons convicted of intimidating or injuring civil rights workers and African Americans engaged in activities related to schooling, housing, voting, registering to vote, jury duty, and the use of public facilities. The act also extended the Bill of Rights to Native Americans living on reservations under tribal government and made it a federal crime to travel from one state to another or to use radio, television, or other interstate facilities with intent to incite a riot.

SIGNIFICANCE

It is difficult to determine the impacts that resulted from the passage of the 1968 Civil Rights Act. The act cannot be assessed in isolation. It was but one of a series of statutory actions to integrate minorities, especially African Americans, into American life. Moreover, decisions

of the Supreme Court on the issue of open housing carried far-ranging potentials.

In the end, however, the fair housing law did little to quell the problem of housing discrimination, as its enforcement provisions were weak. The Department of Housing and Urban Development (HUD) was empowered to investigate complaints and to negotiate voluntary agreements with those found guilty of discrimination. If this conciliatory approach failed, the attorney general was authorized to bring lawsuits, an expensive and time-consuming process. Because the act failed to afford timely redress, victims of discrimination largely ignored it. Fewer than fifteen hundred complaints were filed during the first two years that the act was in effect. A 1974 study of real estate practices in major cities by the U.S. Commission on Civil Rights and another at the University of Michigan in 1976 showed that housing discrimination was widespread but subtle. Steering remained a common practice.

The Civil Rights Act of 1968 was amended on September 13, 1988, to eliminate defects. The amendments provided HUD with authority to forward class-action cases to the Department of Justice (DOJ) for prosecution, empowered the DOJ to initiate class-action suits on its own initiative, and increased monetary penalties.

A noticeable decline in residential segregation has occurred since the bill was enacted. Segregation in the twenty-five cities with the largest black populations declined 1 percent between 1960 and 1970 and 6 percent between 1970 and 1980. The decline for Asian Americans and Latinos was much greater. Preliminary statistics suggest that the decline in segregation accelerated for all groups between 1980 and 1990. Court decisions also advanced the cause of open housing. A study by HUD in 2000 indicated that over the previous decade even more substantial declines in the level of discrimination occurred for both Latinos and African Americans attempting to purchase homes. That same study also showed a modest decline in discrimination against African Americans attempting to rent, but Latinos were more likely to be discriminated against in the rental market. The study also collected data for the first time on discrimination against Asian Americans and Pacific Islanders, finding that about one-fifth of them were discriminated against when trying either to rent or buy a home in the eleven U.S. metropolitan areas examined.

In 1967, the Supreme Court had invalidated California's Proposition 14, which had been adopted by voters in 1964 to negate a fair housing bill enacted by the legislature.

In ruling against Proposition 14, which gave property owners an absolute right to dispose of their property as they saw fit, the Court, in *Reitman v. Mulkey*, held that although the state was not obligated to enact nondiscriminatory housing legislation, it could not enact provisions which had the effect of encouraging private discrimination.

Much more significant, a few weeks after enactment of the new civil rights law, the Supreme Court made open housing a legal reality with the decision in *Jones v. Alfred H. Mayer Company*. That decision resurrected a provision of the 1866 Civil Rights Act. Codified as section 1982, the provision reads that "All citizens of the United States shall have the same right, in every State and Territory, as is enjoyed by white citizens thereof to inherit, purchase, lease, sell, hold, and convey real and personal property." The resurrection of section 1982 made the heart of the Civil Rights Act of 1968 dispensable.

—*Ashton Wesley Welch*

See also: Truman Orders Desegregation of U.S. Armed Forces; Supreme Court Ends Public School Segregation; Congress Passes the Civil Rights Act of 1964; Supreme Court Prohibits Racial Discrimination in Public Accommodations; Supreme Court Upholds Ban on Housing Discrimination.

POOR PEOPLE'S MARCH ON WASHINGTON

April 28-May 13, 1968

The failure of the Poor People's March on Washington reflected the public's lack of interest in the complex problem of economic injustice and the difficulty of solving such a problem.

The Event: Unsuccessful attempt to broaden the Civil Rights movement into a nonracial national campaign to reduce poverty
Place: Washington, D.C.

In 1967, after passage of federal laws designed to end racial segregation and disfranchisement of African American voters, including the Civil Rights Act of 1964 and Voting Rights Act of 1965, the Southern Christian Leadership Conference (SCLC) decided that federal legislation was needed to address joblessness and homelessness.

BACKGROUND TO THE MARCH
To draw attention to the problems of poor Americans and push Congress to pass laws to expand employment and low-income housing opportunities, the SCLC developed plans for a nonviolent march to Washington, D.C., in the spring of 1968. The march would be followed by the construction of Resurrection City, a temporary community for poor people, on federal property in Washington. The SCLC hoped that these actions, labeled the Poor People's Campaign, would unify impoverished people of various ethnic and racial backgrounds. Although Martin Luther King, Jr., strongly supported the campaign, others in SCLC were critical of it and argued that Congress was unlikely to respond to the protesters. Public support for marches had faded considerably since 1965, partly because people believed that protest marches tended to provoke urban rioting.

On April 4, 1968, with the march just weeks away, King was assassinated in Memphis, Tennessee. Although his death represented a tremendous loss to SCLC and march organizers were in mourning, plans for the Poor People's Campaign continued. Ralph Abernathy, King's successor as leader of the SCLC, became spokesperson for the march. On April 28, groups of poor people left their communities to

Demonstrators participating in the Poor People's March at Lafayette Park and on Connecticut Avenue, Washington, D.C. by Warren K. Leffler, U.S. News & World Report

travel to Washington, D.C. Although some southern participants actually walked from town to town en route to Washington, others from the North, Midwest, and West Coast traveled by bus toward the nation's capitol. Marchers made designated stops during their journeys to hold rallies and recruit additional participants.

MARCHERS CONVERGE ON WASHINGTON, D.C.

Marchers began to arrive in Washington on May 11, and on May 13, the Poor People's March officially marked its end with Abernathy driving a construction stake into the grounds of a fifteen-acre section of West Potomac Park that became Resurrection City, where the marchers would live during the next phase of the campaign. The demonstrators erected wooden shacks and tents designed to draw the government's attention to the plight of poor people. On June 24, police moved in with tear gas and razed the buildings. Abernathy and a group of

followers held a march in protest of the destruction of Resurrection City and were arrested.

The Poor People's March drew media attention to SCLC's decision to focus national attention on the need for federal legislation to address the problems of people living in poverty. However, neither the public nor Congress responded with support for new programs for the poor. The failure of the Poor People's Campaign reflected the loss of King's leadership and a shift in public attention from problems of racism and poverty to the war in Vietnam and the 1968 presidential campaign.

—Beth Kraig

See also: Birmingham March; Chisholm's election to Congress; Economic trends; Million Man March; Million Woman March; Selma-Montgomery march; Southern Christian Leadership Conference

GREEN V. COUNTY SCHOOL BOARD OF NEW KENT COUNTY

May 27, 1968

In this Supreme Court case, the Court ruled for the first time that school boards have an affirmative duty to desegregate their schools, and it disallowed freedom-of-choice desegregation plans that do not result in substantial pupil mixing.

The Case: U.S. Supreme Court ruling on school integration and busing

In the wake of the Court's 1954 decision in *Brown v. Board of Education* that outlawed school segregation, few southern school boards took action to integrate their schools. Finally, in the mid-1960's, under the threat of federal fund cutoffs and adverse court decisions, most southern school boards made some effort to integrate their schools. Many such school boards did so by adopting an assignment system whereby students were permitted to choose which school they wished to attend. Most such freedom-of-choice plans resulted in little racial integration. Black students typically chose to attend traditionally black schools, whereas white students chose to attend traditionally white schools. As a result, schools remained racially segregated in many southern school districts following the introduction of free-choice plans.

One school district that adopted a free-choice plan during the 1960's was the school district in New Kent County, Virginia. New Kent County is a rural county; its student population was about half black and half white, with black and white people scattered throughout the county. Prior to 1965, the schools in New Kent County had been completely segregated, with all the black students attending the county's one black school and all the white students attending the county's one white school. In 1965, the school board adopted a free-choice plan whereby every student was permitted to choose between the two schools. As a result of the free choice, all the white students chose to remain in the white school and 85 percent of the black students chose to remain in the black school.

A group of black parents, with the assistance of the National Association for the Advancement of Colored People (NAACP) Legal Defense and Educational Fund, filed a lawsuit challenging this free-choice plan. These parents contended that the plan was deficient because it did not effectively dismantle the old dual school system. The Supreme Court, faced with thirteen years of southern school board recalcitrance on school desegregation, agreed that the school board's free-choice plan did not satisfy constitutional standards and announced that the school board had an affirmative duty to devise a desegregation plan that actually resulted in substantial pupil mixing. This decision, the Supreme Court's most important school desegregation decision since the 1954 *Brown* decision, helped transform school desegregation law by forcing school boards to devise assignment plans that resulted in greater integration. In the wake of the *Green* decision, lower courts throughout the South required school boards to take additional action to integrate their schools.

—*Davison M. Douglas*

See also: *Alexander v. Holmes County Board of Education; Brown v. Board of Education;* Civil Rights movement; National Association for the Advancement of Colored People; Segregation

SUPREME COURT UPHOLDS BAN ON HOUSING DISCRIMINATION
June 17, 1968

In Jones v. Alfred H. Mayer Company, the U.S. Supreme Court ruled that discrimination in the sale or rental of residential property violated U.S. law.

Also known as: *Jones v. Alfred H. Mayer Company*
Locale: Washington, D.C.
Categories: Laws, acts, and legal history; civil rights and liberties; social issues and reform

KEY FIGURES

Potter Stewart (1915-1985), associate justice of the United States, 1958-1981, who delivered the *Jones* decision
Lyndon B. Johnson (1908-1973), president of the United States, 1963-1969, who backed the Civil Rights Act of 1968, calling for a ban on all housing discrimination
Martin Luther King, Jr. (1929-1968), African American civil rights leader whose assassination prompted House passage of the 1968 Civil Rights Act

SUMMARY OF EVENT

As an official response to the movement for the rights of African Americans in the 1960's as well as to an additional array of social protests, U.S. president Lyndon B. Johnson initiated, and the U.S. Congress passed, the 1964 Civil Rights Act. It soon became clear that subsequent civil rights legislation was politically essential.

Accordingly, the Johnson administration directed its efforts toward passage of a fair housing bill in 1966. The heart of the bill, Title IV, sought to outlaw housing discrimination "by property owners, tract developers, real estate brokers, lending institutions and all others engaged in the sale, rental, or financing of housing." Although superficially the bill appeared to be sweeping in scope, its enforcement provisions were feeble and procedures for redress by alleged victims of these widespread forms of discrimination were prohibitively expensive and time-consuming. The bill languished in Congress.

As a further step toward creation of an effective federal fair housing law, Congress in 1968 enacted another Civil Rights Act, the major provision of which, Title VIII, decreed a general ban on racial and religious discrimination in the sale and rental of housing. The ultimate effectiveness of Title VIII was dependent on judicial decisions, fresh legislation, and the outcomes of a volatile social situation across the nation.

Impetus behind fair housing legislation and the passage of a series of federal civil rights acts came in important ways from a number of African American and liberal campaigns, some of long duration. For example, trade unions, churches, and civil rights organizations had formed an alliance called the National Committee Against Discrimination in Housing. It had been active since 1950 and already had by the mid-1960's played an important role in securing enactment of open housing laws, municipal ordinances, and administrative regulations pertaining to housing in seventeen states and in sixty major cities.

Fair housing laws complicated what during the 1950's and 1960's had become a "white flight" from inner cities to suburbs that was imputed largely to racial prejudice. Governmental attempts to implement or enforce open housing policies often produced a so-called white backlash. Nowhere was this more manifest than in California. There, in 1964, voters approved Proposition 14 in a state referendum.

Proposition 14 declared that the state could not interfere with anyone's right to sell or rent property, or conversely the right not to sell or rent property. In effect, the proposition abrogated a number of California statutes, including the Rumford Fair Housing Act of 1963, which banned racial discrimination in housing. Proposition 14's constitutionality was soon tested before the U.S. Supreme Court, in *Reitman v. Mulkey* (1967). The proposition was judged to be a violation of the Fourteenth Amendment because it would have authorized the state of California to engage in discrimination. Nevertheless, the proposition was indicative of widespread white reactions to one major thrust of the black and liberal drive toward winning expanded civil liberties. Opposition sentiments such as those embodied in Proposition 14 had been responsible for stalling Johnson's fair housing bill in Congress for two years. Only the assassination of Martin Luther King, Jr., as the bill was being debated, led to its passage, transformed into the Civil Rights Act of 1968.

Only weeks after President Johnson signed the act into law, the Supreme Court assumed its own initiative in hearing the case of *Jones v. Alfred H. Mayer Company.* Joseph Lee Jones, an African American, alleged that the Alfred H. Mayer Company had refused, on racial grounds, to sell him a home in the suburban Paddock Woods community in St. Louis County, Missouri.

In considering the case, Justice Potter Stewart, who was to deliver the majority opinion, and his affirming colleagues premised their decision not on Title VIII of the Civil Rights Act of 1968 but on an obscure law, section 1982, that had become part of the U.S. Code upon passage of the Civil Rights Act of 1866. Originally intended as an enforcement provision of the Thirteenth Amendment applicable to the District of Columbia, the law was nevertheless interpreted by the Court's majority to bar "*all* racial discrimination, private as well as public, in the sale or rental of property." Justice Stewart made it clear that section 1982 was not a comprehensive open housing law and that it did not address discrimination based on religion or national origins.

It likewise did not deal with the provision of services or facilities in connection with the sale or rental of dwellings, as might be performed by a realty company. Nor did it apply to advertising, financial arrangements, and brokerage services that might be involved in sales or rentals of dwellings. Stewart's point in enumerating precisely what section 1982 covered was to emphasize the significance of the newly enacted Civil Rights Act, stressing the need for such legislation and underscoring the responsibilities of the federal government in enforcing the rights of petitioners such as Jones.

For the majority, Justice Stewart explained the resort to section 1982, which had been section 1 of the Civil Rights Act of 1866. In *Hurd v. Hodge*, decided by the Court in 1948, the identical law had been invoked to respond to a situation in which an African American had been denied the chance to buy the home of his choice "solely because of [his] race and color." The source of Hurd's injury was the action of whites who agreed to bar African Americans from a particular residential area. In that case, a federal court had aided in the enforcement of the white homeowners' intentions. Thus the *Hurd* case did not, as the *Jones* case did, present the question of whether purely private discrimination, without the intervention of government, would violate section 1982.

In Stewart's opinion, the *Jones* case represented the first chance for the Court squarely to confront the question of whether a wholly private conspiracy to deny the right to buy or rent property solely because of race or ethnicity was legally sustainable. The Court majority determined for Jones. It decided that historical evidence overwhelmingly supported the notion that the 1866 Civil Rights Act was intended to "secure for all men, whatever their race or color, . . . the great fundamental rights" to acquire property; to buy, sell, or rent as one chose; and to "break down *all* discrimination between black men and white men."

SIGNIFICANCE

Ten years after passage of the Civil Rights Act of 1968 and the decision in *Jones*, an exhaustive study by the federal Department of Housing and Urban Development (HUD) concluded that "a vast residue of discrimination" in the housing market remained. Black ghettos continued to exist within almost all major cities as well as in smaller communities.

Although the 1968 Civil Rights Act aimed to establish a fair housing market, in practice, as civil libertarians, black leaders, and legal scholars observed, it was more gesture than substance. The act provided no enforcement mechanisms, such as cease-and-desist orders aimed at violators. Charged with implementing the act, HUD, for example, lacked authority to ask for more than voluntary compliance when complaints came before it. It was incapable of imposing remedies.

Similarly, as historians noted, the Justice Department, which did have authority to bring housing discrimination suits where patterns of discrimination existed, avoided tackling a number of exclusionary practices. The Justice Department, for example, made little effort to cope with "redlining," which in the arena of housing discrimination took the form of mortgage lenders marking out areas, primarily on the basis of racial composition, in which they would not lend. Although the country's financial regulatory bodies were legally required to act affirmatively to ensure fair housing, they were, many authorities concluded, derelict in issuing rules mandating nondiscrimination in mortgage lending and were slow to enforce the rules they did issue.

Notwithstanding these serious weaknesses, the act as implemented in the *Jones* decision did have positive effects. At the least, housing discrimination became less flagrant. A number of political scientists also found evidence in the 1970 U.S. census that there had been some progress. The census indicated a light but definite trend toward residential desegregation. Moreover, spurred by largely black riots in more than one hundred American cities during 1968, President Johnson presented Congress with the most extensive federal housing program in the nation's history, an initiative calling for federal subsidization of 600,000 units annually for ten years.

The president also drew many of the same banking and construction interests that had previously abetted housing discrimination into profitable participation in his housing reform through his 1968 Housing Act's subsidization of 1.7 million units over the following three years. Johnson's successor, Richard M. Nixon, continued the program with the unprecedented federal construction of 1.3 million low-income housing units during the early 1970's.

Meanwhile, the Supreme Court hewed to the course in regard to housing discrimination that it had plotted in the *Jones* decision. The City of Akron, Ohio, for example, had adopted a fair housing ordinance in 1964. Its dissatisfied electorate thereafter amended the city charter to provide that any ordinance regulating the sale or rental of real property had to win the approval of a majority of voters before it could become effective. The amendment, in short, nullified the city's fair housing law and reinstated customary patterns of housing discrimination.

The issue came to the Supreme Court in the case of *Hunter v. Erickson* in 1969. It afforded the liberal Court, which for fifteen years had been presided over by Chief Justice Earl Warren, an opportunity to review favorably Title VIII of the 1968 Civil Rights Act. Speaking through Justice Byron White, the Court acknowledged that it was confronted by a law that resorted to "an explicitly racial classification treating racial housing matters differently" from other legislative affairs. White declared that the charter provision was a violation of the equal protection clause of the U.S. Constitution's Fourteenth Amendment and was therefore invalid.

Court decisions and legislative actions aside, in the early 1980's the Justice Department's Civil Rights Division declared that housing discrimination remained "rampant." Moreover, HUD estimated that there were two million instances of illegal race discrimination pertaining to housing annually and that it received only forty thousand complaints about them. In addition, the 1968 Civil Rights Act covered only 80 percent of the nation's housing units. Congress seemed willing to leave matters as they were.

Legislation and Supreme Court decisions tried to establish a healthier social environment within which beneficial change could occur, but only changes in traditional attitudes over time, it seemed, could alter the facts of daily life. Evidence for such a change in attitudes was reflected in the 1980's and 1990's, as studies demonstrated that the level of discrimination in housing dropped considerably, though not to the point of elimination.

—Clifton K. Yearley

See also: Truman Orders Desegregation of U.S. Armed Forces; Supreme Court Ends Public School Segregation; Congress Passes the Civil Rights Act of 1964; Supreme Court Prohibits Racial Discrimination in Public Accommodations; Fair Housing Act Outlaws Discrimination in Housing.

JONES V. ALFRED H. MAYER COMPANY

June 17, 1968

The Case: U.S. Supreme Court ruling on housing discrimination

In this landmark decision, the Supreme Court used the Thirteenth Amendment banning slavery to outlaw racial discrimination in housing.

Joseph Lee Jones, alleging that a real estate company had refused to sell him a house because he was African American, sought relief in a federal district court. Since the case appeared before the passage of the Civil Rights Act of 1968, Jones and his lawyer relied primarily on a provision of the 1866 Civil Rights Act that gave all citizens the same rights as white citizens in property transactions. Both the district court and the court of appeals dismissed the complaint based on the established view that the 1866 law applied only to state action and did not address private acts of discrimination. The U.S. Supreme Court, however, accepted the case for review.

All the precedents of the Supreme Court supported the conclusions of the lower courts. In the *Civil Rights* cases (1883) the Court had ruled that the Thirteenth Amendment allowed Con gress to abolish "all badges and incidents of slavery," but the Court had narrowly interpreted these badges or incidents as not applying to private acts of discrimination. In *Hodges v. United States* (1906) the Court held that Congress might prohibit only private actions that marked "a state of entire subjection of one person to the will of another," and even in *Shelley v. Kraemer (*1948) the Court recognized the right of individuals to make racially restrictive covenants.

In *Jones v. Alfred H. Mayer Company*, however, the Court surprised observers by voting 7 to 2 to overturn its precedents. Writing for the majority, Justice Potter Stewart asserted that Congress under the Thirteenth Amendment possessed the power "to determine what are the badges and incidents of slavery, and the authority to translate that determination into effective legislation." In addition, the majority reinterpreted the 1866 law so that it proscribed both governmental and private discrimination in property transactions—an interpretation that is questioned by many authorities.

Justice John M. Harlan wrote a dissenting opinion which argued that the majority probably was wrong in its interpretation of the 1866 law. Harlan also wrote that the passage of the Fair Housing Act of 1968 eliminated the need to render this decision that relied on such questionable history.

Since the *Jones* decision was based on the Thirteenth rather than the Fourteenth Amendment, it was important in diluting the Court's traditional distinction between state and private action, and it appeared to grant Congress almost unlimited power to outlaw private racial discrimination. *Jones* became a precedent for new applications of the almost forgotten post-Civil War statutes in cases such as *Griffin v. Breckenridge* (1971) and *Runyon v. McCrary* (1976). In the quarter-century after *Jones*, however, the Congress did not pass any major legislation based upon the authority of the Thirteenth Amendment.

—*Thomas Tandy Lewis*

See also: Civil Rights Act of 1968; Civil Rights Acts of 1866-1875; *Civil Rights* cases; *Griffin v. Breckenridge; Moose Lodge v. Irvis; Patterson v. McLean Credit Union*; Restrictive covenants; *Runyon v. McCrary*; Segregation; *Shelley v. Kraemer*

YORK RACE RIOT OF 1969

July 1969

The York race riot of 1969 was a city-wide riot between white and African American residents fueled by a conflict between African American and white street gangs after a series of high profile incidents involving attacks on African Americans.

Identification: Race riot that occurred in July of 1969 in York, Pennsylvania.

York, Pennsylvania, was a predominantly white city with a sizeable African American minority in the late 1960s. On July 17th, when a 17-year-old African American Taka Nii Sweeney was shot by an unknown assailant. When white and African American gangs began fighting in the streets, responding police officer Henry Schaad was killed, reportedly by an African American gang member. After Schaad's death, several days of riots occurred, with white mobs burning down buildings and attacking residents of the town's African American neighborhoods. On July 21st, African American Lillie Belle Allen was shot and killed by members to two white street gangs who encountered Allen and her family driving through the city. The murder reignited the riots which lasted for several days until the National Guard was called in to quell the violence. In 1999, a series of retrospective articles about the riots inspired renewed interest in the death of Lillie Allen, leading to a new investigation. Four former members of the street gangs involved in Allen's death were arrested in 2001 and later, York City Mayor Charles Robertson was arrested after former street gang member Rick Knouse testified to a grand jury that Robertson, then a police officer, had given him ammunition and had

encouraged him to use the ammunition to kill African Americans. Robertson was later acquitted for his role in the murder, but admitted to having made racist statements during the incident and subsequently dropped his bid for reelection.

—Micah Issitt

CHICAGO RIOTS MAR THE DEMOCRATIC NATIONAL CONVENTION

August 24-30, 1968

Antiwar protesters interrupted the Democratic National Convention with rioting that was met by indiscriminate police violence, representing one of the most tumultuous years in mid-twentieth century U.S. political history. The riots helped change the traditional "back-room" selection of candidates for office to a more open and participatory process involving the citizenry.

Locale: Chicago, Illinois

Categories: Wars, uprisings, and civil unrest; government and politics; Vietnam War; social issues and reform

KEY FIGURES

Lyndon B. Johnson (1908-1973), president of the United States, 1963-1969, who escalated the war in Vietnam

Hubert H. Humphrey (1911-1978), vice president of the United States under Johnson and the Democratic nominee for president in 1968

Eugene McCarthy (1916-2005), U.S. senator from Minnesota and antiwar candidate for the Democratic presidential nomination in 1968

Richard Daley (1902-1976), mayor of Chicago and head of the Illinois Democratic political machine at the time of the convention

Rennie Davis (b. 1941), antiwar activist and cofounder of the National Mobilization to End the War in Vietnam

David Dellinger (1915-2004), antiwar activist and cofounder of the National Mobilization to End the War in Vietnam

Tom Hayden (b. 1939), New Left political organizer, founder of Students for a Democratic Society, and later state senator for California

Abbie Hoffman (1936-1989), author, political activist, and cofounder of the Youth International Party, or Yippies

SUMMARY OF EVENT

By all measures, 1968 was one of the most tumultuous years in twentieth century American political history. The Vietnam War increased in intensity, escalating American casualties and citizen disillusionment with the conflict. Racial tensions exploded into riots in many cities, particularly after the assassination of Martin Luther King, Jr. Demonstrations on college campuses against the war brought students into conflict with police who were often called to maintain order. Lyndon B. Johnson, who had been elected president with one of the largest pluralities in U.S. history four years earlier, responded to the turmoil by deciding not to run for a subsequent term in office.

Frustrations with the political process mounted on both the Left and the Right. Left-wing thinkers attributed problems to the underlying causes of the demonstrations, notably the continuing war in Vietnam and the government's failure to address racial and social inequities quickly enough. These individuals often argued for radical change in the political, judicial, and executive systems. Rightwing politicians argued that the demonstrators themselves were the problem and blamed the confrontations on indulgent political officials who failed to use sufficient force to suppress protests. George C. Wallace ran for the presidency as an independent candidate, demanding "law and order"—a catchphrase that became synonymous with the repression of political dissent.

Most American citizens fell somewhere between these two extremes. There was a growing feeling that the government's Vietnam policy was not working and that many social injustices went unaddressed. Most citizens also feared the increased polarization of the society and hoped that the conflicts would be worked out within the confines of the present political system. Many young people who opposed the war expressed this hope by working on Eugene McCarthy's or Robert F. Kennedy's campaigns for the Democratic presidential nomination. Both candidates enjoyed success in the Democratic primaries by taking a stance against Johnson's war policies; McCarthy continued this crusade after Kennedy's assassination.

Many McCarthy delegates perceived the Democratic National Convention as a forum for challenging the administration's Vietnam policy and its candidate, Vice President Hubert H. Humphrey. The Democratic National Convention, for several reasons, proved a suitable place for the conflict between left- and right-wing extremists to boil over into violent confrontations.

First, the city was run by Mayor Richard Daley, an old-style political boss who controlled the state Democratic Party system with unchallenged authority. Daley viewed disruptive demonstrations and calls for more participation in the choice of presidential candidates as a direct affront. He made this position clear during disturbances following the death of Martin Luther King, Jr., and during a peace march in Chicago in April, 1968. When police acted with restraint in the first case, they were chastised by Daley, who had issued a command to "shoot to kill arsonists and shoot to maim looters." When police attached demonstrators, bystanders, and media personnel in the second case, the mayor's office ignored the violence.

Second, several groups planned to organize demonstrations against the war and called upon supporters to join them in Chicago for the convention. Four of the main groups were the National Mobilization to End the War in Vietnam, led by David Dellinger and Rennie Davis; the Yippies, led by Jerry Rubin and Abbie Hoffman, who attempted to combine dhte counter-culture lifestyle of the hippies with a political statement against the war; Students for a Democratic Society (SDS), a campus antiwar group led by Tom Hayden; and the Coalition for an Open Convention, led by Martin Slate, which attempted to bring together antiwar and anti-Humhrey forces in the Democratic Party.

Some McCarthy supporters also cam to Chicago, despite the senator's warning to stay away. The first four groups officially intended to demonstrate and rally but avoid disrupting the convention. Rumors and careless statements by some group leaders, and the presence of more military minor groups, undermined these peaceful intentions. All four groups applied unsuccessfully for permits for marches, rallies, and access to the public parks for sleeping. The seemingly inevitable public assemblies were therefore illegal from the start, increasing the potential for confrontation.

Finally, the Chicago convention became a symbolic forum for the conflict between "old" and "new" politics. For many demonstrators, Humphrey's presidential candidacy represented a continuation of the back-room politics that ignored public dissent on Vietnam and other issues. They viewed the convention as a confrontation between traditional machine politics, represented by Daley and the Democratic Party's old guard, and the new (and often idealized) politics of increased citizen participation, represented by McCarthy supporters and young protest leaders.

As expected, the city's prohibition of demonstrations was only partially successful in stopping protesters from arriving in Chicago. Group leaders' early estimates of the number of participants proved to be overly optimistic, but approximately five thousand protesters had gathered in Lincoln Park by the Sunday evening before the convention was to begin. The first confrontations between demonstrators and law enforcement officials occurred following a peaceful afternoon march. The police, enforcing a ban on overnight camping in the park, randomly attacked protesters, bystanders, and media personnel, chasing them into the city's Old Town district.

This pattern was repeated on August 28, following a legal rally in Grant Park, across from the Hilton Hotel, where a number of delegates were staying. The rally was attended by SDS, Yippie, National Mobilization, and Open Convention protesters in addition to a number of older, nonviolent demonstrators, including disillusioned McCarthy supporters. Altercations began at a flagpole, where an American flag was lowered. Police attacked Davis when he attempted to restore order by assembling rally marshals between the protesters and the police.

The rally concluded and the demonstrators marched out with unclear objectives, eventually joining a legal march by the Southern Christian Leadership Conference (SCLC). Approximately seven thousand people eventually massed in front of the Hilton, where television cameras were present. Police allowed the SCLC marchers to pass but began clearing other protesters from the site.

Suddenly, several police officers stormed the crowd and began indiscriminately attacking protesters and innocent bystanders with clubs, mace, and fists. A few protesters fought back with rocks and other projectiles. The violence continued for about three hours in front of the hotels occupied by Humphrey, George McGovern, and McCarthy. Television cameras recorded the entire confrontation despite police attacks on media personnel.

The antiwar protesters retreated back to Grant Park for an all-night rally just as Humphrey received the Democratic nomination for president. Humphrey's victory was to be remembered for the clashes between police and demonstrators that were televised as the final convention votes were tallied.

SIGNIFICANCE

The immediate impact of the events in Chicago were felt within an already divided Democratic Party. There was an upsurge of support for the law-and-order stances of Wallace and, in a milder version, Richard M. Nixon. Humphrey's standing in the polls suffered accordingly, even though he regained most of his support and lost the November election to Nixon by only 0.7 percent of the vote.

Longer-term effects involved the way in which the public regarded the press and its role in covering political upheavals. The Federal Communications Commission answered many complaints about the media's coverage of the violence. The National Commission on the Causes and Prevention of Violence held public hearings in late 1968 to evaluate whether the press contributed to such confrontations in Chicago and other cities. The press was cleared of complicity, but arguments about the impact of mass media on protest activity were to continue for years to come.

Also charged with complicity in the Chicago violence were Davis, Hayden, Dellinger, Bobby Seale, Hoffman, Rubin, and Mobilization officials Lee Weiner and John Froines. These individuals became known as the Chicago Seven after Seale was removed from the courtroom and tried separately. All were charged with conspiracy to riot by U.S. Attorney General John Mitchell, even though most had never even met one another until the convention. By this action, Nixon signaled his intolerance of protests and demonstrations. He made attacks on protesters one cornerstone of his 1972 presidential campaign, adapting

---

Sentencing at the Chicago Seven Trial

On February 20, 1970, at the sentencing of the Chicago Seven, Judge Julius Hoffman asked each of the defendants—Abbie Hoffman, Jerry Rubin, David Dellinger, Rennie Davis, Tom Hayden, John Froines, and Lee Weiner—if he wished to make a statement before the court passed sentence. Here is Hoffman's statement:

I feel like I have spent fifteen years watching John Daly shows about history. *You Are There.* It is sort of like taking LSD, which I recommend to you, Judge. I know a good dealer in Florida. I could fix you up.

[Prosecutor Thomas] Foran says that we are evil men, and I suppose that is sort of a compliment. He says that we are unpatriotic? I don't know, that has kind of a jingoistic ring. I suppose I am not patriotic.

But he says we are un-American. I don't feel un-American. I feel very American. I said it is not that the Yippies hate America. It is that they feel that the American Dream has been betrayed. That has been my attitude. . . .

It wasn't funny last night sitting in a prison cell, a 5 × 8 room, with no light in the room. I could have written a whole book last night.

Nothing. No light in the room. Bedbugs all over. They bite. I haven't eaten in six days. I'm not on a hunger strike; you can call it that. It's just that the food stinks and I can't take it.

Well, we said it was like Alice in Wonderland coming in, now I feel like Alice in 1984 [a reference to George Orwell's dystopian novel *Nineteen Eighty-Four*], because I have lived through the winter of injustice in this trial.

And it's fitting that if you went to the South and fought for voter registration and got arrested and beaten eleven or twelve times on those dusty roads for no bread, it's only fitting that you be arrested and tried under the civil rights act. That's the way it works.

Just want to say one more thing.

People—I guess that is what we are charged with—when they decide to go from one state of mind to another state of mind, when they decide to fly that route, I hope they go youth fare no matter what their age.

Wallace's hard-line law-and-order stance to a more moderate audience.

Perhaps the farthest reaching effects of the Chicago demonstrations, however, were the changes they prompted in the procedures for choosing presidential candidates. The unrest was interpreted as one sign that the back-room selection of candidates for office needed to be opened up to wider citizen participation. By 1972, the rules governing selection had been changed dramatically, providing for an expanded primary system and a selection process for delegates to the Democratic convention including significant numbers of women, young people, and racial minorities. In a final ironic footnote, the Daley delegation to the 1972 convention failed to meet the national party quotas for women and minorities and was not seated.

The changes in the presidential selection process, cannot, of course, be traced solely to the events in Chicago in 1968. The clashes, however, remained a major

symbol of the conflict between the old and new politics, a conflict that redefined the direction and agenda of American politics for decades.

—*Frank Louis Rusciano*

See also: Kerner Commission Explores the Causes of Civil Disorders; Assassination of Martin Luther King, Jr.

CARROLL BECOMES THE FIRST AFRICAN AMERICAN WOMAN TO STAR AS A NON-DOMESTIC ON TELEVISION

September 17, 1968

In the fall of 1968, with the debut of the situation comedy Julia, singer and actor Diahann Carroll became the first African American woman to star as a non-domestic in a weekly television series—comedy or drama.

Locale: United States
Categories: Radio and television; popular culture; social issues and reform; women's issues

KEY FIGURES
Diahann Carroll (b. 1935), American singer and actor
Lloyd Nolan (1902-1985), American actor
Lurene Tuttle (1906-1986), American actor

SUMMARY OF EVENT

The premiere of *Julia* in the late 1960's did not mark the first time that an African American woman took the leading role in a television series. In the 1940's, the popular radio series *Fibber McGee and Molly* featured in its supporting cast a maid called Beulah, who became so popular with listeners that she was spun off into her own radio series. In 1950, when the American Broadcasting Corporation (ABC) decided to bring *Beulah* to television, producers faced a serious problem: the role had been played for years by a white man.

The decision was made to recast the role for TV. The widely respected and admired African American singer and actor Ethel Waters was hired to star as Beulah, now employed—on the comedy—by a family called Henderson, whose problems she sorted out in each week's episode. The series was an enormous hit, but, dissatisfied with its stereotyped portrayal of African

Americans, Waters left the series at the end of its second season. Character actor Louise Beavers replaced her, but she too soon left the show, and the series was canceled at the end of its third season.

Thereafter, a number of African American actresses were featured in supporting roles in series, but always as servants of some sort. It was not until the 1963-1964

Julia and Corey at home. NBC Television

season that an African American woman appeared in a supporting role in a series as something other than a domestic: Cicely Tyson played George C. Scott's secretary in *East Side/West Side* on the Columbia Broadcasting System (CBS). When Diahann Carroll debuted in the lead role in the half-hour comedy series *Julia* on September 17, 1968, she was making U.S. television history as the first African American woman to head the cast of a series in which that lead character did not play a domestic servant.

Julia may not have appeared until the decade was almost over, but it was nevertheless very much in the best spirit of the 1960's: idealistic, optimistic, millennial. The racial environment depicted by the series may not have been strictly realistic, but it reflected quite faithfully the goal toward which civil rights workers and social activists of the decade strove: an America in which ethic diversity is a given and in which harmony among races seems the natural order of things.

Julia may not have depicted African Americans in a realistic struggle for equality but it certainly provided a glowing model for the hopes and dreams of Americans of all ethnicities. This matter of models figures in another important positive aspect of *Julia*, the role model that the heroine provided. For the very first time, young people watching television across America were presented with an African American woman—who was young and professional—as the focus of attention within a series.

On the question of realism and sociopolitical issues, many critics of the time who dismissed the series often overlooked a small but important fact about the background story for *Julia*. Julia Baker was a widow, because her husband was killed in Vietnam. The primary memento that Julia and Corey had of their deceased husband and father, one that was shown from time to time throughout the run of the series, was a photo of him in uniform, gently reminding the audience of how

and where he had died. At a time in U.S. history during which even dramatic television series and mainstream films were reluctant to treat the war in Vietnam, this small element in an otherwise genial situation comedy was almost as groundbreaking as Diahann Carroll's position as lead actor in her own series.

SIGNIFICANCE

The significance of any first accomplishment is that it provides a precedent for a second, a third, and more to follow. *Julia* proved to television executives and programmers that a series headed by an African American woman could be a success. However, perhaps just as important as the series' status as a breakthrough event in American entertainment is its apparent influence on what later became the single most successful situation comedy to feature an African American cast, *The Cosby Show*, which debuted in September, 1984, becoming a runaway hit that appeared on television for more than a decade. In designing this series, Bill Cosby and his producers clearly had studied the approach taken by the creators of *Julia*, for they followed it to the letter.

Sixteen years earlier, *Julia* took an almost trite sitcom formula—a single parent with a cute, mischievous kid, involved in amusing interactions with crusty bosses and wacky neighbors—and used its safe format as a way to ensure the success of an African American-themed series.

Cosby did precisely the same: it relied on the tried-and-true template of a classic American family sitcom (somewhat bumbling, laid-back dad, no-nonsense mom, sarcastic teenagers, cute moppets) to make something new—a series about an African American upper middleclass family—seem familiar and thereby more accessible to viewers.

—*Thomas Du Bose*

SHIRLEY CHISHOLM BECOMES FIRST AFRICAN AMERICAN WOMAN TO SERVE IN CONGRESS

November 1968

Chisholm was the first African American woman to serve in Congress and to run for president of the United States. She was a student activist, a New York state legislator, an active member of Congress, and an outspoken presidential campaigner who said she felt

more discriminated against as a woman than as an African American.

Born: November 30, 1924; Brooklyn, New York
Died: January 1, 2005; Ormond Beach, Florida

Also known as: Shirley Anita St. Hill Chisholm; Shirley Anita St. Hill (birth name)

Areas of achievement: Education; Government and politics

EARLY LIFE

Shirley Anita St. Hill Chisholm (CHIHZ-ohlm) was born in Brooklyn, New York, one of eight children of Guyanan immigrant Charles St. Hill and Barbados native Ruby Seale. When Chisholm was three, she and three sisters were sent to live with their grandmother in Barbados for eight years. She attributed her later success to the strict British education she received there. Back in Brooklyn, she attended Girls' High School, graduated cum laude in sociology as a scholarship student at Brooklyn College in 1946, and received a master's degree in elementary education from Columbia University in 1952.

She was married to Jamaican private investigator Conrad O. Chisholm from 1949 to 1977 (they divorced) and to Buffalo businessman Arthur Hardwick from 1977 until his death in 1986.

Chisholm worked in New York City as a teacher at Mount Calvary Child Care Center, as director of the Friends Day Nursery, and at Hamilton-Madison Child Care Center. From 1959 to 1964, she served as an educational consultant in the city's Bureau of Child Welfare. She became an activist as a member of Brooklyn College's Harriet Tubman Society and went on to serve as a board member for the Brooklyn Home for Aged Colored People, a member of the Brooklyn branch of the National Association for the Advancement of Colored People (NAACP), a volunteer at the Democratic Women's Workshop, and a member of the League of Women Voters and Bedford-Stuyvesant Political League.

Although her forthright and outspoken manner made her unpopular with local Democratic Party leaders, her community work helped her win election to two terms in the New York state legislature, where she worked to pass bills providing scholarships and remedial training for poor African American students, state funding for day care centers, and unemployment insurance for domestic workers. She also supported a bill that eliminated the practice of stripping tenure from woman teachers who took maternity leave. In 1968, Chisholm won a seat in Congress by a large margin over a prominent liberal white Republican civil rights leader. Her campaign slogan, "Unbought and Unbossed," became the title of her first book, published in 1970, and the basis for a later PBS documentary.

LIFE'S WORK

Chisholm started her first term in the U.S. House of Representatives with characteristic courage. Named to the Forestry Subcommittee of the Agriculture Committee, she protested on the floor of the House that there were no forests in Bedford-Stuyvesant for her to represent and that she wanted to serve on committees that dealt with racism, poverty, and urban decay. Within weeks she was named to the Veterans' Affairs Committee.

In her seven terms in the House, she also was appointed to the Education and Labor Committee and ultimately became the only woman on the Rules Committee. Throughout her tenure, she opposed war and defense expenditures and worked for employment, housing, education, and anti-hunger programs for the poor. She also worked against laws and customs that limited women's careers and supported abortion rights and the Equal Rights Amendment. Her women's liberation views made her a popular speaker on college campuses. She also was an active member of its Congressional Black Caucus.

In 1972, Chisholm decided to run for president. She fought to appear on television's *Face the Nation* alongside three other Democratic hopefuls, George McGovern, Henry Jackson, and Ed Muskie. In recognition of her efforts, fellow candidate Hubert Humphrey assigned his delegates to her at the Democratic National Convention, where the party named McGovern as its candidate. Chisholm had not expected to win the nomination, but in her 1973 book *The Good Fight*, she declared that someone had to do it first, and while her attempt did not open the door to women or African Americans, it pushed it ajar. She was named woman of the year by Clairol in 1973.

Chisholm retired from Congress in 1982. From 1983 to 1987, she was Purington Professor of politics and women's studies at Mount Holyoke College in Massachusetts, taking a year off (1985) to serve as a visiting scholar at Spelman College. In 1984, she cofounded the National Political Congress of Black Women and became its first president. Chisholm was a member of the advisory council of the National Organization for Women (NOW) and an honorary committee member of the United Negro College Fund. In 1988, she worked for the presidential campaign of Jesse Jackson. She continued to support early sex education in order to combat teenage pregnancy, urged more African Americans to become college professors, and opposed the Persian Gulf War in 1991, the same year she moved to Florida. In 1993, President Bill Clinton nominated her for the position of ambassador to Jamaica, but she declined because of declining health. That year, she was inducted into the National Women's Hall of Fame. Chisholm died January 1, 2005, in Florida after a series of strokes.

SIGNIFICANCE

In 1968, Chisholm became the first African American woman to be elected to Congress, and in 1972, she became the first major-party black candidate for president and the first woman to run for the Democratic presidential nomination (Margaret Chase Smith previously tried for the Republican nomination). She was outspoken about racial and economic conditions in the United States and what she considered the waste of war, as well as about her role as a trailblazer for future African Americans and women. Her significance was acknowledged even before Hillary Clinton and Barack Obama battled for the Democratic presidential nomination in 2008. In 2002, scholar Molefi Kete Asante included Chisholm on his list of One Hundred Greatest African Americans. She is celebrated in lyrics to songs such as "Nobody Beats the Biz" (1988) by Biz Markie, "Maaaad Crew" (1999) by Redman and Method Man, "Spread" (2003) by Andre 3000 of Outkast, "Mama and Me" (2005) by Nellie McKay, and "George Bush Is the Prez" (2006) by L. L. Cool J.

Chisholm's book *Unbought and Unbossed* was expanded and rereleased in 2010. It describes her 1968 campaign for the hotly contested new Seventeenth District congressional seat in a largely African American and Hispanic section of New York City. Her advantage was having worked for years for its citizens as an educator and New York state assemblywoman, her ability to

---

Chisholm's Campaign for the Presidency

Throughout her political career, Shirley Chisholm was guided by two beacons.

The first was expressed in all her political campaigns as well as in her speeches and formed the title of her first autobiography: her determination to remain "Unbought and Unbossed." The second was her desire to open doors for women and African Americans who aspired to high political office. She declared that she had felt more discrimination as a woman than as an African American, but she was fully aware of both forms of discrimination. Chisholm's disdain for the established Democratic Party bureaucracy won her no help in her campaigns, but her work in support of victims of race and class discrimination endeared her to her Bedford-Stuyvesant constituents and to national African American and women's liberation leaders. When she decided to become a presidential candidate, she did not expect to win. Her campaign's goal was to prepare voters for a time when women and African Americans would be accepted as serious candidates.

---

speak Spanish on the campaign trail, and her self-styled "Fighting Shirley Chisholm" image. In the PBS documentary based on *Unbought*, Chisholm expressed her wish to be remembered after her death as someone who dared to be a catalyst of change.

—*Erika E. Pilver*

REPUBLIC OF NEW AFRICA

Founded in 1968

Never more than a fringe movement, the Republic of New Africa is significant mostly for keeping alive the concept of reparations for slavery.

Identification: Revolutionary black nationalist organization
Place: Detroit, Michigan

Founded in 1968, the Republic of New Africa (RNA) was a revolutionary black nationalist organization whose primary objective was the territorial separation of African Americans from the rest of the United States. Its leaders proposed to make the five southern states considered the "Black Belt"—Mississippi, Louisiana, Alabama, Georgia, and South Carolina—an independent black-ruled nation. The organization also advocated cooperative economics and community self-sufficiency (as defined by the Tanzanian principles of "Ujamaa"); and the collection of reparations from the U.S. government in the amount of ten thousand dollars per person to compensate for retrenchment of the Reconstruction promise of "forty acres and a mule" to freed slaves.

The Republic of New Africa formed a government for the "non-self-governing African Americans held captive within the United States." "Consulates" were established in New York, Baltimore, Pittsburgh, Philadelphia, Washington, D.C., and Jackson, Mississippi. The RNA was seen as an internal threat to the security of the United States and targeted for attack by the U.S. federal government. In 2005, the organization still maintained an office in Washington, D.C., and claimed a membership of ten thousand people.

—*M. Bahati Kuumba*

See also: Black Christian Nationalist Movement; Black Power movement; National Coalition of Blacks for Reparations in America

"BLACK MANIFESTO"

April 26, 1969

The initial reaction to the demands of the "Black Manifesto" was positive with promises of support coming from several denominations and groups, but soon the religious press across the spectrum attacked the manifesto and its strategies.

The Event: Call by militant black leaders for white Christian churches and Jewish synagogues to pay reparations to African Americans for the hardships of slavery

Place: Detroit, Michigan

The "Black Manifesto" was presented by Student Nonviolent Coordinating Committee (SNCC) member James Forman to the National Black Economic Development Conference in Detroit, Michigan, and was adopted on April 26, 1969. The manifesto was a call to arms for African Americans to overthrow the current U.S. government, which it characterized as capitalist, racist, and imperialist, and to set up a black-led socialist government. The "Black Manifesto" demanded the payment of $500,000,000 in reparations to African Americans by white churches and Jewish synagogues to compensate for the hardships of slavery. Churches were specifically targeted because they were seen as agents of U.S. imperialism. The monies that were demanded in the manifesto were to be used to establish land banks, television studios, universities, and black presses. To pressure churches to pay the reparations, the manifesto advocated the disruption of church services and the seizure of church property.

The initial reaction to the demands of the "Black Manifesto" was positive with promises of support coming from several denominations and groups, but soon the religious press across the spectrum attacked the manifesto and its methods, which echoed Malcolm X's "by any means necessary" revolutionary strategies. The manifesto particularly alienated Jewish groups.

—*C. A. Wolski*

See also: Crown Heights conflicts; Nation of Islam; Student Nonviolent Coordinating Committee

RUSSELL RETIRES AS THE CELTICS TAKE AN ELEVENTH NBA TITLE

May 5, 1969

Bill Russell, perhaps the greatest U.S. professional basketball player of all time, retired after thirteen seasons, eleven of which his Celtic teams won the league championship. He also was the team's head coach from 1966 to 1969, making him the first African American head coach in U.S. professional sports history.

Locale: Inglewood, California

Category: Sports

KEY FIGURES

Bill Russell (b. 1934), professional basketball player and coach of the Boston Celtics, the Seattle Supersonics, and the Sacramento Kings

Wilt Chamberlain (1936-1999), professional basketball player for the Philadelphia Warriors, Harlem

Russell defending against Wilt Chamberlain of the Philadelphia 76ers in 1966 by New York World-Telegram and the Sun staff photographer

Globetrotters, Golden State Warriors, Philadelphia Seventy-Sixers, and Los Angeles Lakers

Jerry West (b. 1938), professional basketball player, coach, and administrator for the Los Angeles Lakers and the Memphis Grizzlies

John Havlicek (b. 1940), professional basketball player for the Boston Celtics

Elgin Baylor (b. 1934), professional basketball player for the Los Angeles Lakers, coach for the New Orleans Jazz, and administrator for the Los Angeles Clippers

Sam Jones (b. 1933), professional basketball player for the Boston Celtics

SUMMARY OF EVENT

On May 5, 1969, Bill Russell played his last game as a professional basketball player, helping the Boston Celtics to its eleventh National Basketball Association (NBA) championship in thirteen years. Many basketball historians believe that the seven-game championship series between the Celtics and the Los Angeles Lakers in 1969 was one of the greatest of the league's history.

The decisive game seven was played on the Lakers home turf, leading most experts to choose the Lakers to win. Game day started, however, with a costly psychological and strategic mistake by the Lakers' owner, who had placed hundreds of balloons along the ceiling of the Forum that were to be released after the expected Lakers victory. Celtics players noticed the balloons and were greatly motivated to ruin the Lakers' anticipated victory. Also, Celtics' players knew that there was a chance that Russell, their great center and coach, could retire at the end of this season-ending game, and they determined that he would go out a winner.

Game seven, another classic confrontation between Russell and Chamberlain and one that had its share of controversy, also turned out to be a late-in-the-game comeback victory for the Celtics. Chamberlain, who had twenty-seven rebounds to Russell's twenty-one, had hurt his knee with five minutes and forty-five seconds left in the game and had to sit out the last several minutes.

It has been said that during the last two or three minutes of the game, Chamberlain wanted to return to the game, telling his coach that he could play despite his injury. During those last two to three minutes, though, the Lakers lead disappeared and the Celtics came from behind to win.

The teams on which Russell played rarely lost. At the University of San Francisco, his team won the National Collegiate Athletic Association (NCAA) championship in 1955 and 1956 and even had a fifty-five-game winning streak. In the fall of 1956, Russell was captain of the gold-medal-winning U.S. men's Olympic basketball team. Shortly after, he had joined the Boston Celtics.

During his thirteen-year playing career with the Celtics, the team won the NBA league championship eleven times. He was voted the league's most valuable player five times and in 1975 was voted into the Basketball Hall of Fame. In 1980, Russell was voted the greatest player in the history of the NBA by the Professional Basketball Writers Association of America.

SIGNIFICANCE

The 1969 championship season was the culmination of a great basketball career for Russell. This successful season had confirmed Russell's selfless, team-first philosophy, which emphasized a defensive style of play characterized by rebounding, blocking opponents' shots, and passing the ball to open teammates. His leadership reflected his friendly personality, high level of intelligence, and worthiness as a role model for youth. Making his career even more remarkable is that Russell played during the 1950's and 1960's, a troubled time in the United States that saw explicit racism and bigotry, especially against African Americans.

—*Alan Prescott Peterson*

LEAGUE OF REVOLUTIONARY BLACK WORKERS

Founded in June, 1969

This organization was formed to fight racism within the United Auto Workers union. The group encompassed the Dodge Revolutionary Union Movement and similar groups.

Identification: Radical African American labor organization
Place: Detroit, Michigan

In 1967, African American autoworkers at the Detroit-area Dodge main plant formed the Dodge Revolutionary Union Movement (DRUM), a rank-and-file union caucus. DRUM accused both the company and the United Auto Workers (UAW) of racism, citing evidence that the best positions went to whites, while African Americans had the dirtiest, most dangerous jobs. The group charged that the nearly all-white local union leadership perpetuated this system by inadequately addressing the grievances of African American workers. Scores of other "RUMs" formed, including ELRUM at the Eldon Avenue plant, FRUM at the Ford plant, and UPRUM among United Parcel Service workers. The League of Revolutionary Black Workers, founded in June, 1969, acted as their umbrella group.

League organizations conducted demonstrations and wildcat strikes in response to unfair working conditions. DRUM believed racism was intentionally cultivated by employers and the union to divide African American, white, and Arab workers (who were numerous in Detroit). League members picketed the UAW International convention and ran against incumbents in union elections. The league gained broad left-wing support, but the UAW responded with red-baiting and called the league's publications "extremist hate sheets" and its members "black fascists."

The league voiced a powerful critique of racism in the union movement. Strongly influenced by black nationalism and Marxism-Leninism, it was one of the most prominent radical labor groups of the 1960's. Several League activists helped launch the Black Workers Congress in 1970; shortly afterward, the league disintegrated amid internal disputes.

—*Vanessa Tait*

See also: Black nationalism; Black Panther Party; Black Power movement; Employment; Race riots of the twentieth century

DAVIS INTRODUCES JAZZ-ROCK FUSION

August, 1969

Miles Davis's jazz-rock fusion album Bitches Brew shook jazz out of its commercial doldrums and spawned a style that characterized much of the jazz produced during the 1970's.

Also known as: *Bitches Brew*
Locale: United States
Category: Music

KEY FIGURES
Miles Davis (1926-1991), distinctive and influential trumpeter responsible for many innovative approaches to jazz
Chick Corea (b. 1941), *Bitches Brew* keyboardist whose later groups reflected jazz-rock tendencies
John McLaughlin (b. 1942), *Bitches Brew* guitarist who later led the Mahavishnu Orchestra, an important fusion band

Wayne Shorter (b. 1933), *Bitches Brew* saxophonist who was later a coleader of the creative jazz-rock combo Weather Report

Joe Zawinul (1932-2007), *Bitches Brew* keyboardist who was later a coleader of Weather Report

Summary of Event

The integration of jazz and rock—long awaited and often prematurely announced during the 1960's—was fully achieved for the first time on Miles Davis's album *Bitches Brew* in 1969. Making frequent use of electronic instruments and sophisticated studio techniques, the resulting "fusion" jazz style was based on a synthesis of modern jazz with elements of rock, pop, and soul music of the 1960's. A trumpeter known for his influential tone and distinctive improvisations, Davis had been a dominant force in jazz since the late 1940's, changing jazz perhaps more deeply and in more varied ways than anyone else.

Though fusion jazz had forerunners prior to the appearance of *Bitches Brew*—for example, the music of Soft Machine and the Gary Burton Quarter—Davis was influenced very little, if at all, by those artists. His work had always demonstrated his compulsion to explore new musical territory on his own terms. By the time he recorded *Bitches Brew* in August, 1969, he had played in the classic bebop style with Charlie Parker, broken new ground with the cool style of his Capitol band in the late 1940's, played first hard bop and then a pioneering modal style during the 1950's, and then had experimented in the 1960's with a style that was based on modal concepts but was more open in its harmonic structure and was played with sharper accents.

By the late 1960's, Davis's creativity was by no means exhausted. He was listening to many rock and rhythm-and-blues artists, especially James Brown, Jimi Hendrix, and Sly and the Family Stone. Electronic instruments caught his ear as early as 1967. By 1968, Davis was incorporating electronic instruments and rock rhythms into his music. The effect varied—sometimes the new approach produced a collage of sound, at other times a danceable ostinato, or "ground," beat with garish harmonies and exotic melodies floating above it.

Although Davis's *In a Silent Way* (1969), with its multiple percussionists and electric piano players, came first, his *Bitches Brew*, which was recorded six months later, represents the full flowering of the jazz fusion style. Breaking radically with tradition, this two-disc album captures a collage of jam sessions characterized by impressionistic soloing over shifting, rock-influenced rhythms and a continuous interplay of electronic keyboards, guitar, and percussion instruments. *Bitches Brew* pulled out all the stops, as Davis superimposed the sophisticated, modally based harmonies and more flexible phrasings of jazz on rock's intensity. Furthermore, Davis produced new, brilliantly colored sound surfaces through his combination of sonorities, as in "Spanish Key," which features a soprano saxophone over a bluesy electric piano and guitar with a rich bass clarinet droning underneath.

The working principles of the *Bitches Brew* band—like those of all the previous Davis groups—were spontaneity and Davis's uncanny ability to capitalize on every idea, no matter how small, which he encountered. Davis was as much influenced by his sidemen as they were by him, but for Davis, such influence meant that he used creatively everything he heard. There were virtually no rehearsals for the *Bitches Brew* sessions, and the resulting music reflects the unpredictability and boldness of its methodology.

The most tightly organized track on the album is "Miles Runs the Voodoo Down." It is perhaps the track most likely to appeal to fans of Davis's earlier styles. His melodic trumpet lines dovetail well with the rock-like beat underneath (a characteristic not to be found in the looser structure of the twenty-minute-long "Pharoah's Dance"). Davis's solo on "Voodoo" varies effectively quick phrases and long tones, a recognizable element in his straightahead jazz playing. The track is punctuated heavily with the sounds of South American and African percussive instruments (percussion would blossom throughout the 1970's). By contrast, "Bitches Brew" is an impressionistic and expansive twenty-seven-minute vamp-plus-improvisation.

Davis's open trumpet sound reverberates through an electronic Echoplex unit, surrounded by chord splashes from a guitar and an electric piano. On top of an ostinato bass, Davis's trumpet pierces and unites the various elements of a Charlie Mingus-like instrumental conversation. Sustained energy and sensitivity characterize Wayne Shorter's "Sanctuary," which elicits one of Davis's longest solos. "Spanish Key," by John McLaughlin, features straight-out rock rhythm with numerous stoptime breaks that became a formula for the fusion style in later years.

In 1968, Davis had announced his intention of forming the best rock-and-roll band in the world. As far as jazz-rock was concerned, he succeeded in gathering the most original and prolific one. Musicians apply the term "bitch" only to the finest of improvisers. Given the

Bitches Brew sessions' improvisational nature and assembled talent, the album's title proved quite appropriate.

The album quickly sold 400,000 copies, four times the number sold for Davis's previous best seller, *Sketches of Spain*, another fusion of sorts done with composer-arranger Gil Evans. So-called pure jazz had never fared so well commercially, especially since the rapid development of rock and its commercial domination of the music business.

SIGNIFICANCE

Davis received equal amounts of praise and scorn for *Bitches Brew*. Some saw his fusion style as little more than inspired mercantilism. Yet objective critics, who judged the music on its merits rather than on Davis's intentions, recognized it as coherent, highly improvisational, exciting, and evocative. Unquestionably, it jolted jazz out of its commercial doldrums and expanded jazz's horizons.

The ingredients of *Bitches Brew*—though Davis's combination of them was unmatched—became the recipe for much of the jazz produced during the 1970's. The success of the *Bitches Brew* band and of those that had preceded it during the 1960's—many of whom became well known individually—serves as a barometer of Davis's impact on yet another generation of jazz musicians.

The degree and consistency of the fusion synthesis is attributable in part to the unprecedented impact of rock and soul music on American listening habits. Jazz musicians have always absorbed the sounds around them, and the aesthetic development of rock and soul, along with the increased availability of electric pianos, guitars, and synthesizers, thus made the cross-fertilization that led to *Bitches Brew* inevitable. Fusion developed more purposefully than earlier jazz styles, with bands making significant use of electronic instruments and overdubbing and editing separately recorded tracks—factors that had played a minimal role in jazz prior to 1969. The advantages of electronic sound, noted enthusiasts, were multiple. It captured the tones, timbres, and energy of much rock and soul music; it became easier to play louder and faster, an asset in the cavernous halls needed to house fusion audiences; and, given programmable synthesizers, it offered new tone colors with which to work.

Some argued that electronic instruments, which abandoned the subtlety and nuances of the acoustic for volume and gadgetry, could not communicate the personality of the musician. Fusion musicians, however, having discovered the power of modern recording equipment to improve on what had been played in a studio or even to record music that was physically unplayable by a band performing live, insisted that the electronics were just as appropriate to fusion as acoustic instruments had been to modern jazz.

Fusion exploded on the music scene after the appearance of *Bitches Brew*. Davis continued to play fusion until ill health and an accident led to a seven-year retirement beginning in 1974 (after his return in 1981, he performed a pop-oriented type of jazz-rock). In 1973, keyboardist Herbie Hancock, a Davis alumnus (from the 1963-1968 bands), recorded jazz's first gold album by combining funky and danceable rhythms with a modicum of jazz melodic and harmonic feeling. Fusion's commercial peak was reached as early as 1976, when George Benson, a superb improvising jazz guitarist of the 1960's who had played briefly with Davis, was transformed into a semipop vocalist with the album *Breezin'*, which went on to sell four million copies by 1980. The leaders of the major fusion bands of the 1970's—Chick Corea of Return to Forever, John McLaughlin of the Mahavishnu Orchestra, and Joe Zawinul and Wayne Shorter of Weather Report—all came from the ranks of the *Bitches Brew* group.

Fusion, the dominant strain of jazz during the 1970's and 1980's, has been both lucrative and controversial. Critics maintain that its profits and popularity have far exceeded its durability, aesthetic value, or contribution to the development of jazz. Defenders point out that, for all of fusion's limitations, it helped overcome the uncommunicative and elitist image that jazz had projected in the 1960's, thus gaining a much wider audience for jazz in the era of rock. Fusion is an eclectic rather than an innovative jazz style, and its coupling of repetitive rhythms with electronically amplified instruments led in time to the creation of a formulaic music characterized by a finely detailed yet passive musical fabric. Nevertheless, jazz fusion was responsible for some undeniably exciting music in its heyday during the 1970's.

—*L. Moody Simms, Jr.*

See also: Parker's Playing Epitomizes Bebop; Mahalia Jackson Begins Her Recording Career; Davis Develops 1950's Cool Jazz; Berry's "Maybellene" Popularizes Rock and Roll; Gordy Founds Motown Records; Brown Introduces Funk Music; Hendrix Releases Acid Rock Album *Are You Experienced?*

HAMPTON-CLARK DEATHS

December 4, 1969

Black Panther members Fred Hampton and Mark Clark were killed by Illinois state police officers.

The Event: Concerted effort by law enforcement to destroy New Left and African American radical organizations
Place: Illinois

Twenty-one-year-old Fred Hampton and twenty-two-year-old Mark Clark were leaders in the Illinois branch of the Black Panther Party, a radical African American organization that had a reputation for militancy and was dedicated to equality between whites and African Americans; the group was particularly active in Chicago, where it had a large membership.

On December 4, 1969, Clark and Hampton were killed during an early-morning raid on their apartment by members of the Illinois state police. The police fired between eighty-two and one hundred shots through the door at the apartment's inhabitants. Hampton, chairman of the Illinois branch of the Black Panther Party, was hit four times, twice in the head. Clark, a Panther leader from Peoria, Illinois, fired a single shot at the police (the only shot fired during the incident by those inside) before being killed. Four of the seven other Panthers in the apartment, including Hampton's pregnant girlfriend, were wounded. Hampton was probably drugged the previous evening by police and Federal Bureau of Investigation (FBI) informant William O'Neal, who had provided police and members of the FBI with a map of the apartment showing where Clark and Hampton slept.

After the killings, the Panthers opened the apartment for public viewing. Thousands walked through the quarters and saw for themselves the damage the police had done. The Illinois attorney general filed charges of attempted murder against the surviving Panthers. His office supported police attempts to characterize the attack as a shootout in which police acted in self-defense. These attempts included lying to the media about a gun Hampton was said to have fired (paraffin tests later proved Hampton had not fired any weapon) and stating that nail holes in the apartment door were actually bullet holes from weapons fired by the Panthers.

AFTERMATH

The Hampton-Clark killings convinced many Americans that the U.S. government meant to eradicate the Panthers and other African American radicals. That police would kill citizens as they slept and execute a concerted coverup dramatized the extremes to which government agencies would go. The overall, eventual effect of the murders was to create sympathy for the Panthers among whites and African Americans.

A federal grand jury was empaneled in January, 1970, and was subsequently disbanded four months later without indicting anyone. Charges against the Panthers were dropped soon after. A state grand jury was empaneled and in April, 1971, indicted twelve police officers, the state attorney general, and another member of his office for obstruction of justice. The case went to trial in July, 1972. In October, 1972, the judge acquitted the defendants on all charges without requiring them to present their case.

Hampton and Clark's families sued the state of Illinois, the state attorney general, and the police in 1970, but the case was delayed until all criminal proceedings were through. A third criminal trial began in 1976 and ended in another acquittal by the bench, despite a deadlocked jury. This acquittal was overturned in a federal appeals court in 1979 and was upheld by the U.S. Supreme Court in June, 1980. Meanwhile, declassified FBI files revealed the existence of a concerted FBI offensive against the Panthers and other African American and left-wing organizations. The civil trial brought by the slain men's families began in 1976 after a series of government delays. On February 28, 1983, the families of Hampton and Clark received a settlement of $1.85 million.

—Ron Jacobs

See also: "Black Manifesto"; Black nationalism; Black Panther Party; Black Power movement; Civil Rights movement

MITCHELL AND SHOOK FOUND THE DANCE THEATRE OF HARLEM

1969

The Dance Theatre of Harlem, founded by ballet dancer Arthur Mitchell and ballet teacher Karel Shook, became the first world-renowned African American ballet company. The company's success continues into the twenty-first century.

Also known as: School of Dance Theatre of Harlem
Locale: New York, New York
Categories: Dance; organizations and institutions; education

KEY FIGURES

Arthur Mitchell (b. 1934), principal dancer with the New York City Ballet, who became cofounder of the Dance Theatre of Harlem

Karel Shook (1920-1985), ballet teacher, choreographer, and former director of the Netherlands Ballet, who became cofounder of the Dance Theatre of Harlem

SUMMARY OF EVENT

Arthur Mitchell, a principal dancer with the New York City Ballet, was at a New York airport en route to Brazil on April 4, 1968, the day Martin Luther King, Jr., was assassinated. The idea to develop a black ballet company germinated that same day. Mitchell noted, "I sat there the whole time, thinking to myself, here I am running around the world doing all these things, why not do them at home?" Mitchell was commuting to Brazil, where he was establishing that country's first national ballet company under the auspices of the United States. He was asked to head the Brazilian group as permanent artistic director; the event of April 4, though, lingered in his thoughts.

Mitchell declined the offer and returned to New York. He felt that he should go to Harlem, the community of his youth, to open a school and pass on his knowledge to other African Americans. Mitchell thus aimed both to open a school and to found a company in which the school's graduates could perform; he believed that,

with talent and given proper instruction, African Americans could achieve success in ballet.

Mitchell approached Karel Shook, ballet master of the Netherlands Ballet and Mitchell's former teacher at the Katherine Dunham School of Dance, to assist in the undertaking. The two established the Dance Theatre of Harlem as a school of allied arts and as a professional dance company. Their goal for the Dance Theatre was "to promote public interest in and support for the aims of the organization, while providing role models and professional goals for aspiring students." With the financial assistance of the Ford Foundation, the school opened in a garage and a church basement belonging to the Harlem School of Arts. The original student body of thirty increased to four hundred within two months. Many of the students had at first been curious onlookers, since the garage doors were left open for ventilation and light.

The primary purpose of the school was "to promote interest in and teach young black people the art of classical ballet, modern and ethnic dance, thereby creating a much-needed self-awareness and better self-image of the students themselves." The instructors at the school included Mary Hinkson, a renowned Martha Graham dancer who taught modern dance, and Pearl Reynolds,

Young dancers from the Dance Theatre of Harlem perform during a dinner held at the White House on February 6, 2006. President George W. Bush and Laura Bush are in attendance.

who instructed the ethnic dance classes. Classical ballet classes were conducted by Mitchell and Shook.

Strained relations with the Harlem School of Arts and the advice of George Balanchine and Lincoln Kirstein led to Mitchell's opening the school as an independent endeavor. The school and company moved to new premises.

The long-range goal of the Dance Theatre was the production of dancers soundly trained in the classical tradition. Mitchell noted, "We have to prove that a black ballet school and a black ballet company are the equal of the best of their kind, anywhere in the world." The performing company was inaugurated in February of 1969, with Balanchine and Kirstein as members of the company's first board of directors.

Since funding from the Ford Foundation was provided via a matching grant, the Dance Theatre of Harlem began performances as a means of raising money. The programs also provided the dancers with an opportunity for development as artists. In addition, frequent lectures and demonstrations were given for a range of audiences, from neighborhood children to corporate executives. The school also expanded to include classes in related aspects of theater production. Lighting, sound, music, costuming, stage management, and accounting became part of the curriculum.

During this period, Mitchell was still performing with the New York City Ballet. As he became increasingly involved with the operation of his organization, however, Mitchell's performances became fewer. In 1970, Mitchell resigned from the New York City Ballet, informing Balanchine of his need to stop dancing to devote his full attention to the Dance Theatre of Harlem.

The first extended performance of the Dance Theatre of Harlem took place in August of 1970 at Jacob's Pillow, Lee, Massachusetts. The official debut of the company occurred in 1971 at the Guggenheim Museum in New York. In 1974, the Dance Theatre of Harlem presented its first Broadway season at the Anta Theatre.

SIGNIFICANCE

Following the official debut of the Dance Theatre of Harlem, the company built its international reputation. In 1971, the company participated in the Festival of Two Worlds in Spoleto, Italy, and played other Italian engagements. Cities in Switzerland and the Netherlands were also included on the performance schedule. The Dance Theatre gained recognition within the United States as well through its touring. The repertoire of the Dance Theatre diversified under the artistic direction of Mitchell, and Balanchine ballets were added to the repertoire.

The Dance Theatre is acknowledged as one of the world's finest ballet companies. Initially predominantly composed of black dancers, the company has come to include several white dancers, underscoring its initial concept and attesting to the universality of classical ballet. In this regard, Mitchell has commented, "Blackness is now irrelevant in ballet."

—*Mary Pat Balkus, updated by Patricia A McDaniel*

BLACK UNITED STUDENTS IS FORMED

Founded during the late 1960's

These students, spurred by the Black Power movement, worked toward establishing black studies departments in colleges and universities.

Identification: Militant organization of African American college students

In the latter half of the 1960's, African American college students, inspired by the Black Power movement, formed collectives in colleges and universities throughout the United States in order to improve the lives of African American students and institute black studies departments. The first record of students organizing as the Black United Students was at San Francisco State University in 1968. The group was organized by Professor Nathan Hare, who later denied his part in the student strike, and supported by the Third World Liberation Front, a coalition of minority groups.

In November, 1968, the Black United Students, with the encouragement of the Black Panther Party, called for a student strike at San Francisco State University. The group presented the campus administration with fifteen nonnegotiable demands relating to the creation of a black studies department and the improvement of black student life. In response to the students' protest, San Francisco State University created the first integrated black studies program in 1969. Previously, Meritt Junior College in nearby Oakland, California, had begun offering a few courses in black studies, primarily to appease some members of the Black Panther Party, such as Huey P. Newton, who were attending the junior college, but it did not create a complete black studies department.

In addition to their efforts toward establishing black studies departments, the Black United Students actively joined with other campus groups in antiwar, antiestablishment protests in the late 1960's and early 1970's. The most noteworthy of these protests occurred in 1970, when the Students for a Democratic Society (SDS) and the Black United Students cosponsored a demonstration at Kent State University in Ohio, where four young people were killed by the Ohio National Guard.

IMPACT

The efforts of the Black United Students and similar African American groups helped establish black studies departments in numerous colleges and universities in the late 1960's and the following decades. By the 1990's, approximately two hundred black studies programs had been created across the nation. These programs have evolved from the original 1960's programs, which were sometimes cursory and not very well thought out, into degree-granting, three-tiered programs. At the first level, these programs provide an introduction to African history and to the African experience in the Americas and in other parts of the world. At the second level, they begin to include more specific courses and examine current issues and research, delving into issues such as the place of African Americans in American society. At the third level, the programs offer an integrated look at African influences on and experiences of psychology, economics, political science, sociology, history, and literature.

In the late 1990's, a number of organizations calling themselves the Black United Students were located on campuses across the United States. These organizations act to further the interests of African American students.

—Annita Marie Ward

See also: Black Panther Party; Civil Rights movement; Education; Student Nonviolent Coordinating Committee

CONGRESSIONAL BLACK CAUCUS

1970

The caucus also strove to ensure that the government assisted others in need, including children, the elderly, and the physically and mentally ill.

Identification: Group comprising African American members of Congress formed to advance the concerns of African Americans and other members of minority groups

The Congressional Black Caucus, a group comprising African American members of the U.S. Congress, was established in 1970 by thirteen members of the House of Representatives who joined together "to promote the public welfare through legislation designed to meet the needs of millions of neglected citizens." Before that year, the House had never had so many African Americans among its 435 members, yet thirteen was still a small minority. The founders of the Congressional Black Caucus hoped that they could gain more visibility and power working together than they could acting alone.

In 1971, the Congressional Black Caucus was granted a meeting with President Richard M. Nixon, during which its members presented a document describing sixty actions the government should take on domestic and international issues. The president promised to promote desegregation by seeing that civil rights laws were more stringently enforced (later, caucus members came to believe that he did not work hard enough to fulfill his promise). Media coverage of the meeting helped the group gain recognition. Over the next quarter-century, members of the caucus built and strengthened ties with other influential members of the black community, including educators, community and religious leaders, and local and state legislators, which enabled the group to influence public policy at all levels of government.

Although originally formed to promote the concerns of African Americans and other members of minority groups, the caucus also worked to ensure that the government assisted others in need, including children, the elderly, and the physically and mentally ill. The group asserts that it is possible and desirable to develop a national African American position on matters of federal policy, and it has sought to direct that effort. Since its founding, the group has introduced and supported legislation concerning domestic issues such as employment, welfare and health care reform, education reform, small business development, urban revitalization, and federal disaster relief.

In 1981, members of the caucus spoke out against the budget proposed by President Jimmy Carter, believing that it devoted too much funding to the military and too little to social programs. At House Judiciary Committee hearings in 1996, following a rash of fire-bombings of black churches across the South, the caucus criticized the federal government's apparent failure to prosecute those guilty of the crimes. Many of the group's positions have been unpopular, even among some African Americans; in the late 1990's, for example, the caucus strongly endorsed the work of the controversial leader of the Nation of Islam Louis Farrakhan, who was accused by many of teaching anti-Semitism.

As the visibility and influence of the caucus increased, the group called for action on international issues of special concern to African Americans, including human rights. It was one of the earliest and strongest voices urging that the United States use pressure against apartheid in South Africa and to call for increased attention and aid to other African nations.

—*Cynthia A. Bily*

See also: Black nationalism; Chisholm's election to Congress; Church burnings; Politics and government; Summit Meeting of National Negro Leaders

BLOODS AND CRIPS GANGS

1970-

The Crips and Bloods are two, formerly rival, street gangs that formed in urban Los Angeles in the early 1970s and came to national prominence in the 1980s. Due to widespread media coverage during the 1980s and 90s, the Crips and Bloods gained national attention with groups claiming Crip and Blood membership arising in cities around the nation.

Identification: The Bloods and Crips were predominantly African American street gangs, founded in Los Angeles, California in the early 1970s.

Historians examining the history of African American street gangs in the United States, point to the economic depression hitting American cities at the end of the 1950s as one of the factors that led to the emergence of the large gangs like the Crips and Bloods. High unemployment rates, racism fomenting antagonism between young African American men and police, and the deterioration of the Black Pride Movement, largely due to police and FBI persecution, helped to create an impetus for young African Americans to band together in street gangs. While street gangs had long been a part of urban youth culture in California, the Crips and Bloods became internationally famous, inspiring Crip and Blood sets in numerous cities and hundreds of imitators trying to create similar street gangs.

The Crips was founded by Raymond Lee Washington and Stanley Tookie Williams, both of whom ran small gangs in South Central Los Angeles before deciding to combine their forces to control a larger territory. The gang was originally called the "Cribs" because of the youth of their members, but as members later became known for carrying canes in an effort to cultivate a "pimp" aesthetic, neighborhood residents began calling them the "cripples" or "crips." As the gang grew, it began splitting into different "sets," or local crews, such as the "Main Street Crips," and the "Rolling 20 Crips." Though all operating under the Crips banner, the smaller sets were in competition and often fought one another at the edges of each set's territory and in the city's public schools, which became a focal point for gang recruitment and conflict. In 1979, founder Raymond Washington was killed by a rival gang member, while Tookie Williams was incarcerated on four counts of murder. According to the autobiography of founder Tookie Williams, the Crips started wearing blue bandanas and blue clothing after one member, known as Buddha, inspired the trend with his all blue outfits accessorized with a bandanna. Blue was also the color of Washington High School where many of the original Crips were students.

The Crip's rival, the Bloods was formed in the early 1970s by Sylvester Scott and Vincent Owens, who originally called the gang the "Compton Pirus." The group formed to protect themselves from the increasing dominance of the Crips and began incorporating members from other gangs from the area who had been attacked or threatened by Crips members. By the late 1970s, the gang was known as "the Bloods," and, as they were still outnumbered by Crips, Bloods members became famous for their aggression, escalating violence to protect their territories. Members also began wearing red and sporting red bandannas to represent their gang affiliation, which was the color of Centennial High School where many early Bloods were students.

The rivalry between the Crips and Bloods escalated markedly in the 1980s when both gangs became involved in the sale of crack cocaine. With drug sale territory becoming a premium in Los Angeles, violence between Crips and Bloods intensified and national news agencies began covering the fued. Many historians have since criticized the national response to the issue, which involved militarizing local police forces to fight a "war on drugs" in America's cities. With police treating the street gangs like paramilitary organizations, and largely ignoring or downplaying any alternative methods of addressing the rising violence, animosity between African American youth and police intensified markedly. In 2015, it was estimated that the rivalry between the Bloods and Crips resulted in more than 15,000 deaths. The 1984 film *Colors*, exploring the rise of youth gang culture in Los Angeles, combined with the proliferation of "gangsta rap," from California, helped to make the Crips and Bloods national brands with satellite Crips and Bloods sets emerging in cities around the nation.

The feud between the Crips and Bloods died out in the 1990s, though both organizations remain active in many cities. However, the militarization of police is an ongoing phenomenon that contributes to antagonism between African American youth and police, encouraging members of both groups to view members of the opposite group as potential enemies. This ongoing pattern plays a role in the widely reported instances of police violence against African American youth in the 2010s that created national activist movements like *Stop the Killing* and *Black Lives Matter*.

—*Micah Issitt*

EVANS V. ABNEY

January 29, 1970

The Supreme Court imposed a racially neutral principle to decide a question of the legitimacy of race-based restrictions on parkland donated to a municipality.

The Case: U.S. Supreme Court ruling on restrictive covenants

Justice Hugo L. Black wrote the 6–2 majority opinion upholding a decision of a Georgia court that a park built on land donated to the city of Macon explicitly for use as a whites-only park had to be closed and the property returned to the heirs of the person donating the land. Previous decisions made it clear that Macon was barred on equal protection grounds from operating the park on a racially restrictive basis. Because the benefactor had been explicit in his instructions, the Court decided the only proper course of action was to return the land to the heirs.

Although African Americans were still denied access to the park, so were whites, thus preserving racial neutrality. Justices William O. Douglas and William J. Brennan, Jr., dissented, and Thurgood Marshall did not participate.

—*Richard L. Wilson*

See also: Segregation

NATIONAL BLACK WOMEN'S POLITICAL LEADERSHIP CAUCUS

Founded in 1971

This organization is dedicated to helping African American women work toward equality and increase their knowledge of the role of women in the political process.

545

Identification: Organization that encourages African American women and youth to participate in the country's economic and political systems

Founded in 1971, the National Black Women's Leadership Political Caucus is committed to helping African American women work toward equality and increase their knowledge of the role of women in the political process. The organization has its headquarters in Washington, D.C., but it also has groups in three regions and thirty-three states throughout the United States. Aside from its primary members, the caucus has an auxiliary membership that includes men, senior citizens, and youth. The organization encourages African American women and youth to participate in the country's economic and political systems. In addition, the caucus enables women to familiarize themselves with the

functions of city, state, and federal government. The group is also involved in research, conducting studies in the areas of African American families, politics, and economics. A variety of other services are provided by the National Black Women's Political Leadership Caucus, such as training in public speaking; legislative federal, state, and local workshops; children's services; charitable programs; awards for humanitarianism; and placement services. The organization publishes a semi-annual newsletter and has published election tabloids.

—K. Sue Jewell

See also: Colored Women's League; Combahee River Collective; Million Woman March; National Association of Colored Women; National Council of Negro Women.

ALL IN THE FAMILY CONFRONTS CONTROVERSIAL ISSUES
January 12, 1971-September 16, 1976

Norman Lear's All in the Family *revolutionized the content of situation comedies by dealing with currently controversial topics, many previously taboo for television, in both humorous and touching ways.*

Locale: United States
Category: Radio and television

KEY FIGURES
Norman Lear (b. 1922), creator of *All in the Family*
  Robert D. Wood (1925-1986), president of the Columbia Broadcasting System
Bud Yorkin (b. 1926), producer and director of *All in the Family Carroll O'Connor* (1924-2001), actor who played the role of Archie Bunker on *All in the Family Jean Stapleton* (b. 1923), actor who played the role of Edith Bunker
Sally Struthers (b. 1948), actor who played the role of Gloria Stivic
Rob Reiner (b. 1947), actor who played the role of Mike Stivic

SUMMARY OF EVENT
On January 12, 1971, the Columbia Broadcasting System (CBS) broadcast the first episode in a situation comedy (sitcom) series that would soon change the course of television comedy. Critic Dwight Newton

said of this show, *All in the Family*, "In one half hour, CBS destroyed old taboos and liberated comedy writing." The program had a simple premise. A working-class family of father, mother, and daughter, in a blue-collar neighborhood of New York City, portrayed the

When Archie visits a local blood bank to make a donation, he meets his neighbor, Lionel Jefferson, who is there to do the same thing. CBS television.

ambitions, concerns, and fears of millions of Americans who faced the changing social values and conditions of the 1970's. The father, Archie Bunker, was especially concerned over the changes wrought by the Civil Rights movement and the youth culture prevalent on many college campuses at that time. The very forces he feared were brought into his own home as his daughter, Gloria, fell in love with and eventually married Mike Stivic, a liberal college student. When the young couple moved in with Archie and his wife, Edith, the stage was set for regular confrontations between the reactionary views of Archie and the liberal opinions of "Meathead," as Archie referred to Mike.

Television critics and social commentators noted that the broadcast of this program represented a new peak in the social revolution of the 1960's and that the medium of television entertainment would now aid in spreading the revolutionary liberal views. The basic theme of the show was that of young people with 1960's values trying to make a life for themselves while being forced by circumstances to live under an imposed arbitrary authority.

Unlike the popular television series of the 1950's *Father Knows Best*, on *All in the Family*, the daughter, the son-in-law, and even the mother all had something to say about what was "best." Jean Stapleton, in the role of Edith Bunker, portrayed the changes affecting millions of American women at that time. Edith was a housewife, and she knew herself to be one of a dying breed. Many of her fictional contemporaries worked outside the home. Edith did not expect her daughter, Gloria, to have the same relationship with her husband, Mike Stivic, that she had with Archie. Although not ready to join the National Organization for Women or to demonstrate in the streets, Edith still saw new vistas of opportunity opening before her as a woman, and she occasionally shocked her husband by exploring one of those new avenues. Although bumbling in physical actions and often under assault from her husband as a "dingbat," Edith maintained her essential personal dignity and often brought to the resolution of problems a warmhearted dose of common sense.

If television critics and social commentators thought *All in the Family* to be new and wonderful, the public had different views. The pilot episode for the series had been offered to the American Broadcasting Company (ABC), which showed it to a test audience and received such poor responses that the network declined to purchase the show. Some sociologists have suggested that many members of the test audience probably actually liked the show but were ashamed to say so because some of the opinions expressed by the actors were not considered socially acceptable, even though many viewers agreed with those opinions.

Robert D. Wood, president of CBS, was determined to replace the aging stories and actors making up the CBS lineup with fresh, contemporary material. He saw the social mood of the United States in 1971 as a mixture of anxiety and hope. To him, *All in the Family* reflected these dual notes. Bud Yorkin, producer and director of *All in the Family*, agreed. He believed that young people in particular were ready for a new approach to television entertainment. Many of them were challenging established assumptions or had peers who were, and they wanted entertainment that dealt with these same real issues.

On these assumptions, CBS purchased the show. In a move unusual for television, the network allowed the show to stay on the air despite a slow start. Its audience grew as viewers became accustomed to the radical change in television conventions represented by the show.

These changed conventions included episodes in which the show dealt with abortion, homosexuality, impotence, menopause, civil disobedience, and a host of other topics not previously dealt with in any depth by television shows, either drama or comedy. Archie Bunker's blatant racism was featured in virtually every episode, and other previously taboo topics were fair game. Among other "firsts" on the show were the sound of a toilet flushing and a discussion of toilet paper. Never before had there been any evidence on American television that people go to the bathroom.

All in the Family was not an original idea. Norman Lear, creator of the series, stated that he was inspired by the British program *Till Death Us Do Part*, which featured a blue-collar worker in an urban setting. Topics were updated, however, for relevance to contemporary American life.

Despite its ever-increasing popularity, CBS was not always comfortable with the content and direction of the show. Numerous battles were fought within the standards and practices division of CBS over the content of various episodes. *All in the Family*, however, became the nation's most-watched regular television show in its first season, and it retained that position for five seasons. After that, it was consistently in the top fifteen shows in viewership until it was canceled at the beginning of the 1982-1983 season.

SIGNIFICANCE

The enormous popularity of *All in the Family* made it clear that people were ready for a new approach that dealt with contemporary issues in a way that reflected the concerns of society. Rather than restricting comedy to sanitized presentations of family life as in previous shows, *All in the Family* allowed reality to tint comedy to some extent. This does not mean that the show offered solutions to social problems. Archie Bunker was a narrow-minded character who often expressed bigoted views. He portrayed those views honestly and unapologetically. Because he was also a lovable and ineffective character, his views were not taken seriously or viewed as threatening. Some viewers saw Archie as a hero, able to express opinions no longer socially acceptable even though they were still commonly held. Others reveled in the putdowns that Archie suffered as a racist.

In the same way, Mike Stivic represented new liberal values but also could not support his views completely. As a student who had not yet assumed the responsibility of holding a job and supporting a family, his liberal views could be seen as idealistic but not practical. *All in the Family* thus effectively presented the controversies of the 1970's without being didactic. This approach reflected the social and political interests of the show's creator, Norman Lear. Lear described himself as a social and political liberal whose politics informed his sense of comedy. Lear believed that people laugh hardest when they are the most concerned.

Going beyond his television presentations, Lear founded the political lobbying organization People for the American Way. He brought to this organization all the skills of Hollywood in raising money, recruiting celebrities, and producing advertisements capable of conveying a powerful message in a short time. The most notable activity of this group was its successful opposition to the nomination of Robert H. Bork to the Supreme Court of the United States. Such political involvement, along with continuing frank discussion of sexuality and changing forms of the family, made Lear, by the 1980's, one of the chief targets of the religious and political fundamentalist right. The controversy, however, did not prevent Lear from producing other shows in the mold of *All in the Family* or from keeping up his constant barrage of social commentary from the mouths of his characters. Lear and *All in the Family* proved that controversy can be the stuff of comedy.

All in the Family had a continuing impact by bringing social tensions into the open. Many critics have assumed that Lear meant to discredit conservative views by placing support for them in the hands of Archie Bunker, an obviously flawed character tending toward bigotry.

Other critics argued that *All in the Family* took on issues only tangentially instead of confronting them head-on. These critics point to evidence that there was widespread sympathy for Archie Bunker and his views. In reality, the narrow-minded character of Archie Bunker raised sensitive social issues and got people to talk about them. Carroll O'Connor, in a superbly shrewd performance, kept Archie from becoming a buffoon. Archie expressed some viewers' anxieties about the changes sweeping across the nation. As these changes and issues were introduced on the show, and as various aspects of them were raised by the show's characters, the fallacies of beliefs of both the left and the right were exposed.

As one critic stated, "The best preachers deliver sermons without preaching." Lear and his show helped the nation look at problems and deal with them within the family. The popularity of *All in the Family* seems to have come from its ability to transform, or even deform, the tensions of real-life conflicts. The predictable, almost ritual, confrontations between Archie Bunker and Mike Stivic were actually taking place across the country. The social and psychological cracks in the nation's cultural landscape were real. The reaction to the show, and its characters, was ambivalent because the United States was and is a mixed culture, with few ideas approaching anything near universal acceptance.

All in the Family prompted a new wave of television situation comedies dealing with relevant subjects. Having proved that society would accept such shows, *All in the Family* set the stage for *Sanford and Son, Maude, M*A*S*H, The Jeffersons, Good Times, Married . . .with Children, Roseanne,* and *The Simpsons.* Lear showed an uncanny ability to reach American audiences through comedy. Social relevance and an acceptance of controversy are now a part of television comedy and are no longer subjects limited to drama or documentaries.

—*Michael R. Bradley*

GRIGGS V. DUKE POWER COMPANY

March 8, 1971

In this case, the Supreme Court interpreted Title VII of the Civil Rights Act of 1964 to require employers to show that hiring practices that disfavor members of minorities or women are clearly based on applicants' job skills.

The Case: U.S. Supreme Court ruling on employment discrimination

The Civil Rights Act of 1964, Title VII, prohibited workplace segregation. Shortly after the law took effect in mid-1965, Duke Power Company in North Carolina rescinded its policy of restricting African Americans to its labor department, so in principle they could transfer to other departments. Nevertheless, according to a company policy, begun in 1955, all employees but those in Duke's labor department had to have a high school diploma. Therefore, all those applying for a transfer from the labor department in 1965 needed a diploma. For those lacking a high school diploma (African Americans were far less likely to have completed twelve grades than whites in that part of North Caro lina), an alternative was to score at the national median on two standardized aptitude tests.

Willie Griggs and coworkers in the labor department at the company's Dan River steam-generating plant filed a class-action charge with the Equal Employment Opportunity Commission (EEOC), which ruled in favor of Griggs. When the company refused to conciliate the case, Griggs and his coworkers filed suit in district court. The court held that a claim of prior inequities was beyond the scope of Title VII and that the requirements for a high school diploma or a passing score on standardized tests were not intentionally discriminatory.

The district court's decision was overruled by the Supreme Court. Chief Justice Warren Burger delivered a unanimous Supreme Court opinion (8 to 0), setting forth the adverse impact test. According to this principle, if statistics show that a job requirement screens out one race, the employer must prove that the requirement is relevant to the performance of the job. Since the percentage of black high school graduates and percentages of African Americans who passed the two tests were substantially below percentages for whites, Duke Power had to prove that the jobs sought by Griggs and his coworkers required completing high school or having a level of intelligence at the national median. Since the company advanced no such evidence, the Court ruled that Title VII discrimination had occurred and decreed that "any tests used must measure the person for the job and not the person in the abstract."

The decision had an extremely broad impact: It called into question all lists of qualifications for every job in the United States. Employers were called upon to review job qualifications and to recalibrate job duties to job qualifications or risk successful discrimination suits.

In the 1980's the Supreme Court began to chip away at the *Griggs* ruling. In *Wards Cove Packing Company v. Atonio* (1989), the Court shifted the burden of proof so that those filing suit must prove that specific job requirements alone cause statistical disparities. Congress responded by passing the Civil Rights Act of 1991, codifying the original *Griggs* ruling into law.

—Michael Haas

See also: *Adarand Constructors v. Peña*; Affirmative action; *Albemarle Paper Company v. Moody*; Civil Rights Act of 1964; Civil Rights Act of 1991; Equal Employment Opportunity Commission; *Washington v. Davis*.

US SUPREME COURT ENDORSES BUSING TO END SCHOOL SEGREGATION

April 20, 1971

In its decision in the case of Swann v. Charlotte-Mecklenburg Board of Education, the U.S. Supreme Court endorsed the use of busing to desegregate the public schools of Charlotte, North Carolina, opening the way for federal judges throughout the United States to impose busing as a means of racial desegregation in public schools.

Also known as: *Swann v. Charlotte-Mecklenburg Board of Education*, 402 U.S. 1

Locale: Washington, D.C.
Categories: Education; laws, acts, and legal history; civil rights and liberties; social issues and reform

Key Figures

Julius LeVonne Chambers (b. 1936), attorney for the NAACP who represented black students and parents in litigation seeking desegregation of Charlotte schools

James B. McMillan (1916-1995), federal district judge in North Carolina

Warren E. Burger (1907-1995), chief justice of the United States, 1969-1986

William J. Brennan (1906-1997), associate justice of the United States, 1956-1990

Richard M. Nixon (1913-1994), president of the United States, 1969-1974

Summary of Event

Although the Fourteenth Amendment to the U.S. Constitution, enacted in 1868, required that states provide equal protection of the laws for all persons, African Americans continued to suffer from severe discrimination in education, employment, housing, and other aspects of American life. In 1896, in *Plessy v. Ferguson*, the Supreme Court formally endorsed racial segregation as an acceptable practice that did not violate the equal protection clause of the Constitution. Cities and states were permitted to create laws that forced blacks to attend separate schools, ride on separate train cars, and even drink from separate drinking fountains in public buildings.

Many kinds of local facilities, such as municipal swimming pools and golf courses, were reserved for whites only. The facilities provided for blacks, if there were any at all, were often shabby and grossly inferior to those provided by the government for whites. For example, African American students were frequently forced to receive their education in unheated, one-room shacks with virtually no funding for paper, pencils, desks, or other supplies. Meanwhile, white students in the same districts attended well-equipped schools with superior resources.

During the twentieth century, civil rights lawyers filed lawsuits seeking judicial decisions that would outlaw racial segregation in schools. The lawyers wanted to stop state and local governments from providing inferior educational resources to blacks. Because most black children had access only to inferior educational resources, they had little hope of attending college in the

future or of competing with whites for good jobs. The inferior schooling provided to African American children helped to ensure that many of them would spend their lives as poor laborers in the employ of whites.

The Supreme Court finally gave meaning to the constitutional right of equal protection by declaring, in the 1954 landmark case of *Brown v. Board of Education of Topeka, Kansas*, that segregated public schools violated the U.S. Constitution. The Court declared that racial discrimination in public schools caused damage to the personal development and life prospects of black children.

The Court's opinion in *Brown*, delivered in 1955, was supposed to tell the nation how to dismantle school segregation. The Supreme Court said only that desegregation should proceed with "all deliberate speed."

Federal district judges were instructed to examine school systems on a city-by-city basis in order to develop individual remedies that would correct illegal segregation.

Because the Supreme Court did not provide clear guidance on how and when schools were to end racial segregation, many school systems remained segregated for years after the *Brown* decision. Black students continued to be barred from attending the well-equipped, all white public schools. In many cities, government officials intentionally delayed making any changes in the schools because they did not agree with the judicial decisions mandating desegregation.

As a result of widespread resistance to the Supreme Court's decision against racial segregation, civil rights lawyers filed new lawsuits on behalf of black parents and children seeking judicial orders that would mandate specific desegregation plans for individual cities. Frequently, the parents and children were represented in court by lawyers from the National Association for the Advancement of Colored People (NAACP), a public interest organization that had pursued school desegregation cases since the 1930's. In a 1969 decision, *Alexander v. Holmes County Board of Education*, the Supreme Court indicated that it would no longer tolerate delays in implementing school desegregation. The Court said that

"every school district is to terminate dual school systems at once," but it did not say how schools should achieve desegregation. Julius Le Vonne Chambers, a lawyer for the NAACP, initiated a lawsuit in 1965 that sought to end racial segregation in the Charlotte, North Carolina, public schools.

The preliminary court decision in *Swann v. Charlotte-Mecklenburg Board of Education* did not require significant changes in the school system. Initially, the school district purported to eliminate segregation by permitting students to transfer between schools voluntarily if there were open places available. This freedom of choice plan did little to change the fact that schools were essentially either all-white or all-black. Only 490 of the 20,000 black students attended schools that contained any white students, and most of these students were in one school that happened to have only 7 white students. The few black students who attempted to attend all-white schools were often attacked by mobs of angry whites.

Chambers filed a legal action in 1969 to ask the court to force the schools to end segregation. After hearing evidence during a trial, Judge James B. McMillan, the federal district judge in Charlotte, found that the Charlotte schools were illegally segregated. Judge McMillan gave the Charlotte-Mecklenburg Board of Education an opportunity to develop a plan for desegregating the schools, but he subsequently rejected the board's proposals as inadequate.

With the assistance of education consultants, McMillan developed and imposed a desegregation plan in the public schools that involved transporting white children to previously all-black schools and black children to previously all-white schools in order to achieve desegregation. By mixing black children and white children in every school building, the school officials would no longer be able to provide adequate educational resources only for white students.

Many white residents did not want their children to attend schools with black children. Judge McMillan received threatening telephone calls and was ostracized by the community. Chambers was victimized by more specific attacks, with his office, car, and home damaged by firebombs and dynamite. Amid the controversy, the school board still sought to avoid implementing desegregation. The school system asked the Supreme Court to overturn Judge McMillan's busing plan.

Since 1954, even with changes in the composition of the Supreme Court, the justices had always unanimously supported desegregation whenever school districts challenged court orders against racial segregation. In the *Swann* case, however, many people expected at least some of the justices to be critical of busing as a tool for desegregating schools. The use of busing had become a controversial political issue, and President Richard M. Nixon had campaigned against the forced busing of schoolchildren. Nixon's two appointees to the Supreme Court, Chief Justice Warren E. Burger and

Associate Justice Harry A. Blackmun, were presumed to agree with the president's view that courts should be less active in forcing school districts to desegregate.

When the Supreme Court considered the *Swann* case, Chief Justice Burger and Associate Justice Hugo L. Black initially disagreed with Judge McMillan's busing order. Burger circulated several draft opinions that were critical of busing. Associate Justice William J. Brennan and other justices made repeated suggestions for revisions in the opinion that would support Judge McMillan's order. Ultimately, because a majority of justices supported the busing order, Burger accommodated the other justices and wrote an opinion supporting the use of busing. On April 20, 1971, the Court announced that judges could order school districts to use busing as a means to desegregate schools. Because all nine justices supported the opinion, the Court gave busing the full weight of its authoritative endorsement. The unanimous decision was regarded as a political defeat for the Nixon administration, which urged the Court to invalidate Judge McMillan's busing order.

SIGNIFICANCE

The Court's decision opened the way for federal judges throughout the United States to impose busing as a means of ending racial segregation in public schools. The use of busing spread as federal judges began to hear more lawsuits challenging discriminatory conditions in school systems. A 1973 case in which Denver, Colorado, was ordered to implement a busing plan demonstrated that the judges were willing to examine segregation in northern school systems. The results of busing plans have been mixed. Initially, there were highly publicized protests against busing by many white people. In Boston, Massachusetts, for example, residents of several white neighborhoods threw rocks at buses and attacked black passersby. As schools in many cities became integrated after decades of operation as single-race institutions, there were sometimes fights between black and white students.

Eventually, however, most schools adjusted, and desegregation became an accepted component of normal school operations. In smaller cities and countywide systems, such as Charlotte-Mecklenburg County, transportation of students to desegregated schools gave black students the opportunity to receive educational benefits that had previously been denied to them. Black students were no longer trapped in inferior schools with limited resources.

Public opinion research indicated that, especially in southern states, the implementation of desegregation orders was accompanied by an increase in racial tolerance. Fewer people expressed the racial prejudice that had once been a component of many Americans' attitudes. In many large metropolitan areas, however, schools failed to become racially mixed. They would have had to mix their schools with neighboring suburban schools in order to desegregate.

In 1974, however, after President Nixon had appointed a total of four justices to the Supreme Court, the Court issued a divided five-to-four decision in *Milliken v. Bradley* that prevented most busing plans from crossing school district boundaries. As large cities experienced economic decline and shrinking tax bases, deteriorating central city schools often contained predominantly poor, minority student bodies that resembled those in illegally segregated schools. Many big-city school systems had significantly fewer resources than neighboring suburbs for maintaining school buildings and for providing quality educational programs. Black students thus continued to receive inferior educational resources in many large cities.

—Christopher E. Smith

SWANN V. CHARLOTTE-MECKLENBERG BOARD OF EDUCATION
April 20, 1971

The Supreme Court ruled that federal courts may order local school boards to use extensive busing plans to desegregate schools whenever racial segregation had been supported by public policy.

The Case: U.S. Supreme Court ruling on school integration and busing

The original catalyst for this case was the plan of the school board of Charlotte, Mecklenburg County, North Carolina, to close some African American schools, create attendance zones for most of the schools in the district, and allow a "freedom-of-choice" provision under which students could transfer to any school in the district, provided that they could furnish their own transportation and the school was not already filled to capacity. The litigation began on January 19, 1965, when eleven African American families, including Vera and Darius Swann and their son James, were convinced by attorney Julius L. Chambers to sue the district for relief. The plaintiffs challenged the plan on the premise that the closing of the African American schools would place the burden of desegregation on the African American students, and that the other features would only perpetuate segregation.

THE APPELLATE PROCESS
In 1965, federal district court judge J. Braxton Craven rejected the plaintiff's challenge and approved the school board's plan. A year later, the Court of Appeals for the Fourth Circuit affirmed Craven's ruling. At this point, Chambers opted not to appeal to the Supreme Court, because he feared that the Court would only affirm the lower rulings under the precedents established at that time.

After the Supreme Court's ruling in *Green v. County School Board of New Kent County, Virginia* in 1968, however, Chambers decided to petition for further relief. In *Green*, the justices ruled that freedom-of-choice plans did not aid in the process of desegregation, and that other methods must be used to comply with *Brown v. Board of Education* (1954). On September 6, 1968, the *Swann* plaintiffs filed a motion for further relief in the federal district court in Charlotte. The motion came before Judge James B. McMillan. Both parties agreed that the school system fell short of achieving the unitary status required by *Green*. Two plans were submitted, one by the school board and the other by a court-appointed expert from Rhode Island College, Dr. John Finger.

Judge McMillan essentially accepted the Finger plan, which required more desegregation than the school board was willing to accept. The board plan would have closed seven schools and reassigned the students involved. Attendance zones were to be restructured to achieve greater racial balance, but the existing grade structures were left intact. Furthermore, the board plan would modify the free transfer plan into an optional majority-to minority transfer system (students in a racial majority in one school could transfer to another where they would be in the minority).

Under the board plan, African American students would be reassigned to nine of the ten high schools in the district, thereby producing in each an African American population of between 17 and 36 percent. The tenth high school would have an African American population of 2 percent. The junior high schools would be rezoned so that all but one would have from none to 38 percent African Americans. One junior high school would have an African American population of 90 percent. Attendance at the elementary schools, however, still would be based primarily on the neighborhood concept. More than half the African American children at this level would remain in schools that were between 86 and 100 percent black.

The Finger plan used the board zoning plan for high schools, with one modification. Three hundred additional African American students would be transported to the nearly all-white Independence High School. This plan dealt similarly with the junior high schools. Nine satellite zones would be created, and inner-city African American students would be assigned to nine outlying, predominantly white junior high schools. As was typically the case, the biggest controversy concerned the elementary school students. Rather than simply relying on zoning, Finger proposed that pairing and grouping techniques be used as well, with the result that all elementary schools would have a black student proportion that would range from 9 to 38 percent. Pairing occurs when two schools, one predominantly white and one predominantly black, are combined by either sending half the students in one school to the other for all grades or by sending all the children to one school for certain grades and then to the other school for the remaining grade levels. Bus transportation would be used for the affected students. After the district court's busing order, McMillan was hanged in effigy. Crowds demonstrated at the courthouse, in front of the judge's house, and at the *Charlotte Observer*, a newspaper that had supported busing. McMillan and his family received threatening phone calls, his law office was fire-bombed by an arsonist, his car was dynamited, and his home was vandalized.

NEW APPEALS

The Charlotte-Mecklenberg Board of Education appealed McMillan's busing order to the Fourth Circuit Court of Appeals. The appellate court vacated McMillan's order respecting elementary schools, and affirmed his ruling only on the secondary school plans. This time, because of the *Green* case, Chambers appealed the decision to the Supreme Court.

By the time the Supreme Court ruled on *Swann* in 1971, Earl Warren had retired as Chief Justice, and President Richard Nixon (who had publicly condemned forced busing) had filled Earl Warren's seat on the Court with Warren Burger in 1969. *Swann v. Charlotte-Mecklenberg Board of Education* dealt with the constitutionality of several different techniques to achieve desegregation.

In writing the unanimous decision, Burger admitted that the Court had not, as of that time, provided federal district courts with comprehensive guidelines for implementing its 1954 landmark case, *Brown v. Board of Education of Topeka, Kansas*. He declared:

Understandably, in an area of evolving remedies, those courts had to improvise and experiment without detailed or specific guidelines. This Court . . . appropriately dealt with the large constitutional principles; other federal courts had to grapple with the flinty, intractable realities of day-to-day implementation of those constitutional commands. Their efforts, of necessity, embraced a process of "trial and error," and our effort to formulate guidelines must take into account their experience.

In accepting the Finger plan, the justices ruled that federal district courts could decree as tools of desegregation the following: reasonable bus transportation, reasonable grouping of noncontiguous zones, the reasonable movement toward the elimination of one-race schools, and the use of mathematical ratios of black and white people in the schools as a starting point toward racial desegregation. Thus, the nation's highest tribunal had ruled that school districts could transport students in an effort to implement different techniques for the purpose of desegregating their schools.

—Brian L. Fife

See also: *Brown v. Board of Education*; Little Rock school desegregation crisis.

GRIFFIN V. BRECKENRIDGE

June 7, 1971

This decision extended federal civil rights guarantees of equal protection of the law to the protection of personal rights not only from state action but from personal conspiraces as well.

The Case: U.S. Supreme Court ruling on equal protection of the law

The Supreme Court's *Griffin v. Breckenridge* decision extended federal civil rights guarantees of equal protection of the law to the protection of personal rights. On July 2, 1966, a group of African Americans who were suspected of being civil rights workers were halted on a Mississippi highway near the Alabama border by Lavon and Calvin Breckenridge, who purposely blocked the road with their car. The Breckenridges forced the passengers from their vehicle and then subjected them to intimidation with firearms. The travellers were clubbed about their heads, beaten with pipes and other weapons, and repeatedly threatened with death.

Although terrorized and seriously injured, the travellers (who included Griffin) survived. They subsequently filed a suit for damages, charging that they had been assaulted for the purpose of preventing them and "other Negro-Americans" from enjoying the equal rights, privileges, and immunities of citizens of the state of Mississippi and of the United States, including the rights to free speech, assembly, association, and movement and the right not to be enslaved.

A federal district court dismissed the complaint by relying on a previous U.S. Supreme Court decision, *Collins v. Hardyman (*1951), which in order to avoid difficult constitutional issues had held that federal law extended only to "conspiracies" condoned or perpetrated by states. That is, the Court tried to avoid opening questions involving congressional power or the content of state as distinct from national citizenship, or interfering in local matters such as assault and battery cases or similar illegalities that clearly fell under local jurisdiction.

The *Collins* case, however, had been decided a decade before the nationwide Civil Rights movement of the 1960's, a period marked by the enactment of a new series of federal civil rights laws as well as by attentive regard by the U.S. Supreme Court of Chief Justice Warren Burger to cases involving civil rights violations. The Burger court heard the *Griffin* case on appeal.

The Supreme Court's unanimous decision in *Griffin* was delivered by Justice Potter Stewart on June 7, 1971. The Court broadly interpreted the federal statute under which Griffin brought damages, Title 42 of the U.S. Code, section 1985. Section 1985 stipulated that if two or more persons conspired or went in disguise on public highways with the intent to deprive any person or any class of persons of equal protection of the laws or of equal privileges and immunities under the laws, a conspiracy existed and damages could be brought. The Court waived consideration of whether the *Collins* case had been correctly decided. Instead, reviewing previous civil rights legislation, starting in 1866, the justices determined that the language of the federal statute clearly indicated that state action was not required to invoke federal protection of constitutionally guaranteed personal rights from impairment by personal conspiracies. *Griffin* effectively extended federal safeguards of civil rights to reach private conspiracies under the Thirteenth Amendment as well as under congressional powers to protect the right of interstate travel.

—*Clifton K. Yearley*

See also: *Palmer v. Thompson*

PALMER V. THOMPSON

June 14, 1971

In this ruling, the U.S. Supreme Court refused to seek out racially discriminatory intent in cases in which local government decisions appeared to be neutral.

The Case: U.S. Supreme Court ruling on racial discrimination in public accommodations

Justice Hugo L. Black wrote the opinion for the 5-4 majority, upholding the decision of the city of Jackson,

Mississippi, to close a public swimming pool rather than operate it as an integrated facility. Lower federal courts had ordered the pool to be integrated, and the city closed it rather than comply. African Americans thought this showed a clear discriminatory intent, but the Supreme Court was reluctant to go beyond the plausible non-discriminatory reason the city offered for its decision. Chief Justice Warren E. Burger concurred, and Justices William O. Douglas, Byron R. White, Thurgood Marshall, and William J. Brennan, Jr., dissented, finding that there was sufficient evidence of discriminatory intent to justify overturning this local government decision as a violation of the Fourteenth Amendment's equal protection clause. The Court subsequently moved more in the direction of the dissenters' point of view.

—*Richard L. Wilson*

See also: Fourteenth Amendment; Segregation; Civil Rights movement; Civil rights worker murders; *Jones v. Alfred H. Mayer Company*

CIVIL RIGHTS GROUPS INVESTIGATE THE FBI AND CIA

1971-1974

In the early 1970's, a number of civil rights groups—including the Citizens' Commission to Investigate the FBI, the Committee for Public Justice, and the Woodrow Wilson School at Princeton University—investigated documents of the Federal Bureau of Investigation and the Central Intelligence Agency that suggested these federal agencies had conducted intrusive, if not illegal, campaigns against a number of antiwar and leftist organizations during the 1960's.

Locale: United States

Categories: Civil rights and liberties; organizations and institutions

KEY FIGURES

J. Edgar Hoover (1895-1972), director of the Federal Bureau of Investigation, 1924-1972

Richard Helms (1913-2002), director of the Central Intelligence Agency, 1965-1973

Lyndon B. Johnson (1908-1973), president of the United States, 1963-1969

Richard M. Nixon (1913-1994), president of the United States, 1969-1974

Gerald R. Ford (1913-2006), president of the United States, 1974-1977

SUMMARY OF EVENT

For many years, the U.S. Federal Bureau of Investigation (FBI) enjoyed a sterling reputation under the leadership of its longtime director, J. Edgar Hoover. In the later years of Hoover's administration, however, questions about overzealousness and abuse began to arise. Similar questions were raised about the U.S. Central Intelligence Agency (CIA), which always had been more controversial.

Most of the CIA controversy focused on its foreign operations, for it was forbidden a domestic intelligence role. In the early 1970's, however, evidence emerged of illegal or improper domestic activity by both agencies, a significant part of that activity targeted against civil rights and anti-Vietnam War groups and individuals.

In 1971, a group calling itself the Citizens' Commission to Investigate the FBI broke into a two-man FBI office in Media, Pennsylvania, stole over 1000 classified documents and sent them out to various media outlets. A number of FBI documents that suggested that the agency had conducted intrusive, if not illegal, campaigns against a number of antiwar and leftist organizations. In October of the same year, the Committee for Public Justice and the Woodrow Wilson School at Princeton University sponsored a conference titled "Investigating the FBI," which focused media attention on alleged FBI abuses in investigating civil rights and antiwar activities. Little evidence for these abuses could be produced, as the bureau closely guarded what it considered to be privileged information.

After the death in 1972 of the FBI's powerful director, J. Edgar Hoover, and with the Watergate scandal in 1972 through1974, public pressure mounted for further investigation. Finally, suits filed in December, 1973, and March, 1974, under the Freedom of Information Act resulted in publication of a number of FBI Counter Intelligence Program (COINTELPRO) files. The information in these files, coupled with documentation implicating the CIA in domestic intelligence abuses, prompted congressional investigation into the activities of both agencies. Although many FBI and CIA files had been destroyed or altered, the investigations revealed that both organizations had carried out a number of programs intended to undermine, discredit, or destroy civil rights and antiwar movements in the 1960's.

In 1964, following a number of race-related incidents, President Lyndon B. Johnson ordered the FBI to investigate the causes of racial unrest. In April, 1965, the bureau began investigating student antiwar groups for communist influence. When neither of these investigations found illegal or communist activity, Hoover intensified the programs. By 1968, the FBI had established two counterintelligence programs to gather data on black and student movements. COINTELPRO-Black Nationalist-Hate Groups extended to all forty-one FBI field offices authority for collecting information on civil rights groups. COINTELPRO-New Left attempted to undermine the activities of alleged campus radicals, with authority again given to all FBI field offices. Tactics included extensive wiretapping; planting listening devices in homes, hotel rooms, and meeting places of various organizations; infiltrating groups; and fabricating documents to create hostility within and among the organizations.

Specific evidence derived from the FBI's COINTELPRO files reveals that the bureau found certain individuals to be of particular interest. The Reverend Martin Luther King, Jr., civil rights leader and recipient of the Nobel Peace Prize, was under intense FBI scrutiny from 1963 until his death in 1968. In 1964, shortly before King was to receive the Nobel Prize, the FBI sent him a tape of damaging information it had collected regarding his private life and threatened to make the data public if he did not commit suicide.

Leaders of the Black Panther Party and the Student Nonviolent Coordinating Committee (SNCC) were also targets of FBI activity. When the two groups proposed a merger in 1968, the FBI engineered a rift between the groups. The rift contributed to decisions of high-ranking members of both groups, Stokely Carmichael of SNCC and Eldridge Cleaver of the Black Panthers, to go underground.

The FBI accomplished this and other similar operations by fabricating stories and circulating them among members of targeted organizations. For example, the bureau leaked information that Carmichael was a CIA informant. It also telephoned his mother claiming that members of the Black Panthers had threatened to kill Carmichael because of his alleged CIA affiliation. Carmichael left for Africa the next day.

FBI infiltrators at times encouraged illegal activities among groups that they had joined in order to create public disapproval of the organizations. These agents were known as provocateurs. One of the best-known provocateurs, Thomas Tongyai, traveled throughout western New York encouraging students to participate in violent activities such as bombing buildings and killing police.

The FBI's disruptive capabilities were enhanced by using local police and other federal agencies to collect data. For example, from 1968 through 1974, the FBI obtained confidential tax information from the Internal Revenue Service on 120 militant black and antiwar leaders.

The CIA also became an important source of documentation and information for the FBI. Although the CIA has no authority to gather information regarding domestic matters, that agency began collecting information on American citizens at the request of President Johnson. The agency's Special Operations Group, later known as CHAOS, was begun in August, 1967, to determine the role of foreign influence in the American peace movement. President Richard M. Nixon increased the demands on the CIA in 1970 by requiring that it become involved in evaluating and coordinating intelligence gathered on dissident groups. Some of the groups targeted for infiltration by the CIA included SNCC, the Women's Strike for Peace, the Washington Peace Center, and the Congress of Racial Equality.

CIA director Richard Helms was aware of the implications of the agency's operating outside its jurisdiction. In a cover memo to a 1968 report on student revolutionary activities around the world, including the United States, Helms noted: "This is an area not within the charter of this Agency. Should anyone learn of its existence it would prove most embarrassing for all concerned." The report concluded that student unrest was a product of domestic alienation, not of foreign manipulation, but the CIA continued to gather data on American citizens. By the early 1970's, the CIA had accumulated open files on more than 64,000 citizens and a computerized index of more than 300,000 individuals and organizations.

SIGNIFICANCE

Following the revelation of FBI and CIA abuses, there was a public outcry for curbs on both organizations. In 1975, President Gerald R. Ford ordered the creation of a special commission to establish the extent of CIA activities and to report findings and recommendations. The commission found that the CIA had indeed conducted improper investigations. Further, the commission recommended that the scope of CIA procedures be limited to foreign intelligence.

Also in 1975, a federal court awarded $12 million in damages to persons who had been arrested in Washington, D.C., while participating in antiwar demonstrations in May, 1971. The arrests were believed to have been a result of police coercion in which the FBI collaborated with local and national officials.

Because both the FBI and the CIA often deal with what is considered to be "sensitive" information, there was a large amount of controversy over what the public had a right to know and what should be withheld to protect national security. In 1974, Congress amended the Freedom of Information Act (FOIA) to allow private review of documents by federal district courts in order to determine whether publication of information would pose a security risk. Although this amendment to the FOIA resulted in the declassification of many COINTELPRO documents, in many instances text was deleted.

Participants in FBI and CIA abuses during the COINTELPRO era generally went unpunished. Richard Helms, former director of the CIA, was fined only $2,000 and given a suspended sentence of two years in jail.

In 1980, the only two FBI personnel tried and found guilty of COINTELPRO abuses were pardoned by President Ronald Reagan. In 1981, the FBI settled a $100 million suit for abuses committed against former members of the Weathermen, a radical student group.

Changes were made in leadership, administrative rules, and legislation. Recurrences of abuses, however, are possible because of the natural tensions between individual civil liberties on one hand and the demands of national security and civil order on the other.

—Laurie Voice and Robert E. Biles

The FBI's Blackmail Note to Martin Luther King, Jr.

Following the revelation of the FBI's counterintelligence program, COINTELPRO, federal authorities were found to have investigated "radical" organizations ranging from violent hate groups such as the white supremacist Ku Klux Klan to nonviolent groups such as Martin Luther King's Southern Christian Leadership Conference. According to a 1976 Church Committee report, the FBI attempted to infiltrate such groups and to undermine the character of their leaders. In 1964, the FBI mailed King a tape recording made from its surveillance coverage that contained evidence of the civil rights leader's extramarital activities. According to the head of the FBI's Domestic Intelligence Division, William C. Sullivan, the tape was intended to precipitate a separation between King and his wife and thus reduce King's stature.

The tape was accompanied by the following note, which King and his advisers interpreted as a threat that the tape would be released unless he committed suicide. King received the note thirty-four days before he was to receive the Nobel Peace Prize.

King, look into your heart. You know you are a complete fraud and a great liability to all of us Negroes. White people in this country have enough frauds on their own but I am sure they don't have one at this time that is any where near your equal. You are no clergyman and you know it. I repeat you are a colossal fraud and an evil, vicious one at that. . . .

King, like all frauds your end is approaching. You could have been our greatest leader. . . .

But you are done. Your "honorary" degrees, your Nobel Prize (what a grim farce) and other awards will not save you. King, I repeat you are done. . . .

The American public, the church organizations that have been helping— Protestant, Catholic and Jews will know you for what you are—an evil, abnormal beast. So will others who have backed you.

You are done.

King, there is only one thing left for you to do. You know what it is.

You have just 34 days in which to do it (this exact number has been selected for a specific reason . . .) You are done. There is but one way out for you. You better take it before your filthy, abnormal, fraudulent self is bared to the nation.

EQUAL EMPLOYMENT OPPORTUNITY ACT OF 1972

March 13, 1972

Landmark legislation helps redress historic discrimination against women and members of minorities in hiring and promotion.

The Law: Federal legislation that prohibited government agencies and educational institutions from discriminating in hiring, firing, promotion, compensation, and admission to training programs

The Equal Employment Opportunity (EEO) Act of 1972 was an omnibus bill appended to Title VII of the Civil Rights Act, which had been enacted on July 2, 1964, to meet a need for federal legislation dealing with job discrimination on the basis of "race, color, religion, sex or national origin." The 1964 act was charged to enforce the constitutional right to vote, to protect constitutional rights in public facilities and public education, to prevent discrimination in federally assisted programs, and to establish an Equal Employment Opportunity Commission (EEOC). Title VII did not, however, give comprehensive jurisdiction to the EEOC.

A series of laws and executive orders has built up over the years to add to the momentum against discrimination in all areas of American life. With enactment of the Fourteenth and Fifteenth Amendments, the Civil Rights Acts of 1866 and 1875, and a series of laws passed in the mid- and late 1880's, the government and the president, in theory at least, gained sufficient authority to eradicate racial discrimination, including employment bias. No president, however, used his constitutional power in this regard. With the peaking of the Civil Rights movement in the early 1960's, the pace of progress toward equal opportunity accelerated. President John F. Kennedy's Executive Order 10925 established the Committee on Equal Employment Opportunity, the predecessor of the EEOC. Numerous other executive orders by succeeding presidents followed, each chipping away at discrimination in employment.

ANTI-DISCRIMINATION LEGISLATION

The first modern federal legislation to deal specifically with employment discrimination, however, was the Equal Pay Act of 1963. As a result of this act, more than $37.5 million was subsequently found to be due to 91,661 employees, almost all of them women, for the years between 1963 and 1972. Then followed the momentous Civil Rights Act of 1964, which contained the

provision for equal employment opportunity that would be expanded with the 1972 law.

The push for the Equal Employment Opportunity Act was a natural result of many forces in the early 1970's: The economic disparity between white men, on one hand, and members of minorities and women, on the other, had become more apparent and disturbing. Women and members of minorities were generally last hired and first fired, with little chance for promotion. Yet, one-third of the U.S. workforce were women. Although most women worked in order to support themselves and their families, many people still considered their employment to be expendable and marginal. This was especially true for poor women, minority women, and female heads of household. Female college graduates earned only slightly more per year than the average white man with an eighth-grade education. In the 1960's, female-headed households were largely black women with one thousand dollars less than their white counterparts in annual median income. The median annual income for white women in 1971 was slightly more than five thousand dollars, and for nonwhite women, four thousand dollars. African Americans in general suffered more from lower salary and lower job security and benefits because, in part, they either were discouraged or, in many cases, were not permitted to join labor or professional unions. In 1972, some 88 percent of unionists—about 15 million—were white, while only 2.1 million were from minority groups.

COMBATTING UNEMPLOYMENT

Another motivation to push for the EEO Act was unemployment. In 1971, the general unemployment rate was close to 6 percent as compared to 3.4 percent as recently as 1969. Rates of joblessness were highest among the veterans returning from Vietnam (12.4 percent), and in cities with high minority populations such as Jersey City (9 to 11.9 percent) and Detroit (6 to 8.9 percent). The U.S. Department of Labor reported in 1972 that one-fifth of all wage and salary earners were unionized and males outnumbered females four to one.

The unemployment issue had plagued government and business ever since Congress passed the Employment Act of 1946, which declared, among other things, that it was federal policy to promote "maximum employment."

On March 13, 1972, the EEO Act was passed by Congress, and on March 24, it was signed into law by President Richard M. Nixon. Primary responsibility for eliminating employment discrimination was entrusted to the Equal Employment Opportunity Commission. Congress increased EEOC's authority dramatically by giving it power to issue cease-and-desist orders, to receive and investigate charges, and to engage in mediation and conciliation regarding discriminatory practices. Jurisdiction of the EEOC was extended to cover all companies and unions of fifteen or more employees, private educational institutions, and state and local governments. The EEOC found broad patterns of discrimination. It resolved most of them and referred unresolved cases to the attorney general, who had authority to file federal lawsuits.

AFFIRMATIVE ACTION

Affirmative action became one means to promote equal employment opportunity. It was a controversial measure from the start. Opponents of affirmative action viewed it as preferential treatment or "reverse discrimination," often invoking the decision in *Griggs v. Duke Power Company* (1971), in which the Supreme Court noted that Congress did not intend to prefer the less qualified over the better qualified simply because of minority origin. Proponents of affirmative action believed that when properly implemented, the policy did not do away with competition but, rather, leveled the playing field to create equal opportunity for jobs in hiring, on-the-job treatment, and firing policies. Affirmative action, according to proponents, meant a conscious effort to root out all types of inequality of employment opportunity, such as unrealistic job requirements, non-job-related selection instruments and procedures, insufficient opportunity for upward mobility, and inadequate publicity about job openings.

The U.S. Civil Service Commission provided technical assistance to state and local governments in developing affirmative action plans and provided training manuals for the purpose. The thrust of EEO guidelines, however, was that gender, racial, ethnic, national origin, or religious status alone should be avoided as an employment consideration. Women and members of minorities had taken the lead in getting the EEO proposal through Congress, thus making EEO a women's and minority issue.

The EEO Act dealt with areas where discrimination had been blatant, such as hiring and promotion by small businesses and by police and fire departments, as well as admission to local unions such as branches of the longshoremen in the Northeast and Southeast. Discrimination in some areas was so blatant that the federal appeals courts actually had to order hiring of members of minorities to rectify the situation. For example, after the passage of the EEO, Minneapolis hired its first minority-group fireman in twenty-five years.

The EEO Act also dealt with various forms of discrimination against women, such as denying employment because there were no toilet facilities for women. The act required that women receive equal opportunities for sick leave, vacation, insurance, and pensions. It also became illegal to refuse to hire or to dismiss an unmarried mother as long as unwed fathers were holding jobs. Newspaper classified sections were no longer permitted to segregate help-wanted listings under male and female headings. Only a few jobs, such as that of actor, could be proved to have a bona fide occupational qualification on the basis of sex.

OPPOSITION

Opposition forces focused on the confusion created by the passage of the EEO Act. Many of the existing labor laws protecting women and members of minorities seemed to become invalid in the context of the act. For example, the classic prohibition on work that would require a woman to lift more than a specified maximum weight could not stand. Qualification for employment would have to be based on ability to meet physical demands, regardless of gender. Banning women from certain jobs because of the possibility of pregnancy appeared to be impermissible. Leaves or special arrangements for the rearing of children would have to be available to the father, if the couple decided he was to take over domestic duties. In fact, "Men's Lib" became a new trend in the 1970's. Women's campaigns for full equality prompted men to reassess their own situation. The result was that "liberation" was becoming an issue for both men and women.

Men began moving into jobs once reserved for women, seeking alimony from wives, and demanding paternity leaves. The Supreme Court ruled that airlines could not limit flight attendant jobs to women, and most airlines began hiring some male stewards. AT&T had filled 25 percent of its clerical positions and 10 percent of its telephone operator positions with men by 1974. More men enrolled in nursing schools.

On the other hand, by the time the EEO was enacted in 1972, 31 percent of black families were headed by women. One decade later, in 1982, this figure had

grown to 45 percent as compared to 14 percent of families headed by white women in the same year.

The EEO Act worked in tandem with or initiated
investigations into other areas of discrimination, such
as education. For example, by the late 1960's, more
than a decade after the Court struck down "separate but
equal" laws, more than 75 percent of the school districts
in the South remained segregated. This meant markedly
disproportionate employment opportunities for African
Americans.

IMPACT

Armed with its new authority, field investigators, and
two hundred newly hired lawyers, the EEOC was able
to respond effectively to complaints of discrimination.
Within a few weeks of assuming its new, authoritative
position, the EEOC had filed suits against many big
companies. The actionable charges of sex discrimination surged from 2,003 cases in 1967 to 10,436 by June
of 1972. Sex discrimination cases, in only three years
from 1970 through 1972, increased by nearly 300 percent. By June 30, 1972, however, only 22 percent of
cases involved sex discrimination and 58 percent racial
and ethnic discrimination, with 11 percent involving national origin and 2.5 percent religious discrimination.
In 1972, the EEOC forced employers to give raises to
some twenty-nine thousand workers, mainly women,

after finding violations of the law. The total underpay-
ment of wages amounted to about fourteen million dollars.

Much of the business sector objected to the EEOC's
efforts, contending that the new law would permit employees to file class-action suits without the employer's
being given fair notice of the identity of its accusers.
Such criticism protested that as many as eight different laws gave employees an unfair advantage in pressing charges. Nevertheless, companies—including many
large corporations that did work for the government—
were forced to change their employment policies to
comply, and the composition of the workforce began to
change. The Equal Employment Opportunity Act, along
with subsequent follow-on legislation, opened the door
for many women, African Americans, and members
of ethnic minorities to rise out of poverty and begin a
movement toward middle- and upper-middle-class status that later would begin to change the power structure
in the United States.

—*Chogollah Maroufi*

See also: Affirmative action; Civil Rights Act of 1964;
Economic trends; Employment; Equal Employment
Opportunity Commission; Fair Employment Practices
Committee

MOOSE LODGE V. IRVIS

June 12, 1972

*The Supreme Court held that a state agency did not
violate the equal protection clause of the Fourteenth
Amendment when it issued a liquor license to a private
club that practiced racial discrimination.*

The Case: U.S. Supreme Court ruling on state action
and private discrimination

Moose Lodge No. 107, a private club in Harrisburg,
Pennsylvania, allowed only white men to use its premises. One member of the club tried to bring Leroy Irvis, a
prominent African American politician, as a guest. After
Irvis was refused service, he brought a civil suit in federal court. He contended that the state, by providing the
club with a license, was unconstitutionally participating in the club's policy of racial exclusion. Irvis pointed
to *Burton v. Wilmington Parking Authority* (1961), in

which the Court had ruled that a state agency did not
have the right to lease property to a restaurant practicing
racial segregation.

By a 6-3 vote, the Supreme Court rejected Irvis's
claim. Speaking for the majority, Justice William H.
Rehnquist interpreted the doctrine of state action narrowly and concluded that the mere licensing of the lodge
did not constitute enough state involvement to bring the
lodge's policies under the umbrella of the Fourteenth
Amendment. The state played "absolutely no part" in
determining the membership or guest policies of organizations receiving state licenses. The circumstances were
considered different from the "symbiotic relationship"
that had existed between a lessor and a lessee in the *Burton* case. Because states commonly provide regulations
for many necessary services, Rehnquist feared that a ruling upholding Irvis's claim would "utterly emasculate"

the long-standing distinction between private conduct and state action.

Dissenting, JusticeWilliam J. Brennan, Jr., argued that the state was an "active participant" in the Moose Lodge bar, and he noted that the liquor licensing laws included "pervasive regulatory schemes" for many aspects of the licensee's business. JusticeWilliam O. Douglas emphasized that liquor licenses were very scarce and that therefore the state's policy restricted the equal access of African Americans to liquor. Ironically, Irvis was able to find recourse under Pennsylvania's public accommodations law.

—*Thomas Tandy Lewis*

See also: *Burton v.Wilmington Parking Authority; Civil Rights* cases; *Jones v. Alfred H. Mayer Company; Shelley v. Kraemer.*

KEYES V. DENVER SCHOOL DISTRICT NO. 1

June 21, 1973

In its first school desegregation case involving a major city outside the South, the Supreme Court held that a district-wide busing plan was an appropriate remedy for a situation in which official policies had encouraged the establishment of racially segregated schools in any section within the district.

The Case: U.S. Supreme Court ruling on school integration and busing

Decided June 21, 1973, this ruling outlawed de facto desegregation and expanded prohibitions on segregation. *Brown v. Board of Education* (1954) invalidated laws that required or permitted segregated black and white schools. Nevertheless, many school districts remained segregated, in part because of de facto segregation (segregation "in fact" rather than de jure, or "by law"). Wilfred Keyes did not want his daughter, Christi Keyes, to attend any kind of segregated school in Denver. In 1970, when a newly elected school board rescinded a desegregation plan adopted by the previous board in 1969, he brought a class-action suit.

In 1970, the district court ordered Park Hill schools desegregated after hearing evidence that the school board deliberately segregated its schools through school site selection, excessive use of mobile classroom units, gerrymandered attendance zones, student transportation routes, a restrictive transfer policy, and segregated faculty assignment to schools. Keyes was also successful before the court in arguing that inner-city schools, with substantial black and Hispanic student populations, should also be desegregated, but Denver prevailed on appeal in 1971, arguing that the large percentages of black and Hispanic students in these schools resulted from a "neighborhood school" policy.

Justice William J. Brennan delivered the opinion of the U.S. Supreme Court. Six justices joined Brennan, one justice affirmed the decision in part and dissented in part, and the remaining justice dissented. The Supreme Court ruled that since intentional segregation was proved in one part of the city, there was a presumption of intentional discrimination in the other case. The burden of proof thus shifted to the school board to prove that the intentional segregation of one section of the district was isolated, separate, and unrelated to the pattern of pupil assignment to the "core city schools."

When the case was sent back to the district court in 1973, Denver was determined to have practiced unlawful segregation in both areas of the city, and the school board was required to desegregate. When the school board failed to design an adequate plan to desegregate by 1974, the court drew up a plan of its own.

The effect of *Keyes* was to open all northern school districts to the possibility of desegregation lawsuits. Eventually almost every city of at least moderate size then grappled with desegregation plans, voluntary or court ordered. The lone exception is the statewide school district of Hawaii, which has never been desegregated despite the existence of schools situated to serve certain geographic areas where only persons of Hawaiian ancestry by law can reside.

—*Michael Haas*

See also: *Brown v. Board of Education;* Gerrymandering; Segregation; *Sweatt v. Painter.*

WONDER RELEASES *INNERVISIONS*

August, 1973

Innervisions *demonstrated Stevie Wonder's musical maturity and propelled the singer-songwriter-activist to a series of Grammy Awards and even more original music making.*

Locale: United States
Category: Music

KEY FIGURES

Stevie Wonder (b. 1950), singer and songwriter
Berry Gordy, Jr. (b. 1929), founder of Motown Records
Martin Luther King, Jr. (1929-1968), charismatic preacher and civil rights leader who inspired Wonder

SUMMARY OF EVENT

The release of *Innervisions* in August, 1973, marked Stevie Wonder's musical maturity. At the age of twenty-three, he had found freedom from the formulas of the Motown Records assembly-line method of producing hits so popular and successful in the 1960's. Then he was "Little Stevie Wonder, the twelve-year-old genius." Now he was revealed as a consummate African American musician: singer, songwriter, instrumentalist, arranger, and producer.

Innervisions remained on the pop charts for fifty-eight weeks, reaching as high as number four. Both it and *Talking Book* of 1972 sold better than any of Wonder's albums since his first back in 1963. Two top-ten singles were drawn from *Innervisions*: "Higher Ground" and "Living for the City," both of which signaled Wonder's increasing proclivity for adult songs about social conditions.

The National Association of Recording Arts and Sciences (NARAS) presented Wonder with four Grammy Awards at its 1974 show: Album of the Year, for *Innervisions*; Best Pop Vocal Performance, Male, for "You Are the Sunshine of My Life" (from *Talking Book*); Best R&B Vocal Performance, Male, for "Superstition"; and Best R&B Song, also for "Superstition." The conservative NARAS had finally recognized a Motown artist; in its prime in the 1960's, Motown had won nothing. By 1977, however, Wonder had won twelve Grammys. Three albums in a row won Album of the Year awards.

In 1971, when he was twenty-one and free of the restrictions the Motown organization had placed on him as a minor and as its "discovery," Wonder refused to

Rehearsing for a performance on Dutch TV in 1967 by Nijs, Jac. de / Anefo

renew his Motown contract. He moved from Detroit to New York City so that he could control all aspects of his music.

Setting up his own studio and publishing company and soon working with a new electronic instrument, the synthesizer, he was able to oversee in great detail and with startling musical acuity the creation of whole albums conceived as units from start to finish. If not exactly "concept" albums in the popular sense (a series of songs entirely united by theme or focus), they were designed less to produce singles than to allow Wonder a chance to improvise and jam, to play all the instruments on an album himself and to mix the results, to expand songs beyond the time limits of cuts aimed solely at the singles market, and to explore new themes and song types.

Wonder did eventually sign again with Motown, but with guarantees that he would have freedom to produce his own material, which the company would then distribute. For both parties, it turned out to be an ideal arrangement.

Motown had moved to Los Angeles; Berry Gordy, Jr., its charismatic founder and creative leader, had moved his headquarters there in 1971. The glory days of the 1960's were over: Even the label's star attraction, the Supremes, had broken up, as leader Diana Ross wanted to explore a solo career. Only the new Jackson Five created a sensation echoing that of the early and mid-1960's. Having started out as teenagers with Motown, the label's major stars now wanted more freedom to choose songs and the sounds they wanted behind them in the studio.

As a teenage sensation, Stevie Wonder had had his first number one pop hit with "Fingertips (Part Two)" in 1963, and he had followed up with some lively dance tunes and love songs that featured his high-pitched young voice. Sometimes he would still play his harmonica on recordings, but more and more a kind of standard treatment was applied to his recordings, a sort of blandness creeping even into his forays into jazz and standards. He was increasingly frustrated. The new approach, however, heralded the changes and freedom that *Innervisions* best represents.

As a singer, songwriter, and instrumentalist, Wonder needed new contexts, a broader repertoire, and openness to other musical styles. By the late 1960's, the "Motown sound" and the pop-song crossover formulas for soul music restricted Wonder too much. As a live performer, he loved to improvise and jam, demonstrating his skills on instruments that included harmonica, piano, organ, and drums. He wanted to arrange and produce his own records—an idea unheard of at Motown, with its tight control from the top down.

Wonder had pushed the parameters a bit when he recorded Bob Dylan's "Blowin' in the Wind" in 1966, but it was a hit single. After 1971, he extended his reach to a broader white audience that had grown up with the Beatles and Dylan and that expected its artists to show independence and creativity beyond the confines of one style. With albums such as *Music of My Mind* and *Talking Book* (both released in 1972), Wonder took complete charge of his work.

Innervisions continued to chart new paths in this line with extended songs and a sharper look at life. Wonder's voice had become deeper and richer; he could still croon, but now he convincingly shouted and used a wide range to handle all kinds of material, from the soft and romantic to the raw power of tough rhythm and blues. He could put across densely worded pieces and build a sound made up of complex rhythms and cross-rhythms—largely because he could now work slowly and carefully in his own studio, at his own direction, to get just the soundscape he wanted for any particular song.

Variety became the norm in Wonder's work. "Too High" faulted a drug-taking woman; "Visions" was one of the first of Wonder's philosophical songs about dreams of a better world. At seven and a half minutes, "Living for the City" was one of the highlights of the album: A rap-like mini-drama or dramatic scene, it pictured the harshness of urban life, particularly that of New York City, and incorporated actual city sounds into the musical track. "Higher Ground," with harder rhythm-and-blues singing, was a warning of potential world collapse (an apocalyptic strain in Wonder's work that would surface again). In the same manner, "Jesus Children of America" and "He's Misstra Know-It-All" represented Wonder's social and religious concerns, the first a plea for a more truly open and giving religious sensibility and the latter a sharp critique of self-centered and false authority figures. *Innervisions* was the boldest and most original album of Wonder's career to that point.

SIGNIFICANCE

Among other awards, Stevie Wonder won a Grammy Award for Album of the Year for his follow-up to *Innervisions*, the almost equally original *Fulfillingness' First Finale*. A number one pop album, two of its cuts were pop singles hits: "Boogie on Reggae Woman" and "You Haven't Done Nothin.'" The first was a shouting dance song with extended instrumental passages in Wonder's best improvisatory manner. The second song was a piece of sharp social criticism about the lack of significant action to lessen the hardships of the disadvantaged.

Another innovative cut was "Heaven Is Ten Zillion Light Years Away," an evocatively scored song about the inability to embrace humanitarianism, peace, universal brotherhood, and harmony. Lyrically, the song enunciated themes Wonder would treat many times in later albums through the 1970's and 1980's. Musically, it was a sort of chanted spiritual, with a repeated throbbing bass and chorus setting up its hypnotic effect and rich chordal harmonies.

Wonder's albums continued to integrate reggae, rap, jazz, blues, gospel, rock, and even classical elements. Echoes of Johann Sebastian Bach in some chorale-like pieces were mixed with complex African rhythms and the use of actual African instruments in his orchestrations.

With his complete control of arrangement and production, Wonder was in essence scoring and orchestrating his songs as complex soundscapes and as extended compositions rather than as simple songs. His double album of 1976, *Songs in the Key of Life*, went on to garner Grammys in 1977. Here, Wonder continued to explore social themes in pieces such as "Black Man," an eight-minute tribute to black leaders and heroes done in a rap-like style. "Sir Duke" (a hit single) was a tribute to jazz great Duke Ellington. "Village Ghetto Land" continued in the vein of "Living for the City," while "Love's in Need of Love Today" reiterated a favorite Wonder theme. The latter piece was a fascinating example of Wonder's studio and production art. With its pattern of lead voice overlapped by a responding or echoing chorus, the work achieved an odd, compelling effect. A seven-minute composition, it consisted of an opening plea for love and then burst into a polyphonic main segment, and throughout was marked by a flowing, gently propulsive bass rhythm. "Contusion" exemplified Wonder's instrumental jamming skills. One song used only a harp and harmonica to back the vocal; another included a long jam with a prominent flute part.

In 1978 and 1979, Wonder became actively involved in lobbying for a national holiday on the birthday of slain civil rights leader Martin Luther King, Jr. Wonder's 1980 album *Hotter than July* included his own song "Happy Birthday," a tribute to King, and also included a picture sleeve with a photo of King, a montage of scenes from the turbulent civil rights struggles of the 1960's, and Wonder's own prose comments on King's significance.

At a rally held January 15, 1981, in Washington, D.C., to celebrate King's birthday and to lobby Congress for official recognition of the day as a holiday, Wonder sang his "Happy Birthday" and "We Shall Overcome." Motown then released the Wonder song as a single backed with excerpts from four speeches by King. Congress finally made the holiday official in 1986. Wonder's albums of the 1970's and his campaign for broader recognition of King's significance are really congruent aspects of Wonder's art as singer and composer. His philosophy of love and understanding among

Wonder's Best-Selling U.S. and U.K. Albums			
From 1963 through 2005, twelve Stevie Wonder albums reached the top ten on the popular music charts in the United States, the United Kingdom, or both.			
Year Released	Title	U.S. Rank	U.K. Rank
1963	*Recorded Live: The Twelve Year Old Genius*	1	—
1972	*Talking Book*	3	—
1973	*Innervisions*	4	8
1974	*Fulfillingness' First Finale*	1 5	
1976	*gs in the Key of Life*	1	2
1979	*Journey Through the Secret Life of Plants* (sound track)	4	8
1980	*Hotter than July*	3	2
1982	*Stevie Wonder's Original Musiquarium*	4	8
1984	*he Woman in Red* (sound track)	4	2
1985	*In Square Circle*	5	5
1995	*Conversation Peace*	—	8
2005	*A Time to Love*	5	—

all races and countries and his criticisms of hate and narrow religious sectarianism pervade his music.

Even the less successful—and distinctly experimental—double album of 1979, *Journey Through the Secret Life of Plants*, explored his common themes of the inner life, peace, and communication with any kind of sensate world. Planned as a sound track for a documentary film about plants, the album featured Wonder on harmonica, organ, and African instruments, which were used to suggest the sensate life of plants themselves. Though not aimed at easy commercial success (though it did reach a number four position on the charts), the album represented the achievement of Wonder as a composer and not simply as a pop songwriter.

Wonder established himself as one of the few popular music figures who could break through the stereotypes and narrow musical categorizations of the music industry. Like his hero, Duke Ellington, Wonder had become a composer; his compositions were the albums he created as musical units. He absorbed many musical influences without becoming a dilettante, and he managed to create a kind of musical universalism. As a major step in Wonder's transition from child prodigy to master musician, *Innervisions* indicated that the

designation "twelve-year-old genius" was not unwarranted.

—*Frederick E. Danker*

See also: Marsalis Revives Acoustic Jazz; *Thriller* Marks Jackson's Musical Coming-of-Age; Rap Goes Platinum with Run-D.M.C.'s *Raising Hell*.

BAKKE CASE

1973–1978

In this ruling, the Supreme Court held that educational institutions may not use rigid quotas in their admissions policies but may take race into account in order to increase minority enrollment.

The Case: U.S. Supreme Court ruling on affirmative action in education

During the 1950's and 1960's, the United States made substantial progress in civil rights, aided by Supreme Court decisions that found state-sponsored segregation of the races to be unconstitutional. With its decision in *Brown v. Board of Education* (1954), the Court signaled that the equal protection clause of the Fourteenth Amendment to the Constitution could not be reconciled with public policy that discriminated on the basis of race. The Civil Rights Act of 1964 enacted this idea into legislation. The 1960's also heralded the beginning of a new effort to correct the wrongs of racial discrimination through the adoption of affirmative action programs.

Supporters of affirmative action contended that the removal of legal barriers was inadequate to ensure equality of the races. For example, President Lyndon B. Johnson argued that the effects of years of discrimination could not be erased by the dismantling of legal segregation and that affirmative action to aid those who had been the victims of that discrimination was necessary. Agencies throughout the federal bureaucracy adopted regulations requiring or encouraging the use of affirmative action programs by recipients of federal funds. In response to a regulation of this type from the Department of Health, Education, and Welfare, many colleges and universities throughout the country altered their admissions policies in order to recruit members of minorities more actively.

THE UNIVERSITY OF CALIFORNIA

The University of California at Davis Medical School (UCDMS) enrolled its first class in 1968. There were fifty students, three of whom were Asian and none of whom were African American, Hispanic, or American Indian. Almost immediately, the school decided to create a special admissions program that would provide seats in each class for members of disadvantaged minorities. In 1970, eight seats were reserved for special admissions. In 1971, the total class size of the school was doubled to one hundred and the number of special admissions slots was doubled to sixteen. The admissions process became a two-track one, with applicants indicating whether they wanted to be considered as a disadvantaged minority. Persons found to qualify for special admissions competed against each other for the sixteen seats while all other applicants competed for the remaining seats. Applicants for special admissions did not have to meet the same requirements in terms of grade point averages and test scores as those competing in the general admissions process. Between 1968 and 1973, the year Allan Bakke first applied to Davis, the number of minority students enrolled in the medical school rose from three to thirty-one.

Allan Bakke was employed as an engineer with the National Aeronautics and Space Administration in California when he decided to apply to medical school in the fall of 1972. He had come to the decision that his true calling was in the practice of medicine. He applied to twelve medical schools that year and was rejected by all of them. Several of the schools cited Bakke's age, thirty-three, as the cause of the rejection. Bakke had an admissions interview at UCDMS and received high marks in the ranking of candidates for admission but, because of his late application, missed by a few points the cut-off score for the few seats left at that time. Bakke visited the school after being rejected and talked with an admissions officer who encouraged him to apply again the next year and to consider challenging the special admissions program. Bakke believed that he would have been admitted to the school in 1973 if sixteen places had not been set aside.

REVERSE DISCRIMINATION

Bakke applied for the 1974 class and was again rejected. This time it appeared that his views on the special admissions program, which he had discussed with an administrator during his interview, had kept him from gaining admission. Bakke decided to sue the medical school, arguing that the special admissions program violated his equal protection rights because the sixteen-seat quota was allocated purely on the basis of race. Bakke's case brought to the limelight a new equal protection question: Can members of the white majority be the victims of racial discrimination? Bakke contended that affirmative action programs like the one at the medical school created "reverse discrimination" and were no less a violation of the equal protection clause because the victim was a member of the majority race instead of the minority.

UCDMS argued that it had compelling reasons for creating the racial classification. It sought to remedy past societal discrimination that had kept members of minorities from becoming doctors. Additionally, it believed that upon completion of their medical training, minority doctors would be more likely to return to their communities and provide much-needed medical care. Finally, the school contended that ethnic diversity was an important asset to the educational environment and that the special admissions program helped ensure a more diverse student body. The question of "reverse discrimination" had been before the courts only once before. In 1971, Marco DeFunis had challenged a similar special admissions program at the University of Washington Law School which he believed had kept him from being accepted at that school. The trial court agreed with DeFunis's claim and ordered the school to admit him. The law school complied but appealed the decision against its program. At the appeals level the court sided with the school and the case reached the U.S. Supreme Court in 1974, the same year Bakke began his suit. The *DeFunis* case received considerable attention and clearly contributed to Bakke's decision to go ahead with his suit. In April of 1974 the Court decided to dismiss the *DeFunis* case as moot. DeFunis was about to graduate from the law school and the Court held that no

true legal controversy existed any longer. This decision opened the way for Bakke's case to be the flag bearer for the reverse discrimination argument.

The Superior Court of California agreed with Bakke's position. It found that the special admissions program constituted a racial quota in violation of the constitutions of the nation and the state and the Civil Rights Act of 1964. It said that UCDMS could not take race into account in its admissions decisions. It refused, however, to order Bakke's admission to the school, finding no evidence that Bakke would have been admitted had there been no affirmative action program. Both Bakke and the medical school appealed the decision. In 1976, the Supreme Court of California ruled in Bakke's favor, holding that the special admissions program was a violation of the Equal Protection Clause of the Fourteenth Amendment and that Bakke must be admitted to the medical school. The medical school appealed this decision to the U.S. Supreme Court.

BAKKE CASE RESOLVED

At the end of its 1977–1978 term, the Supreme Court announced its decision. Four justices, led by John Paul Stevens, believed the program to be a violation of Title VI of the Civil Rights Act of 1964, which forbids discrimination on the basis of race in any program receiving federal funds. These justices believed that the Court should go no further than this in ruling on the case. Four other justices, led by William Brennan, argued that affirmative action programs were acceptable because they remedied the effects upon members of minorities of centuries of discrimination. These justices distinguished between invidious discrimination, which was forbidden by the Fourteenth Amendment, and what they saw as a benign discrimination, which was at the root of affirmative action programs. Some discrimination in favor of members of minorities was necessary if real equality instead of theoretical equality was the goal. Justice Harry Blackmun wrote, "In order to get beyond racism, we must first take account of race. . . . And in order to treat some persons equally, we must treat them differently."

Justice Lewis Powell wrote the decision that, because it allowed each of the other justices to join in at least part, became the ruling of the Court. Powell found that the UCDMS special admissions program was indeed unconstitutional. He argued that the equal protection clause prohibited policies based solely on racial factors unless there was some compelling state interest that could override the very high barrier to such classification. In examining the justifications offered by the medical school, he found only the academic interest in diversity convincing. He rejected the argument that past societal discrimination justified affirmative action. Reverse discrimination required a showing that the agency practicing it (in this case, UCDMS) had in the past discriminated. Since the school had opened in 1968 and begun its special admissions program in 1970, no such history of discrimination existed. Powell also rejected the argument that the program was justified because it served the medical needs of disadvantaged minority communities. The medical school could provide no evidence that special admissions doctors were any more likely than others to return to these communities to practice medicine. Powell held that the program could not stand. In this part of his opinion, he was joined by the four justices in the Stevens coalition, creating a majority to strike down the special admissions program and compel Bakke's admission.

Powell did not rule out all affirmative action programs as violations of equal protection. In the medical school's third justification, diversity, he found some legitimacy because of the traditional freedom granted to academic institutions to set their educational goals. Powell said that the desire for diversity justified some consideration of race as a factor in admissions decisions. The flaw in the UCDMS program was that race appeared to be the only factor shaping decisions for the sixteen seats. In this part of his decision, Powell was joined by the four justices in the Brennan coalition, thus creating a majority for the position that race may be considered as one factor among others in admissions decisions.

IMPACT

The landmark *Bakke* case provided something for both opponents and supporters of affirmative action. While it accepted the idea of "reverse discrimination" made by Allan Bakke and vindicated his rights, it refused to reject the concept of affirmative action altogether. For college admissions officers, it provided a roadmap for how to go about pursuing affirmative action in admissions decisions without violating the equal protection clause. For policymakers in general, it warned against the use of numerical quotas for accomplishing affirmative action

ends. The division on the Court heralded an extended battle in the courts over which kinds of affirmative action programs would be found to be constitutional and which would not. In the years after Bakke, the courts struggled repeatedly, and contentiously, with questions regarding affirmative action in employment. Bakke raised more questions than it answered and brought to the forefront the breakdown of consensus on civil rights questions in the United States. When the issues of civil rights had been about the dismantling of legal barriers to equality, a broad consensus had existed about the justice of this course of action. It was generally agreed that the Constitution could not permit a legally segregated society. After the landmark desegregation decisions of the 1950's and 1960's, the questions became more complicated and the moral imperatives less clear. What kind of equality did the Constitution require? Once the legal requirements of segregation were removed, was there any further affirmative obligation for society to remedy the wrongs of the past? To what extent could individuals not responsible for past discrimination be made to bear the burden for the past? These were questions much more difficult to navigate in the murky waters of constitutional interpretation.

For Allan Bakke, the impact was more clear cut. He enrolled in the University of California at Davis Medical School in the fall of 1978. In the spring of 1982, he graduated to a loud round of applause from the audience. For thousands of minority students around the country, the Bakke decision provided new opportunities in higher education. The Court majority permitting race to be considered as one factor ensured that special admissions programs would continue. What can never be calculated is whether more or fewer of these students were provided educational opportunities because of the decision.

—*Katy Jean Harriger*

See also: *Adarand Constructors v. Peña*; Affirmative action; Education; Equal Employment Opportunity Commission; *Sweatt v. Painter*; *United Steelworkers of America v. Weber.*

COMBAHEE RIVER COLLECTIVE

Founded in 1974

This group of black feminists challenges multiple sources of oppression, including racial, sexual, heterosexual, and class oppression.

Identification: Group consisting of black feminists and lesbians
Place: Boston, Massachusetts

The Combahee River Collective, consisting of black feminists and lesbians, was first organized in 1974 and took its name from Harriet Tubman's 1863 military campaign to free slaves. The members of this Boston-based group are committed to combating multiple systems of oppression and to enacting revolutionary social and political changes.

Many black feminists of the twentieth century saw themselves as continuing the "herstory" of African American women, including such early activists as Sojourner Truth, Harriet Tubman, and Mary Church Terrell. They located their contemporary roots in both the black liberation movements (including the Civil Rights and Black Nationalist movements) and the American women's movement. By necessity, however, they also found themselves challenging the sexism in predominantly male-centered liberation groups, as well as the elitism and racism of white feminism. Thus, beginning in the late 1960's, black feminists and other feminists of color took part in the second wave of the American women's movement, in which many women of color challenged the racist and elitist blind spots in the American feminist movement. By 1973, some New York-based black feminists felt the need to form an independent coalition that came to be known as the National Black Feminist Organization (NBFO).

Some members of the NBFO, unhappy with what they perceived to be the organization's "bourgeois-feminist stance" and "lack of a clear political focus," left to form the Combahee River Collective. Although they suffered from internal disagreements influenced by differences related to class, politics, and sexuality, by 1976 the remaining group had decided to function as a study group, committed to publishing black feminist writings and working on specific social and political projects. While editing *Capitalist Patriarchy and the Case for Socialist Feminism* (1978), Zillah Eisenstein asked the Combahee River Collective to contribute to her anthology. In response, three members of the group—Demita Frazier, Beverly Smith, and Barbara Smith—drafted the *Combahee River Collective Statement* in April, 1977.

Subsequently, the statement was published in several other anthologies, and in 1986, it was finally published as a pamphlet by Kitchen Table: Women of Color Press. The statement focuses on four major areas: the general development of black feminism; the collective's statement of beliefs; a history of the Combahee River Collective, highlighting the problems of organizing black feminists; and a brief outline of the issues and projects of black feminism.

In the *Combahee River Collective Statement*, the members of the collective noted that although they are dedicated to advancing the struggle of black women, they do not support a philosophy of feminist/lesbian separatism, and they believe in forming coalitions with other progressive liberation groups. As politically committed socialists, they believe in the liberation of all oppressed people and believe that racial, sexual, heterosexual, and class oppression are often enacted simultaneously. Thus, in their brief pamphlet, the Combahee River Collective articulated an important concept concerning black feminist history, theory, and practice.

See also: Colored Women's League; Million Woman March; National Association of Colored Women; National Black Women's Political Leadership Caucus; National Council of Negro Women

AARON BREAKS RUTH'S HOME RUN RECORD

April 8, 1974

Hank Aaron's 715th career home run broke a record that many had thought would never be broken, and

Aaron used the position of influence he gained with his achievement to argue for fairer treatment of minorities.

Hank Aaron

Locale: Atlanta, Georgia
Categories: Sports; social issues and reform

KEY FIGURES

Hank Aaron (b. 1934), professional baseball player
Babe Ruth (1895-1948), professional baseball player
Al Downing (b. 1941), professional baseball player
Eddie Mathews (1931-2001), manager of the Atlanta
    Braves baseball team

SUMMARY OF EVENT

Milwaukee Braves outfielder Bobby Thomson broke his leg during spring training in 1954, and twenty-year-old Hank Aaron, who was expecting to play another year in the team's minor-league system, was assigned to play left field in Thomson's place. Forty years earlier, in 1914, Babe Ruth broke into the big leagues, playing in five games for the Boston Red Sox. Ruth made the home run a central offensive weapon in baseball. In 1914, Frank Baker led the American League in home runs with 8; he had a career total of 94 when he retired in 1922, and he was known as "Home Run" Baker. In contrast, Ruth hit 59 home runs in 1921 and 60 in 1927. By the time Hank Aaron was two years old, Ruth had hit 714 home runs, far more than anyone else. It was a record that no one thought could be broken. Certainly, no one thought Aaron would break that record.

He was a highly regarded hitter, but he was known as a line-drive hitter, not one who lofted towering home runs as Babe Ruth did. It was not that Ruth and other home run hitters hit the ball any harder than Aaron did; rather, the blistering line drives Aaron hit were expected to stay in the ballpark for doubles and triples, not carry out of the park for home runs. Aaron's line drives were different, however; an infielder might just miss a leaping catch of an Aaron shot, and the outfielder behind him might watch it clear the fence for a home run. In 1957, his fourth year with the Braves, Aaron led the National League in home runs with 44. Still, he received little attention as a threat to Ruth's 714 until he passed 500 and began to approach 600, showing no sign of slowing down.

By that time, the Braves had left Milwaukee for Atlanta, Georgia, and around then, Aaron began receiving negative mail from people who were upset that Aaron, an African American, might break the record established by baseball legend Ruth, a white man. In 1947, just seven years before Aaron joined the Braves, Jackie Robinson had become the first African American to play on a major league baseball team. Aaron had grown up in Mobile, Alabama, and he was among the first blacks to play in the South Atlantic League, in the heart of the segregationist South, so he had firsthand knowledge of southern racial attitudes. Black players could not stay at the same hotels, eat at the same restaurants, or drink from the same water fountains as the white players. None of Aaron's background, however, fully prepared him for the abuse he endured as he neared Ruth's record.

Some letter writers threatened Aaron that he would be killed if he did not retire or if he approached Ruth's record. Others threatened Aaron's family. The letters came from northerners and southerners alike. The authorities took the threats seriously and gave Aaron and his family members special protection, although it must have been clear to everyone that no amount of security could completely ensure their safety. Despite the concerns he must have had for his own safety and that of his family, Aaron kept producing on the field. He played in fewer games each year, a concession to advancing age, but his batting average, runs scored, and runs batted in, as well as his home run totals, held near the exceptional levels he had always produced. Rather than responding in kind to the abuse, Aaron let his performance speak for him.

In the next-to-last Braves game of 1973, Aaron hit the 713th home run of his career and his 40th of the year. He had three hits the next day, to push his batting average over .300, but all were singles, so Ruth's record had to wait until 1974. Still, 1973 was a stellar year for Aaron, with 40 home runs, a .301 batting average, 84 runs scored, and 96 runs batted in, all in just 120 games. The disturbing mail continued through the winter off-season, but its effects were mitigated some-what by the supportive letters that began to pour in after it became widely known that Aaron was receiving hate mail. The positive letters, many from children, far out-numbered the negative.

The 1974 baseball season began in controver-sy. Eddie Mathews, manager of the Atlanta Braves, shared a big part of Aaron's baseball history. The two had been teammates for thirteen years, batting next to each other in most games, each making the other a better hitter. Even by the beginning of the twenty-first century, these two men still held the record for the most career home runs by two players on the same team. Mathews had planned to keep Aaron out of the lineup for the season-opening games in Cincinnati so that he could break the record at a home game in At-lanta, but the commissioner of Major League Base-ball, Bowie Kuhn, ordered Aaron to play in at least two of the three Cincinnati games. Aaron started in the opening game. Facing Cincinnati Reds pitcher Jack Billingham with two runners on and one out in the first inning, Aaron watched three balls and one strike go by. Billingham then threw a low, hard pitch that Aaron lined over the wall for his 714th career home run. Aaron hit no more home runs in Cincinnati; he sat out the second game and batted three times without a hit in the third. That set the stage for eleven straight games in Atlanta.

In the second inning of the first game in Atlanta, Al Downing of the Los Angeles Dodgers walked Aaron without giving him a pitch to hit. Aaron batted again in the fourth inning, with two outs and a runner on first. Downing bounced the first pitch at the plate for ball one.

The next pitch he threw was a low slider, closer to the middle of home plate than he wanted it to be. Aaron's legendary wrists snapped the bat around, the shortstop started to jump but never finished the ef-fort, and the left fielder started for the wall to make a leaping attempt of his own, but that effort too was left incomplete. Braves relief pitcher Tom House caught number 715 in the Atlanta bullpen. Aaron circled the bases, accompanied part of the way by two college-age men who were quickly removed from the field. He was greeted at the plate by his teammates, his mother (who hugged him so tightly he remarked later that he did not realize she was so strong), and House, who handed him the ball.

SIGNIFICANCE

Aaron hit 40 more home runs before he retired, ending his career with 755—a Major League Baseball record that stood for decades. Aaron also long held the career records for most runs batted in, most extra-base hits, and most total bases and was, ironically, in a tie with Babe Ruth for third place in runs scored. He finished with a career batting average of .305. It was, however, the 715th home run more than any other accomplish-ment that put Aaron in a position to lobby for more op-portunities for black baseball players in management positions and for black people in other venues. In ad-dition, the events surrounding Aaron's pursuit of that 715th home run, especially the racist letters he received and the public's response with even more letters of sup-port, made important inroads into the racial divide that still troubles the United States. That division may be a little less deep because of the courageous and gracious example of Hank Aaron as he strove to break Babe Ruth's home run record.

—Carl W. Hoagstrom

See also: Robinson Becomes Baseball's First African American Manager.

MILLIKEN V. BRADLEY
July 25, 1974

In this case, the Supreme Court held that federal judges could not order the busing of students across school district lines into other districts that had done nothing to promote racial segregation.

The Case: U.S. Supreme Court ruling on mandatory school busing

By the early 1970's, many urban school districts contin-ued to operate schools with a majority black population because of the dearth of white students in those school districts. In 1971, the U.S. Supreme Court in *Swann v. Charlotte-Mecklenberg Board of Education* had held that urban school boards could be required to engage in extensive school busing to integrate their schools.

The *Swann* decision, however, did not address the issue of how to integrate urban school districts that had few white students.

In the early 1970's, a group of black parents, with the assistance of the National Association for the Advancement of Colored People Legal Defense and Educational Fund, brought suit seeking to desegregate the Detroit school system. In 1972, federal district court judge Stephen Roth ruled that the Detroit schools were in fact illegally segregated and ordered a multidistrict desegregation plan involving the Detroit city school district along with fifty-three surrounding suburban school districts. One year later, the U.S. Court of Appeals for the Sixth Circuit affirmed, holding that the Detroit schools could not be adequately desegregated without such a multidistrict plan. Shortly thereafter, the U.S. Supreme Court agreed to hear the case.

In 1973, the Supreme Court had considered a similar multidistrict desegregation plan involving the Richmond, Virginia, schools. In that case, the Court had divided 4 to 4, with Justice Lewis Powell recusing himself because of his prior membership on the Richmond School Board. The Court took the Detroit case to decide the question of whether multidistrict desegregation plans were required when inner-city school districts could not otherwise be desegregated. In the meantime, the specter of multidistrict desegregation prompted a firestorm of activity in Congress, as many members of Congress backed both legislation and amendments to the Constitution restricting the ability of federal courts to order extensive desegregation plans.

In its 5-4 vote in the *Milliken v. Bradley* decision, the Supreme Court held that a district court should not order an interdistrict remedy unless it could be shown that the school district lines had been constructed in a manner to preserve segregation or unless state government officials had taken other action that contributed to the interdistrict segregation. This was a burden of proof that would prove difficult to meet. The *Milliken* decision marked the first time that the Supreme Court had declined to refine existing school desegregation jurisprudence to further integrationist goals.

In the wake of the *Milliken* decision a few metropolitan areas did adopt interdistrict desegregation remedies, but, for the most part, the decision undermined desegregation efforts in America's cities. Unable to utilize an assignment plan that included children from surrounding suburban school districts, inner-city school boards were greatly restricted in their efforts to desegregate their schools.

—*Davison M. Douglas*

See also: *Brown v. Board of Education*; Segregation

ALI AND FOREMAN RUMBLE IN THE JUNGLE

October 30, 1974

When heavyweight boxing champion George Foreman faced challenger and former champ Muhammad Ali in a title fight in Kinshasa, Zaire, Ali knocked Foreman out and became the second boxer to lose and regain the heavyweight title.

Locale: Kinshasa, Zaire (now Democratic Republic of the Congo)
Category: Sports

KEY FIGURES
Muhammad Ali (b. 1942), former heavyweight boxing champion
George Foreman (b. 1948), heavyweight boxing champion

SUMMARY OF EVENT
The heavyweight boxing title bout between champion George Foreman and challenger Muhammad Ali, held in Kinshasa, Zaire, on October 30, 1974, was one of the most significant fights of the twentieth century. The match, during which Ali regained the heavyweight title that had been taken from him after his conviction for evading the U.S. military draft, solidified Ali's reputation as one of the century's greatest fighters and one of the world's most popular athletes.

Three great boxers dominated the heavyweight boxing division during the late 1960's and early 1970's: Ali (the former Cassius Clay), Foreman, and Joe Frazier. As amateurs, all three had won Olympic gold medals. Ali, the oldest of the three fighters, won the heavyweight

Portrait of Muhammad Ali in 1967. World Journal Tribune photo by Ira Rosenberg.

title, at age twenty-two, from Sonny Liston in 1964 and held the title until 1967, when the World Boxing Association and the New York State Athletic Commission canceled his boxing license and stripped him of his title for refusing to be drafted into the U.S. Army. Ali cited his opposition to the Vietnam War as his reason for refusing to serve in the military.

During Ali's absence from the ring, Frazier gained the heavyweight title. Ali, whose conviction for draft evasion was ultimately reversed by the U.S. Supreme Court, returned to the ring in 1970 and fought Frazier for the heavyweight title in 1971. Frazier bested Ali in that bout at New York City's Madison Square Garden but lost his title to Foreman in two brutal rounds in Kingston, Jamaica, in 1973. Ali beat Frazier in a rematch early in 1974, and later that year, Don King, an ex-convict new to the world of boxing promotion, arranged for Ali to fight Foreman for the heavyweight title in Kinshasa, Zaire. Promotional material dubbed the fight the "Rumble in the Jungle." Each fighter would receive $5 million for the fight, then the largest purse in boxing history. The bout was scheduled for 4:00 a.m. local time so that it could be broadcast in prime viewing time in theaters on the East Coast of the United States.

King's success in arranging and promoting the Ali-Foreman fight established him as boxing's most important promoter. "Smokin' Joe" Frazier attended the fight, anxious for a chance to challenge the winner and regain the heavyweight title.

Inside and outside the ring, Ali and Foreman were a study in contrasts. Foreman was a bruising toe-to-toe fighter who relied on a strong knockout punch to demolish his ring opponents. As he entered the ring in Kinshasa, Foreman, who was undefeated, had scored thirty-five knockouts, all but three of which came before the fifth round. Ali danced in the ring. He relied on his quickness and constant movement around the ring to avoid punches and tire his opponent, then he moved in for the knockout when the other boxer was exhausted and rubbery-legged. Ali was talkative and quick-witted, a public man who spoke out forcefully about the Vietnam War, civil rights, and other social issues of the day; he also was known for predicting the outcomes of his fights in rhyme. Foreman was private and subdued, often even sullen, in public appearances.

For their Zaire bout, Foreman was the betting favorite, but Ali was the fan favorite. During the short time that he held the title, and during his three-year forced absence from the boxing ring, Ali had built a worldwide fan base. He stepped into the ring in Zaire as the most recognized athlete in the world, a hero to both the world's poor and downtrodden, who admired his rise from poverty, and the educated elite, who admired his willingness to articulate unpopular stands on public issues. Ali embraced the religion of Islam as well as his African roots, which made him the hometown favorite in Kinshasa.

Before the fight, Ali boasted that he would dance all night against Foreman. Early in the fight, however, it became clear to spectators that Ali had developed a different strategy for his rumble with Foreman. The two fighters exchanged punches in the middle of the ring during the first round, but early in round two, Ali backed himself against the ropes, covered his face with his gloves and his body with his forearms, and allowed Foreman to punch away. Against a strong puncher like Foreman, leaning back against the ropes and absorbing blows was a questionable strategy. Spectators expected Ali to move around the ring to avoid Foreman's formidable punches, but for the next few rounds, Ali spent most of the time leaning on the ropes—a tactic later dubbed the "rope-a-dope" strategy.

Ali blocked most of Foreman's fiercest punches, and Foreman, clearly frustrated by Ali's refusal to come to the center of the ring and box, often swung wildly and missed. By the fifth round, Foreman, who was used to dispatching his opponents inside of four rounds, began to tire. During the last half minute of the fifth round, Ali bounced off the ropes and savagely attacked his fatigued opponent, landing twenty unanswered punches before the round ended. The crowd cheered, and journalists covering the fight began to sense an upset.

By the eighth round, Foreman was exhausted; his punches lacked the snap and crispness needed to knock out an opponent. With twenty seconds left in the round, Ali, confident that he could block or absorb any of the champion's punches, moved off the ropes and forced Foreman to the center of the ring. Ali staggered Foreman by hitting him with consecutive left-right combinations. Two hard rights from Ali then sent the champion spinning forward, arms outstretched, toward the canvas. The referee counted Foreman out, and Ali had regained the heavyweight boxing title.

SIGNIFICANCE

By winning the match in Zaire, Ali became the second boxer (after Floyd Patterson) to regain the heavyweight title. Although he never faced Foreman again, Ali defended his title against Frazier in 1975, beating Smokin' Joe in a brutal battle in Manila. Ali lost his title again to Leon Spinks in 1978, then again regained the title later that year by besting Spinks. Ali retired from boxing in 1980. Already a world celebrity, he became,

in retirement, active in social and philanthropic causes and an unofficial American ambassador to the world. The onset of Parkinson's syndrome during the 1990's curtailed Ali's activities and public appearances.

Foreman used his defeat in Zaire to remake himself. He fought a few more matches during the next three years, then retired in 1977 to become a minister and operate a youth center. After retirement, he gained more than one hundred pounds, but in 1987, he shocked the boxing world by shedding some of his weight and returning to the ring. He quickly regained his ranking as a top heavyweight. Then, in 1994, at age forty-five, Foreman knocked out Michael Moorer, the reigning heavyweight champion, to regain the heavyweight title. By the time he had returned to the boxing ring, Foreman had cast off his image as a brooding, brutish man and had become a garrulous, witty, and self-effacing fan favorite. When he finally retired from boxing for good, he became a popular television pitchman for a variety of consumer products.

The Ali-Foreman fight in Zaire marked a high point in boxing history. Three great fighters dominated the heavyweight division at the time of the Ali-Foreman fight. Ali, with his victory over Foreman in Zaire and his subsequent victory over Frazier in Manila, proved that he was the greatest of them all.

—James Tackach

ALBEMARLE PAPER COMPANY V. MOODY

June 25, 1975

Referring back to Title VII of the Civil Rights Law of 1964, the Supreme Court found that an employer's screening tests were discriminatory and that the employer must provide back pay for employees who suffered monetary loss as a result of racial discrimination.

The Case: U.S. Supreme Court ruling on employment discrimination

African American employees in a North Carolina paper mill, the Albemarle Paper Company, charged that the company's pre-employment tests and seniority system perpetuated the discrimination that had existed before

the passage of Title VII, and they sought back pay relief. By a 7–1 vote, the Supreme Court ruled in favor of the employees. Because the tests were judged to be not sufficiently job related to be valid, they had to be discontinued. The awarding of back pay, moreover, provided an appropriate incentive for compliance with the law. The Albemarle Paper Company decision provided a useful framework for resolving numerous claims under Title VII.

—Thomas Tandy Lewis

See also: Civil Rights Act of 1964; *Griggs v. Duke Power Company*

MARLEY'S *NATTY DREAD* ESTABLISHES REGGAE'S POPULARITY

February, 1975

Natty Dread was the first reggae album to achieve widespread popularity outside Jamaica. The album's success brought reggae, a previously obscure musical form, to the attention of a worldwide audience, and it subsequently became a powerful tool of social and political change.

Locale: Kingston, Jamaica
Category: Music

KEY FIGURES

Bob Marley (1945-1981), Jamaican musician whose songs espoused social and political change and the Rastafarian way of life

Rita Marley (b. 1946), member of the Wailers' backup singers, the I-Threes, and Bob Marley's wife

Chris Blackwell (b. 1937), white Jamaican record producer and founder of Island Records

Family Man Barrett (b. 1946), bass player for the Wailers, 1969-1981

Carlton Barrett (1950-1987), percussionist for the Wailers, 1969-1981

Al Anderson (b. 1953), black American rock guitarist who joined the Wailers in 1974 and played on *Natty Dread Touter Harvey* (b. 1958), organ player for the Wailers on *Natty Dread Peter Tosh* (1944-1987), original member of the Wailers who went on to a successful solo career after leaving the group

Bunny Livingston (b. 1947), childhood friend of Bob Marley and original member of the Wailers who had a successful solo career after leaving the group

SUMMARY OF EVENT

The 1975 release of the album *Natty Dread*, by Bob Marley and the Wailers, and the tour that followed marked the first time that Jamaican reggae music achieved widespread international success and recognition.

Although reggae enjoyed tremendous popularity in Jamaica, it had registered only an occasional hit, such as Jimmy Cliff's "Wonderful World, Beautiful People" (1969), Desmond Dekker's "Israelites" (1969), and Johnny Nash's "I Can See Clearly Now" (1972), on the European and American charts. Paul Simon's reggae-inspired "Mother and Child Reunion," recorded in Jamaica in 1971, and Eric Clapton's immensely successful 1974 cover version of Marley's "I Shot the Sheriff" also helped to bring reggae to the attention of a wider

Bob Marley on stage by Eddie Mallin

audience, but it was Marley's compelling aura of moral authority, social commitment, and personal charisma, coupled with the Wailers' masterful musicianship on *Natty Dread*, that first inspired a worldwide interest in the music called reggae.

Reggae, like American blues, is "hard times" music that appeals directly to the downtrodden and disenfranchised. It is characterized by a distinctive, complex rhythm that emphasizes the first instead of the second beat; in reggae, the guitar functions mainly as a rhythm instrument, and the bass offers a melodic counterpart to the vocals. The tempo is slow, and the lyrics are often esoteric, containing references to Rastafarianism, African folktales, and Jamaican politics. Reggae's roots are in the traditional Jamaican folk music known as mento and American rhythm-and-blues and soul music, which reached Jamaica for the first time from Miami and New

Orleans in the 1950's with the introduction of the transistor radio.

The radio, along with sound systems—huge speakers and generator-powered stereos mounted on the backs of flatbed trucks—brought the hottest new sounds, including the work of such favorite artists as Fats Domino, Johnny Ace, and Louis Jordan, to the Kingston slums. Competition for new hits was fierce; sound system disc jockeys scratched the labels off hit singles to obscure the records' origin, and violence was routine, as disc jockeys sent gangs of thugs out to steal hits from the competition.

When the supply of hot rhythm-and-blues records began to dry up in the 1960's, Jamaican artists started to produce their own music to fuel the sound systems. The first of this home-produced popular music was known as ska. Ska, bouncy music with the emphasis on the off-beat, enjoyed a brief spurt of popularity in Britain and was popularized in the United States with Millie Small's recording of "My Boy Lollipop" in 1964. By 1965, ska had been replaced in Jamaica by "rock steady,"

which was slower and had a heavier rhythm. Rock steady evolved into reggae, which was heavily influenced by American soul music, particularly that of James Brown.

The derivation of the word "reggae" is not known, although many believe the word is simply a description of the music's beat; it first appeared in the title of a 1968 Toots and the Maytals release, "Do the Reggay." Bob Marley, whose music followed the course from ska to rock steady to reggae, was born in the isolated rural parish of St. Ann's on February 6, 1945, to nineteen-year-old Cedella Malcom Marley and Captain Norval Marley, a white Jamaican attached to the British West Indian Regiment. Captain Marley, bowing to family pressure, soon deserted his wife and son, and Cedella, tiring of country life, moved to the teeming slums of Kingston.

Bob joined her there at age fourteen and, like most Kingston youths, became enthralled with the American music he heard throughout the slums. Introduced to record producer Leslie Kong by fellow musician Jimmy Cliff, Marley recorded his first single, "Judge Not," in 1962. It attracted little attention, but a year later, Marley and his friends Peter Tosh and Bunny Livingston, along with vocalist Junior Braithewaite and two female backup singers, recorded "Simmer Down" for record producer Clement Dodd, and the record became a big hit in Jamaica.

Known as the Wailing Wailers, Marley and his friends quickly became Jamaica's top group, addressing themselves directly to the "rude boys," tough ghetto youths who fashioned themselves after American gangsters. For the next eight years, the Wailers recorded for nearly every producer in Kingston, turning out hits but making little money until they signed with Chris Blackwell of Island Records in 1972. Blackwell, a white Jamaican with aristocratic roots and a reputation for honesty and artistic integrity, advanced the group money and allowed them the freedom to create more sophisticated and political music. The result, *Catch a Fire*, the band's first album to be released in the United States, was critically well received but did not attract a popular audience.

Later in 1973, *Burnin'*, considered by many to represent the purest of Marley's music, was released but also received little popular recognition. With the release of *Natty Dread* in 1975, reggae found a wide international audience. Now billed as Bob Marley and the Wailers, the group no longer included Peter Tosh and Bunny Livingston, who had left to pursue solo careers.

The Wailers in 1975 consisted of Marley, Aston "Family Man" Barrett on bass, his brother Carlton on percussion, Al Anderson on guitar, Touter Harvey on organ, and the backup singers the I-Threes, including Bob's wife, Rita. The album contained the Wailers' most sophisticated and political music to date, including "Them Belly Full (But We Hungry)," a warning to Jamaican prime minister Michael Manley that "a hungry crowd is an angry crowd"; "Revolution," a declaration of revolutionary struggle; "Rebel Music (Three O'Clock Roadblock)," a condemnation of random roadside searches by army troops; and the title track, an anthem glorifying the Rastafarian life.

Reggae became closely associated with Rastafarianism, a religious movement founded in Jamaica and based on the belief that the former Emperor Haile Selassie I of Ethiopia was god, or "Jah," on Earth and that he would arrange for the return of all people of African ancestry to Africa. Rastas shun alcohol, tobacco, meat, and shellfish, outlaw the combing or cutting of their hair (thus the "dreadlocks," the long matted plaits of hair worn by most Rastas), and consider the smoking of marijuana, or "ganja," to be a religious rite.

From 1976 on, Marley's concerts were sellouts throughout the world; he toured Canada, the United States, France, England, Italy, West Germany, Spain, Scandinavia, Ireland, Holland, Belgium, Switzerland, Japan, Australia, New Zealand, and Ivory Coast. He sold more than $240 million worth of albums, including *Bob Marley and the Wailers Live!* (1975), *Rastaman*

Vibration (1976), *Exodus* (1977), *Kaya* (1978), *Survival* (1979), and *Uprising* (1980). Marley died from cancer in 1981 at the height of his popularity and influence, leaving an enormous legacy of music and political and social change.

SIGNIFICANCE

After the release of *Natty Dread*, reggae found an audience outside Jamaica, particularly in Europe, South America, and Africa, and became a powerful tool of social and political change in Third World countries. Bob Marley became an influential figure not only in the music world but in the realms of politics and religion as well.

More than a rock star, Marley was a hero of almost mythic proportions in the Caribbean and Africa. Reporters from around the world made the trek to Kingston to interview Marley, who used the opportunity as a kind of ministry to expound on his religion and philosophy and the plight of his country, bringing the tenets of a previously obscure religion and a small developing country to the attention of the world.

Marley's musical success allowed him to become an extremely successful spokesman for the Rastafarian faith. Largely as a result of the missionary zeal with which Marley and the Wailers spread the message through their music, Rastafarianism grew from a fringe cult in Jamaica to a widely practiced belief. Songs such as "Natty Dread" portrayed Rastas as cultural heroes rather than as dangerous "crazies" and did much to change the public perception of the religion. Marley himself was thought by many Jamaicans to be a "myla-man," or holy man, with the power to banish or destroy evil spirits.

Marley's political influence was equally great, although he often disavowed any interest in politics or politicians. He was sometimes aligned with Michael Manley's People's National Party (PNP), and his words were carefully heeded by Edward Seaga and the Jamaica Labour Party (JLP) as well, for both politicians were keenly aware of the massive sway Marley held over the Jamaican people. On December 3, 1976, Marley and his friends and family were targets of an assassination attempt only two days before Marley was to give a free concert in Kingston in an attempt to bring warring factions together. Although injured, Marley performed the concert as planned, singing before fifty thousand people; Rita Marley performed in her hospital robe and bandages. The assassins were never apprehended or identified, but the attempt testifies to Marley's immense political and social influence in Jamaica.

Marley's reputation as a black freedom fighter and reggae's powerful message reached much farther than Jamaica. In 1980, he was invited to perform at the official Independence Day ceremonies of the new nation-state of Zimbabwe to celebrate the end of British rule. Marley's appearance created such hysteria that the ceremonies had to be stopped for forty-five minutes until the crowd could be controlled.

Reggae achieved its peak of worldwide popularity from 1975 to 1980. The success of *Natty Dread* paved the way for other Jamaican artists such as Jimmy Cliff and Toots and the Maytals to reach a wider audience. Former Wailers members Peter Tosh and Bunny Livingston, both of whom had successful solo careers in Jamaica, also began to reach a wider audience. Burning Spear (Winston Rodney, also born in St. Ann's Parish), whose music continues the Marley tradition of reggae concerned with political oppression and mystical transcendence, remained popular into the twenty-first century. Several of Marley's children performed and recorded as the Melody Makers, and Bob's son, Ziggy, went on to a successful solo career.

Many other bands were strongly influenced by reggae, including the English punk bands of the 1970's; in particular, the adventurous and critically praised band the Clash, who had several songs produced by Jamaican record producer Lee "Scratch" Perry, drew from reggae sources. The success of reggae also inspired a brief revival of ska in Britain, performed by such bands as the Specials and the English Beat. The most successful pop band to incorporate reggae was the Police, who used a reggae beat in such hit songs as "Roxanne" and "Can't Stand Losing You." Many other popular musical artists and groups, including Paul Simon, Stevie Wonder, Blondie, the Grateful Dead, Jimmy Buffett, Elvis Costello, Ry Cooder, Joan Armatrading, the J. Geils Band, and the Rolling Stones, incorporated reggae influences into their music.

—*Mary Virginia Davis*

See also: Wonder Releases *Innervisions*; Rap Goes Platinum with Run-D.M.C.'s *Raising Hell*.

THE JEFFERSONS SIGNALS SUCCESS OF BLACK SITUATION COMEDIES

January 18, 1975-July 23, 1985

The Jeffersons, a spin-off from All in the Family, became an immensely successful situation comedy, one of the first to put a black cast into nonstereotyped scripts.

Locale: United States
Category: Radio and television

KEY FIGURES

Norman Lear (b. 1922), television producer and director who created *The Jeffersons* and numerous other shows of the 1970's and 1980's

Sherman Hemsley (b. 1938), actor who played George Jefferson

Isabel Sanford (1917-2004), actor who played Louise Jefferson

Mike Evans (1949-2006), actor who played Lionel Jefferson when the show went on the air

Marla Gibbs (b. 1931), actor who played Florence, the Jeffersons' maid

Roxie Roker (1929-1995), actor who played Helen Willis, one of the Jeffersons' neighbors

Franklin Cover (1928-2006), actor who played Tom Willis, Helen's husband

Paul Benedict (b. 1938), actor who played Harry Bentley, one of the Jeffersons' neighbors

SUMMARY OF EVENT

"Getting taken to the cleaners" took on a whole new meaning when, in January, 1975, *The Jeffersons* came on the air. Originally, the characters George and Louise Jefferson, with their son, Lionel, had been next-door neighbors to Archie and Edith Bunker on *All in the Family*. In that capacity, they fulfilled the role of allowing a humorous discussion about urban race relations. The Jeffersons proved to be economically upwardly mobile, finding business success as their single dry-cleaning shop in Queens turned into a chain of seven shops covering several areas of New York City. In celebration of their success, they moved out of their working-class neighborhood to an apartment on the upper East Side of Manhattan. This was where their own show was set.

The launching of *The Jeffersons* was testimony to the fact that, in the mid-1970's, television was producing spin-off series at a furious rate. No show produced more spin-offs than the grandfather of the socially relevant situation comedy, Norman Lear's *All in the Family*.

George and Louise Jefferson bid farewell to Edith and Archie Bunker because the Jeffersons had established a television identity of their own that could support a separate series.

The strength of situation comedies, or sitcoms, tends to be more in characters than it is in plots. The plots of sitcoms are, generally, routine and predictable. The strength of a program can be seen when a character is able to leave the original setting and establish a free-standing spin-off. It is astonishing that Norman Lear created so many strong characters.

All in the Family spun off *The Jeffersons* and *Maude*, the title character of which was introduced on *All in the Family* as Edith Bunker's cousin; *Maude* later spawned *Good Times*, which featured the character who had been Maude's maid. Gloria Bunker even had her own show, *Gloria*, in 1982 and 1983. The basic situation pursued in *The Jeffersons* was the misplacement of a family in a social class. The Jeffersons had money, but they did not have the education or the social skills of their new associates. This was far from a new premise. Television had used the same concept a decade earlier with *The Beverly Hillbillies*. *The Jeffersons* was basically *The Beverly Hillbillies*, but with black characters. One twist was that while Jed Clampett tried to hold on to the old ways, George Jefferson was attempting to learn new ones. *The Jeffersons* also had elements reminiscent of the 1950's situation comedy *Father Knows Best*: George Jefferson tried to be the all-knowing father for his brood and usually made a mess of things in the attempt.

At the beginning of the series, George Jefferson was probably the most unsympathetic character on American television. He had few redeeming qualities, was devoid of warmth, was verbally abusive to his wife and son, harassed his maid, and was a bigoted, social-climbing snob who did not understand the social code of the class he was attempting to enter. Even the huge business and financial success he achieved with his dry-cleaning business did not change him. He remained short-tempered, bigoted, pompous, and a know-it-all. One critic noted that George Jefferson was an African American version of Archie Bunker, except that George had money while Archie was struggling to make ends meet.

The public responded to George, sensing that behind his blustery exterior there was insecurity and sadness. George had always believed that money was the key to the American Dream. Once he had acquired money, it was devastating to him that he still could not find acceptance.

Sherman Hemsley, who played George, had grown up as a member of a street gang in Philadelphia. Four years in the Air Force gave him discipline and direction in life and, on his discharge, he attended the Philadelphia Academy of Dramatic Arts. In 1967, he went to New York City to perform on Broadway. Norman Lear saw Hemsley in a performance and recalled him years later when he was casting for *All in the Family.* Isabel Sanford played Louise, George's long-suffering wife. The function of her character was to smooth out the feathers George ruffled and to remind him of his roots.

Whenever George engaged in delusions of grandeur and narcissistic self-involvement, Louise would prick his bubble and put his feet solidly back on the ground. Even in their high-rise luxury apartment, Louise was a very down-to-earth person. She had known hard work and economy before their marriage, and she retained a practical outlook on life.

Sanford grew up in New York City and was so enamored of acting that she began doing nightclub acts without her mother's knowledge or permission. She joined the American Negro Theatre and acted whenever and wherever she could. Her goal was to become a black comedian, and she pursued that goal by moving to Hollywood.

Marla Gibbs played Florence, the Jeffersons' maid. Her ambition long had been to become a television star. She studied singing and acting in Hollywood before appearing on the situation comedy *Barney Miller*. From there she became a regular on *The Jeffersons*. Although some critics thought her portrayal of Florence perpetuated stereotypes about lazy black workers, Gibbs rejected this criticism by saying that she worked against such stereotypes by talking back to her employers and insisting that they do some of their own menial work. In her view, Florence was the representative of a common black heritage, that of the servant.

It is requisite of sitcoms that there be eccentric neighbors for the major characters to react to. Paul Benedict played such a character with his role of Harry Bentley. Occasionally, the character would suffer from back problems. On those occasions, Bentley would lie on the floor and ask George Jefferson to walk on him—symbolism carried to its ultimate degree. The microcosm inhabited by the characters on *The Jeffersons* gave Americans of the mid-1970's to the mid-1980's a chance to laugh at themselves and at the racial tensions of the time.

SIGNIFICANCE

The Jeffersons was part of the new wave of socially relevant situation comedies that began to come on the air in the 1970's. These relevance shows, which can be attributed to Norman Lear, with assistance from Mary Tyler Moore, all involved a degree of social consciousness and dealt with current issues of concern and controversy. By being a part of this line of approach, *The Jeffersons* helped change the face of television. Beginning in 1971, topics and even language that once had been taboo were made legitimate by the impact of such shows.

The Jeffersons broke ground beyond what had been accomplished by *All in the Family* and *The Mary Tyler Moore Show*. *The Jeffersons* portrayed an atypical black family and its issues, which often came up in comical ways. American audiences had been slow to accept black characters in serious roles on television. Exceptions to this rule include Diahann Carroll in *Julia* and Bill Cosby in *I Spy*, but most black characters prior to the 1970's were used to provide comic relief. *The Jeffersons* used several stock characters in this respect, but they all had more than one dimension to them. George Jefferson often portrayed a loud-mouthed, opinionated windbag; Florence was an "uppity" black woman, even though she worked as a maid. In many ways, *The Jeffersons* was no more than another domestic comedy, one that happened to be about an African American family. This in itself set a precedent, in that it showed that black actors could play mainstream roles and be accepted by viewers.

The serious side to the program came through the character of George Jefferson, whose bluster belied a sensitive nature that was hurt and bewildered by the failure of the American Dream to be fulfilled by his financial success. The show also presented to the public subjects not previously explored in great depth on entertainment television, subjects such as integrated neighborhoods and interracial marriage. Franklin Cover and Roxie Roker appeared on *The Jeffersons* as the Willises, prime time's first interracial married couple. To the extent that *The Jeffersons* helped open the way for racial tolerance, the show had social significance.

The secret to the success of Norman Lear, in this respect, was his use of humor to attract viewers. Then, once they had become involved in the show, Lear stimulated them to think about their prejudices. It is impossible to say how effective this relevance approach was in changing attitudes and opinions. Many studies indicate that the initial reaction of viewers was reinforcement of the attitudes they held before they watched the show; in short, they saw what they wanted to see. The long-term impact was to wear down resistance to unfamiliar social situations such as integrated neighborhoods, although this did not mean that viewers came to approve of these conditions.

It is noteworthy, however, that the liberal social context of *The Jeffersons* met with little resistance from ultra-conservative groups, and no stations canceled their broadcast of the program. Although set in radically different social conditions, *The Jeffersons* was a lineal descendant of *Amos 'n' Andy*.

The picturesque characters of the old radio show, which made the transition to television, made their comedy work by tricking other black people and had only minimal contact with white society. George Jefferson tried to outwit all of society and integrate himself into white society when it suited his purposes. *Amos 'n' Andy* was about black people, but the intended audience was largely white. The heavily stereotyped characters appealed to the ignorance and prejudice of whites who

lived in a segregated society, but the black community recognized the program for what it was. *The Jeffersons* was clearly about black people and targeted a black audience as well as the large white audience. Perhaps the major difference between *Amos 'n' Andy* and *The Jeffersons,* and a measure of the impact of relevance programming, can be seen in the roles of the two Georges.

George "The Kingfish" Stevens on *Amos 'n' Andy* ducked his head, shuffled his feet, and said, "Yas, suh, Boss." On *The Jeffersons*, George Jefferson looked the world in the eye becuse he was the boss, a successful independent businessman.

The Jeffersons remained a hit well into the Ronald Reagan years, going off the air in 1985. By that time, socially conscious shows generally had lost their appeal. Their legacy, and the legacy of *The Jeffersons* in particular, can be seen in the shows that developed later.

—*Michael R. Bradley*

See also: *Roots* Dramatizes the African American Experience; Innovative Black Filmmakers Achieve Success; *The Cosby Show* Makes Television History.

SOUTHERN SCHOOLS ARE FOUND TO BE THE LEAST RACIALLY SEGREGATED

March 11, 1975

Twenty years after the landmark U.S. Supreme Court decision declaring school segregation unlawful, schools in the South had achieved a greater degree of desegregation than had schools in the North. A report published by the U.S. Commission on Civil Rights noted that a long history of housing discrimination in northern cities had adversely affected minorities' opportunities to attend superior, predominantly white, schools, especially in the suburbs of large cities.

Locale: Washington, D.C.
Categories: Civil rights and liberties; education

KEY FIGURES

Arthur S. Flemming (1905-1996), former U.S. secretary of health, education, and welfare and chair of the U.S. Commission on Civil Rights, 1974-1981
Richard M. Nixon (1913-1994), president of the United States, 1969-1974

James S. Coleman (1926-1995), author of a report used to support desegregation plans who later criticized the use of busing for school desegregation
Thomas F. Pettigrew (b. 1931), social psychology professor who critiqued studies arguing against the potential effectiveness of school desegregation

SUMMARY OF EVENT

It was not until 1954 that the U.S. Supreme Court took a dramatic step against the well-established and accepted policy of racial segregation in such areas as public facilities and government services. In 1896, the Court had approved "separate but equal" facilities for blacks and whites. That decision effectively permitted states to operate separate and decidedly inferior schools for African American children. Black students were crammed into crumbling buildings with few supplies while white students within the same districts had superior buildings, programs, and equipment. Fifty-eight years later, the Supreme Court's landmark decision in *Brown v. Board of Education of Topeka, Kansas* declared that separate schools were inherently unequal and therefore in violation of the equal protection principles in the U.S. Constitution.

American school districts were informed that they could no longer practice racial segregation in public schools. The decision was aimed primarily at southern states and border states in which segregation was maintained by official government policies.

Very little changed in the immediate aftermath of the *Brown* decision. Many school districts took no action to correct the thorough segregation within their schools. In many southern districts, elected officials and school administrators openly defied the Court's decisions. They tried various tricks to prevent the dismantling of segregation.

In one town, public schools were abolished and then reopened as whites-only private schools, thus leaving black students with no schools at all. In other cities, freedom-of-choice plans created the hypothetical possibility that blacks could transfer to previously all-white schools.

In practice, however, spaces were not made available to students wishing to transfer. If black students did succeed in transferring, they often faced harassment by mobs that hounded and threatened them.

African American students continued to be deprived of access to the best programs and facilities, which were almost always reserved for white students. Because the Supreme Court has little ability to enforce its decisions immediately and effectively, it took time and additional lawsuits by black parents before school districts began to reduce the barriers of racial discrimination.

Ten years after the *Brown* decision, only 1.2 percent of the nearly three million black students in the South attended schools with whites, and most of these students were in Texas. No black students in Mississippi attended schools with whites, and only ten black students attended schools with whites in South Carolina. Black students had won a significant legal victory in the *Brown* case, but they still had little to show for it. Although the existence of segregated schools violated constitutional law, few school systems in the South had changed their segregated structures.

In 1964, after finally overcoming the previously successful obstructionist tactics of southern senators and representatives, Congress passed a comprehensive civil rights law. The Civil Rights Act of 1964 contained a number of provisions aimed at ending racial

discrimination in, among other things, employment and public accommodations.

The act also provided for federal administrative enforcement to push recalcitrant school districts to desegregate. Under Title IV of the act, the U.S. Department of Health, Education, and Welfare (HEW) was empowered to provide funding and technical assistance to schools undergoing desegregation. Schools embarking seriously on a course of desegregation could now be rewarded with federal funds. Title VI of the act gave HEW the power to initiate proceedings to remove all federal assistance from schools that failed to desegregate. This was a potentially powerful weapon because many schools benefited from a variety of federal programs. If they continued to disobey the Supreme Court's directives, these schools could lose money that they were accustomed to receiving.

As HEW began to use its "carrot" (Title IV) and its "stick" (Title VI) in the South, school systems finally began to dismantle the segregated school systems that had been in place for decades. School systems were pushed into remedial action through the intervention of the federal government (involving actions byHEWand the Department of Justice) and through lawsuits filed by black parents seeking to implement the *Brown* decision.

During the 1968 presidential campaign, Richard M. Nixon spoke against the use of busing to achieve school desegregation. Busing was unpopular with many southern whites, and Republican candidate Nixon attracted many people who had traditionally voted for Democratic candidates. Republicans and southern Democrats in Congress proposed legislation that would have limited the ability of HEW to enforce desegregation orders against school districts. When Nixon was elected president, he reduced enforcement efforts by HEW and the Justice Department against segregated southern schools, and he declined to employ vigorously HEW's power to withdraw funding from schools that refused to comply with desegregation orders.

In 1975, an advisory agency for the federal government, the U.S. Commission on Civil Rights, issued a series of reports concerning the state of racial equality. The reports examined the existence of racial disparities in housing, employment, public accommodations, education, and the administration of justice. The reports were designed to assess how much change had occurred during the twenty years since the Supreme Court's historic 1954 decision against racial segregation in *Brown*. The visible spokesperson and leader for the commission was Arthur S. Flemming, a former secretary of HEW under President Dwight D. Eisenhower. Because Flemming was a respected Republican, his participation in organizing and disseminating studies that were critical of racial progress within the United States gave bipartisan credibility to the belief that the country still had much work ahead before racial discrimination would be reduced meaningfully.

The commission's report on education, titled *Twenty Years After Brown: Equality of Educational Opportunity,* was issued in March, 1975. The report made strong recommendations for increasing the government's enforcement efforts by withdrawing financial assistance from school districts that did not comply.

In addition to recommending increased enforcement, the report assessed the state of school desegregation throughout the country. Among the most striking findings contained in the report was evidence that southern

schools were actually less racially segregated than northern schools. Although southern schools had remained segregated until the period of vigorous federal enforcement from 1964 to 1969, during 1968 and 1969 the percentage of minority students in the South who attended predominantly white schools climbed to over 40 percent. By 1972, this percentage had moved only slightly higher, to 46 percent. This was well above the 28 percent figure for the North.

The report noted that a long history of housing discrimination in northern cities had adversely affected minorities' opportunities to attend superior, predominantly white, schools, especially in the suburbs of large cities. While many minority students in the South had gained access to the same educational resources enjoyed by white students, fewer minority students in the North enjoyed comparable opportunities.

SIGNIFICANCE

The report of the Commission on Civil Rights marked the final chapter in the national policy debate about desegregation. By showing that schools had been more effectively desegregated in the South than in the North, the report exacerbated continuing controversies about both the extent of discrimination in the North and the usefulness of busing as a tool to overcome segregation.

The busing controversy moved from the South to the North in 1973, when a Supreme Court decision affecting the Denver schools elicited adverse political reactions from northern whites who did not wish to have their children participate in such programs. Northerners

in Congress joined their southern colleagues in increased efforts to pass legislation designed to limit the power of courts and the federal government to implement desegregation plans.

During the 1970's, members of Congress frequently cited the views of James S. Coleman, a prominent sociologist at the University of Chicago, whose earlier work had been used to justify the use of busing but who later voiced criticism of busing's effectiveness. Coleman and other critics of busing suggested that whites were leaving city school systems because of desegregation plans, thereby defeating the possibility of eliminating single-race schools in large cities. The "white flight" issue raised by Coleman and others was refuted by other scholars, such as Thomas F. Pettigrew, a social psychologist at Harvard University. Their studies indicated that the gradual movement from city to suburb was a longstanding phenomenon not tied to busing.

Just as Congress and the president acted to limit the expansion of desegregation, the Supreme Court, which included four Nixon appointees, changed its previous role as a staunch advocate of desegregation. In 1974, a Supreme Court decision concerning the Detroit schools effectively eliminated the possibility of imposing desegregation plans that would include affluent suburbs in city school districts.

The 1975 report by the Commission on Civil Rights further fueled the debate about the desirability and effectiveness of busing, but it did not lead to increased efforts to desegregate schools. By 1975, all three branches of the federal government had acted to limit busing. The commission's report was a final, ineffective warning that racial separation through residential patterns between city and suburb was a primary source of segregation and unequal educational opportunities for northern African American children. As soon as racial discrimination was recognized as a serious problem that extended outside of the South, the governmental institutions that had imposed changes on the southern schools diminished their enforcement efforts. Millions of students in big-city school systems thus continued to attend deteriorating, overcrowded, predominantly minority schools that, when compared with the resource-rich suburban schools nearby, looked very much like the openly segregated schools that *Brown v. Board of Education* had purported to outlaw in 1954.

—*Christopher E. Smith*

See also: U.S. Supreme Court Endorses Busing to End School Segregation; Supreme Court Bans Racial Quotas in College Admissions; U.S. Supreme Court Upholds Goals, Not Quotas, to Remedy Discrimination.

U.S. Congress Bans Literacy Tests for Voting

August 6, 1975

The Voting Rights Act of 1975 formally ended use of literacy tests for the purpose of denying voting rights to language minorities in the United States.

Also known as: Voting Rights Act of 1975; U.S. Statutes at Large 89 Stat. 402; Public Law 94-73; U.S. Code 42 § 1973

Locale: Washington, D.C.

Categories: Laws, acts, and legal history; civil rights and liberties

Key Figures

Mike Mansfield (1903-2001), U.S. senator from Montana

Robert Byrd (b. 1917), U.S. senator from West Virginia

Peter Rodino (1909-2005), U.S. congressman from New Jersey and chair of the House Judiciary Committee

Don Edwards (b. 1915), U.S. congressman from California who supported the bill and chaired the House Civil and Constitutional Rights Subcommittee

Gerald R. Ford (1913-2006), president of the United States, 1974-1977

Summary of Event

Civil rights became a central concern of American politics in the 1960's. Numerous civil rights acts were passed during that decade, and none was more important for the extension of voting rights in particular than the Voting Rights Act 1965. The 1975 extension of this act included a ban on literacy tests for minorities. Many consider these acts to be the most important extensions of rights ever granted by Congress. In American history, the only actions that surpass the 1965 and 1975 voting rights acts in importance for extending voting rights are the Fifteenth (1870) and Nineteenth (1920) Amendments to the U.S. Constitution, which, respectively, prohibited denial of voting rights on the basis of race, color, or previous servitude and granted the vote to women.

By the mid-1960's, the number of demonstrations by civil rights groups had increased considerably.

Violence surrounding even the "peaceful" demonstrations had intensified their impact. President Lyndon B. Johnson had hoped that the states would address voting rights problems within their own borders. The federal government attempted to assist states by removing some of the obstacles to voting rights. One clear example was President Johnson's leadership in securing the passage of the Twenty-fourth Amendment in 1964, outlawing the use of poll taxes as a necessary prerequisite of voting in federal elections. This was a major step in encouraging minorities to exercise their voting rights.

Although the Twenty-fourth Amendment was a major electoral breakthrough, it had the same shortcoming as the civil rights acts Congress approved in 1957, 1960, and 1964: It left the federal government in a passive role in the crucial area of voter registration. The voting rights acts of 1965, 1970, and 1975 overcame this critical shortcoming. The history of the Voting Rights Act of 1965 is also the history of the Voting Rights Act of 1975, since the later action was an extension of the earlier act. The 1965 act largely was forced on President Johnson and others who hoped that the federal government could avoid direct intervention in what historically had been a local prerogative. Public opinion grew intolerant and impatient after a series of bloody demonstrations. By most accounts, the decisive event that led to congressional action in 1965 was the Freedom March from Selma to Montgomery, Alabama. The Reverend Martin Luther King, Jr., organized this march to protest the registration process in Dallas County. Like other marches during this period, it drew marchers from the entire nation. What distinguished this particular march was the violence that erupted when Governor George C. Wallace called out state troopers to stop the march. The clash between marchers and troopers resulted in the deaths of two marchers and severe injuries to scores of others.

This conflict produced an outburst of demonstrations and protest across the nation. The cries for an end to this violence forced President Johnson to introduce a comprehensive voting rights bill to the U.S. Congress.

The final version of this bill, which Johnson signed into law on August 6, ended literacy tests in the states of Alabama, Georgia, Louisiana, Mississippi, South Carolina, and Virginia and in thirty-nine counties in North Carolina. The other key provision of this law was the authorization of federal examiners to conduct registration and federal observers to oversee elections. The states and counties within the affected jurisdictions also had to submit any changes in their election laws and procedures to federal examiners for clearance. The literacy provision affected southern states primarily, but the broader jurisdic- tion of the act affected states in every region of the nation.

The voting rights act was due for renewal in 1970. In June of that year, Congress extended the act and made some significant changes. The major changes in the 1970 amendments were a ban on literacy tests in all states, prohibition of long-term residency requirements for voting in presidential elections, and establishment of eighteen as the legal age for voting in national elections. Like the 1965 act, this legislation had a five-year life. The 1970 act created two distinct legal categories, general and special. The general provisions dealt with literacy tests, voting age, residency requirements, and penalties for interfering with voting rights. The general provisions were permanent laws that were applied nationally.

The special provisions, like the 1965 act, were selectively applied to areas where such provisions were deemed necessary. States or counties were subjected to the special provisions if they had any test or device established as a prerequisite to either registration or voting and had less than half of the registered voters participate in the presidential elections of 1964 or 1968. The courts could also apply the special provisions to other electoral districts if the attorney general successfully brought suit against them for violating the Fifteenth Amendment. Areas subjected to the special provisions were placed under additional federal controls. There was a provision for the suspension of literacy and other test devices beyond the ban. Federal examiners were assigned to these areas to conduct registration drives, and federal observers were sent into these areas to monitor elections. In addition, similar to the 1965 act, these areas had to submit any changes in voting laws or procedures to the federal government for clearance. The special provisions could be lifted from a state or county if it successfully filed suit in a three-judge federal district court in Washington, D.C. Such suits had to convince the court that the voter tests or devices in use were not discriminatory.

Like the 1965 act, the 1970 amendments required reconsideration and renewal after five years. In preparation for this renewal, the U.S. Commission on Civil Rights prepared an extensive report for the president and Congress in January of 1975. The report, *The Voting Rights Act: Ten Years After*, set the tone for the congressional debate that was to follow. In general, the report found that minority participation in the electoral process had increased significantly since 1965. Discriminatory practices, however, were still hampering minority registration and voting. The report suggested a number of changes, the most controversial of which were its recommendation of a ten-year extension of the act and its call for greater attention to language minorities, or those who did not speak English.

In February, the House Judiciary Subcommittee on Civil and Constitutional Rights began hearings on extending the Voting Rights Act. Although many different bills were introduced in both the House and the Senate, the one that worked its way successfully through both chambers was H.R. 6219. After swift movement through the committee system, this bill passed the House of Representatives on June 4 by a vote of 341 to 70.

Efforts to stall this bill when it was sent to the Senate proved unsuccessful. Senator James Eastland, chair of the Senate Judiciary Committee and a strong opponent of the bill, put off action until mid-July. The tactics used by Senator Eastland proved unsuccessful when the Senate leadership under Mike Mansfield managed to bring the House bill directly to the Senate floor. When it appeared that the bill's opponents would stall it on the Senate floor. Majority Leader Mansfield and Majority Whip Robert Byrd skillfully passed two cloture motions (limiting debate) to get the bill passed. After considerable parliamentary maneuvering, the Senate leadership managed to get seventeen proposed amendments rejected or tabled. The one area where the bill's opponents succeeded was an amendment that limited the extension to seven years instead of ten. Once this issue was settled, the Senate passed the bill by a vote of 77 to 12.

The House quickly made some expedient rules changes that allowed it to accept the Senate version of the bill without going to a conference committee. The House then voted 346-56 to accept the Senate version and sent the bill to President Gerald R. Ford. President Ford signed the voting rights extension into law on August 6, 1975.

SIGNIFICANCE

The passage of the Voting Rights Act of 1975 extended the rights secured by the initial 1965 act through August 6, 1982. This portion of the act, Title I, added little to the previous legislation. The most significant changes were the result of Titles II and III of the 1975 act. Title II of the new act expanded the basic protection of the old legislation to certain language minorities: persons of Spanish heritage, American Indians, Asian Americans, and Native Alaskans. Federal observers could be sent into areas if more than 5 percent of the voting-age population was identified by the Census Bureau as a single-language minority, election material for the 1972 presidential election was printed in English only, or less than half of the voting-age citizens had voted in the 1974 presidential election.

As with the earlier acts, areas could be removed from Title II jurisdiction by appealing their case successfully to the federal district court in Washington, D.C. They had to prove that their election laws had posed no barrier to voting over the past ten years. The provisions in Title III of the act required certain jurisdictions, those with at least 5 percent non-English-speaking populations, to conduct bilingual elections.

The interesting twist to this provision was that areas could drop the bilingual elections if they could prove that the illiteracy rate among their language minority had dropped below the national illiteracy rate.

States and their subdivisions could free themselves from these federal regulations by improving the educational opportunities of their language minorities. Many people believe the 1975 Voting Rights Act to be the most significant expansion of suffrage rights outside the South since the passage of the Nineteenth Amendment. It was clearly the most significant ever for language minorities. The legislation gave access to the electoral process to a significant number of language minorities and expanded voting rights enforcement to numerous jurisdictions outside the South. The Justice Department identified 513 political jurisdictions in thirty states that provided bilingual elections in 1976. All of these bilingual elections were a direct result of the Voting Rights Act of 1975. The number of electoral districts required to seek clearance for changes in their election laws increased by 279 after this enactment.

—*Donald V. Weatherman*

See also: U.S. Supreme Court Bans Discrimination in Hiring; U.S. Congress Mandates Equal Employment Opportunity; U.S. Supreme Court Rules on Affirmative Action Programs; U.S. Supreme Court Upholds Goals, Not Quotas, to Remedy Discrimination; U.S. Congress Mandates Nondiscriminatory Practices by Recipients of Public Funds; U.S. Congress Strengthens Equal Opportunity Laws.

VOTING RIGHTS ACT OF 1975

August 6, 1975

By eliminating discriminatory and often arbitrarily applied literacy tests, the Voting Rights Act of 1975 expanded voting rights to large numbers of poorly educated citizens and members of language minorities throughout the United States.

The Law: Federal law abolishing the use of literacy tests for voters

Civil rights became a central concern of American politics in the 1960's. Strong civil rights acts were passed during that decade, and none was more important for the extension of voting rights in particular than the Voting Rights Act of 1965. The 1975 extension of this act included a ban on literacy tests for members of language minorities. Many consider these acts to be the most

important extensions of suffrage rights ever granted by Congress. In American history, the only actions that surpass the 1965 and 1975 voting rights acts in importance for extending voting rights are the Fifteenth (1870) and Nineteenth (1920) amendments to the U.S. Constitution, respectively prohibiting denial of voting rights on the basis of race, color, or previous servitude and granting the vote to women.

By the mid-1960's, the number of demonstrations by civil rights groups had grown considerably. Violence surrounding even the "peaceful" demonstrations had intensified their impact. President Lyndon B. Johnson had hoped that the states would address voting rights problems within their own borders. The federal government attempted to assist states by removing some of the obstacles to voting rights. One clear example was

President Johnson's leadership in securing the passage of the Twenty-fourth Amendment in 1964, outlawing the use of poll taxes as a necessary prerequisite to voting in federal elections. This was a major step in encouraging members of minorities to exercise their voting rights.

THE NEED FOR NEW LEGISLATION

Although the Twenty-fourth Amendment was a major electoral breakthrough, it had the same shortcoming as the civil rights acts Congress approved in 1957, 1960, and 1964: It left the federal government in a passive role in the crucial area of voter registration. The voting rights acts of 1965, 1970, and 1975 overcame this critical shortcoming.

The history of the Voting Rights Act of 1965 is also the history of the Voting Rights Act of 1975, since the later action was an extension of the earlier act. The 1965 act largely was forced on President Johnson and others who hoped that the federal government could avoid direct intervention in what historically had been a local prerogative. Public opinion grew intolerant and impatient after a series of bloody demonstrations. By most accounts, the decisive event that led to congressional action in 1965 was the Freedom March from Selma to Montgomery, Alabama. The Reverend Martin Luther King, Jr., organized this march to protest the registration process in Dallas County. Like other marches during this period, it drew marchers from the entire nation. What distinguished this particular march was the violence that erupted when Governor George Wallace called out state troopers to stop the march. The clash between marchers and troopers resulted in the death of two marchers and severe injuries to scores of others.

This conflict produced an outburst of demonstrations and protest across the nation. The cries for an end to this violence forced President Johnson to introduce a comprehensive voting rights bill to the U.S. Congress. The final version of this bill, which Johnson signed into law on August 6, 1965, ended literacy tests in the states of Alabama, Georgia, Louisiana, Mississippi, South Carolina, and Virginia and in thirty-nine counties in North Carolina.

The other key provision of the Voting Rights Act of 1965 was the authorization of federal examiners to conduct registration and federal observers to oversee elections. The states and counties within the affected jurisdictions also had to submit any changes in their election laws and procedures to federal examiners for clearance. The literacy provision affected southern states primarily, but the broader jurisdiction of the act affected states in every region of the nation.

THE 1970 ACT

The voting rights act was due for renewal in 1970. In June of that year, Congress extended the act and made some significant changes. The major changes in the 1970 amendments were a ban on literacy tests in all states, prohibition of long-term residency requirements for voting in presidential elections, and establishment of eighteen as the legal age for voting in national elections. Like the 1965 act, this legislation had a five-year life.

The 1970 act created two distinct legal categories, general and special. The general provisions dealt with literacy tests, voting age, residency requirements, and penalties for interfering with voting rights. The general provisions were permanent laws which were applied nationally. The special provisions, like those in the 1965 act, were selectively applied to areas where such provisions were deemed necessary. States or counties were subjected to the special provisions if they had any test or device established as a prerequisite to either registration or voting and had less than half of the registered voters participate in the presidential elections of 1964 or 1968. The courts could also apply the special provisions to other electoral districts if the attorney general successfully brought suit against them for violating the Fifteenth Amendment.

Areas subjected to the special provisions were placed under additional federal controls. There was a provision for the suspension of literacy and other test devices beyond the ban. Federal examiners were assigned to these areas to conduct registration drives, and federal observers were sent into these areas to monitor elections. In addition, similar to the 1965 act, these areas had to submit any changes in voting laws or procedures to the federal government for clearance. The special provisions could be lifted from a state or county if it successfully filed suit in a three-judge federal district court in Washington, D.C. Such suits had to convince the court that the voter tests or devices in use were not discriminatory.

RENEWING THE 1970 ACT

As with the 1965 act, the 1970 amendments required reconsideration and renewal after five years. In preparation for this renewal, the U.S. Commission on Civil Rights prepared an extensive report for the president and Congress in January of 1975. The report, *The Voting Rights Act: Ten Years After*, set the tone for the congressional debate that was to follow. In general, the report found that minority participation in the electoral process had increased significantly since 1965. Discriminatory practices, however, were still hampering minority registration and voting. The report suggested a number of changes, the most controversial of which were its recommendation of a ten-year extension of the act and its call for greater attention to members of language minorities, or those who did not speak English.

In February, the House Judiciary Subcommittee on Civil and Constitutional Rights began hearings on extending the Voting Rights Act. Although many different bills were introduced in both the House and the Senate, the one that worked its way successfully through both chambers was H.R. 6219. After swift movement through the committee system, this bill passed the House of Representatives on June 4 by a 341–70 vote.

Efforts to stall this bill when it was sent to the Senate proved unsuccessful. Senator James O. Eastland, chair of the Senate Judiciary Committee and a strong opponent of the bill, put off action until mid-July. The tactics used by Senator Eastland proved unsuccessful when the Senate leadership under Mike Mansfield, managed to bring the House bill directly to the Senate floor. When it appeared that the bill's opponents would stall it on the Senate floor, Majority leader Mansfield and Majority whip Robert Byrd skillfully passed two cloture motions (limiting debate) to get the bill passed.

After considerable parliamentary maneuvering, the Senate leadership managed to get seventeen proposed amendments rejected or tabled. The one area where the bill's opponents succeeded was an amendment that limited the extension to seven years instead of ten. Once this issue was settled, the Senate passed the bill by a vote of 77–12.

The House quickly made some expedient rules changes which allowed it to accept the Senate version of the bill without going to a conference committee. The House then voted 346 to 56 to accept the Senate version and sent the bill to President Gerald Ford. President Ford signed the voting rights extension (PL 9473) on August 6, 1975.

IMPACT

The passage of the Voting Rights Act of 1975 extended the rights secured by the initial 1965 act through August 6, 1982. This portion of the act, Title I, added little to the previous legislation. The most significant

changes were the result of Titles II and III of the 1975 act. Title II of the new act expanded the basic protection of the old legislation to members of certain language minorities: persons of Spanish heritage, American Indians, Asian Americans, and Alaskan natives. Federal observers could be sent into areas if more than 5 percent of the voting-age population was identified by the Census Bureau as a single language minority, election material for the 1972 presidential election was printed in English only, or less than half of the voting-age citizens had voted in the 1974 presidential election.

As with the earlier acts, areas could be removed from Title II jurisdiction by appealing their case successfully to the federal district court in Washington, D.C. They had to prove that their election laws had posed no barrier to voting over the past ten years.

The provisions in Title III of this act required certain jurisdictions, those with at least 5 percent non-English-speaking populations, to conduct bilingual elections. The interesting twist to this provision was that areas could drop the bilingual elections if they could prove that the illiteracy rate among their language minority had dropped below the national illiteracy rate. States and their subdivisions could free themselves from these federal regulations by improving the educational opportunities for members of their language minorities.

The primary accomplishment of this legislation was that it gave access to the electoral process to a significant number of members of language minorities. It also expanded voting rights enforcement to numerous jurisdictions outside the South. The Justice Department identified 513 political jurisdictions in thirty states that provided bilingual elections in 1976. All of these bilingual elections were a direct result of the Voting Rights Act of 1975. The number of electoral districts required to seek clearance for changes in their election laws increased by 279 after this enactment.

Many people believe the 1975 Voting Rights Act to be the most significant expansion of suffrage rights outside the South since the passage of the Nineteenth Amendment. It was clearly the most significant ever for members of language minorities.

—Donald V. Weatherman

See also: Gerrymandering; Politics and government; Twenty-fourth Amendment; Voting Rights Act of 1965

U.S. CONGRESS PROHIBITS DISCRIMINATION IN THE GRANTING OF CREDIT

October 28, 1975

The Equal Credit Opportunity Act passed in 1975 included policies to eliminate credit discrimination and eased the ability of women and minority group members to get loans. The act had major effects on those involved in granting, receiving, and regulating consumer credit; in 1986, those effects were extended to those involved with loans to small businesses and to the businesses themselves.

Also known as: Equal Credit Opportunity Act; U.S. Statutes at Large 88 Stat. 1521; Public Law 93-495; U.S. Code 15 § 1691

Locale: Washington, D.C.

Categories: Banking and finance; laws, acts, and legal history

KEY FIGURES

William Emerson Brock III (b. 1930), U.S. senator from Tennessee

Joe Biden (b. 1942), U.S. senator from Delaware

William Proxmire (1915-2005), U.S. senator from Wisconsin

Jake Garn (b. 1932), U.S. senator from Utah

Parren James Mitchell (b. 1922), U.S. congressman from Maryland

Lindy Boggs (b. 1916), U.S. congresswoman from Louisiana

Pat Schroeder (b. 1940), U.S. congresswoman from Colorado

Frank Annunzio (1915-2001), U.S. congressman from Illinois

Fernand J. St. Germain (b. 1928), U.S. congressman from Rhode Island

SUMMARY OF EVENT

Portions of the Equal Credit Opportunity Act (ECOA) were enacted in 1974. The intent of this act was to protect individuals applying for credit from facing discrimination based on gender and marital status. In 1975, the act was amended several times to prohibit credit discrimination based on race, color, national origin, religion, and age. The prohibition on age discrimination has one exception: An individual applying for credit must have reached the age of majority in his or her home state and must be deemed competent to sign a legally binding contract.

On January 29, 1975, Senator William Emerson Brock III proposed a bill in Congress to amend the ECOA to ban age discrimination. Further amendments were proposed on June 9, 1975, when Senator Jake Garn suggested that the act encompass not only consumer loans but also all consumer lease agreements, since they were also forms of consumer credit. Later in the month, Senators William Proxmire and Joe Biden proposed further legislation related to consumer leasing requiring lenders to disclose all terms of leases to borrowers. On June 12, 1975, Senators Biden and Proxmire proposed a bill encompassing criteria to prohibit consumer credit discrimination based on the following personal characteristics: race, color, religion, national origin, political affiliation, sex, marital status, receipt of public assistance, or exercise of rights under this act. Both the original act and its amendments applied only to individuals applying for consumer credit, not business credit.

Credit is the process of obtaining funds from a lending institution in order to purchase goods and services. The ability of a consumer to obtain credit substantially raises his or her standard of living, as items can be obtained in the present and can be paid for with future income. The creditor (lender) has the ultimate authority as to whom will be granted credit and thus who will have this opportunity. Traditionally in American society, those deemed by lenders as worthy credit applicants were white and male.

There was some logic to this in the fact that prior to the 1960's a majority of the better-paid workforce with greater likelihood of repaying loans fell into these two categories. The composition of the U.S. workforce began to change drastically in the 1960's as women and minority group members began to enter the workforce in large numbers and take jobs with better pay, more responsibility, and greater longevity. This change increased the ability of women and minorities to derive incomes and to be able to repay their debts. Old paradigms die hard, however, and lenders were conditioned to believe that these groups were poor credit risks. Congress recognized the social changes taking place and the civil unrest erupting during this time period and enacted various legislation to guarantee equal opportunity. Equality in the process of receiving credit was a relatively low priority, so legislation regarding it was proposed relatively late.

The Federal Reserve Board was the primary regulator involved in monitoring banks' compliance with this act. Federal Reserve Regulation B was incorporated into the guidelines of banks and was monitored through bank examinations. This regulation codified the intent of the act.

Creditors are in the business of assessing and managing risk, or the chance of loss. Creditors need to assess five different things when evaluating a consumer credit request: character (will the borrower pay), capacity (can he or she pay), conditions (anything particular or unique to the loan request), capital (the borrower's accumulated wealth), and collateral (the security for the loan). A prudent lender would apply these "five C's" of credit to make a credit decision. These are the criteria that theoretically determine the creditworthiness of a borrower; factors such as age, sex, race, national origin, and religion are not accurate predictors of a borrower's willingness and ability to repay a debt and therefore should not be part of the lending decision. Passage of the amended Equal Credit Opportunity Act on October 28, 1975, thus reflected Congress's desire to exclude irrelevant factors from lending decisions.

SIGNIFICANCE

The passage of the ECOA affected all parties involved in the granting and monitoring of consumer credit. This act was directly related to consumers and their attempts to obtain credit. It stipulated that creditors could not ask the sex, race, color, religion, or national origin of an applicant for credit. Loans using real estate as collateral or for home purchases were exempt because of dower rights of married applicants and government monitoring of other categories for fair housing.

The law also established that no individual can be discouraged from applying for credit, each individual is entitled to have credit files maintained in his or her own name, a spouse is not required to sign a loan agreement unless he or she would be responsible for the credit (with the exceptions related to real estate mentioned above), and poor credit obtained with a former spouse cannot be used against a borrower who has established good credit in his or her own name. Creditors may ask about obligations to pay child support or alimony and if applicants are receiving alimony, child support, or public assistance, but applicants do not have to reveal this information, and creditors are not allowed to use receipt of public assistance as a reason for denial of credit. In the case of female applicants, questions regarding types of birth control methods used and plans to have children are illegal.

Creditors have the right to determine whether applicants have reached the age of majority but cannot deny a consumer credit because of his or her inability to obtain life insurance. Any other discrimination based on age is prohibited. In the event that a consumer is denied credit, the ECOA spells out the procedures that must be followed. The lender has thirty days from the date of the application to inform the borrower of the decision on the loan.

The creditor has to provide the borrower with the following information in writing: the action that has been taken (acceptance of the agreement, denial, or change in the terms), a statement of the consumer's rights, the name and address of the federal agency responsible for credit regulation, and whether information was obtained through a credit reporting agency.

Consumers were not the only parties affected by the passage of this legislation. Everyone in the business of granting credit to consumers was forced to comply with new law. The process of conforming began when a lender started to discuss the process of credit with an applicant. Lenders could not use sexist, racist, or other types of discriminatory language that might discourage or offend applicants applying for credit. Credit applications reflected the impact of this law when they began to include the statement that the lender does not discriminate based on the disallowed factors. Individuals involved in the credit application process needed to have proper training to ensure that they were meeting the requirements of the law. Lenders needed not only proper training but also clerical staff to support the paperwork required by the law, such as the written denial notices that had to be sent out on time. The act added direct costs to lenders through the paperwork, training, and compliance measures required. The paybacks for these added costs to lenders were better customer relations, a more positive image of business, and the possibility of entering new and profitable markets as new groups were able to obtain credit.

The passage of any regulation requires monitoring by appropriate regulators. The Equal Credit Opportunity Act covers a vast spectrum of businesses, with different regulators all responsible for their own areas. Commercial banks were regulated either by the Comptroller of the Currency or by the Federal Reserve Board. Savings and loans were regulated by the Federal Home Loan Bank Board, and credit unions were regulated by the National Credit Union Association. Individual states also had responsibilities in ensuring compliance with the law.

Each regulator had various mechanisms to enforce the law. For example, a major portion of a commercial bank's examination dealt with consumer credit compliance. Bank examiners were often more concerned with loans that were denied than with loans that were made. Regulators have used compliance with ECOA and other consumer regulations in deciding whether to allow banks to merge with or acquire other banks.

Prior to 1986, small-business owners were not protected under the ECOA. Small businesses are viewed as high credit risks. Statistics show that more than half of new small businesses will fail within their first few years, with the most frequent cause of small business failure being inadequate financing brought about by inadequate cash flow. Applicants for small-business loans commonly were bad at providing the following information to the lender: cash flow forecast, a clearly stated purpose for the loan, the amount of the loan, and the time frame and source of repayment. Lenders often required a loan proposal including the above information and a detailed business plan. Most small businesses and their owners are one and the same. Even though loan requests are for business purposes, loans are made to individuals. Congress decided to extend equal credit opportunity to business owners as well as consumers.

On March 19, 1985, Parren James Mitchell and Lindy Boggs proposed a bill to the House of Representatives to amend the Equal Credit Opportunity Act to include owners of small businesses. The bill particularly focused on small-business loans to women and minority group members. Congresswoman Patricia Schroeder, cochair of the Congressional Caucus on Women's Issues, presented details regarding the discrimination women experienced in obtaining credit to finance small businesses. Her arguments included the fact that women were rapidly entering the workforce as the owners of their own companies and that women were playing a critical role in the creation of jobs. Congressmen Frank Annunzio and Fernand J. St. Germain also played critical roles in the passage of this amendment through their work as members of the Subcommittee on Consumer Affairs and Coinage of the Committee on Banking, Finance, and Urban Affairs. St. Germain remarked that this bill was special to him because he had been the floor manager for the original act in 1974. The amendment exempted large businesses from protection. All banks, savings and loans, credit unions, department stores, credit card issuers, and car and appliance dealers had to comply with this regulation and act without discrimination in their credit decisions regarding loans to small businesses.

The Equal Credit Opportunity Act had major effects on those involved in granting, receiving, and regulating consumer credit. The 1986 amendments extended those effects to those involved with loans to small businesses and to the businesses themselves. The economic environment from the late 1980's into the early twenty-first century favored small businesses, and women and minority group members were the fastest-growing segments of small-business owners. This occurrence was brought about in large part by the ECOA amendments prohibiting credit discrimination and increasing opportunities for all borrowers.

—*William C. Ward III*

See also: U.S. Supreme Court Bans Discrimination in Hiring.

SHANGE'S *FOR COLORED GIRLS* ... PRESENTS THE BLACK FEMALE PSYCHE

April-June, 1976

With her choreopoem for colored girls who have considered suicide/ when the rainbow is enuf, *Ntozake Shange dramatically increased public awareness of the black female search for self-identity.*

Locale: New York, New York
Category: Theater

KEY FIGURES

Ntozake Shange (b. 1948), poet, actor, and playwright
Paula Moss (fl. late twentieth century), actor and choreographer who was instrumental in the "choreo" aspect of Shange's choreopoem
Oz Scott (b. 1949), theatrical director who developed the staging for the New York productions of Shange's choreopoem
Judy Grahn (b. 1940), poet whose work provided the model for the development of the seven female characters in Shange's choreopoem

Ntozake Shange, author of for colored girls by Barnard College

Halifu Osumare (b. 1946), dancer and choreographer with whose troupe Shange danced

Amiri Baraka (b. 1934), poet and playwright whose work influenced Shange

Adrienne Kennedy (b. 1931), poet and playwright who was instrumental in Shange's development of a female aesthetic

SUMMARY OF EVENT

Following a two-month run at Off-Off Broadway's Henry Street Settlement New Federal Theater, Ntozake Shange's first play, *for colored girls who have considered suicide/ when the rainbow is enuf*, opened Off- Broadway on June 1, 1976, at Joseph Papp's New York Shakespeare Festival Public/Anspacher Theater. After 120 performances, *for colored girls . . .* closed on August 29, 1976, to open September 15, 1976, on Broadway for 746 shows at the Booth Theatre. Shange's choreographed poetry, or "choreopoem," broke barriers in both content and form by sharing the experiences and emotional lives of seven women of color through language, music, and motion.

Shange began to develop her choreopoem in San Francisco's coffeehouses, bars, and studios, improvising with five female poets and dancers, seeking first to explore their unique and communal identities and then to communicate their discoveries. Sonoma State College's women's studies program provided her with a historical context, and Shange's study of dance gave her a pervasive sense of familiarity and comfort with her body as an instrument of communication.

After seeing the group's typically informal presentation of the work during a summer music festival, theatrical director Oz Scott recognized the inherent quality of the production and proposed to give the show a more polished staging. Shange later noted that the moment she relinquished directorial control to Scott was the first time she could see the twenty individual poems as an integrated whole, a choreopoem. Even so, the show's evolution in content and in form continued until, seven years after its inception, *for colored girls . . .* overwhelmed the Broadway stage and the hearts of audiences at the Booth Theatre.

On a stage bare of a traditional set or props, seven female characters are identified simply by the colors they wear as Lady in Brown, Lady in Yellow, Lady in Red, Lady in Green, Lady in Purple, Lady in Blue, and Lady in Orange. These colors are reinforced by the set's lighting scheme. The only additional distinguishing descriptors are the entrances and exits unique to each character. Absent also is the traditional three-act linear plot, as well as the classic dramatic monologue. No one character holds center stage or her own character boundaries. Instead, in a pulsating series of vignettes in which the women relinquish their own identities to play whatever role best supports the spotlighted figure's tale, stereotypes are demolished. The internal anguish of living in a world where being both black and female seems to negate a character's right to exist is revealed, and the will to survive is celebrated.

With humor, music, dance, black dialects, and movement, the characters explore themselves and their relationships. They acknowledge their complicity through passive subjugation in destructive relationships. They reveal their profound sense of emptiness, anguish, and loss. As they and their audience embrace and move through the mutual pain, the sharing gradually transmutes grief and rage into a vital strength, a resilience. Acceptance of self as powerful and recognition of the crucial significance of female bonding in a relentlessly antipathetic world transcend the learned behavior of silent, suffering subjugation and open the way of the heart to rebirth, to actualization.

Audience members, female and male, involved in *for colored girls* . . . leave the theater viscerally moved by their experience, perhaps without the consolation of the classic catharsis, but infinitely more aware of themselves, of others, and of the hope of transcendence. Dramatic production of Shange's choreopoem reaches beyond gender and beyond race to sound a universal human chord.

for colored girls . . . was nominated for a Tony Award and a Grammy Award. The choreopoem won Obie Awards for playwriting, directing, and ensemble acting. It also won the Outer Critics' Circle Award and four AUDELCO Awards. Acknowledgment that Shange's creation had shattered invisible, perhaps unconscious, barriers was instantaneous. Despite the awards, the critical acclaim, and the overwhelming audience response, Shange moved toward performance art pieces as her stated dramatic preference. As a performance artist, she prefers alternative spaces, intimate audiences, and experimental theater pieces. Nevertheless, after having been a playwright, actor, dancer, and director, she still considers herself a poet first.

SIGNIFICANCE

Although a few critics see Shange's *for colored girls* . . . as underdeveloped and label any positive reviews as pandering, the impact of the choreopoem is both immediate and continuing. The most immediate impact is that, for the first time, a black female playwright was successful in rendering an accurate dramatic portrayal of the black female psyche: her grief, her rage, her loss of self, her endurance, and her infinite capacity to love. This capacity to love, turned inward, is her saving grace; turned outward, it is the healing laying on of hands for others.

Shange has stated her belief that women can best understand and depict other women. Even though she may have alienated some by her lack of focus on male characters in *for colored girls* . . . , she would have belied her own beliefs in attempting to draw as accurate a depiction of men. Shange's message is clear: The black female is worthy of as much dramatic attention as is the black male. The message is an explosive suspension of the widespread notion that the black woman should sacrifice herself if necessary for the well-being of her family. Similarly, Shange's smashing of the traditional fourth wall that distances the audience emotionally from the action onstage facilitated the expression of the idea that the female is as worthy of dramatic attention as is the male. In 1976, that women could experience and suppress such traumata was eye-opening to the general public and evoked an emotional bonding among those who chose to heal themselves through sharing and forgiveness.

Shange's rhythms and verbal patterns are reminiscent of those of poet and playwright Amiri Baraka. As such, the choreopoem, while shattering black cultural myths, also has its roots in the Black Arts movement inspired by Baraka in the 1960's and 1970's. Thus the complexities of being black and female are unavoidably conjoined with the seeming contradictions of being a black feminist dramatic experimentalist. Shange's work is a balancing act to which women of all races can relate.

When Shange successfully broke with traditional dramatic form to create a form (the choreopoem) more reflective of her black heritage in its integration of language and movement, she also helped to free other playwrights from the obligation to adhere to Aristotelian conventions. Playwright and director Emily Mann has used the versatility of performance art and juxtaposed monologues to create in her audiences intense emotional responses. She, too, smashes through the fourth wall. Mann has credited Shange as having had significant influence on her dramatic style.

The liberating effects of Shange's impact extend beyond sexual preference and racial and cultural boundaries. Poet and playwright Alexis DeVeaux maximizes the shattering experiences of black lesbians with a dramatic structure similar to that employed by Shange. David Henry Hwang is a Chinese American playwright whose plays invariably reflect explorations into self-identity and the conflicts that inevitably arise with society, tradition, and loved ones. His characterizations, influenced by *for colored girls* . . . , are nonlinear; his action is rhythmic and free-flowing. Hwang's attempts to draw his characters well enough that they become universal rather than sociocultural figures is one result of his fascination with the performances of Shange's choreopoem. With the emergence of Shange and other female playwrights, many male playwrights became more aware of their female characters and became less likely to subvert these characters' humanity into plasticity. As a result, some male playwrights became more concerned with women's speech patterns, subtexts, and motivations. Additionally, some male playwrights became more conscious of their facilitation or violation of the male aesthetic.

These changes enriched contemporary dramatic productions, from the traditional to the nontraditional.

Beyond her influence on American theater, Shange enhanced awareness of the mutual human condition across genders and races. She helped to bring down cultural barriers by creating an environment that unites people in the struggle toward higher consciousness. In *for colored girls who have considered suicide/ when the rainbow is enuf*, Ntozake Shange demonstrated that through

sharing comes healing and that, with healing, "the rainbow" is indeed enough.

—*Kathleen Mills*

See also: *The Wiz* Brings African American Talent to Broadway; Joplin's *Treemonisha* Is Staged by the Houston Opera.

WASHINGTON V. DAVIS

June 7, 1976

The Supreme Court ruled that plaintiffs must show a discriminatory intent, not merely a disparate impact, to prevail under the equal protection requirements of the Fifth and Fourteenth Amendments.

The Case: U.S. Supreme Court ruling on employment discrimination

In 1970 African American plaintiffs challenged the constitutionality of a hiring and promotion policy of the District of Columbia police department. They objected to the use of Test 21, which attempted to measure verbal skills and reading ability, because African American applicants failed the test at a rate four times that of white applicants. They were encouraged by *Griggs v. Duke Power Company* (1971), when the Supreme Court interpreted Title VII so that employers had to demonstrate the business necessity of any employment policies having a disparate impact on members of racial minorities. The plaintiffs in the *Washington* case had to rely on the Fifth Amendment because at the time they filed suit Title VII did not apply to governmental agencies.

By a 7–2 vote, the Court upheld the use of the examination. Justice Byron R. White's opinion for the majority emphasized that an employment practice is not unconstitutional "solely because it has a racially disproportionate impact." Citing numerous precedents, White concluded that the Court had employed the "purposeful discrimination" test when examining claims of a constitutional violation.

Addressing the questions of when and how one might infer discriminatory intent, White wrote that disproportionate impact was "not irrelevant," but that it had to be considered within the context of the totality of relevant facts. The Constitution did not require scientific proof that requirements were related to job performance, but employers had to show that there was a reasonable relationship between the two. White found that Test 21 was neutral on its face and rationally related to the legitimate governmental purpose of improving the communication skills of police officers.

The *Washington* decision did not disturb the Court's earlier rulings in regard to Title VII of the Civil Rights Act of 1964, prohibiting many employment requirements that had a disproportionate effect on members of minorities. It also actually had little influence in regard to the racial effects of employment requirements because Title VII was expanded to include governmental employees in 1972. The decision was important, however, for nonemployment cases such as *McCleskey v. Kemp* (1987), in which the Court disregarded statistical studies when examining the constitutionality of capital punishment.

—*Thomas Tandy Lewis*

See also: *Griggs v. Duke Power Company*; *McCleskey v. Kemp*.

RUNYON V. MCCRARY

June 25, 1976

In this case, the Supreme Court broadened the meaning of Title 42, section 1981 of the 1866 Civil Rights Act to outlaw discrimination in all contracts.

The Case: U.S. Supreme Court ruling on private school segregation

Parents of African American children brought suit in federal court against private schools in Virginia that had denied their children admission. Disregarding the defendant schools' argument that a government-imposed obligation to admit African American students to their unintegrated student bodies would violate constitutionally protected rights of free association and privacy, the district and appellate courts both ruled in the parents' favor, enjoining the schools from discriminating on the basis of race.

The parents had based their case on a section of the 1866 Civil Rights Act that was still in effect. In 1968, the Supreme Court had held in *Jones v. Alfred H. Mayer Company* that section 1982 of the act prohibited racial discrimination among private parties in housing. In *Runyon*, the Court broadened this holding to imply that section 1981, the act's right-to-contract provision, outlawed all discriminatory contracts, whether involving public or private parties—including one between private schools and the parents of student applicants.

In the wake of *Runyon*, lower federal courts employed section 1981 to outlaw racial discrimination in a wide variety of areas, including banking, security deposit regulations, admissions to amusement parks, insurance, and mortuaries. The breadth of the Court's interpretation in *Runyon* of section 1981 also caused it to overlap with Title VII of the Civil Rights Act of 1964, governing employment contracts. This overlap,

together with ongoing concern about the extensiveness of the interpretation of section 1981, caused the Court to consider overruling *Runyon* in *Patterson v. McLean Credit Union* (1989). Instead, *Patterson* severely restricted *Runyon* by declaring that section 1981 did not apply to postcontractual employer discrimination.

Patterson went so far as to declare that although section 1981 protected the right to enter into employment contracts, it did not extend to future breaches of that contract or to the imposition of discriminatory working conditions. Congress in turn overruled this narrow reading of section 1981 in the Civil Rights Act of 1991, which includes explicit language permitting courts to prohibit employment discrimination that takes place after hiring.

The reason for the Court's about-face with regard to section 1981 can be found in its changing political composition. *Runyon* was decided midway through Chief Justice Warren Burger's tenure, when the Court was dominated by justices who occupied the middle of the political spectrum. In 1986, however, one of two dissenters in *Runyon*, Justice William H. Rehnquist, succeeded Burger, carrying with him his conservative agenda. Rehnquist, who had always been outspoken in his criticism of what he regarded as the Court's excess of liberalism under Chief Justice Earl Warren, dissented in *Runyon* on grounds that the Warren-era *Jones* case had been improperly decided. By 1989, when the Court handed down its decision in *Patterson*, Rehnquist had been joined by enough fellow conservative thinkers to overrule *Runyon*'s interpretation of section 1981 by one vote.

See also: Civil Rights Act of 1991; Civil Rights Acts of 1866-1875; *Jones v. Alfred H. Mayer Company*; *Patterson v. McLean Credit Union.*

ROOTS DRAMATIZES THE AFRICAN AMERICAN EXPERIENCE

January 23-30, 1977

Roots, the history of an African American family—from freedom in Africa to slavery in the United States to emancipation—brought the experience and history of African Americans to mainstream attention.

Locale: United States
Category: Radio and television

Key Figures

Alex Haley (1921-1992), writer who produced the best-selling book on which the miniseries was based

David Wolper (b. 1928), producer of *Roots Fred Silverman* (b. 1937), head of programming for the American Broadcasting Company

LeVar Burton (b. 1957), actor who played the role of Kunta Kinte

Ben Vereen (b. 1946), actor who played the role of Chicken George

Summary of Event

Alex Haley, an established writer who previously had authored *The Autobiography of Malcolm X* (1965) and who had done numerous interviews with well-known figures for *Playboy* magazine, published *Roots: The Saga of an American Family* in 1976. Within a month of the book's release on October 1, it was a best seller. It was a mix of careful historical research and imagined fictional detail that began with Haley's ancestors in the village of Juffure in Gambia, West Africa, and ended with the former slaves gaining their freedom and moving to a farm—still in the Haley family possession—in Henning, Tennessee. Even before the book was published, the American Broadcasting Company (ABC), under programming executive Fred Silverman, had made a decision to produce a made-for-television special based on the book. It soon became obvious that a movie of the usual two to three hours could not encompass the length and content of Haley's book. Because the book had become so popular, ABC did not want to disappoint viewers by overcondensation in its presentation, so a decision was made to film twelve hours of material.

In many ways, the book was well suited for adaptation to television. It was not an academic history but instead a somewhat fictionalized account in which actual lives were re-created. Events were telescoped and sometimes fictionalized while being cast against a mosaic that was factual. At the time of its publication, various historians commented that there were numerous inaccuracies in *Roots*, yet Haley himself said that the book, and the series based on it, were not so much history as a study in mythmaking. Haley commented that "what *Roots* gets at in whatever form, is that it touches the pulse of how alike we human beings are when you get down to the bottom, beneath these man-imposed differences." In its book form, *Roots* won the National Book Award for 1977 and also received a special Pulitzer Prize. The book sold more than one million copies

during 1977. Its popularity was reinforced by the television miniseries: On the third day of the broadcast, the book sold sixty-seven thousand copies.

The success of the book heightened expectations but did not guarantee the success of a miniseries based on the published work. No one knew that *Roots* would be the most-watched dramatic show in the history of television. Instead, there were many unanswered questions.

British television had pioneered the miniseries, but the idea had not been used widely in the United States except on public television. ABC, however, had experienced success in the 1975-1976 season with *Rich Man, Poor Man*. This success encouraged the network to finance additional miniseries, including *Roots*.

As the filming was completed, network executive Silverman began to plan the price of commercials on the programs. He projected this cost on the basis of a rather modest share of the national audience. He expected thirty of every hundred television sets in the nation to be tuned to *Roots*. As the time for the broadcast drew closer, more problems were raised. The series was about a black family and had only black heroes. Would this subject attract a large audience? Would all network affiliates carry the show, or would sensitivity to racial questions cause some stations to bypass the broadcast? In the face of these types of questions, Silverman made a decision that was risky but seemed the best way to handle the matter. He decided to run *Roots* for eight consecutive nights, an hour or two each night, rather than broadcasting the show once a week. If the program was a failure, the damage would be confined to a single week rather than spread across the rest of the season. By parceling out

Roots in short segments following already popular shows, ABC hoped to minimize the impact of potential failure.

On the positive side for planning purposes, the series was well written. Each episode was complete within itself, yet each show led into the next. In addition, each episode, except the sixth and seventh, ended on a positive, hopeful note.

ABC need not have been worried. *Roots* proved to be the supreme example of a miniseries. Seven of its eight segments placed on the top ten list of most-watched television programs of all time, and the remaining segment was thirteenth on the list. The final episode was the most highly watched program ever broadcast on television to that time. In all, more than 130 million Americans watched at least some of *Roots*. Dozens of cities declared the eight-day broadcast period to be "*Roots* Week," more than twenty of these being in the South. More than 250 colleges and universities offered courses based on the telecast and the book.

Roots demonstrated that white Americans would respond positively to a show about black people in a socially and historically significant situation. The miniseries was basically conservative, presenting a family as a major source of stability in the midst of stress. The central element of *Roots* was the favorite American theme of family and family values.

SIGNIFICANCE

Although *Roots* was not the first television miniseries, its sweeping success established that genre as a permanent part of the American television industry. In so doing, *Roots* provided a valuable service to television in the United States. The miniseries, as a new form of programming, allowed television to achieve the thematic power and sweep of narrative that previously had been reserved for films. The extended narrative form provides an opportunity for actors to become a part of their characters and also allows the characters to take hold of the imagination of the viewer. *Roots* lengthened the attention span of its viewers and helped prepare the way for other extended, in-depth treatments of significant subjects. The twelve hours of viewing time was analogous to the time necessary to read a book of medium length. The detail that the miniseries achieved was much greater than the normal thirty-minute or one-hour television program length permits. Although no network would choose to have a miniseries of one kind or another constantly in broadcast, *Roots* determined that there would always be a place for such shows.

Roots also gave historical subjects a prominent place on television. Historic sites are popular vacation destinations in the United States among a significant part of the population, but the study of history is not popular. *Roots* helped create a taste for history that has been pursued by later miniseries, the best example being the 1990 public television broadcast of Ken Burns's multipart documentary *The Civil War*.

The relationship between commercial television and historians was uneasy at the time of the broadcast of *Roots*, and it has remained so. The presentation of historical subjects on television is not accurate enough to satisfy most academic historians. Many insist that programs such as *Roots* be labeled as "docudramas" and not as documentaries.

Some television critics and producers agree with this point of view. As a docudrama, *Roots* was a melodrama with stereotypes that sometimes disclosed the point of view of those who, historically, have been victims. David Wolper, the producer of *Roots*, recognized this fact when he commented that *Roots* was not intended to be a reference work for historical information.

The focus of *Roots* was to be emotional impact; it was intended to show how it felt to be a slave. Because of its vivid historical imagination and its careful attention to re-creation, *Roots* became a powerful tool to achieve this end. The miniseries was, after all, the first television program to address the issue of slavery from the point of view of slaves.

Roots directly challenged what was, in 1977, a major academic theory in the interpretation of slavery. In 1959, historian Stanley M. Elkins had published an important book titled *Slavery: A Problem in American Institutional and Intellectual Life*. In this book, Elkins argued that slavery was a highly coercive, closed system with a modern analogy in the Nazi concentration camps. In the camps of the Nazi era, it was observed that some inmates identified with their guards and adopted the type of behavior the guards wanted. Elkins argued that this was a means of accommodation through role playing that allowed the inmates to deal psychologically with being oppressed. Elkins then argued that slaves did the same thing—they dealt with oppression by psychologically identifying with the masters. The psychological characteristic that developed from this Elkins called the "Sambo" role. Black slaves were like children: "docile but irresponsible, loyal but lazy, humble but chronic liars and thieves." In 1977, this was a widespread view of slavery. *Roots* directly challenged this view of black history and helped open the way for another evaluation of the black experience of slavery. Kunta Kinte, the single most important character, never became docile, despite several severe punishments and eventual amputation of a foot for his repeated attempts to run away. None of the descendants of Kunta Kinte looked at their owners as "good fathers"; indeed, Chicken George had to be restrained from killing the white man who was his biological father when the man made it clear that Chicken George was only a valuable piece of property and not a son. Neither is it the case, as Elkins contends, that black people were so shocked and traumatized by the experience of enslavement that they gave up all ties to their African culture to become white people with black skins.

Roots showed that the African heritage was not wiped out during the first generation of slaves and that aspects of tribal culture endured even into the twentieth century. Kunta Kinte, Chicken George, and Tom all functioned, even in slavery, as traditional African patriarchs. African humor, songs, dances, words, speech patterns, tales, games, folk beliefs, and sayings all were shown surviving the process of enslavement and transportation.

One of the most powerful visual images of these African cultural survivals shown in *Roots* was the practice of naming a newborn child by lifting it upward toward a full moon, a symbol of renewing the link to Africa.

Another important impact of *Roots* was that the miniseries provided a source of national unity by keeping blacks and whites tuned in to acts of moral witness, of compassion, and of expiation. In short, *Roots* was a learning experience and seems to have had a positive impact on race relations. A nationwide survey by the National Association for the Advancement of Colored People (NAACP) reported that, except for a few isolated incidents, the showing of *Roots* strengthened black history offerings in schools and colleges and enlightened whites about the black heritage in both the United States and Africa. In this sense, critic Karl Meyer commented that *Roots* was like a medieval morality play, neither fact nor fiction but serving a didactic purpose.

In November 2013, the History channel announced that it was developing an eight-hour Roots miniseries with Mark Wolper, son of the original show's original producer David L. Wolper. This version aired on May 30, 2016 and combined elements from both Haley's book and its 1977 adaptation. Directors include Mario Van Peebles, Thomas Carter and Phillip Noyce, Executive Producers include Will Packer and LeVar Burton, while cast members include Malachi Kirby as Kunte, Forest Whitaker, Anna Paquin, Laurence Fishburne, Mekhi Phifer, Jonathan Rhys Meyers, Derek Luke, Anika Noni Rose, and Chad L. Coleman.

—*Michael R. Bradley*

UNITED STEELWORKERS OF AMERICA V. WEBER
June 27, 1979

In this case, the U.S. Supreme Court ruled that an employer could establish voluntary programs, including quotas, to eliminate a manifest racial imbalance, even without evidence that the employer had previously discriminated.

The Case: U.S. Supreme Court ruling on affirmative action

Title VII of the Civil Rights Act of 1964 made it unlawful "to discriminate against any individual because of his race, color, religion, sex, or national origin." Based on this law, President Lyndon B. Johnson issued Executive Order 11246, which required all companies doing business with the federal government to take "affirmative action" to eliminate discrimination. Shortly thereafter, federal agencies began to use "numerical imbalance" as *prima facie* evidence of invidious discrimination, and they encouraged employers to use numerical goals, timetables, and sometimes quotas to advance the employment opportunities of underrepresented minorities and women.

In the Equal Employment Opportunity Act of 1972, the majority of Congress rejected Senator Samuel Ervin's amendment that would have barred all "preferential treatment," but the law did not make clear how far employers were expected to go. Meanwhile, lower courts were endorsing strict quotas in situations where intentional discrimination was proven.

EARLIER COURT DECISIONS
In a 1976 case, *McDonald v. Santa Fe Transportation Company,* the Court ruled unanimously that Title VII forbade discrimination against whites as well as members of minorities, but this case avoided the question of whether employers might sometimes use affirmative-action programs that presented comparative disadvantages for whites. In the famous *Regents of the University of California v. Bakke* case (1978), the Court decided against rigid quotas in education. Many people expected the Court to take a similar position on questions of employment opportunity.

The Kaiser Corporation aluminum and chemical plant of Gramercy, Louisiana, had never made employment decisions explicitly on the basis of race, but African Americans were not represented in the plant in proportion to their percentage in the local population, especially in the higher-paying craft positions. Because Kaiser Corporation did business with the federal government, its employment practices were examined by the Office of Federal Contracts Compliance. The agency was naturally critical of the fact that although African Americans made up 39 percent of the local workforce they occupied fewer than 2 percent of the craft positions at the Gramercy plant. Fourteen other Kaiser plants were found to have similar patterns of black employment.

Because a costly legal challenge appeared likely, the Kaiser Corporation and the United Steelworkers of America jointly agreed to begin "voluntary" affirmative-action programs for the fifteen plants, including both goals and quotas. In the Kaiser plant, there was to be a special program to train craft workers, with thirteen positions the first year. Admission to the program was based on seniority, but at least half the positions were reserved for African Americans even if they had less seniority. This quota was to continue until the number of African Americans was commensurate with their percentage in the local labor force.

Brian Weber, who had been active in union affairs, was a white employee who had five years of experience at the Gramercy plant. Disappointed not to receive one of the thirteen positions, he became angry when he learned that two African Americans with less seniority had been admitted to the program. After reading the Civil Rights Act, he decided to sue both the company and the union on the grounds that Title VII prohibited employment practices that favored one race over another.

In 1977, a federal district court ruled in Weber's favor, and the following year he again received a favorable judgment from the Fifth Circuit Court of Appeals. At the appeals court, however, Justice John Wisdom dissented from the argument that statistical disproportion created a presumptive case of discrimination that merited remediation, and he referred to the fact that Congress in 1972 had not banned preferential treatment. The Supreme Court agreed to a writ of *certiorari*, and the Court listened to oral arguments on March 28, 1979. Justice Louis Powell, who was recovering from surgery, did not participate in the case, and Justice John Paul Stevens did not participate for unstated reasons.

THE SUPREME COURT'S RULING

On June 27, the Court announced a five-to-two decision that reversed the lower courts. The senior member of the majority, Justice William Brennan, Jr., decided to write the controversial opinion, and he was joined by Justices Harry Blackmun, Potter Stewart, Thurgood Marshall, and Byron White, with Blackmun writing a concurring opinion. Stewart's vote was a surprise and seemed to contradict his position in similar cases. Chief Justice Warren Burger and Justice William Rehnquist both dissented and wrote strongly worded opinions.

Speaking for the majority, Brennan stressed the narrowness of the decision, indicating that the Court was not ruling on all possible forms of preferential treatment. He argued that Weber's case was based on a "literal" interpretation of Title VII, but that the "spirit" or purpose of the law had to be considered within the framework of its legislative history. Since the goal of Title VII was to promote "the integration of blacks into the mainstream of American society," the law should not be used to prohibit reasonable means designed to achieve that end. Since section 703(j) stated that the statute was not to be interpreted "to require" preferential treatment, Brennan concluded that this wording gave an employer the freedom to institute a voluntary program.

In defending the Kaiser program, Brennan presented three principles. First, the program did "not unnecessarily trammel the interests of the white employees," because they were not discharged or barred from future advancement. Second, the plan was a "temporary measure" that would end when the specific target had been achieved. Third, the program did not aim for a permanent quota but was a limited measure "to eliminate a manifest racial imbalance." Brennan implied that programs violating these principles would likely be declared invalid.

Justice Blackmun's concurring opinion accepted the majority outcome but took a less expansive approach to Title VII. Rather than emphasizing the voluntary nature of the Kaiser program, Blackmun followed Justice Wisdom's contention that statistical imbalance was evidence of an "arguable violation" of the law, allowing employers "to make reasonable responses without fear of liability." Finally, he noted that if the Court had "misperceived" the intent of Congress, this could be corrected easily by legislative action.

In his thirty-seven page dissent, Justice Rehnquist emphasized the actual language of the 1964 law, criticizing Brennan's method of stressing the goals at the expense of the literal words of the law. He noted that Section 703(j) was joined to Section 703(e), with the latter explicitly prohibiting any classifications that might deprive an individual of equal opportunity because of race or sex. He also quoted extensively from supporters of the law during the eighty-three-day debate in the Senate, including Senator Hubert Humphrey's statement that Title VII "forbids discrimination against anyone on account of race." Rehnquist charged that the majority holding was "a *tour de force* reminiscent not of jurists . . .but of escape artists such as Houdini."

In a more restrained dissent, Chief Justice Burger declared that the majority opinion "effectively rewrites Title VII to achieve what it regards as a desirable result." He declared that he would be inclined to allow preferential treatment if he were a member of a legislative body, but that it was incompatible with the principle of separation of powers for the Court to rule "contrary to the explicit language of the statute." In looking for the "spirit" of a law, he asked: "How are judges expected to ascertain the purpose of a law except through the words Congress used and the legislative history of the statute's evolution?"

Impact

When the *Weber* decision was announced, it created much controversy. Defenders included most civil rights groups and officials of the administration of President Jimmy Carter. Some supported the ruling because of the assumption that preferential treatment and numerical remedies were necessary to counteract the "institutional racism" that was endemic in American society, and others believed that such policies were justified in order to compensate for the socioeconomic disadvantages of African Americans and members of other minorities. In contrast, critics of affirmative action feared that the *Weber* ruling would give a green light to quotas and "reverse discrimination," with innocent whites being punished for past injustices for which they were not responsible. Jewish organizations such as B'nai B'rith were especially outspoken in their disagreement, for historically quotas had been used to place limits on opportunities for Jews.

Formally, the *Weber* ruling was limited to voluntary programs of racial preference for private businesses that had manifest racial imbalance when compared with the local labor force. It did not draw a clear line of demarcation between permissible and impermissible forms of affirmative action. Since the majority

chose to ignore the fact that Kaiser Corporation and the union were acting because of federal pressure under Executive Order 11246, the ruling did not address the constitutionality of this kind of state action, but the silence of the Court on this crucial issue appeared to give tacit approval. Informed observers generally agreed that there was unlikely to be an epidemic of voluntary affirmative action without the "prodding" of governmental agencies.

During the 1980's, the Court, although becoming more conservative, made decisions that generally were consistent with the key points of *Weber*. In *Fullilove v. Klutznick* (1980), the majority upheld a congressional public works law that stipulated that 10 percent of contracts had to be reserved for minority-owned businesses. When there was evidence that either public or private employers had demonstrated bad faith in the employment of members of minorities, the Court supported the right of lower courts to impose rigid quotas. In several cases, the Court allowed statistical evidence of racial or sexual imbalance to be used as one of the indicators of possible discrimination. When employees lost their jobs because of economic difficulties, however, the Court did not permit racial quotas to determine who was to be laid off. Despite public opposition to preferential treatment, by the early 1990's it appeared very unlikely that *Weber* would be reversed.

A quarter of a century after the passage of the Civil Rights Act of 1964, African Americans and members of other minorities had made a number of gains in the realm of employment, although statistics made it clear that they were far from achieving parity with whites. By that time, the vast majority of Americans said that they agreed with the goal of equal opportunity, but there was no consensus on the goal of equality of outcomes. Few observers denied that African Americans continued to face negative stereotypes and discrimination, and race relations did not seem to be improving for the better. The principles of the *Weber* decision continued to elicit emotional debates.

—Thomas Tandy Lewis

See also: *Adarand Constructors v. Peña*; Affirmative action; *Bakke* case; *Fullilove v. Klutznick*.

INNOVATIVE BLACK FILMMAKERS ACHIEVE SUCCESS

1980's-1990's

After a number of gifted black actors had established during the 1980's that a crossover audience existed for films dealing with black subjects, a renaissance of black films and directors emerged.

Locale: Hollywood, California
Category: Motion pictures and video

KEY FIGURES

Spike Lee (b. 1957), young black film director, one of the most popular of the era

John Singleton (b. 1968), director who astonished the film industry with the quality of his first feature film, *Boyz n the Hood* (1991)

Mario Van Peebles (b. 1957), film director and actor, son of filmmaker Melvin Van Peebles

Robert Townsend (b. 1957), actor and comedian who went on to direct *Hollywood Shuffle* (1987), a comedy that commented on black stereotypes

Bill Duke (b. 1943), actor, television director, and film director

Matty Rich (b. 1971), youngest of the new wave of black filmmakers

Denzel Washington (b. 1954), stage and film actor

Morgan Freeman (b. 1937), stage and film actor

Whoopi Goldberg (b. 1949), comedian and stage and film actor

SUMMARY OF EVENT

During the late 1980's and early 1990's, a substantial wave of serious black films entered the mainstream of American filmmaking, utilizing a growing number of African American talents—actors, writers, directors, and composers who managed to redefine the American cinema and expand its horizons to pay closer attention to black culture. The catalyst for this revolution—it was more than simply a trend—was the controversial success of Spike Lee's *Do the Right Thing* (1989) following the more marginal success of his earlier films, *School Daze* (1988) and *She's Gotta Have It* (1986). By 1990, Lee had become both a national celebrity, appearing in television commercials for Nike shoes, and a respected major filmmaker, creating opportunities for other African American talents such as Mario Van Peebles, whose *New Jack City* was released early in 1991, and John Singleton, whose semiautobiographical *Boyz*

n the Hood was released later in that year to high critical acclaim.

These films grew out of the black urban experience and reflected the concerns and culture of African Americans in new and vital ways. What was especially significant was the mainstreaming of those concerns and the development of a substantial crossover audience. There had always been an ethnic audience for films treating African Americans, who earlier in the century had their own film industry that produced pictures outside the mainstream, starring black actors, made for black audiences in segregated theaters. That industry was separate but unequal, serving a limited market.

On occasion, Hollywood had experimented with novelty pictures starring African Americans, such as King Vidor's *Hallelujah* (1929); Andrew L. Stone's *Stormy Weather* (1943), noteworthy for the vitality of a cast that included Lena Horne, Bill Robinson, Fats Waller, Cab Calloway, and the Nicholas brothers; and Otto Preminger's *Carmen Jones* (1954), which adapted the opera as a musical starring Dorothy Dandridge, Pearl Bailey, and Harry Belafonte. In addition, occasional pictures attempted to treat significant racial issues, ranging from Elia Kazan's *Pinky* (1949), starring Jeanne Crain as a black girl passing for white in the South, to Stanley Kramer's *Guess Who's Coming to Dinner* (1967), with Sidney Poitier supporting Spencer Tracy and Katharine Hepburn; Poitier played the fiancé of their daughter in this film exploring interracial relationships. In 1961, Daniel Petrie adapted Lorraine Hansberry's 1959 play *A Raisin in the Sun*, providing starring roles for Sidney Poitier and Ruby Dee, and in 1964, Michael Roemer's *Nothing but a Man* dramatized the struggle of a black worker (Ivan Dixon) to protect his family against racial inequality. Such efforts as these were few and far between, however.

During the early 1970's, a trend for black films developed, led by Ossie Davis, Melvin Van Peebles, and Gordon Parks, Sr. *Cotton Comes to Harlem* (1970), directed by Davis from a story developed by Chester Himes, and *Shaft* (1971), directed by Parks, presented black policemen as hero figures. In a television interview aired November 9, 1971, in New York City, Davis noted that "the choice of materials and employees is determined by those who have no direct knowledge of the black experience." Melvin Van Peebles, the director of

Watermelon Man (1970) and *Sweet Sweetback's Baadasssss Song* (1971), asserted that black films "should all work toward the decolonization of black minds and the reclaiming of black spirit," goals that were not to be widely achieved for another twenty years. The most lucrative films of the 1970's trend were Parks's *Shaft* and, later, the drug drama *Super Fly* (1972), directed by Parks's son, Gordon Parks, Jr.

The number of films directed by African Americans increased in the early 1970's, but each year brought only a few dozen. Clearly, a market was developing, but the audience was largely ethnic and the films produced were by and large regarded as "blaxploitation" pictures, sexually oriented films with a focus on action and violence. A substantial crossover audience was needed, and that was not to come until the end of the 1980's, when the content of black films had developed. Film critics of the mid- 1970's were unsure about where black filmmaking would go or whether black directors would ever reach more than an ethnic audience.

The widening of the crossover audience took place during the 1980's, thanks to the efforts of white filmmakers who were determined to make films that would treat the black experience honestly and were willing to risk experimenting with predominantly black casts. Leading the way was Norman Jewison with *A Soldier's Story* (1984), adapted by the African American playwright Charles Fuller from his own stage work *A Soldier's Play* (1981) and featuring an amazing cast that included Howard E. Rollins, Jr., Denzel Washington, Robert Townsend, and Adolph Caesar. Steven Spielberg directed *The Color Purple* (1985), which was adapted from Alice Walker's 1982 novel but not scripted by the novelist herself. Spielberg's film made Walker's story less grim and ornamented it with sentimentality, but the Spielberg touch also made it a popular success and turned Whoopi Goldberg into a major star. These two films opened the mainstream market to stories about the black experience.

Another significant development was the rise of an increasingly large pool of gifted black actors with drawing power at the box office. Denzel Washington shot to prominence as a consequence of *A Soldier's Story*, for example, as did Robert Townsend. Howard E. Rollins, Jr., established his credentials forcefully in *Ragtime* (1981), directed by Miloš Forman. Danny Glover gave a memorable performance as a loyal black farmhand in *Places in the Heart* (1984) and went on to star in *Grand Canyon* (1991) and with Mel Gibson in *Lethal Weapon* (1987). Morgan Freeman gained notice for his acting

ability in *Driving Miss Daisy* (1989). Eddie Murphy became a major star during the 1980's in such films as *Beverly Hills Cop* (1984), *Beverly Hills Cop II* (1987), and *Trading Places* (1983). Gregory Hines made his film debut in *Wolfen* (1981), a supernatural thriller, and was transformed into a leading actor by Francis Ford Coppola's *The Cotton Club* (1984), in a role appropriate for a dancer who began performing at the Apollo Theater at the age of six. The career of television talk-show host Arsenio Hall received a tremendous boost when Hall appeared as Eddie Murphy's comic sidekick in *Coming to America* (1988) and in a smaller part in *Harlem Nights* (1989). Oprah Winfrey, another talk-show host, became a national celebrity after costarring with Whoopi Goldberg in *The Color Purple*.

Many of the popular stars of the 1980's, both in film and on television, were black, reflecting mainstream acceptance. *The Cosby Show* completed an eight-year television run in 1992 after frequent appearances at the top of the ratings. Bill Cosby's earlier work with Robert Culp in the television series *I Spy* established the black-white buddy formula in the 1960's. The black renaissance of the 1980's and 1990's represented a culmination of audience acceptance by both black and white audiences and the appearance of a large number of African American artists capable of doing original, entertaining work. The transition from bebop to hip-hop culture can be dated to *Beat Street* (1984), the first film to popularize rap culture. The success of that film might suggest that American culture had become less racist and more will- ing to accept, or at least examine, black culture. Spike Lee explored racial tensions, however, in *Do the Right Thing* and *Jungle Fever* (1991), showing that tensions and racism still existed. Certainly the films of the 1990's were far different from such black exploitation features as *Super Fly*, less superfluous and ephemeral, more realistic, original, and inventive. This was particularly true of the films of Spike Lee, John Singleton, and Matty Rich, which examined social problems and attitudes in depth from a distinctly black perspective.

The black renaissance hit full force in 1990 in two separate but related ways, in films directed by mainstream directors who used black actors and in films directed by African Americans. One of the very best films of 1989, for example, was *Driving Miss Daisy*, directed by Australian Bruce Beresford and adapted from Alfred Uhry's Pulitzer Prize-winning play (pr. 1987), starring Morgan Freeman as Hoke Colburn, Miss Daisy's compassionate chauffeur, and Esther Rolle as Idella, her sardonic cook. The same year saw *Glory*, directed by Edward Zwick, a film that told the story of a black regiment that fought against the Confederacy during the Civil War, starring Morgan Freeman and Denzel Washington, with Matthew Broderick as Robert Gould Shaw, the white colonel who organized and led the regiment. Washington won the Academy Award for Best Supporting Actor for his portrayal of a runaway slave turned soldier in *Glory*. In 1991, he starred with rap music artist Ice-T in the police drama *Ricochet*. *Driving Miss Daisy* received Academy Award nominations for Best Actor, Best Actress, and Best Picture, but at the same time the Academy of Motion Picture Arts and Sciences virtually ignored Spike Lee's *Do the Right Thing*.

With a new generation of African American directors in place by the 1990's, it became less likely that films dealing with black topics would be made by white directors. Spike Lee continued to stabilize his reputation with *Mo' Better Blues* (1990), which featured strong performances from Denzel Washington and Wesley Snipes, followed by *Jungle Fever* (1991) and the controversial *Malcolm X* (1992), which went over budget and resulted in a public argument between Lee and the studio over funding to complete the picture.

Although still the most visible of black directing talents, Lee faced strong competition by 1991. The first to challenge Lee was Mario Van Peebles, whose *New Jack City* (1991), a film about a police crackdown on drug dealers, received nationwide attention when riots broke out in theaters where it opened. John Singleton's *Boyz n the Hood* eclipsed both *New Jack City* and *Jungle Fever* when it was released at midyear and was the consensus pick of critics around the nation for the top film of 1991. For that film, Singleton became the youngest person and the first African American to be nominated for an Oscar as Best Director.

SIGNIFICANCE

The impact of the black renaissance in film was obvious in the other major black films released in the early 1990's: Matty Rich's *Straight Out of Brooklyn* (1991); Bill Duke's *A Rage in Harlem* (1991), followed by *Deep Cover*, starring Laurence Fishburne and released in early 1992; Robert Townsend's *The Five Heartbeats* (1991); and Topper Carew's *Talkin' Dirty After Dark* (1991). Other films in production in 1991 were released in 1992, such as Ernest Dickerson's *Juice*, extending interest in the problems of black urban neighborhoods, and Reginald Hudlin's *Boomerang*, which undertook to reinvigorate Eddie Murphy's sagging career by starring him in a comedy-romance with Robin Givens, Halle Berry, Grace Jones, and Eartha Kitt. *Boomerang* was dominated by black talent; it was coproduced by Warrington Hudlin, the director's brother and cofounder of the Black Filmmakers Foundation.

The black films of the late 1980's and early 1990's focused, to a greater or lesser degree, on black themes and issues. They reached mainstream audiences with something more than standard Hollywood blockbuster fare, and they showed that African American artists were providing many of the new ideas in American film.

—*James M. Welsh*

MOBILE V. BOLDEN

April 22, 1980

Reaffirming that the Fourteenth and Fifteenth Amendments prohibit only "purposeful discrimination," the Supreme Court upheld an at-large system of voting in which no African American had ever been elected.

The Case: U.S. Supreme Court ruling on one person, one vote concept

The three-member city commission of Mobile, Alabama, had been elected on a citywide basis since 1911. Although African Americans made up almost 40 percent of the population, none had ever been elected to the commission. A district court found that the at-large system was unconstitutional, but the Supreme Court, by a 6-3 margin, reversed the judgment. In evaluating Mobile's electoral system according to the demands of the Fourteenth and Fifteenth Amendments, Justice Potter Stewart's plurality opinion simply followed the Court's many precedents indicating that a state policy that is neutral on its face does not violate the Constitution unless it is "motivated by a racially discriminatory purpose." In an angry dissent, Justice Thurgood Marshall accused the Court of being "an accessory to the perpetuation of racial discrimination" and argued that voting rights should be judged according to a discriminatory effects test rather than a discriminatory intent standard.

In *Rogers v. Lodge* (1982), the Court used the *Bolden* standard to strike down an at-large electoral scheme in Georgia. The Court's ruling in *Bolden*, however, became almost irrelevant after Congress passed the 1982 extension of the Voting Rights Act, which allows plaintiffs to prevail in voting dilution cases on the basis of a modified discriminatory effects test.

—*Thomas Tandy Lewis*

See also: Fifteenth Amendment; Fourteenth Amendment; Voting Rights Act of 1965; Voting Rights Act of 1975

RIOTERS PROTEST MIAMI POLICE BRUTALITY

May 17-19, 1980

The race riot that took place in Miami, Florida, in 1980 gave evidence that the attainment of an American society free of racial conflict was far from being realized.

Locale: Miami, Florida
Categories: Civil rights and liberties; wars, uprisings, and civil unrest; social issues and reform

KEY FIGURES

Arthur McDuffie (1947?-1979), Marine Corps veteran and insurance agent whose death led to the Miami riot

Alex Marrero (fl. late twentieth century), police officer charged with second-degree murder in McDuffie's death

Michael Watts (fl. late twentieth century), police officer accused of manslaughter in McDuffie's death

Herbert Evans (fl. late twentieth century), police sergeant charged with tampering with evidence in the cover-up of McDuffie's death

Ira Diggs (fl. late twentieth century), police sergeant who initially gave chase to McDuffie

William Hanlon (fl. late twentieth century), police officer who participated in McDuffie's arrest

Janet Reno (b. 1938), state attorney for Dade County, Florida

SUMMARY OF EVENT

On May 17, 1980, a sad chapter of racial violence was added to the long and painful history of race relations in the United States. On that date, five white South Florida law-enforcement officers—Herbert Evans, Ira Diggs, William Hanlon, Alex Marrero, and Michael Watts—were acquitted by an all-white jury of charges stemming from the death of Arthur McDuffie, an African American insurance executive. The acquittals precipitated a riot in an area known as Liberty City, a black community of Miami, Florida. Before the riot was brought under control, eighteen people were dead and countless more had been injured. Property damages were assessed in the millions of dollars. Eight of those who died were whites who had been driving through Liberty City unaware of the verdicts.

By the time anger had replaced the initial shock caused by the acquittals, migrants as well as residents had been beaten, stabbed, and burned to death by rioters who were taking out their frustrations on those they believed to be responsible not only for the verdicts but also for their impoverished condition.

Although the immediate cause of this urban and racial violence could be attributed to the Tampa jury's failure to find the police defendants guilty, the underlying cause may be somewhat more difficult to ascertain. It is highly unlikely that any riot would have taken place at all if the defendants had been found guilty. For the African American community, the acquittal was more than simply one more example of unequal justice, and it had a profound meaning that went beyond that community to a much larger audience. It became a symbol for an outpouring of fear, distrust, and hostility, mirroring some of the emotional and violent disturbances and attempts to achieve equal process that had surfaced during the 1960's. That decade had been filled with inner-city frustration that had resulted in a "get whitey" response to real and perceived racial injustices. The Miami riot seemed equally representative of this period in American history. Perhaps most shocking about the Miami riot was the intensity of the rage directed by blacks against whites.

The Miami riot, born of the immediate need to redress a perceived injustice, may also be viewed as a culmination of events that exemplified general policies of official oppression against the African American community. It had been fifteen years since the government had established equal employment opportunity guidelines and affirmative action processes that were supposed to provide equal access for minorities to political decision-making centers. It was therefore only a short step from the perception that an all-white jury had unjustly set free the white police defendants to the recognition that the black community was still being racially discriminated against by a society dominated by white people. Included in this immediate reaction was the idea that the police forces in South Florida were disproportionately white. At the time of the riot, the number of African Americans on the Dade County Public Safety Department (PSD) police force stood at only 7 percent. The upper ranks had only a few black officers, and in the higher ranks, there were no blacks at all.

The violent reaction by blacks also stemmed from frustration over largely ignored accusations of police brutality in the past. Many blacks perceived McDuffie's death as only the most recent in a long series of police transgressions against members of the black community—incidents that, when addressed, had resulted in few or no disciplinary actions against those charged.

On the morning of December 17, 1979, Arthur McDuffie left the home of a friend. He was riding his motorcycle toward his home in northwest Dade County, where he lived with his sister. At approximately 1:00 a.m., McDuffie was observed by PSD sergeant Ira Diggs as having failed to stop for a red light. Diggs began to pursue McDuffie, calling police headquarters for assistance as he did. McDuffie reacted to Diggs's pursuit by increasing his speed. After an eight-minute chase, more than one dozen police cars surrounded McDuffie's motorcycle, forcing him to stop. In an ensuing confrontation between McDuffie and six police officers, McDuffie received severe head wounds that resulted in his death four days later.

The investigation into McDuffie's death led to the eventual prosecution of the officers involved in the incident. During the investigation, it was determined that a cover-up of the cause of McDuffie's death had been instituted by key police personnel, including higher-ranking personnel who were not present during the confrontation with McDuffie. Inconsistencies in official police reports made the police officers' statements surrounding McDuffie's death seem highly suspect. The county medical examiner, for example, did not believe that if

McDuffie's injuries had occurred as stated by the officers that they would have been sufficient to cause death. In the end, State Attorney Janet Reno brought official charges of manslaughter and tampering with evidence against the PSD officers.

Protests over McDuffie's death began almost immediately within the African American community. On January 3, 1980, five days following the official charges, two dozen blacks and a handful of whites marched from Liberty City to the Dade County criminal justice building, where they demanded that the manslaughter charges be changed to charges of murder. Reno issued a public statement rejecting any such change on the grounds of insufficient evidence. Black newspapers and radio stations began to receive angry messages calling for Reno's removal from the case. Reno then handed the prosecution over to a team of mostly white assistant state's attorneys. The trial was eventually moved to the Tampa area, as it was believed that the officers would not be able to receive a fair trial in the heated racial atmosphere of Miami.

On May 17, 1980, after almost four weeks of testimony, an all-white jury took only two hours and forty-five minutes to return not-guilty verdicts for all officers involved.

Shocked reactions to the verdicts surfaced immediately throughout Florida, especially in the Liberty City area of Miami. For Liberty City blacks, the trial and the verdicts seemed to represent a continuation of an inherently unequal judicial process. In reaction to this and other perceived injustices, Liberty City erupted into violence that claimed the lives of eighteen people and injured many others.

The residents of Liberty City did not riot because of the death of Arthur McDuffie at the hands of PSD officers—the riot did not begin until after the officers' trial was completed and the verdicts were announced. Rather, the riot took place in an atmosphere of perceived racial injustice; it was caused by African Americans' belief that the American criminal justice system had failed to punish those they believed were guilty of McDuffie's death.

SIGNIFICANCE

If there are lessons to be learned from the Miami riot of 1980, then certain questions must be addressed regarding the judiciary process surrounding the prosecution of those accused of causing McDuffie's death. Did the system fail? Was racism a factor in the white officers' acquittal?

Was there psychological conflict between the residents of Liberty City and the white government? Do the members of all racial groups in the United States share connected values, assumptions, and perceptions of problems and goals? A good place to start in attempting to answer such questions is to look at readily identifiable values and perceptions that characterize American cultural identity. In the case of the Miami riot, three such values and their interpretations clearly emerge: equality, freedom, and justice.

It was a combination of equality and justice, or a perception of a lack of these, that encouraged the violent response to the trial verdicts by members of the black community. The acquittal of the white police officers by an all-hite jury reawakened age-old fears of racism in the Liberty City section of Miami—in particular, the fear that the American criminal justice system was inherently racist.

In part, this perception was justified. Any system that prevents members of a jury from being seated on the basis of race can surely be labeled as racist. The prosecutors and defense attorneys in the McDuffie case freely applied such a selection process. Prosecutors did not try to exclude black jurors; the defense did. Both sides, whether racist in outlook or not, based their decisions during jury selection on the color of potential jury members, and a racist outcome resulted. In the McDuffie case, whether the racial makeup of the jury affected the verdict was obscured by the confusing and contradictory evidence presented by the prosecution. If the evidence presented did not in fact convince the

jurors beyond a reasonable doubt that the officers were guilty as charged, then charges of procedural racism were irrelevant.

The McDuffie case contained enough racist possibilities to cause concern over the accusations surrounding it. It was not enough that officers of the court maintained that the trial was a fair one; the trial also needed to appear fair to those outside administrative capacities. Blacks in the United States have a long history of racial abuse. A lack of equality of condition and equality of opportunity has kept blacks from participating in the mainstream wealth of the nation. Many laws have been enacted to override discriminatory practices, but those laws have varied in their impacts. The courts have become the vehicle through which minorities experiencing discrimination attempt to achieve redress. The denial of justice in the courts—the chief avenue for the elimination of discrimination—creates the potential for violence.

The death of Arthur McDuffie and the acquittal of those perceived to be responsible for it left the black community with a sense of alienation that was answered by violence. In evaluating the reasons for the Miami riot, it is not necessary to confront the inequalities of condition and opportunity; one can simply look to see if justice was perceived to have been served. In the black community of Liberty City, the perception was clearly otherwise. The resulting frustration quickly grew into rage and violence.

—Thomas Jay Edward Walker

FULLILOVE V. KLUTZNICK

July 2, 1980

The Supreme Court held that setting aside a percentage of federal contracts for minority businesses was constitutional as long as it was intended to remedy demonstrated discrimination.

The Case: U.S. Supreme Court ruling on affirmative action

After Congress passed the Local Public Works Capital Development and Investment Act in 1976, there was an outcry when minority business enterprises (MBEs) received only 1 percent of the contracts. Although members of minorities accounted for at least 15 percent of

the U.S. population, only 3 percent of businesses were MBEs, and they earned only 0.65 percent of gross receipts.

Accordingly, in passing the Public Works Employment Act of 1977, Congress required 10 percent of local public works contracts to be "set aside" for MBEs— businesses with at least 50 percent ownership or 51 percent stockholding by African Americans, Spanish-speaking people, Asian Americans, American Indians, Eskimos, or Aleuts. Nonminority prime contractors were required, in subcontracting to MBEs, to provide guidance and technical assistance in making bids, to lower or waive bonding requirements, and to assist

MBEs in obtaining working capital from financial institutions and government agencies.

Shortly after Juanita Krebs, U.S. secretary of commerce, issued administrative guidelines for bidding under the new law, several potential project grantees (H. Earl Fullilove and trustees of the New York Building and Construction Industry Board of Urban Affairs Fund, two general contractor associations, and a firm engaged in heating, ventilation, and air conditioning work) filed suit against Krebs, the city and state of New York, the New York Board of Higher Education, and the Health and Hospitals Corporation for a temporary restraining order to block implementation of the law. After they lost the case in the district court (in December, 1977) and on appeal (in 1978), they took the case to the Supreme Court. When the case was decided, Philip Klutznick was U.S. secretary of commerce. Chief Justice Warren Burger wrote the majority opinion; three justices provided concurring majority opinions, and two wrote dissents.

The Court answered the argument that government should act in a color-blind manner by noting that Congress had the power to spend money for the general welfare and thus to design a remedy for MBEs. The argument that nonminority businesses were deprived of equal access to contracts was rejected: a 10 percent setaside rate was considered light in view of the larger percentage of members of minorities. The Court responded to the argument that the definition of "minority" was underinclusive and should have added other groups by noting that such a definition was entirely up to Congress. The argument that the "minority" definition was overinclusive and might favor MBEs unqualified to do the technical work was refuted by a reference to the statutory provisions that only members of bona fide minorities were covered by the law and that a waiver from the set-aside could be issued if no MBE was able to do the work.

The Supreme Court thus held that a numerical goal could be designed as a remedy for a statistically demonstrated inequality for members of minorities, with provisions tailored to removing specific, documented barriers to the success of minorities. Plans failing these tests have been consistently rejected by the Court, as in *Richmond v. J. A. Croson Company* (1989).

See also: *Adarand Constructors v. Peña;* Affirmative action; Civil Rights Act of 1964; *United Steelworkers of America v. Weber*

THRILLER MARKS JACKSON'S MUSICAL COMING-OF-AGE

December, 1982

With the release of his album Thriller, *Michael Jackson completed his transformation from a child prodigy into one of the most powerfully talented figures in American popular culture.*

Locale: Los Angeles, California
Categories: Music; radio and television

KEY FIGURES

Michael Jackson (b. 1958), singer, songwriter, and dancer who dominated popular music in the early 1980's

Quincy Jones (b. 1933), musician, bandleader, and songwriter who produced Jackson's most famous records

Berry Gordy, Jr. (b. 1929), Motown Records founder who signed the Jackson Five and persuaded Michael Jackson to perform on a Motown television special

SUMMARY OF EVENT

By the beginning of the 1980's, Michael Jackson had evolved from an instinctive child performer on Jackson Five songs such as "ABC" and "I Want You Back" into a highly self-conscious pop craftsman who had enjoyed considerable chart success with his 1979 album *Off the Wall.* That album, which spawned the hits "Don't Stop 'til You Get Enough" and "Rock with You," brought Jackson an entirely new audience. Seven million album copies were sold, giving him the confidence and artistic freedom to pursue his next project.

In 1982, Jackson began assembling a production team in Los Angeles for a new album. Like *Off the Wall,* the record would be produced by Quincy Jones, with whom Jackson had begun working during the making of the 1978 film version of the Broadway musical *The Wiz.*

Jackson, however, intended to have greater input this time around. In addition to acting as coproducer, he also wrote many of the songs, among them "Wanna

Be Startin' Somethin'" and "Billie Jean." When Jones coaxed Jackson to round out the emerging collection with a solid rock song, Jackson wrote "Beat It," a critique of gang violence. The two enlisted Eddie Van Halen, the virtuoso guitarist of the heavy metal band Van Halen, to contribute a solo. Jackson was also able to draw on the talents of former Beatle Paul McCartney, who agreed to sing a duet with Jackson on "The Girl Is Mine." Although it was not regarded as the strongest song on the album, Jackson released "The Girl Is Mine" as the first single in late 1982, since the pairing of two major stars would attract radio attention. It was not until the release of "Billie Jean" in early 1983 that it became apparent to many that Jackson was offering more than mere pop pap. With its dark lyrics about an illegitimate child and the sinuous rhythms of its bass line and percussion, "Billie Jean" catapulted *Thriller*—and Jackson—to new levels of critical attention.

Jackson then made the unorthodox decision of releasing "Beat It" with "Billie Jean" still on the charts. Despite concern that the two songs would cancel each other out, they ended up in the top ten at the same time. "The Girl Is Mine," "Billie Jean," and "Beat It" were followed in short order by "Wanna Be Startin' Somethin'," "Human Nature," "P.Y.T. (Pretty Young Thing)," and "Thriller." *Off the Wall* had been the first album in popular music history to generate four top-ten singles on *Billboard* magazine's charts; *Thriller* generated seven. The album spent twenty-one weeks on top of the album chart, went on to sell more than forty million copies worldwide, and became the best-selling album of all time.

Music was only one part of the *Thriller* phenomenon, however. Another important component was video. In 1981, a new television network, Music Television (MTV), made its debut. MTV quickly established itself as an extraordinarily popular and influential medium for introducing new acts to the American public. Among the beneficiaries of this development were British performers, who were long familiar with video and who had product on hand to supply MTV's heavy demand. Acts such as Culture Club, Duran Duran, and Australia's Men at Work quickly became inhabitants of the American pop charts.

MTV, however, avoided music videos by African Americans. Some critics charged racism; MTV executives claimed that black music simply was not popular enough to justify airplay. Whatever the reason, the success of *Thriller* was simply too obvious to be ignored.

Jackson's first video, for "Billie Jean," featured an arresting set and some electrifying dancing. "Beat It," which Jackson paid for himself, included elaborate choreography and a dramatic story line. With "Thriller," which Jackson again financed himself, he stretched the boundaries of the form. Shot on film rather than videotape, and directed by noted director John Landis, "Thriller" was less a music video than a short film. Packaged with a documentary about the production of the piece, *The Making of Thriller* became the best-selling music video of all time and buoyed Jackson's musical success. At one point in 1984, he was selling a million records a week.

Other events kept the Jackson juggernaut rolling. On May 16, 1983, Motown Records celebrated its twenty-fifth anniversary with a television gala. Though Jackson had long since left behind the paternalistic strictures of the company, he agreed to perform on the show. His rendition of "Billie Jean," accompanied by a widely remarked-upon dance step called the "moonwalk," won accolades from Fred Astaire and Gene Kelly and introduced Jackson into the homes of millions of Americans previously unfamiliar with his work. The performance (which was soon sold on video) became part of television lore, comparable to Elvis Presley's and the Beatles' appearances on *The Ed Sullivan Show*.

With *Thriller* finally fading from the charts, Jackson turned to other projects. In the summer of 1984, he reunited with his brothers to record *Victory*. The album and subsequent tour proved to be a disappointment, however; the record sold below expectations, and the family came in for criticism in the black community for the high price of tickets, which effectively denied access to the tour to much of the Jacksons' most important constituency. In 1985, Jackson helped raise millions for famine relief in Africa when he and Lionel Richie cowrote "We Are the World," a benefit record on which dozens of famous pop stars appeared. The following year, Jackson teamed up with directors George Lucas and Francis Ford Coppola to appear in *Captain EO*, a three-dimensional video short to be shown at Disney theme parks.

Jackson's follow-ups to *Thriller*, although impressive, did not match its success. His 1987 album *Bad* sold more than seventeen million copies and generated six hit singles—an impressive performance, but far from record-breaking. *Dangerous*, released in 1991 after Jackson signed a precedent-shattering contract with Sony Music, was widely viewed as a disappointment. It remained to be seen whether he—or anyone else—could again scale the heights of success attained by *Thriller*. In so raising the stakes, however, Jackson became the standard by which all performers, including himself, would be measured.

SIGNIFICANCE

In the 1980's, Michael Jackson played a role in popular music comparable to the one Elvis Presley played in the 1950's and the Beatles played in the 1960's. Like those figures, he sold unprecedented amounts of records and became an industry force in his own right; like them, he maintained a presence in other media, a presence that reinforced his musical supremacy and introduced him to other audiences; and like them, too, he influenced much of the music that followed, ranging from the lightweight pop of DeBarge to the more aggressive (and interesting) work of Jackson's own sister Janet.

Perhaps the most important trait Michael Jackson shared with Presley and the Beatles, however, was a powerful ability to synthesize varied strains in popular musical culture and present them in highly original ways. In rock-and-roll history, this has usually meant fusing black and white musical styles, and Jackson was no exception.

Whereas Presley and the Beatles translated and manipulated African American culture for largely white consumption, Jackson began his career immersed in black music and largely shaped it on his own terms. To be sure, he received criticism for pandering to white audiences, and he lost some respect in the eyes of the black musical community—perhaps deservedly—for the saccharine qualities that marred his work. Jackson's lifestyle choices, and the rumors that surrounded them, also raised questions about his judgment. Nevertheless, it would be difficult to question his mastery of gospel, rhythm-and-blues, or rock-and-roll idioms, or the often astounding grace and charisma that characterized his onstage performances.

Thriller is a pivotal record in pop music history because it both caused and reflected the racial convergence of American popular music in the 1980's. By the late 1970's, black urban music was largely segregated on its own radio stations, while white rock and roll, which drew much of its early vitality from African American music, was increasingly distanced from it. In restricting broadcasts of black performers, MTV was merely emulating the dominant assumptions governing the radio industry.

Jackson's success in attracting listeners across race, class, and gender lines helped demonstrate the efficacy

of a contemporary hit radio format that created a vast new center in popular music. The subsequent success of performers such as Prince, Tina Turner (who made a celebrated comeback in 1984-1985), and Tracy Chapman demonstrated the commercial and cultural potential for black performers interested in musically bridging the races.

Perhaps the best example of this in Jackson's own work is "Beat It." Marked by the hypnotic rhythmic grooves that have become Jackson's trademark, the song gained added heft from Eddie Van Halen's guitar work, which appealed to millions of white adolescents only vaguely aware of heavy metal rock's debt to the blues. In so doing, Jackson enhanced white receptivity to other performers, including Prince, who recaptured the black flavor in rock and roll that had ebbed ever since Jimi Hendrix's death in 1970.

Thriller is also a compendium of popular cultural phenomena. Horror films (the title track), the pleasures and dangers of nightlife ("Wanna Be Startin' Somethin'" and "Billie Jean"), traditional romance ("Baby Be Mine" and "The Lady in My Life"), and philosophical meditation ("Human Nature") are among the themes, with influences ranging from James Brown to Vincent Price (who provides a voice-over for "Thriller"). Perhaps it was inevitable that Jackson would go on to make a video featured at Disneyland and Walt Disney World; he so thoroughly imbibed American culture that in many ways he came to embody it.

Jackson's other major achievement stemming from *Thriller* concerns video. In addition to breaking the color barrier on MTV, he also demonstrated the visual possibilities of the form and raised it to new levels of artistry.

By retaining financial control over his work, he retained creative control as well, and he was able to enlist some of the most important directors in the television and film industries to shoot his videos. "Billie Jean," "Beat It," and "Thriller" remain classics of the form and went a long way toward consolidating the legitimacy—and profitability—of MTV.

The years following the release of *Thriller* witnessed a slow but steady ebbing of Jackson's artistic and commercial power. Inevitably, success on the scale he achieved engendered some backlash, and his personal and social isolation made his work seem less in touch with musical currents. This is especially evident in the rise of rap into musical prominence, a form which makes *Thriller* seem dated and which Jackson did not

The Five Most Expensive Music Videos in History

Michael Jackson spent $800,000 on the video for his 1983 hit "Thriller," the most expensive music video up to that time. Jackson continued to invest in other music video projects, with the controversial "Black or White" and "Remember the Time," both from his album Dangerous (1991), costing more than a million dollars each. To date, the most expensive music video production was for Jackson's award-winning "Scream," costing $7 million, with most of that money going to eleven sets.

Artist(s)	Song Title	Production Costs
Michael Jackson and Janet Jackson	"Scream" (1995)	$7 million
Madonna	"Die Another Day" (2002)	More than $6 million
Puff Daddy (with Notorious B.I.G. and Busta Rhymes)	"Victory" (1998)	More than $2.7 million
Mariah Carey (with Jay-Z)	"Heartbreaker" (1999)	More than $2.5 million
Busta Rhymes (with Janet Jackson) "	What's It Gonna Be?!" (1999)	More than $2.4 million

seem able to perform with much conviction. Certainly, he continued to write engaging songs, such as his 1988 hit "Smooth Criminal." Little of his work has had lasting thematic significance, however, and all too often Jackson lapsed into banality in trying to write inspiring songs, as the titles of "Heal the World" and "Keep the Faith" suggest. Moreover, while he had his usual share of hits from *Dangerous* (1991)—including "Black or White," "Remember the Time," and "In the Closet"—the almost frenetic collage of styles contained in those songs gave the impression that Jackson was trying to chase down an audience rather than lead (or better yet, create) one.

Nevertheless, none of this can erase *Thriller*. Without it, Jackson would be considered an important figure in contemporary popular music. Because of it, he has earned consideration as a major American artist of the late twentieth century.

—Jim Cullen

RAINBOW COALITION

Founded in 1983

A multicultural effort to unify racial and ethnic groups that have been marginalized in the U.S. political process, the Rainbow Coalition flourished during the 1980's but began to fragment during the 1990's.

Identification: Multicultural rights advocacy organization founded under the leadership of the Reverend Jesse Jackson.

Historically, racial and ethnic groups in the United States have experienced differing levels of participation in formal political institutions, leading to substantial inequalities in the distribution of political power among various groups. African Americans, for example, were historically excluded from participation in political processes through such legal and extralegal means as poll taxes, intimidation, and gerrymandering.

What political power African Americans did acquire was often symbolic, achieved through appointments of black leaders to high-profile positions. This tradition led to the development of a black elite that accepted the role of junior partner in the process of achieving racial integration. Most of this leadership came from minority group members in nonelected positions and from extrapolitical movements such as strikes, boycotts, and acts of civil disobedience.

In the early 1980's, the Reverend Jesse Jackson organized a united front of liberal integrationists, socialists, trade unionists, feminists, gays, and racial minority constituencies to work together in his 1984 presidential campaign. The Rainbow Coalition platform was based on four premises: that Jackson had a base among the "black masses," that he was an important figure in southern black politics, that the campaign would stimulate registration of black voters, and that Jackson's presidential candidacy would create "coattail" effects that would propel other outsiders into the electoral process. None of these premises was supported by subsequent events.

To appeal to a broad range of voters, Jackson moved the left-leaning Rainbow platform toward the political center for the time of the 1988 presidential campaign. Jackson purged the coalition of its activists by blocking democratic elections of local Rainbow leadership and by placing gag orders on radical dissenters. In 1989, Jackson asserted the right to appoint all coalition leaders at the congressional district rank. In response, thousands of activists left the coalition, and several splinter groups were organized.

In the 1990's, Democratic Party leaders including Bill Clinton acted to undermine Jackson's leadership role in the African American community, severely diminishing the power of the Rainbow Coalition. Clinton's 1992 presidential victory was followed by the political rise of Ron Brown, one of Jackson's protégés, who had become the chair of the Democratic National Committee and was appointed secretary of commerce. Such developments led many members to leave the Rainbow Coalition and to adhere to Clinton's policies.

—Glenn Canyon

See also: Civil Rights movement; Gerrymandering; Jackson's run for the presidency.

JACKSON'S RUN FOR THE PRESIDENCY

1983-1984

As the first African American to mount a serious run for the presidency of the United States, Jesse Jackson offered an unusually strong voice on behalf of the poor and minority groups.

The Event: Civil rights leader Jesse Jackson's bid for the Democratic nomination for president

In a memorable speech of November 3, 1983, Jesse Jackson became the first major African American candidate for the presidency of the United States. Using the rhythms and tones of the Southern Baptist preacher that he was, Jackson lashed out at the administration of President Ronald Reagan, charging that it was anti-black, anti-Hispanic, pro-rich, and pro-military. He also attacked his own party, accusing the Democrats of having been too weak in opposing the many threats posed by the Reagan presidency. The new candidate urged formation of a "rainbow coalition," in which Americans of all races and ethnic groups would come together to oppose policies that hurt the poor and middle classes.

JACKSON'S HANDICAPS

Jackson entered the race under a number of handicaps. Many people saw him as "a black candidate," but far less than half the electorate was African American. Many African American leaders were already backing other Democratic hopefuls, and they made no move to switch to Jackson. While Jackson was a respected

Jesse Jackson was a Presidential candidate in both 1984 and 1988.

minister, community activist, and former associate of Martin Luther King, Jr., he had never held political office and could offer only modest evidence of expertise in foreign policy. The two strongest Democratic contenders, former vice president Walter Mondale and U.S. senator Gary Hart, both had abundant experience as elected officials.

On the other hand, Jackson could boast of a remarkably successful life of devoted public service and prolific achievements in civil rights. While a student at North Carolina Agricultural and Technical State College, Jackson was simultaneously student body president, an honors student, and quarterback of the football team. After graduation, he was on the staff of North Carolina's governor, Terry Stanford, and he attended Chicago Theological Seminary. While working for the Chicago office of Operation Breadbasket, he led protests that forced Chicago stores to hire more African Americans and to stock more goods made by black-owned firms. Soon Jackson was national director of Operation Breadbasket. Jackson was with King the night of the latter's assassination, and he soon went to work as a top executive for King's Southern Christian Leadership Conference. At the time he announced his candidacy for the presidency, Jackson was heading Operation PUSH (People United to Save Humanity), a group designed primarily to help minority-group children excel in school.

Only seven weeks into the campaign, Jackson seized an opportunity to prove his abilities in the foreign policy arena. Syria was holding prisoner a downed U.S. pilot named Robert O. Goodman, Jr. Jackson charged that the Reagan administration was doing little to secure the pilot's release, and stories in the press seemed to support Jackson's charges. Jackson sent a message concerning the pilot to Syrian president Hafez al-Assad, and in response, Assad invited Jackson to come to Syria. Jackson did so and won the release of the pilot. While President Reagan and a number of other politicians initially criticized Jackson for interfering with U.S. foreign policy, all praised Jackson after his success.

THE CAMPAIGN TRAIL

Back on the campaign trail, Jackson was hampered by an inexperienced and disorganized staff and by a scarcity of funds for running television spots.With only a modest advertising budget, Jackson had to rely on reporters for his public exposure. Soon his photograph was on the covers of dozens of magazines, and his voice was heard in scores of radio and television interviews.

Jackson benefited from his speaking skills, which seemed to captivate audiences more than did the efforts of his main rivals, Mondale and Hart.

In the first two contests for the Democratic nomination (those in Iowa and New Hampshire), Jackson was hurt by the lack of large minority populations in those states. In the Iowa caucuses, Jackson finished seventh, with less than 2 percent of the vote; in the New Hampshire primary, he placed fourth, with 6 percent of the total vote. Jackson's first major test came with the Super Tuesday contests in a number of states, held on March 13, 1984. On that day, Jackson won 21 percent of Georgia's vote and 20 percent in Alabama. A number of Democratic hopefuls dropped out of the presidential race, leaving only Mondale, Hart, and Jackson.

As the primary season wore on, Jackson continued to show some real strength. In the important New York primary, Jackson won more than one-quarter of the vote. He placed first in the District of Columbia primary, taking 67 percent of the vote. While this District of Columbia win was expected, given the black majority in the nation's capital, Jackson surprised most observers with his strong victory in Louisiana, where he captured 43 percent of the total vote. In Mississippi, Jackson finished ahead of Hart; in South Carolina, Jackson did better than either of his two rivals. Even in the industrial state of Illinois, Jackson won a respectable 21 percent.

Jackson's biggest stumble came over allegations that he was bigoted. An African American journalist reported that he had overheard Jackson referring to Jews as "Hymies" and to New York City as "Hymietown." Jackson at first ducked reporters' questions about the comments, but later admitted having used the terms. He did say that the remarks were simply slang, and that he used the terms with no animosity. Jackson's reputation as a coalition-builder was also hurt by his friendship with Louis Farrakhan, an African American leader of the Nation of Islam. Farrakhan seemed to make threats against the life of the reporter who broke the "Hymietown" story, and he later referred to Judaism as a "gutter religion." Jackson eventually distanced himself completely from Farrakhan's words, but many liberal Democrats grew lukewarm toward the Jackson candidacy.

THE DEMOCRATICE NATIONAL CONVENTION

Going into the Democratic National Convention in San Francisco, it was clear that Mondale had enough delegates to secure his nomination. Still, Jackson remained a significant force: Many party leaders feared that Jackson would remain aloof from the Democratic campaign. Others feared that he might consider running as an independent. Jackson was able to play on these fears to get the Democratic convention to declare its support for affirmative action and to appoint a committee to consider the changes Jackson sought in delegate selection procedures.

When the roll was called, Mondale had the support of 2,191 delegates, Hart 1,200, and Jackson 465. While Jackson fell well short of a victory, he had broken the color barrier by becoming the nation's first major presidential hopeful who was African Ameri- can. Jackson won more than three times as many delegates as had an earlier African American candidate, Representative Shirley Chisholm, who had run in 1972.

The 1984 Democratic convention also broke a gender barrier, as it tapped the first woman to appear on a major party ticket. Geraldine Ferraro was the convention's choice for vice president. Jackson campaigned on behalf of the Mondale-Ferraro ticket, but the Democrats went down to defeat in 1984. Still, the Jackson candidacy had offered an unusually strong voice on behalf of the poor and minority groups. Such voices have appeared only infrequently on the presidential campaign trail.

—*Stephen Cresswell*

FURTHER READING
Barker, Lucius J. *Our Time Has Come: A Delegate's Diary of Jesse Jackson's 1984 Presidential Campaign*. Urbana: University of Illinois Press, 1988.

Particularly strong first-person account of the Jackson campaign and the 1984 Democratic National Convention.

Barker, Lucius J., and Ronald W. Walters, eds. *Jesse Jackson's 1984 Presidential Campaign: Challenge and Change in American Politics*. Urbana: University of Illinois Press, 1989. Presents the Jackson campaign's history from a variety of perspectives.

Frady, Marshall. *Jesse: The Life and Pilgrimage of Jesse Jackson*. New York: Random House, 1996.

Jackson, Jesse. *A Time to Speak: The Autobiography of the Reverend Jesse Jackson*. New York: Simon & Schuster, 1988. Agood starting point for any study of Jackson's 1984 presidential bid.

Kimball, Penn. *Keep Hope Alive: Super Tuesday and Jesse Jackson's 1988 Campaign for the Presidency*. Washington, D.C.: Joint Center for Political and Economic Studies, 1989. Covers the background and key events of Jackson's 1988 presidential bid.

Reed, Adolph L. *The Jesse Jackson Phenomenon: The Crisis of Purpose in Afro-American Politics*. New Haven, Conn.: Yale University Press, 1986. Reed puts the 1984 Jackson campaign in the larger context of African American political history.

Timmerman, Kenneth R. *Shakedown: Exposing the Real Jesse Jackson*. Washington, D.C.: Regnery, 2002.

See also: Chisholm's election to Congress; Civil Rights movement; Politics and government; Rainbow Coalition; Southern Christian Leadership Conference; Wilder's election to Virginia governorship

MOVE BOMBING

May 13, 1985

The city of Philadelphia's use of bombs to remove illegal squatters from a densely crowded neighborhood resulted in eleven deaths and the destruction of sixty-one homes and brought severe criticism down on the city's government.

The Event: Bungled attempt to evict illegal squatters
Place: Philadelphia, Pennsylvania

Founded in 1972 by Vincent Leaphart, who adopted the name "John Africa," MOVE was a group of

"back-to-nature" activists with an unusual and inconsistent philosophy. Although they advocated going back to nature, they were an urban movement. They shunned modern technology but used an elaborate loudspeaker system to bombard neighbors with their views. They decried pollution but littered property with their garbage and human waste.

The origin of the term "MOVE" is unclear. Not an acronym, it is generally believed to be merely a shortened form for the term "movement." MOVE first received media attention in 1978, when Philadelphia police clashed with members when police tried to evict them from an illegally occupied house. One police officer was killed, and eight officers and firefighters were wounded. Nine MOVE members were convicted of murder.

After failing to win the release of their imprisoned colleagues, MOVE members barricaded their new residence in a middleclass neighborhood, hooked up an elaborate sound system, and bombarded their neighbors for twelve hours per day with their profanity-laced speeches. This continued for more than two years, despite repeated appeals to the city by neighborhood residents. Philadelphia mayor Wilson Goode, that city's first African American mayor, chose to ignore the appeals of local residents. At one point, Mayor Goode announced that he preferred "to have dirt and some smell than to have death." The denouement, however, included dirt, smell, and death.

THE CITY TAKES AGGRESSIVE ACTION

After local residents held a press conference on May 1, 1985, criticizing the city's inaction, city officials decided to take aggressive action. On May 13, 1995, Police Commissioner Gregore Sambor told MOVE members to vacate their two-story row house. Tear gas was fired into the house, and a gun battle commenced. Twelve

hours later, MOVE members still occupied the house. Police officials requested and received Mayor Goode's permission to drop a satchel filled with explosives onto the roof of MOVE's house. The goal was to dislodge a rooftop bunker; the result, however, was a fire that quickly got out of control. By the time the fires were controlled, eleven MOVE members, including four children, were dead. Only one thirty-year-old woman and one thirteen-year-old boy escaped alive. In addition to the deaths, two city blocks were destroyed, and sixty-one homes were reduced to embers.

Newspapers across the nation and throughout the world condemned the mayor's decision to drop the bomb, but a majority of local residents, both black and white, supported Goode and the police department. By the mid-1990's, the MOVE bombing had cost Philadelphia $30 million, and legal action was still pending. The city rebuilt the sixty-one destroyed homes, paid settlements to residents for lost belongings, and paid damages to the families of slain MOVE members. A 1986 citizens' commission concluded that Mayor Goode and the police and fire commissioners had "exhibited a reckless disregard for life and property." Goode was reelected to another four-year term in 1987.

See also: King beating case; Media; Miami riots

THE COSBY SHOW MAKES TELEVISION HISTORY

September 20, 1984-April 30, 1992

With The Cosby Show, *Americans were introduced to a weekly television series about an African American family that broke from standard black situation comedy. Bill Cosby, the program's star as well as its cocreator, coproducer, and executive consultant, had full artistic control.*

Locale: United States
Category: Radio and television

KEY FIGURES

Bill Cosby (b. 1937), actor, writer, and stand-up comedian who portrayed Cliff Huxtable in *The Cosby Show*
Phylicia Rashad (b. 1948), actor who costarred as Clair Huxtable, Cliff's wife
Brandon Tartikoff (1949-1997), president of the National Broadcasting Company

Marcy Carsey (b. 1944), executive producer of *The Cosby Show Thomas Werner* (b. 1950), a producer of *The Cosby Show John Markus* (fl. late twentieth century), writer who headed the writing-producing team for *The Cosby Show* during its peak seasons
Carmen Finestra (b. 1947), actor, writer, and producer for *The Cosby Show* during its years of greatest popularity
Gary Kott (b. 1945), writer and producer for *The Cosby Show* in its most popular seasons
Matt Williams (b. 1952), actor, writer, and producer for *The Cosby Show*, 1984-1987

SUMMARY OF EVENT

By 1984, Bill Cosby was a major figure in American entertainment, especially on television. Although he had been a stage performer and popular nightclub comic in the early 1960's, Cosby did not become a national figure until he costarred with Robert Culp in the action-drama television series *I Spy*, which ran for three seasons from 1965 to 1968. For his portrayal of Alexander Scott in *I Spy*, Cosby won three Emmy Awards. At the same time, as equal costar in the series, he dismantled the television stereotype of the African American as social and psychological subordinate.

In 1969, Cosby had a television series created especially for him, *The Bill Cosby Show*, a situation comedy in which he played Chet Kincaid, a high school coach. The show remained on national television for two seasons.

There followed the award-winning animated series *Fat Albert and the Cosby Kids*, which ran for ten years (1972-1982); the program featured Cosby's stories about growing up in Philadelphia. A concert film, *Bill Cosby—Himself*, was distributed in 1982. By the 1980's, Cosby had become a national icon, appearing in television series and specials, in films, and in stage shows as well as creating comedy recordings.

One story has it that it was an appearance that Cosby made as a guest on *The Tonight Show Starring Johnny Carson* that set in motion the creation of *The Cosby Show*. Brandon Tartikoff, president of the National Broadcasting Company (NBC), had been awakened by his young daughter. To pass time while he soothed his child, Tartikoff turned on *The Tonight Show*, on which Cosby was doing one of his monologues on the vicissitudes of rearing a family. Perhaps Tartikoff, a parent, was struck by the change that had been occurring in Cosby's material, for as Cosby's own family grew, Cosby had switched from creating humor about growing up to creating humor based on parenting. It could also be that Tartikoff was only reacting to an ongoing plea by Thomas Werner and Marcy Carsey, whose production company, Carsey-Werner, had been promoting—perhaps for as long as two years—the idea of a new Cosby show. Whatever the case, Tartikoff became convinced that Bill Cosby should be featured in a comedy series based on parenthood. The idea did not immediately produce positive response.

Certainly, there was reason for network executives to be wary; Cosby was a forceful and determined personality. His celebrity status was significant enough to place him in a powerful bargaining position. Moreover, what he was asking for in creating a series was unprecedented: full artistic and content control. Such terms had led to the an earlier rejection of a show with Cosby by the American Broadcasting Company (ABC).

As discussions evolved, the concept of the show became bolder. First, in an echo of *I Spy*, Cosby was to play a detective. A later proposal was for him to play a chauffeur living in Brooklyn with his wife, who was a plumber. Cosby's final suggestion, Heathcliff Huxtable, M.D., prevailed with NBC. Other series, notably *The Jeffersons* and *Julia*, had starred upwardly mobile African Americans in middle-class settings, but those shows featured blacks working their way into a white world. Moreover, every television series had always been controlled by established producers working with network executives.

Ultimately, negotiations led to an arrangement with the Carsey-Werner Company. Marcy Carsey was named executive producer, with Cosby as co-producer, co-creator, and executive consultant. In essence, Cosby had complete control, and he exercised his rights. He was involved in all artistic decisions, including casting, directing, story, and dialogue. One of the principal staff writers on *The Cosby Show* characterized Cosby as "the emperor." Because he was a professional educator as well as a successful entertainer, Cosby intended that his show provide family education. He also intended that the show should reflect his own positive philosophy and lifestyle; he was known to reject unsuitable scripts even on the day before taping.

It is not surprising, then, that *The Cosby Show* paralleled Cosby's own life. Cosby was a graduate of Temple University and had earned a doctor of education degree from the University of Massachusetts in 1977. His wife, Camille, was a professional woman, and the couple had four daughters and a son. They lived in an upscale neighborhood in Massachusetts. The television family was headed by Heathcliff "Cliff" Huxtable, a successful obstetrician who lived with his family above his office in an upscale neighborhood inNew York City. Huxtable's wife, Clair, was a lawyer. Like the Cosbys, the Huxtables had five children, four daughters and a son.

The Cosby Show introduced important differences from other shows starring African Americans. First, it did not include any featured white performers. The show starred Cosby and Phylicia Rashad as Clair. The Huxtable's children, the other important continuing characters, were played by Lisa Bonet, Tempestt Bledsoe, Sabrina Le Beauf, Keshia Knight Pulliam, and Malcolm-Jamal Warner.

A second innovation was that the Huxtables were a black family without financial concern. As a physician and a lawyer, respectively, Cliff and Clair were members of prestigious professions, and their children would go to college. The family members' speech was not pretentious, but it was clearly educated.

Finally, the episodes focused on simple parenting problems, without tortured plot complications: a daughter wearing too much makeup, a son squandering his allowance, a pet goldfish whose death breaks the heart of the youngest child (the whole family, dressed in funeral attire, holds a burial ceremony next to the toilet). From its first airing on September 20, 1984, the show was an immediate hit, and it quickly moved to the top position in the ratings, a place it held throughout the 1980's. As the series continued, the children matured, and the parents aged so that the Huxtable family was organic, living and changing with the families who watched them for eight years.

SIGNIFICANCE

The impacts of *The Cosby Show* were both immediate and long-lasting. First, the series marked the revival of situation comedy as the basic form of television entertainment in prime time. Of the top ten shows in the A. C. Nielson ratings in the 1982-1983 season, only two were comedies; the 1983-1984 season featured only one comedy.

Critics had begun to discuss the death of situation comedy, but *The Cosby Show* proved their discussion premature. Not only was it an immediate hit, but it also encouraged the development of other situation comedies that became successful, such as *Family Ties* (the NBC companion piece to *Cosby*) and the popular ABC series *Growing Pains* and *Valerie*. Indeed, a new artistic-commercial vision was conceived out of the impetus of *The Cosby Show*. Each network began to attempt to design whole evenings of programming built around appeals to an aggregate market.

On NBC, for example, in the early evening, when the whole family was viewing, there was *Cosby* followed by *Family Ties*. Later in the evening came *Cheers*, followed by more adult fare such as *Night Court* and *Hill Street Blues*.

Nothing, however, not even an aggregate evening of shows, had the impact of Bill Cosby's program. One commentator observed that situation comedy as an art form can be divided into "B.C." (before Cosby) and "A.C." (after Cosby). During the late 1980's, *The Cosby Show* frequently attracted more than 50 percent of the total television audience. During its second year, thirteen of *The Cosby Show*'s episodes were among the fifteen most-watched shows of the entire year. The upshot

of such unprecedented popularity was that NBC had a solid run as the number one television network throughout the 1980's.

In the 1990's, *The Cosby Show* was challenged as the undisputed choice of American television viewers. The challenge came in part from *A Different World*, a series that was spun off from *The Cosby Show*; it featured Lisa Bonet as a Huxtable daughter gone off to college. A more significant challenge came from *Roseanne*, a series that was the artistic and spiritual child of *The Cosby Show*.

Roseanne was created in 1987 by Matt Williams, a longtime writer and producer for Cosby, and was produced by the Carsey-Werner Company. Carsey-Werner went on to produce *Davis Rules*, and Williams joined with Carmen Finestra, another writer from *Cosby*, to follow *Roseanne* with *Home Improvement*.

All these shows were about parenting or the results of parenting. *Roseanne* was clearly a blue-collar twist on *The Cosby Show*. *Home Improvement* probably had the closest affinity to Cosby's formula of straightforward, no-frills episodes, featuring simple, earnest language and gentle, positive humor. The outlandish predicaments of *I Love Lucy*, the overwrought emotions and self-conscious social significance of *All in the Family*, and the fatuousness of *Father Knows Best* were replaced by Roseanne's bluntness, by her overweight husband's cheerful acceptance of life as it is, and by the deadpan humor of the family in *Home Improvement*. "Bill is a genius," said Matt Williams. "We all learned from him and are applying those lessons." "Cosby is brilliant, a mind like a jazz musician," said Carmen Finestra.

Perhaps the most significant of Bill Cosby's lessons, Finestra has argued, is that earnest, positive humor is the funniest. When Clair asks why the Huxtables have five children and Cliff answers that it is because they did not want six, the only possible response is undiluted laughter. Another lesson concerning earnest humor has to do with the great store that the middle class puts in the process of thinking a problem through to a solution. Thinking is hard work, however, and is meant to be done in private, with only the solution being made public.

Thinking in public is thus a sort of embarrassment, a case of being caught with one's intellectual pants down. "We knew that they tuned in to watch Bill think," Matt Williams noted. "It was very funny when Bill thought."

Above all, the lesson of *The Cosby Show* was that Americans love the ideal of the family, especially a traditional family with a frequently present father and an omnipresent mother whose whole concern is the children.

Here, the Huxtables were consummate: Cliff Huxtable's workplace is downstairs; Clair Huxtable has a highly prestigious profession, but she apparently works only when all the children are asleep. Even so, she never discusses her work, never brings work problems home. She represents complete achievement for the American woman: a satisfying profession equal to that of any man and the apparent time off from work to give entirely of herself to her children.

In its last two seasons, *The Cosby Show* slipped steadily in the ratings but remained in the top ten. By that time, most of the original writing team had gone on to other shows. Still, the Cosby mystique drew fifty-four million viewers for the final episode. *The Cosby Show* made all of its featured players stars. Awards of all types—notably Emmy Awards and Peabody Awards—were lavished on the actors, writers, and directors. Cosby himself refused to accept Emmy Awards, but he was without doubt a superstar and a powerful force in American family life.

—*August W. Staub*

See also: *All in the Family* Confronts Controversial Issues; *The Jeffersons* Signals Success of Black Situation Comedies.

U.S. SUPREME COURT UPHOLDS GOALS, NOT QUOTAS, TO REMEDY DISCRIMINATION

1986

In a number of decisions, the U.S. Supreme Court defined the permissible extent of affirmative action programs.

Locale: Washington, D.C.

Categories: Laws, acts, and legal history; business and labor; civil rights and liberties; social issues and reform

KEY FIGURES

William J. Brennan (1906-1997), associate justice of the United States, 1956-1990, who wrote the majority opinions in several affirmative action cases

Warren E. Burger (1907-1995), chief justice of the United States, 1969-1986, who advocated an activist role for the Supreme Court in fostering civil liberties

William H. Rehnquist (1924-2005), chief justice of the United States, 1986-2005

Antonin Scalia (b. 1936), associate justice of the United States beginning in 1986

SUMMARY OF EVENT

Title VII of the Civil Rights Act of 1964, amended by the Equal Employment Opportunity Act of 1972, is intended to eliminate discrimination by employers and labor unions. In addition, Executive Order 11246 regulates employment practices of federal contractors and, in some cases, requires contractors to implement affirmative action programs to improve the opportunities of minorities and women. The implementation of these fair employment regulations led to considerable legal interpretation. In *United Steelworkers of America v. Weber* (1979), the U.S. Supreme Court set down norms for legitimate affirmative action programs. The *Weber* criteria are that any affirmative action program must be part of an overall plan, must be voluntary, must have an objective of remedying imbalances arising from discrimination, must be temporary, and must not trammel the interests of others.

Throughout the early 1980's, the U.S. Justice Department under President Ronald Reagan argued that the objective of civil rights legislation should be to rectify injustices done to specific individuals. Giving a preference to a minority group member who was not a proven victim of discrimination was considered to be a form of "reverse discrimination" against the majority. A number of Supreme Court decisions in the 1986 session served to expand the scope of permissible affirmative action programs.

In *Wygant v. Jackson Board of Education*, the Court supported by a five-to-four vote the concept of an affirmative action plan along the lines spelled out in *Weber* but opposed a provision in the plan that gave preference to black workers in layoff decisions. The plurality view of the Court was that when a person is laid off, the entire burden of the decision is borne by that employee. The rights of the laid-off worker are affected much more than in a case in which a person is not promoted. The effort to remedy discrimination imposes an excessive cost on a single person, the one laid off. In addition, the Court concluded that other remedies that imposed less cost might have been available. The view of the Court was that although seniority could be overridden in promotions and other job assignments, it should not be in layoffs.

In 1975, a New York district court found that the sheet metal workers' union had discriminated against nonwhite workers in its apprenticeship program. The court ordered an end to the discrimination and established a goal of 29 percent nonwhite membership, to be reached by July, 1981. The court arrived at the percentage based on the nonwhite composition of the local New York City labor market. The union was subsequently fined for failing to meet the goal. Both the goal and the date for achieving it were changed. A district court and the court of appeals found the union in contempt for failing to reach the court-ordered revised goals. The union then appealed to the Supreme Court. The union, along with the solicitor general of the United States, argued that the membership goal and the means prescribed to achieve it were in violation of Title VII of the Civil Rights Act, which implies that no court can order admission of an individual to a union if that individual was refused for reasons other than discrimination.

In *Local 28 Sheet Metal Workers International Association v. Equal Employment Opportunity Commission* (1986), the Supreme Court affirmed, by a five-to-four vote, the decision of the district court against the union. Justice William J. Brennan, speaking for the Court, asserted that even though the individuals admitted to the apprenticeship program had not themselves been previously denied admission or discriminated against, the courts had the right to provide relief when the union had been guilty of egregious discrimination or discrimination had been endemic. Brennan concluded that unless courts have the right to require agencies to employ qualified minorities roughly in proportion to their number in the labor market, it may be impossible to provide the equal opportunity that is the intent of Title VII. Brennan made a subtle distinction regarding racial quotas. Although it is clear from congressional deliberations and Title VII that quotas should not be used simply because of the existence of racial imbalance in the workplace, this does not preclude the use of quotas by the courts to rectify racial imbalances in cases in which discrimination is proven to exist. The purpose of affirmative action is not to make whole the victims of discrimination but rather to provide relief to the group discriminated against. The recipients of relief need not have suffered themselves.

In *Local 93 International Association of Firefighters v. City of Cleveland* (1986), the Supreme Court by a sixto- three vote approved a consent decree to eliminate racial discrimination. An association of minority group members brought suit against the city of Cleveland, charging discrimination in the city's fire department. A federal district court approved a consent decree between the city and the firefighters' association to rectify the problem. The decree set forth a quota system for the promotion of minorities over a four-year period. The terms of the decree were arrived at by the parties to a lawsuit and were approved by the court. Local 93 was not a party to the initial suit, and it did not approve the decree. Local 93 appealed to the Supreme Court, arguing that public safety required that the most competent people be promoted.

The Court again affirmed the right of the courts to prescribe corrective plans that benefit individuals who were not actual victims of discrimination. The majority of the Court further held that voluntary consent decrees can go beyond what the courts would have ordered to rectify the problem. The decision did recognize the right to challenge consent decrees in the courts. In the private sector, consent decrees arrived at with the Equal Employment Opportunity Commission (EEOC) could similarly be challenged as violations of collective bargaining agreements, Title VII, or the equal protection clause of the Fourteenth Amendment.

In the light of a 1984 Supreme Court decision, the Reagan administration had advised cities to reexamine consent decrees, believing that less aggressive affirmative action plans might be acceptable. The administration now found itself uncertain as to which way the court was leaning. These 1986 decisions marked the end of the activist approach of the Court under Chief Justice Warren E. Burger while at the same time making the more conservative approach of Chief Justice William H. Rehnquist more difficult to establish.

Significance

Although the 1986 decisions applied specifically to minorities, it soon became clear that affirmative action pro- grams similar to those approved by the Supreme Court could also be applied to women. In *Johnson v. Santa Clara County Transportation Agency* (1987), the Court, by a six-to-three vote, concluded that promoting a woman to the job of dispatcher ahead of more qualified men was acceptable under the provisions of a voluntary affirmative action program in the public sector. The agency was to consider sex as one factor in making promotion decisions for jobs in which women were underrepresented. The long-term objective was to have employment in the agency mirror the composition of the local labor market. No explicit quota was established, but the agency was to examine the composition of its workforce annually and undertake the steps necessary to achieve its long-term goal.

The case arose when a woman was given the job of dispatcher over Paul Johnson, another candidate. Johnson appealed to the Equal Employment Opportunity Commission. The EEOC granted the right to sue, and the lower court held that Johnson's rights under Title VII of the Civil Rights Act had been violated. The court ruled that gender had been the only factor in the promotion of the woman and that the agency program was not "temporary," as required by the *Weber* decision.

In the majority opinion of the Supreme Court, Justice Brennan was careful to avoid the pejorative implications of quotas. He concluded that there was a manifest imbalance in the representation of women in this job classification and that the agency program did not specify a strict number of women that should be hired but rather set aspirations that were subject to change and review. Hiring was not to be based solely on applicants' sex; rather, sex was to be one factor considered. Justice Lewis F. Powell, Jr., pointed out that there were seven candidates who were deemed qualified for the job, so Johnson did not have an unqualified right to the job in the absence of the preference granted to women. Although Johnson was denied promotion, he retained his position in the agency, so that an undue burden was not imposed on him. In dissent, Justice Antonin Scalia interpreted the majority opinion as an unjustified extension of Title VII intended to alter social standards. The case was the first to establish that voluntary affirmative action programs to overcome the effects of societal discrimination are permissible.

In *United States v. Paradise* (1987), the plurality opinion of the Court supported the promotion of one black state trooper for each white state trooper promoted. This course of action was allowed because of the narrowly defined nature of the preference and because of the egregious nature of past violations of equal rights. The Court noted that the plan was flexible and

temporary and that it postponed rather than denied the promotion of white officers.

In *San Francisco Police Officers' Association v. City and County of San Francisco* (1987), a federal appeals court again applied the *Weber* test. The city used three criteria in promoting police officers: a written examination, a multiple-choice test, and an oral examination. After administering the first two parts, the city found that the percentage of minorities who passed was lower than desired. The results were then rescored on a pass-or-fail basis, with the deciding factor for those who passed being the oral examination. The city had thus rescored promotional examinations to achieve racial and gender percentages. The court found that rescoring the examinations unnecessarily trammeled the interests of the nonminority police officers. Candidates for promotion, the court ruled, are denied equal opportunity if test results can be rescored. The practice was deceptive in that candidates had a right to know how the test results were to be weighed as they prepared for the test. In addition, other methods of correcting the racial imbalance were available that were less dramatic or less costly to others.

In 1989, the Supreme Court handed down five decisions, all with five-to-four majorities, that reversed many of the 1986 cases. Essentially, these decisions shifted the burden of proof to the employee, who had to demonstrate that practices by an employer were unrelated to the requirements of a job. Statistical data indicating small proportions of minority group members holding a job were no longer sufficient to claim discrimination. The Court limited the extent to which state and local governments could set aside positions to be filled only by minority group members. The Court also allowed for an affirmative action program to be reexamined if, over the course of the program, employees claimed reverse discrimination.

The view of the courts with regard to employment quotas has been far from unanimous and has continued to evolve. Title VII explicitly states that discrimination based on race is prohibited. In this context, quotas that discriminate are prohibited. Difficulties arise in determining whether these prohibitions are universal. Quotas implemented to achieve racial balance even though discrimination has not been demonstrated would be deemed illegal. Uncertainty occurs when discrimination has been found to exist and either voluntary or court-mandated programs are prescribed to rectify the problem. Critics argue that setting numerical standards in effect discriminates against the majority. Choosing one person over another is discriminatory toward the person not chosen, and the person chosen has not necessarily been discriminated against in the past. Therefore, the person chosen is given a preference that is undue and at the expense of someone else who was not a party to any discrimination.

The advocates of affirmative action argue that in cases in which discrimination has been proven to exist, setting numerical standards may be the only viable way of correcting a demonstrated problem.

The essence of affirmative action is not to compensate actual victims of discrimination but rather to provide opportunities to groups of people who historically have been discriminated against. Individuals are given preference not because of anything done to them but because of something done to their group. Further, the people not chosen do not lose anything they previously had or anything to which they had a unilateral right. In cases in which there is a direct loss, as in layoffs, the courts have been less willing to support numerical quotas. Businesses thus have had to walk a fine line in trying to be fair to all employees while maintaining productive workforces.

—*John F. O'Connell*

See also: U.S. Supreme Court Bans Discrimination in Hiring; U.S. Congress Mandates Equal Employment Opportunity; U.S. Supreme Court Rules on Affirmative Action Programs;

BATSON V. KENTUCKY

April 30, 1986

The Supreme Court ruled that the equal protection clause of the Fourteenth Amendment forbids a prosecutor from using peremptory challenges to remove potential jurors because of their race.

The Case: U.S. Supreme Court ruling on jury selection

James Batson, an African American, was indicted for second-degree burglary. When the judge conducted a voir dire examination (preliminary check of suitability and qualifications) of the potential jurors, the prosecutor used his peremptory challenges to remove all four African Americans from the panel, resulting in an all-white jury. The Supreme Court had refused to disturb the same development in *Swain v. Alabama* (1965). After Batson's conviction, nevertheless, his lawyers asserted that the process of jury selection violated his rights to equal protection and to a jury drawn from a cross section of the community.

By a 7–2 majority, the Court accepted Batson's claim. Speaking for the majority, Justice Lewis F. Powell, Jr., remanded the case and instructed the trial court to require the prosecutor to justify the exclusion of members of the defendant's race from the jury. If the prosecutor were unable to give a racially neutral explanation, Batson's conviction would have to be reversed. Powell's opinion formulated a framework for future voir dire proceedings. The basic idea is that a pattern of exclusion based on race creates an inference of discrimination. Once such an inference is established, the prosecutor has the burden of showing that the peremptories are not discriminatory. Emphasizing that the Constitution does not guarantee a right to peremptory challenges, Powell wrote that potential jurors may not be eliminated simply because of the assumption that people of a particular race might be more sympathetic to a particular defendant. Thus, Powell's opinion requires color-conscious rather than color-blind procedures in jury selection, and it tends to encourage the use of racial quotas.

The *Batson* principles have been significantly expanded. In *Powers v. Ohio* (1991), the Court held that criminal defendants may object to race-based peremptory challenges even if the defendant and the excluded jurors do not belong to the same race. Later that year, in *Edmonson v. Leesville Concrete Company*, the Court applied the Batson framework to the selection of juries in civil trials. In *Georgia v. McCollum* (1992), the Court decided that the *Batson* ruling applies to defense attorneys. In *J. E. B. v. Alabama* (1994), moreover, the Court held that the equal protection clause prohibits discrimination in jury selection on the basis of gender.

—*Thomas Tandy Lewis*

See also: *Edmonson v. Leesville Concrete Company*; *Moore v. Dempsey*; *Norris v. Alabama*; *Powers v. Ohio*; *Strauder v. West Virginia*; *Williams v. Mississippi*

RAP GOES PLATINUM WITH RUN-D.M.C.'S *RAISING HELL*

July, 1986

The increasing importance of rap as a part of multicultural popular music was confirmed when Run-D.M.C.'s album Raising Hell *sold more than one million copies.*

Locale: Los Angeles, California
Category: Music

KEY FIGURES

Joseph Simmons (b. 1964), rapper nicknamed "Run" whose popularity crossed racial lines, bringing the black urban sound to pop music

Russell Simmons (b. 1957), Joseph Simmons's elder brother, who managed and produced many top rap groups, including Run-D.M.C.

Darryl McDaniels (b. 1964), friend of Joseph Simmons and the "D.M.C." of Run-D.M.C.

Jason Mizell (1965-2002), D.J. known as Jam Master Jay who performed with Run-D.M.C.

SUMMARY OF EVENT

Rap music originated in the inner cities of the United States as a new voice for the frustration and hopelessness of ghetto life. A continuation of African American musical culture, rap drew from oral traditions and the rhythmic drumming and syncopation of black music. It was also influenced by the Jamaican "sound system" disc jockeys of the 1960's and the political jazz of Gil Scott-Heron and the Last Poets. Emerging in New York City during the mid-1970's, early rap was performed almost exclusively for black audiences in Brooklyn, Queens, Manhattan, and the South Bronx. Rap remained a predominantly race- and class-specific form of expression until 1986, when two young rappers known as Run-D.M.C. released the album *Raising Hell*. This platinum hit crossed cultural boundaries and firmly established rap as an important part of popular music.

Raising Hell combined metallic rock, rhythm and blues, and rap into a popular mixture that jumped up the pop music sales charts to number three. The album included a collaboration with the hard rock band Aerosmith on a remake of Aerosmith's classic "Walk This Way," which was also released as a music video that received heavy play on the Music Television (MTV) network. "Walk This Way" was the first rap hit to cross over the racial barriers that previously had made rap the domain of black musicians only. *Raising Hell*'s success

Run-D.M.C.

opened the door to Caucasian, Hispanic, American Indian, and Samoan rappers, and encouraged collaborations between rappers and musicians best known for their work in other genres. Rap diversified, branching off from the violent and controversial "gangsta" or "hardcore" genre. The late 1980's and early 1990's saw the emergence of "pop" or "bubblegum," "countercultural" or "hippie-hop," and "party" rap, as well as feminist rappers such as Salt-N-Pepa and Queen Latifah.

Prior to 1986, rap was not completely unknown to the music world. In 1979, songwriter Sylvia Robinson released "Rapper's Delight" by Harlem's Sugarhill Gang.

This rap hit was the first to make a mark on national music sales charts. It was soon followed by "The Breaks" and "125th Street," by Kurtis Blow, and by Grandmaster Flash and the Furious Five's graphic protest "The Message." Rap concerts drew increasingly larger crowds, and the record industry began to take notice.

It was at this time that a young man named Joseph Simmons began developing his own rap style. The son of a civil rights activist and poet, Joseph grew up in the middle-class neighborhood of Hollis, Queens. His elder brother Russell managed Kurtis Blow and sometimes allowed Joseph, a glib fifteen-year-old, a few minutes onstage to do his own thing. Nicknamed "Run" at the age of twelve because of his tendency to run off at the mouth, Joseph was enrolled in college, studying mortuary science, when he teamed up with Darryl McDaniels, his best friend since kindergarten, to form Run-D.M.C.

619

Run-D.M.C.'s first album, *It's Like That*, was released by Profile Records in 1983. Interesting for its dramatic, tense lyrics and the juxtaposition of Simmons's higher, smoother voice and McDaniel's rougher tone, *It's Like That* sold 250,000 copies and went to number fifteen on the black music sales charts. By 1985, Run- D.M.C. had two gold albums and was headlining concerts.

Simmons and McDaniels added Jason Mizell, known as Jam Master Jay, as D.J. and developed a "gangsta"-style look that included black hats and suits and white Adidas shoes. Run-D.M.C.'s major breakthrough came in July, 1986, when their album *Raising Hell* was simultaneously certified gold and platinum. Run-D.M.C. followed up on the record's success with the Raising Hell national tour. The group sold out twenty-thousand-seat arenas across the United States, but the tour was devastated by violence at concerts in at least six cities, including rioting in Pittsburgh, New York, and St. Louis.

In Long Beach, California, gang members tore through the arena before the concert, injuring more than forty people. Although rowdiness at concerts was nothing new, the magnitude of the violence in these cases attracted the attention of the watchdog organization the Parents Music Resource Center. Tipper Gore, a founding member of the PMRC and wife of Senator Al Gore, criticized Run- D.M.C. for the use of provocative lyrics, and many concert promoters reconsidered their decisions to book rap groups.

Simmons argued that he was serving as a role model for inner-city youth: "They listen to me *because* I act tough and cool. I got a lot of juice with them. . . . So when we say don't take drugs and stay in school, they listen." One music critic described *Raising Hell* as "highly moral," and others pointed to Run-D.M.C.'s history of social involvement, including an appearance at the Live Aid concert and participation in public-service announcements aimed at discouraging drug abuse and the risky behaviors associated with exposure to sexually transmitted diseases. After the Long Beach incident, Simmons went on the radio in Los Angeles to urge people to calm down. "I told the gangs," Run said, "if you're listening to me—you're stupid."

The next significant crossover hit was inspired when Russell Simmons teamed up with heavy metal producer Rick Rubin to form Def Jam Records. Def Jam managed more than a dozen rap acts, including Run-D.M.C. and the Beastie Boys, three white punks turned rappers. The two groups collaborated on "Paul Revere," released

in late 1986 on the Beastie Boys' *Licensed to Ill*. This hit album continued the musical direction started by Run-D.M.C. and appealed to black fans as well as white. In 1987, Run-D.M.C. and the Beastie Boys went on the road with the Together Forever tour, selling out major arenas despite bad press and attracting mixed audiences of blacks and whites. Rap had become the music of the youthful masses, a multicultural voice expressing anger, joy, political opinion, and idealism.

SIGNIFICANCE

When Run-D.M.C. went platinum with *Raising Hell* in 1986, rap became an undeniable force in the popular music industry. "Walk This Way," the hit collaboration with Aerosmith, broke the precedent that rap was created by black musicians only for black youth only.

Rap's increased popularity with a racially mixed audience provided incentive for artists of different ethnic backgrounds to experiment with this musical form, and rap diversified and flourished. The impacts of rap were not limited to the music world alone. Heated debates regarding the violence associated with rap concerts and the obscenity, sexism, and hostility prevalent in the lyrics of "gangsta" or "hard-core" rap raged in the media, the courtroom, and the classroom.

Although "gangsta" rap was the most visible because of its controversial nature, a variety of distinct approaches to the genre developed, each with its own stars and audience. "Pop" or "bubblegum" rap, pioneered by M.C. Hammer, was characterized by its repetitive musical samples and innocuous lyrics. Acts such as Hammer, Heavy D. and the Boyz, Sir Mix-a-Lot, and Kris Kross, as well as white rappers Vanilla Ice and Marky Mark, were popular with the media because of their inoffensive style. Pop rap received airtime on MTV, and advertising campaigns targeting teenagers utilized such hits as Hammer's "Can't Touch This" (1990), Vanilla Ice's "Ice Ice Baby" (1990), and Kris Kross's "Jump" (1992). Female rappers assumed a more dominant role with the 1986 release of *Hot, Cool, and Vicious* by Salt-NPepa.

Women had performed in rap since its inception but were usually labeled as novelty acts. Salt-N-Pepa's feminist attitude encouraged other women to respond aggressively to the misogyny of most male rappers. Queen Latifah delivered a powerful message on *All Hail the Queen* (1989) and *Nature of a Sista'* (1991) and created a niche for female fans in a genre known for its endorsement of violence against women.

Another female rapper, Sister Souljah, elicited Democratic presidential candidate Bill Clinton's criticism in response to remarks she made on interracial violence. The militancy of her album *360 Degrees of Power* (1992) is expressive of the politicized rap for which Public Enemy is best known. That group's innovative albums *It Takes a Nation of Millions to Hold Us Back* (1988) and *Fear of a Black Planet* (1990) received the attention of musicologists, jazz musicians, and composers. Director Spike Lee used Public Enemy's "Fight the Power" as the theme song for his film *Do the Right Thing* (1989). Because of Public Enemy's association with the Nation of Islam, the media generalized political rap as Black Nationalistic and anti-Semitic, obscuring the actual diversity of political opinions being expressed. Rap albums released in the late 1980's and early 1990's included the antiapartheid collaboration *Sun City*, the militant *Sleeping with the Enemy* by Paris, the spiritual Afrocentrism of X Clan's *To the East, Blackwards*, and Isis's *Rebel Soul.*

Criticized in its early days for nihilism and lack of utopian vision, rap experienced a resurgence of optimism and ethnic identity common to black music. Combining spiritual and mystical lyrics with the rhythmic textures sampled from 1960's music, P. M. Dawn's *Of the Heart, of the Soul, and of the Cross: The Utopian Experience* united those alienated by other forms of rap. Along with P. M. Dawn, De La Soul, Arrested Development, and A Tribe Called Quest met with great success in the mainstream, receiving acclaim for their work in such popular publications as *Rolling Stone*, *Spin*, *The New York Times,* and the *Village Voice.*

As early as 1980, rap was used by educators who took advantage of its retainability. Douglass "Jocko" Henderson, a radio personality of the 1950's and 1960's, formed Get Ready, Inc., an educational rap program with topics ranging from black history to career preparation skills. Later, performers such as KRS-One (Knowledge Reigns Supreme Over Nearly Everyone), the Poor Righteous Teachers (PRT), and the Intellectual Hoodlum incorporated the message that knowledge is a crucial aspect of survival.

Rap music flourished in the decades after Run-D.M.C. caught the public's attention in 1986, as many artists unique in music and message came on the scene. Rap also influenced American culture more widely. The controversial nature of some rap music encouraged people who had never listened to it to hold strong opinions about it nevertheless. The effect of explicit rap on society (and vice versa) could not be ignored, and rap music contributed to debates concerning censorship and restrictions on material that could be presented to children.

The controversy surrounding the graphically violent and sexist lyrics of 2 Live Crew's *As Nasty as They Wanna Be* came to a head on June 10, 1990, when the group, led by Luther Campbell, was charged with violating obscenity laws in an adults-only concert in Hollywood, Florida. After a two-week trial, the members of 2 Live Crew were found not guilty of all charges. Freedom of speech as guaranteed by the First Amendment to the U.S. Constitution and the limits of this right, if any, are issues critical to American society. When a rap musician expresses him- or herself freely and without censorship in the public eye, the content of rap cannot go unnoticed.

One impact of controversial rap music was to provoke examination and evaluation of the environmental conditions that foster antagonistic philosophies. Rap continues to extend the tradition of African American music. It is the honest voice of a diverse set of people, espousing divergent viewpoints and encompassing many attitudes. Run-D.M.C., the first rap group to enter the limelight of popular music, opened the door for a segment of society that had been shut out for too long.

—*Susan Frischer*

See also: Wonder Releases *Innervisions*; Marley's *Natty Dread* Establishes Reggae's Popularity.

NATIONAL COALITION OF BLACKS FOR REPARATIONS IN AMERICA

Founded in 1987

This coalition seeks a formal apology by the government and supports a congressional bill that demands reparations for African Americans.

Identification: Federation of organizations across the United States that support reparations for African Americans

The National Coalition of Blacks for Reparations in America (N'COBRA) is a coalition of organizations across the United States that support reparations for African Americans. African Americans were supposed to receive "forty acres and a mule" from the U.S. government upon emancipation in reparation for the time they spent in slavery, but this proposal was never actually made law. The newly freed blacks lacked property, capital, education, and job experience, giving them a severely disadvantaged start. In addition, not long after slavery was made illegal, a system of segregation known as Jim Crow took effect. Segregation blocked equal access to home ownership, which is the main source of capital for most Americans, and this government-sanctioned inequality can be seen as the root cause of the wealth gap between black and white Americans in modern times.

N'COBRA supports and lobbies for HR 40, a congressional bill introduced every year since 1989 by John Conyers, a Democratic representative from Illinois, that demands reparations for African Americans not unlike those received by Native Americans for land seized by the government and by Japanese Americans for time spent in internment camps during World War II. While the organization does not specify the exact amount of reparation money that should be paid, its Web site suggested, in 2005, a figure of eight trillion dollars.

—*Eileen O'Brien*

See also: Emancipation Proclamation; Republic of New Africa; Slavery; Slavery and race relations

AFROCENTRISM

1988

Afrocentrism offers an alternative to "Eurocentric" interpretations of history.

Definition: Philosophy of historical analysis and education articulated by Molefi Kete Asante

A professor of African American studies at Temple University, Molefi Kete Asante is the author of *The Afrocentricity Idea* (1987), *Afrocentricity* (1988), and *Kemet, Afrocentricity, and Knowledge* (1990), and other works that define Afrocentrism as the perspective of history that allows students to observe the world from the point of view of the African and African American. Asante created Afrocentrism as a reaction to "Eurocentric" interpretations of history, which, in Asante's view, marginalize members of ethnic and racial minorities by portraying them as victims and passive participants in European-dominated history.

Asante's philosophy advocates a "multi-centered multiculturalism" in which all racial groups are encouraged to write history from their perspective to replace the "monocentric," or European-dominated, historical perspective. Asante's philosophy does not advocate the elimination of the European perspective but rather invites the European perspective to be presented alongside the interpretations of other racial groups. Opponents of the Afrocentric model, however, accuse Asante and his supporters of historical inaccuracy and of using history to promote a racist political agenda. The philosophy of Afrocentrism borrows heavily from the writings of Carter G. Woodson, Asa Hilliard, and Cheikh Anta Diop.

—*Jason Pasch*

See also: Black Is Beautiful movement; Black nationalism; Education

CIVIL RIGHTS RESTORATION ACT

March 22, 1988

Congress required recipients of federal financial assistance to uphold nondiscriminatory requirements of the 1964 and subsequent civil rights legislation in all respects, not merely in activity aided by federal funds.

The Law: Federal legislation devised to clarify earlier mandates regarding the funding of educational institutions

Title VI of the Civil Rights Act of 1964 mandated that federal funds could not be used to support segregation or discrimination based on race, color, or national origin. The law did not affect a number of other civil rights problems, however. At Cornell University's School of Agriculture, for example, women could not gain admission unless their entrance exam scores were 30 percent to 40 percent higher than those of male applicants. Epileptics were often barred from employment, and persons in their fifties were often told that they were qualified for a job but too old. To rectify these problems, Congress extended the scope of unlawful discrimination in federally assisted schools in Title IX of the Education Amendments Act of 1972 to cover gender; the Rehabilitation Act of 1973 expanded the same coverage to people with disabilities; and the Age Discrimination Act of 1975 added age as a protected class.

Enforcement of the statute regarding education was initially assigned to the Office for Civil Rights (OCR) of the U.S. Department of Health, Education, and Welfare, which later became the U.S. Department of Education. OCR ruled that the statute outlawed not only discrimination in the particular program supported by federal funds but also discrimination in programs supported by nonfederal funds. All recipients of federal financial assistance were asked to sign an assurance of compliance with OCR as a condition of receiving a federal grant.

GROVE CITY COLLEGE

From 1974 to 1984, Grove City College in western Pennsylvania received $1.8 million in tuition grants and guaranteed student loans but refused to sign an assurance of compliance. The college argued that the funds were for students, not the college, but OCR insisted that the financial aid was administered as a part of the college's financial aid program and, therefore, the college must pledge as a whole not to discriminate on the basis of race, color, national origin, or gender. OCR instituted enforcement proceedings against Grove City College, and an administrative law judge ruled in 1978 that the college could no longer receive federal student loan moneys.

Grove City College and four students desiring financial aid then sued. In 1980, when the case was first tried, the federal district court ruled in favor of Grove City College on the grounds that no sex discrimination

had actually occurred. On appeal, the court of appeals reversed the lower court's decision, and the matter was taken up by the Supreme Court of the United States, this time with Terrel H. Bell, head of the newly created federal Department of Education, as the defendant.

In *Grove City College v. Bell* (1984), Justice Byron R. White delivered the majority opinion of the Court, which held that OCR did not have sufficient congressional authority to withhold funds from Grove City College for failure to sign the assurance of compliance. Moreover, according to the Court, violations of Title VI could occur only in the specific program or activity supported directly with federal funds, a judgment that went beyond the question raised by the case. Justices William J. Brennan, Jr., and Thurgood Marshall dissented.

A NEW BILL

Shortly after the Supreme Court ruling, OCR dropped some seven hundred pending enforcement actions, resulting in an outcry from civil rights groups over the decision. Representative Augustus F. Hawkins authored the Civil Rights Restoration Act in the House, and Senator Ted Kennedy sponsored the bill in the Senate. Their aim was to amend all the affected statutes—Title VI of the Civil Rights Act of 1964, Title IX of the Education Amendments Act of 1972, the Rehabilitation Act of 1973, and the Age Discrimination Act of 1975. According to the bill, any agency or private firm that wanted to receive federal financial assistance would have to comply with the nondiscrimination requirement as a whole, even if the aid went to only one subunit of that agency or firm.

Although Hawkins's version quickly passed in the House of Representatives, the measure was caught up in the politics of abortion, and the bill died in the Senate. Opponents advanced more than one thousand amendments over a period of four years, and representatives of the administration of President Ronald Reagan testified against passage of the law. A group known as the Moral Majority broadcast warnings that the bill would protect alcoholics, drug addicts, and homosexuals from discrimination, although there were no such provisions in the proposal.

More crucially, the Catholic Conference of Bishops, which was traditionally aligned with the Civil Rights movement, wanted two amendments to the bill. One proposed amendment, which was unsuccessful, would have exempted institutions affiliated with religious institutions from complying with the law if religious views would be compromised thereby. The other proposed amendment, which was opposed by the National Organization for Women, was an assurance that no federal funds would be spent on abortion. Congress delayed finding a compromise.

In 1987, leaving out references to abortion, Congress finally adopted the Civil Rights Restoration Act. By vetoing the measure, Reagan became the first president to veto a civil rights bill since Andrew Johnson. Supporters of the act sought to override the presidential veto. Opponents in the Senate tried to destroy the bill by various amendments in debate on the floor of the Senate on January 28, 1988. Senator John C. Danforth proposed an amendment that would disallow federal payments for abortion. This amendment passed. With the passage of the act by the Senate on March 22, 1988, Congress overrode Reagan's veto, and the law went into effect immediately.

—*Michael Haas*

FURTHER READING

The law is explained and analyzed in Veronica M. Gillespie and Gregory L. McClinton's "The Civil Rights Restoration Act of 1987: A Defeat for Judicial Conservatism" in National Black Law Journal (12, Spring, 1990), Robert K. Robinson, Billie Morgan Allen, and Geralyn McClure Franklin's "The Civil Rights Restoration Act of 1987: Broadening the Scope of Civil Rights Legislation" in Labor Law Journal (40, January, 1989), and Robert Watson's "Effects of the Civil Rights Restoration Act of 1987 upon Private Organizations and Religious Institutions" in Capital University Law Review (18, Spring, 1989). Mark Willen's "Congress Overrides Reagan's Grove City Veto" in Congressional Quarterly Weekly Review (46, March 26, 1988) explains the parliamentary maneuvers required to get the law passed.

See also: Affirmative action; Civil Rights Act of 1964; Education

DO THE RIGHT THING ESTABLISHES LEE AS A WORLD-CLASS DIRECTOR
June 30, 1989

Do the Right Thing, *director Spike Lee's third feature-length film, confronted the existence of racial tension in the United States and confirmed Lee's reputation as a pioneering African American artist.*

Locale: United States
Category: Motion pictures and video

KEY FIGURES

Spike Lee (b. 1957), writer, director, coproducer, and star of *Do the Right Thing*
Ernest Dickerson (b. 1951), director of photography on *Do the Right Thing*
Danny Aiello (b. 1933), actor who played the role of Sal in *Do the Right Thing*

SUMMARY OF EVENT

When *Do the Right Thing* went into production, Spike Lee had already established himself as a provocative filmmaker. He had not, however, completed a project on the scale of *Do the Right Thing*, nor had he shed the label of "promising" young director.

Born in Atlanta, Georgia, in 1957, Lee was reared in Brooklyn, New York. He returned to Atlanta in 1975 to attend Morehouse College, as had his father and

grandfather before him. At Morehouse, Lee met Monty Ross, who would become his longtime coproducer. Lee also wrote his first short film at Morehouse. Titled *Black College: The Talented Tenth*, it examined the minority of African Americans who had entered the American economic mainstream.

After graduating from Morehouse, Lee studied film at New York University (NYU), where he met Ernest Dickerson, who would become the director of photography for Lee's feature films. Lee first attracted notice as a filmmaker while at NYU. After making such student projects as *The Answer* (1980), a provocative retort to the open racism of D. W. Griffith's film classic *The Birth of a Nation* (1915), and *Sarah* (1981), which focuses on a Harlem Thanksgiving Day celebration, Lee teamed up with Dickerson to complete *Joe's Bed-Stuy Barbershop: We Cut Heads* (1983), an hour-long film shot in color.

Joe's Bed-Stuy Barbershop, which successfully portrays nuances of black conversation and culture, won a Student Academy Award from the Academy of Motion Picture Arts and Sciences and was shown on public television.

After Lee left NYU, his first attempts at making a feature film failed. He persisted, however, and began writing and raising funds for *She's Gotta Have It* (1986).

Filmed in black and white for a modest $175,000, *She's Gotta Have It* required Lee to make his first contacts with Hollywood film companies. A candid exploration of a black woman's sexuality, the film was a critical and boxoffice success. It also established the character of Mars Blackmon (played by Lee himself), who would later appear in a popular series of television shoe advertisements made by Lee with basketball star Michael Jordan. Lee's next film, *School Daze* (1988), was shot in color and was completed for about $6 million; the size of the budget made it necessary for Lee to work with a major film company, Columbia Pictures. Although the film, an examination of life at a black college modeled on Morehouse, drew mixed reviews, it earned a profit.

Getting *Do the Right Thing* made constituted a major test for Lee. He arranged for his most substantial budget up to that time, $6.5 million, in a deal cut with Universal Pictures. The sum was less than Lee wanted and far less than some motion pictures received; Hollywood was not yet willing to take a major risk on Lee. Nevertheless, Lee was set to make an aggressive exploration of race relations in the United States.

Do the Right Thing revolves around a cast of characters that includes Sal (played by Danny Aiello) and his two sons (one of whom is a blatant racist), Italian American proprietors of Sal's Famous Pizzeria; Mookie, played by Lee, who delivers pizzas for Sal; Buggin' Out, the neighborhood radical; Smiley, an awkward, stuttering devotee of both Martin Luther King, Jr., and Malcolm X; and Radio Raheem, a massive figure who traverses the neighborhood playing militant rap music on a huge portable cassette player.

The plot unfolds slowly. Buggin' Out has had a conflict with Sal because the pizzeria's "wall of fame" features only photographs of Italian Americans. Buggin' Out believes that black people ought to be represented on the wall, given that nearly all of Sal's customers are black. He tries to organize a boycott against Sal, but he meets with no success until he gets together with Radio Raheem, who has clashed with Sal over the volume of the music Raheem plays, and Smiley. As Sal is about to close the pizzeria for the day, he good-naturedly decides to remain open at the request of some tardy customers.

Buggin' Out and Radio Raheem enter and demand action on the wall of fame. Driven to distraction by Raheem's music, Sal begins to use racial epithets and then destroys Raheem's cassette player.

With this first act of violence, the molehill of a dispute becomes a veritable mountain. Sal and his sons begin to fight with Radio Raheem and his friends, and the fight flows outside the store. Police officers arrive, and one pulls Radio Raheem off Sal by using a choke hold, which he releases only after Raheem is dead. The crowd is stunned and angry. The police leave with Raheem's body, and the crowd begins to turn on Sal and his sons.

Mookie grabs a garbage can and throws it through the pizzeria's plate-glass window. The shop is gutted and burned by the crowd; Smiley puts pictures of his two heroes on the wall of fame just before it burns. The crowd then turns menacingly toward a store across the way but stops when the store's Korean owner pleads that he, too, is "black." The next morning, Mookie and Sal have a reconciliation of sorts, and the film closes with a display of dueling quotations: one from Martin Luther King, Jr., expounding on the futility of violence, and the other from Malcolm X, arguing that the use of violence in selfdefense is justifiable and intelligent.

Do the Right Thing was both a critical and a commercial success. Lee created a compelling if somewhat surrealistic image of Brooklyn's Bedford-Stuyvesant neighborhood (where he filmed on location), and once again Ernest Dickerson's cinematography was riveting. Lee also drew a strong acting performance from Danny Aiello as Sal. Aiello was nominated for an Oscar for his performance, as was Lee for the film's screenplay. The film also made money, becoming Lee's most profitable venture up to that point.

Lee was also the subject of criticism for *Do the Right Thing*, however. He was criticized for making his Bedford-Stuyvesant block appear more like a stage set than a real urban street with real urban characters, for the film's absence of a clear story line, and for the contrived nature of the film's climax. Critics pointed out that police would not likely leave such a violent crowd unsupervised. Added to these aesthetic critiques were allegations of social irresponsibility.

Many observers asserted that Lee's film was dangerous because it seemed to encourage inner-city African Americans to look for violent solutions to their problems. For his part, Lee referred to the film's violent scenes as depicting an "uprising" rather than a riot.

Defenders of the film, including Lee himself, pointed out that Lee did not invent riots or the social conditions that fuel them. In addition, the film presents two sides of the issue: Malcolm X's statement is counterbalanced by King's. Moreover, it is not clear that the burning of Sal's pizzeria is an act of self-defense (Malcolm X's precondition for the intelligent use of violence). Buggin' Out is portrayed as silly and boorish; his cause is made to appear trivial, and the violence he inspires ends up being pointless. The film makes this last point by focusing on an elderly black woman during the riot scene; at first, she cheers the crowd on, but she later cries when she sees the results of the crowd's actions. The sympathetic treatment of Sal (partly a result of Aiello's performance) also tempers Lee's message. Finally, it is possible to see Mookie's breaking of the restaurant's window as an act of moderation, because it draws the crowd's attention away from Sal and his sons and substitutes damage to property for violence against people.

Significance *Do the Right Thing* confirmed Lee's unique combination of artfulness and box-office appeal. It also made him a controversial figure on matters of race, bringing his talent and ideas to a broader audience. The film's boxoffice and critical success had a major effect both on Lee's own career and on the prospects for other African American filmmakers in Hollywood.

In the wake of his third straight box-office success, Lee gained the opportunity to direct *Mo' Better Blues* (1990), about a jazz musician who learns the value of human commitments; *Jungle Fever* (1991), which concerns interracial sexual relations; and the biographical *Malcolm X* (1992). Although the first two of these films were successful, they earned Lee further criticism for his use of questionable plot structure and contrived conclusions.

With *Malcolm X*, Lee benefited from the powerful nature of his subject matter. Moreover, Lee was at last allowed a big Hollywood budget (about $35 million) to make a film on a theme many white Americans were likely to find threatening, and the result was an intense, well-focused film. Had *Do the Right Thing* not succeeded in establishing Lee's credentials as a major voice on racial issues as well as his box-office appeal, Lee would likely not have had the opportunity to direct

Malcolm X. Lee's success created strong pressure on Warner Bros. to use a black director to tell the story of Malcolm X's life.

The success of *Do the Right Thing* and Lee's other films also opened doors for other young African American filmmakers, such as Matty Rich (*Straight Out of Brooklyn*, 1991), Mario Van Peebles (*New Jack City*, 1991), and John Singleton (*Boyz n the Hood*, 1991).

These filmmakers did not imitate Lee's style, nor did they, by and large, show Lee's thematic range. They did, however, begin exploring black themes for black audiences with independence and individuality, and their films attracted substantial white audiences as well.

FILMS DIRECTED BY SPIKE LEE, 1983-2016

Released	Title
1983	*Joe's Bed-Stuy Barbershop: We Cut Heads*
1986	*She's Gotta Have It*
1988	*School Daze*
1989	*Do the Right Thing*
1990	*Mo' Better Blues*
1991	*Jungle Fever*
1992	*Malcolm X*
1994	*Crooklyn*
1995	*Clockers*
1996	*Girl 6*
1996	*Get on the Bus*
1997	*4 Little Girls (documentary)*
1998	*He Got Game*
1999	*Summer of Sam*
2000	*The Original Kings of Comedy (documentary)*
2000	*Bamboozled*
2002	*25th Hour*
2004	*She Hate Me*
2006	*Inside Man*
2008	*Miracle at St. Anna*
	Passing Strange
2009	*Kobe Doin' Work*
	Saint John of Las Vegas
2010	*If God Is Willing and da Creek Don't Rise*
2011	*You're Nobody 'til Somebody Kills You*
	Pariah
2012	*Red Hook Summer*
	Bad 25
2013	*Oldboy*
	Mike Tyson: Undisputed Truth
2014	*Da Sweet Blood of Jesus*
	Evolution of a Criminal
	Manos Sucias
	Katt Williams: Priceless: Afterlife
	Jerrod Carmichael: Love at the Store
2015	*Cronies*
	The Girl Is in Trouble
	Chi-Raq
2016	*Michael Jackson's Journey from Motown to Off the Wall*

Although modest about his influence on younger directors, Lee has noted that he sees himself as a pioneer; in his book *By Any Means Necessary: The Trials and Tribulations of the Making of Malcolm X* (1992), Lee likens himself to baseball star Jackie Robinson, whose uniform number Lee's character wears in *Do the Right Thing*.

Robinson was uniquely suited to the task of integrating professional baseball; Lee believes he was uniquely suited to the task of opening up Hollywood to a variety of black perspectives.

Lee has been a controversial figure, but his films and those of other young black directors have encouraged fresh thought about racial equality and racial harmony in the United States. Black audiences for such films have been drawn by the validation of their hopes and concerns; at the same time, white audiences have been challenged to respond to rather than ignore the feelings of black Americans. Most notable, perhaps, is the way in which such films have led white viewers to a greater understanding of the centrality of anger to the experience of black Americans.

Moreover, Lee demonstrated that appealing films could still be made without blockbuster budgets and special effects. He showed that artfulness and serious ideas are compatible with profitability, a lesson of value to directors and producers of any race.

—*Ira Smolensky*

See also: 1980's-1990's: Innovative Black Filmmakers Achieve Success; July, 1986: Rap Goes Platinum with Run-D.M.C.'s Raising Hell; Oct. 12, 1992: Columbus Day Debates Reflect Cultural Diversity.

WILDER BECOMES THE FIRST ELECTED BLACK GOVERNOR

November 7, 1989

Nearly 125 years after the end of the American Civil War, L. Douglas Wilder became the first African American in the United States to be elected to the position of state governor.

Locale: Virginia
Categories: Government and politics; social issues and reform

KEY FIGURES

L. Douglas Wilder (b. 1931), governor of Virginia, 1990-1994

J. Marshall Coleman (b. 1942), Republican candidate for governor of Virginia in the 1989 election

Gerald L. Baliles (b. 1940), governor of Virginia, 1986-1990

Charles S. Robb (b. 1939), U.S. senator from Virginia

SUMMARY OF EVENT

The 1989 contest for the governor's mansion in Virginia was destined to receive an unusual amount of attention both within the state and around the country. The election offered the possibility of producing the first elected black governor of a U.S. state in the former capital of the Confederacy. In addition, few other election contests of national importance took place in 1989 to attract the interest of the news media. Each of the candidates for the Virginia governorship spent more than $6 million in the general election campaign. History was made when, on November 7, 1989, Democrat L. Douglas Wilder, an African American, was elected governor of Virginia.

Wilder, the incumbent lieutenant governor received the Democratic Party's nomination without challenge. He had proven his ability to win a statewide election when he became lieutenant governor in 1985, demonstrating that he could attract white voters in a state where the electorate was 80 percent white. Wilder received the full support of the state Democratic Party and of outgoing governor Gerald L. Baliles, who could not run again because of Virginia's law limiting the governor to a single term. Wilder also received less-than-enthusiastic endorsement from U.S. senator Charles S. Robb, a popular former governor of Virginia. There was friction between Wilder and Robb, but Robb did support Wilder's candidacy.

J. Marshall Coleman, the Republican gubernatorial candidate, had scored a come-from-behind victory in a hotly contested and often acrimonious three-man race for his party's nomination. For the first time, state Republicans employed a primary election to choose their candidate, and the Coleman campaign was noteworthy for its strong negative content. Coleman had lost the 1981 gubernatorial election and was denied the

Republican nomination for lieutenant governor in 1985, but he was resurrected politically in 1989.

By the 1980's, the United States had witnessed an increasing number of successful African American candidates at the local and state legislative levels. Many of the nation's largest cities had elected black mayors, but the number of blacks in statewide office and at the national level remained low. At the time of Wilder's election, less than 2 percent of the nation's elective offices were held by African Americans, and most of those were in jurisdictions with a majority of black residents. Wilder's candidacy thus was seen as extremely important for the cause of civil rights in the United States, and Wilder himself was viewed as a model for other black candidates.

Wilder's campaign was not based on race; rather, the strategy was to portray Wilder as a moderate alternative to the extremely conservative Coleman. Although his politics were clearly more moderate than the positions favored by former presidential candidate Jesse Jackson, Wilder may have benefited from Jackson's experience.

Black candidates, who had often been dismissed by voters on the basis of their race, may have been taken more seriously after Jackson's campaigns for the Democratic presidential nomination in 1984 and, particularly, in 1988. The opponents of black candidates and the news media, however, still struggled with the issues surrounding the candidacies of African Americans. Heavy criticism of a black candidate could lead to charges of racism, and ignoring or emphasizing the race of a black candidate could be viewed as patronizing.

African Americans faced major electoral hurdles in 1989, not the least of which was the misleading nature of the findings of public opinion polls in black-white contests. Although carefully conducted public opinion polling usually returns reliable results, polls in elections in which a black candidate faced a white candidate tended to overestimate the strength of the black candidate by several percentage points. This phenomenon was evident in the Wilder election as well as in the New York City mayoral campaign of David Dinkins and the unsuccessful California gubernatorial campaign of Los Angeles mayor Tom Bradley. Experts speculated that these inaccuracies might have been caused by racism, by low turnout among black voters, by poll respondents' fears that they might appear racist if they endorsed the white candidate, or by respondents' attempts to offer what might be perceived as the "correct answer."

Although Wilder faced problems in his campaign related to his race, his candidacy also posed problems for his opponent. The race factor was virtually absent from the campaigns of both candidates. Coleman's campaign was relatively negative but was careful not even to allude to the question of race. The only exception to this came late in the campaign, when Coleman complained publicly that he was the victim of a media double standard in which Wilder was not seriously questioned regarding several ethics issues raised by Coleman. Coleman, conversely, was frequently questioned about his position on abortion. The implication was that Wilder was getting preferential treatment from the press because he was black.

For his part, Wilder was equally careful not to raise the race issue. He did discuss his background, but he chose to emphasize how far Virginia had come in matters of race. His attempt to run as a moderate also prevented him from running as a "black" candidate. In his television advertisements, Wilder was usually surrounded by whites. His issue emphasis was almost solely on his stand on abortion—he endorsed a woman's right to choose. His theme was summed up by his campaign slogan, "I trust the women of Virginia."

One of Wilder's most popular campaign advertisements used conservative rhetoric to express a prochoice position. In the advertisement, a narrator claimed that "Doug Wilder believes the government shouldn't interfere in your right to choose. He wants to keep politicians out of your personal life. Don't let Marshall Coleman take us back." This strategy effectively made Wilder look at least moderate, if not conservative, and it may well have been a subtle reference to the overt racism of Virginia's past.

Wilder avoided some more controversial issues. For example, his campaign included no discussion of funding abortions for the poor. Wilder also chose not to associate himself with Jesse Jackson or Molly Yard, president of the National Organization for Women, emphasizing that he had not requested any help from outside the state.

Wilder's qualifications and experience were never questioned. The grandson of slaves, Wilder grew up in a middle-class family in segregated Richmond. He excelled in the segregated schools, and he graduated from Virginia Union College in Richmond. After winning a Bronze Star for his actions in the armed services during the Korean War, he attended law school at Howard University.

In 1959, Wilder became the only African American to pass the Virginia bar exam, and he soon opened his own law practice. Wilder rose rapidly within his profession, and in 1969 he entered politics, winning a seat in the Virginia state senate when two white candidates split the white vote, allowing Wilder to win by a narrow margin. He worked diligently and established a reputation as a powerful individual in Virginia politics. Initially a liberal, Wilder moderated his positions and issues over time. By 1985, he was ready to run for the office of lieutenant governor, and some clever political maneuvering placed him on the Democratic ticket with Gerald Baliles. Successful grassroots campaigning enabled him to win that election and position himself for the gubernatorial race in 1989. With his election as lieutenant governor, Wilder became only the second black elected to a major statewide office since Reconstruction. (Republican Edward W. Brooke of Massachusetts was the first with his election to the U.S. Senate in 1966. P. B. S. Pinchback was acting governor of Louisiana for forty-three days in 1873, but he was not elected to that position.)

On November 7, 1989, Wilder eked out a narrow victory over Coleman, capturing 50.1 percent of the votes cast. Nearly 1.8 million Virginians voted in the gubernatorial contest, which set records both for the total of voters and for the 66.5 percent of registered voters who cast ballots. Although his margin of victory was considerably narrower than those of the Democratic nominees for the Virginia offices of lieutenant governor and attorney general, Wilder had once again fooled the political pundits and accomplished what seemed to be impossible. Many experts attributed his victory to heavy turnout among black voters and his popularity among women, but it should be remembered that Wilder took more than 40 percent of the votes cast by whites and more than 40 percent of the votes cast by men.

SIGNIFICANCE

The impacts of Wilder's election were felt in three specific areas: the national stature and reputation of Wilder himself, the nation's and the state's view of Virginia, and the long-term effects on black candidates nationwide.

Wilder's election propelled him into the national spotlight. Many came to view him as a national spokesperson for African Americans and as a viable candidate for the 1992 Democratic presidential nomination. Wilder welcomed this notoriety and spent much of his time preparing and delivering speeches around the country. Perceptions of Virginia also changed virtually overnight. The state had changed dramatically in the previous two decades, but the changes had gone largely unnoticed.

An urbanized corridor running from northern Virginia through Richmond into Tidewater produced more than 60 percent of the voters. Many of these voters had migrated to Virginia, many from the North, and they voted disproportionately for Wilder. The rural areas of Virginia, which had dominated the state's politics, now accounted for less than one-third of the state's votes. These major demographic changes made Virginia politically more like a Middle Atlantic state than a southern state. In comparison with the nation as a whole, Virginia politics would still be considered conservative, but the state's political leanings had been modified considerably in twenty years.

The lessons of Wilder's election for other black candidates were mixed. Wilder's victory showed that a black willing to run as a mainstream, moderate, nonthreatening candidate could win a statewide election. This contrasted sharply with the liberal approach taken by Jesse Jackson. Jackson's philosophy was successful within the Democratic Party, where liberals wielded considerable power, but Wilder's strategy seemed much more likely to be successful in general elections.

Another lesson drawn from the election was that the journey for a minority candidate was still a long and difficult one. Wilder had many advantages in the campaign: He was the heir apparent to two popular Democratic administrations, he won the party's nomination unopposed, and he was supported by a united party. In addition, his campaign was well financed. Wilder ran a strategic campaign, played the issues correctly, and was opposed by a relatively weak opponent. Despite all these advantages, he won by an extremely narrow margin.

Some observers saw Wilder's win, combined with the election of David Dinkins as the first black mayor of New York City, as the vanguard of more political successes by blacks. Andrew Young's losing campaign for the governorship of Georgia the following year caused much of that optimism to disappear, however.

The long-term effects of the Wilder victory on Virginia politics and public policy are difficult to assess. By the beginning of the twenty-first century there were still relatively few black politicians in the state, and state policy making remained largely unchanged. Governor Wilder was prevented from proposing any governmental initiatives by a continuing budget crisis that allowed him to show his fiscal conservative stripes through a steadfast refusal to raise taxes and an insistence on serious budget cuts. The consequences of these actions were a decline in Wilder's popularity within the state and a rise in his stock nationally. After he completed his term as governor, Wilder remained in the public eye and decided to call himself an independent. He became the mayor of Richmond, Virginia, in 2005, after winning that city's first ever mayor-at-large election by a landslide.

—Harry L. Wilson

HAWKINS MURDER

August 23, 1989

The Yusuf Hawkins murder was racially motivated and the tragedy came to symbolize racial divisions that lay under the surface of New York City.

The Event: Killing of a sixteen-year-old African American boy by young Italian Americans
Place: Brooklyn, New York

Yusuf Hawkins, a sixteen-year-old African American, was confronted and killed by a group of Italian American young men in the predominantly white Bensonhurst section of Brooklyn, New York, on August 23, 1989. His murder was clearly racially motivated and served as a sign of the deep-seated animosities and racial divisions that existed in New York City.

Hawkins and three African American friends had traveled to Bensonhurst from their home in East New York to look at a used car for sale. They were confronted by a group of white youths with baseball bats led by Keith Mondello, Joseph Fama, and others. Hawkins was trapped by the group when four shots from a .32-caliber automatic pistol were fired. Hawkins was hit once in the hand and twice in the chest and died shortly after.

Police reported that the white youths mistakenly believed that Hawkins and his companions were friends of a white neighborhood girl, Gina Feliciano. Feliciano, who once dated Mondello, had reportedly begun a series of friendships with African American and Hispanic men. The night that Hawkins was killed, Mondello was reportedly told either by Feliciano or someone else that a group of her black and Hispanic friends would arrive with bats to beat up him and his friends.

Eight men were charged in the attack. The eighteen-yearold Fama was the only one convicted of

Mural of Yusef Hawkins in Bedford-Stuyvesant, Brooklyn; photo taken in 2012, by Blacren

second-degree murder and sentenced to the maximum sentence on June 11, 1990. The nineteen-year-old Mondello was convicted of riot, unlawful imprisonment, discrimination, menacing, and criminal possession of a weapon and sentenced on June 11, 1990, to five and one-third to sixteen years in prison. Joseph Serrano, John Vento, and Pasquale Raucci were convicted on lesser charges. Three others were acquitted of all charges.

—Erica Childs

See also: Civil rights worker murders; Crown Heights conflicts

EDMONSON V. LEESVILLE CONCRETE COMPANY

JUNE 3, 1991

The Supreme Court extended its ruling that potential jurors could not be peremptorily excluded on the basis of race from criminal trials to include civil trials.

The Case: U.S. Supreme Court ruling on jury composition

Thaddeus Edmonson, an African American construction worker, sued his employer, the Leesville Concrete Company, in 1988, claiming compensation for injuries suffered in a workplace accident. Edmonson invoked his right to a trial by jury. During the pretrial examination of potential jurors, the company's lawyers used their peremptory challenges to excuse two of the three black members of the panel. Edmonson asked the district court to require the company to provide a race-neutral explanation of the dismissals of the black panelists. Under *Batson v. Kentucky* (1986), racial motivation for juror challenges was held unconstitutional in criminal cases. In *Batson*, the U.S. Supreme Court had reasoned that the use of race as a criterion in jury challenges by the prosecution violates the equal protection clause of the U.S. Constitution. Edmonson's case presented the issue of whether such dismissals are improper in civil cases. The trial court denied Edmonson's request and, after conflicting decisions in the court of appeals, he appealed to the Supreme Court.

In 1991, Justice Anthony Kennedy wrote for the Court in a 6–3 decision holding that racially based juror challenges are unconstitutional even in civil cases. Because the juror challenges use the power of the government to select jury members, the discrimination becomes "state action" even though invoked by a private litigant. All state action must be consistent with constitutional rules forbidding racial discrimination.

Justice Sandra Day O'Connor dissented, arguing that only governmental discrimination is forbidden by the equal protection clause and that the act of Leesville Concrete's counsel was not state action.

—*Robert Jacobs*

See also: *Batson v. Kentucky*; *Moore v. Dempsey*; *Norris v. Alabama*; *Powers v. Ohio*; Strauder v. West Virginia; Williams v. Mississippi.

BUSH NOMINATES SECOND AFRICAN AMERICAN TO THE SUPREME COURT

July 1, 1991

When Thurgood Marshall, the nation's first African American Supreme Court justice, retired in 1991, President George H. W. Bush nominated another black judge, Clarence Thomas, to replace Marshall. Thomas's confirmation hearings, contentious from the start, became truly sensational when Thomas was accused of sexual harassment by Anita Hill, a law professor who had previously worked for Thomas.

Locale: Washington, D.C.
Categories: Organizations and institutions; government and politics

KEY FIGURES

Clarence Thomas (b. 1948), associate justice of the United States beginning in 1991
George H. W. Bush (b. 1924), president of the United States, 1989-1993

Thurgood Marshall (1908-1993), first African American to serve as associate justice of the United States, 1967-1991
Anita Hill (b. 1956), law professor who worked for Clarence Thomas at the Equal Employment Opportunity Commission

SUMMARY OF EVENT

Thurgood Marshall was the first African American to serve as a justice on the U.S. Supreme Court. At the time of his appointment in 1967, he was a renowned advocate for civil rights. As counsel for the National Association for the Advancement of Colored People (NAACP), Marshall had argued thirty-two civil rights cases before the Supreme Court, winning twenty-nine, including the landmark school desegregation case, *Brown v. Board of Education of Topeka, Kansas* (1954). He had been a federal appeals court judge and U.S. solicitor general. He was known for his concern for racial equality and the rights of the criminally accused. When Marshall retired from the Supreme Court in 1991, President George H. W. Bush, a Republican, was under intense political pressure to replace Marshall with another African American. On July 1, 1991, President Bush nominated Clarence Thomas, an African American, for Marshall's seat on the Court. Thomas was as conservative as Marshall had been liberal.

In 1987, President Ronald Reagan had nominated Robert H. Bork to the Supreme Court. Bork, like Thomas, was known to have a conservative judicial philosophy. Acrimonious hearings before the Senate Judiciary Committee culminated in the Senate's rejection of Bork's nomination by a vote of fifty-eight to forty-two. The approach taken by Bork's opponents to attack him personally led to the coining of the term "to bork," which is defined in the *Oxford English Dictionary* as follows: "To defame or vilify (a person) systematically, esp. in the mass media, usually with the aim of preventing his or her appointment to public office." Four years later, abortion rights activists and other liberal interest groups mobilized for the "borking" of Clarence Thomas. They attacked on two fronts, emphasizing Thomas's purported lack of qualifications and his ultraconservative judicial philosophy.

Announcing the appointment, President Bush called Thomas "the best person for this position." Critics of the nomination pointed out Thomas's slight judicial experience, only a year and four months on the U.S. Court of Appeals for the District of Columbia Circuit. His other experience included eight years as chairman of the Equal Employment Opportunity Commission (EEOC). Thurgood Marshall, by comparison, had authored ninety-eight majority decisions in his four years on the U.S. Court of Appeals for the Second Circuit. Thomas's supporters countered that many Supreme Court justices had little or no judicial experience before they were named to the Court, including such highly esteemed justices as Joseph Story, Earl Warren, William H. Rehnquist, Felix Frankfurter, and Louis D. Brandeis. At the heart of the confirmation controversy, however, were Thomas's views on such contentious issues as abortion rights, affirmative action, and the constitutional role of the Supreme Court vis-à-vis the legislative and executive branches of the U.S. government.

Clarence Thomas was born in 1948 in the small town of Pin Point, Georgia. He was raised by his grandparents, attended Catholic schools, and graduated from Holy Cross College in 1971 and Yale Law School in 1974. During his confirmation hearings, Thomas explained how the values imparted to him by his grandparents and the nuns who taught him led him to believe that hard work and the overcoming of obstacles, rather than preferential treatment based on race, would lead to a better life for black Americans. He expressed his beliefs that affirmative action had been of greatest benefit to middleclass rather than poor blacks and that government entitlements create a cycle of dependence and poverty, ultimately doing more harm than good for the poor. Thomas's detractors saw him as a beneficiary of affirmative action who was hypocritically attempting to deny the same help to others.

Thomas's confirmation hearings before the Senate Judiciary Committee began on September 10, 1991. The first attack on Thomas targeted his affinity for "natural law." Some senators worried that such a belief might lead Thomas to subordinate constitutional principles to principles of dubious provenance, such as the notion that an unborn child has the rights of persons, a position that could lead to the overturning of abortion rights. Thomas explained that he viewed certain principles of natural law—such as equality and limited government with the consent of the governed—as guides for how properly to interpret the U.S. Constitution, so as to guard against both run amok majorities and run-amok judges.

Thomas was asked numerous times for his views on abortion, which he resisted providing. He claimed that he had never "debated" the 1973 abortion case *Roe v. Wade.* This response was met with skepticism, and Thomas lost some credibility that he would need when the hearings soon took a dramatic turn.

The Judiciary Committee sent the nomination to the full Senate without a recommendation for confirmation. The Senate vote was originally scheduled for October 8, but on October 6, the existence of sensational allegations of sexual impropriety against the nominee were leaked to the press. Thomas requested a delay so that the Judiciary Committee would have time to investigate the charges before the Senate voted. On October 11, the hearings reopened, with the public's attention firmly riveted by the sensational allegations.

The accuser was Anita Hill, a law professor at the University of Oklahoma who had worked for Thomas in the past, first at the U.S. Department of Education and later at the EEOC, when Thomas became the commission's chair. Thomas testified first, making a statement in which he categorically denied Hill's allegations. Hill then testified. She related that when she and Thomas worked together at the Department of Education, Thomas had repeatedly asked her out on dates;

she further stated that in workplace conversations he had described acts he had seen in pornographic films and that he had bragged about his sexual prowess. Hill admitted that when Thomas left the Department of Education to take the EEOC job, she agreed to go with him. That admission cost Hill some credibility, as many observers wondered why someone who had been treated so shabbily would agree to accompany her harasser to another job.

Later that day, Thomas gave a second, highly emotional and dramatic statement in which he described the proceedings as a "high-tech lynching for uppity blacks who in any way deign to think for themselves." Witnesses were then brought in to corroborate both Thomas's and Hill's testimony, but ultimately the Judiciary Committee concluded its hearings without making a determination on the charges. On October 15, 1991, the Senate voted to confirm Thomas as an associate justice of the United States by a vote of fifty-two to forty-eight, the slimmest margin in history.

SIGNIFICANCE

Public opinion at the time of Thomas's confirmation hearings was as closely divided as the Senate vote, and debates about who was telling the truth continued for years afterward. Some observers vilified Thomas as an Uncle Tom, a race traitor who served his (conservative) white masters. Some were embarrassed that Thomas had been portrayed in the mass media as the negative stereotype of the black man who could not control his sexual appetites. Thomas's defenders saw him as a latter-day Booker T. Washington, a man who had pulled himself up out of poverty by his own bootstraps and who believed that progress for blacks would come from hard work and the self-esteem that one earns by overcoming obstacles, rather than from special treatment or government handouts.

Some saw Anita Hill as a feminist heroine who struck a blow against the sexual harassment of women. Others saw her as a liar who was simply determined to destroy Clarence Thomas for personal reasons or who, for political reasons, was a conspirator in the borking of a conservative nominee who happened to be black.

The Thomas hearings served to increase public awareness of the problem of sexual harassment in the workplace, and in subsequent years, additional scandals arose involving accusations of unwanted sexual advances by public figures. Senator Robert Packwood of Oregon was forced to resign in 1995 following complaints from several female employees, and President

Judge Thomas Responds

At the evening session of the hearing of the Senate Judiciary Committee on the nomination of Clarence Thomas to the U.S. Supreme Court on October 11, 1991, Thomas lashed out after testimony was presented against him by Anita Hill, a former employee:

Senator, I would like to start by saying unequivocally, uncategorically, that I deny each and every single allegation against me today that suggested in any way that I had conversations of a sexual nature or about pornographic material with Anita Hill, that I ever attempted to date her, that I ever had any personal sexual interest in her, or that I in any way ever harassed her.

A second, and I think more important point, I think that this today is a travesty. I think that it is disgusting. I think that this hearing should never occur in America. This is a case in which this sleaze, this dirt, was searched for by staffers of members of this committee, was then leaked to the media, and this committee and this body validated it and displayed it at prime time over our entire nation. How would any member on this committee, any person in this room, or any person in this country, would like sleaze said about him or her in this fashion? Or this dirt dredged up and this gossip and these lies displayed in this manner? How would any person like it?

The Supreme Court is not worth it. No job is worth it. I'm not here for that. I'm here for my name, my family, my life and my integrity. I think something is dreadfully wrong with this country when any person, any person in this free country would be subjected to this.

This is not a closed room. There was an FBI investigation. This is not an opportunity to talk about difficult matters privately or in a closed environment.

This is a circus. It's a national disgrace. And from my standpoint as a black American, as far as I'm concerned, it is a high-tech lynching for uppity blacks who in any way deign to think for themselves, to do for themselves, to have different ideas, and it is a message that unless you kowtow to an old order, this is what will happen to you.

You will be lynched, destroyed, caricatured by a committee of the U.S. Senate rather than hung from a tree.

Bill Clinton was accused of sexual impropriety by Paula Jones and others.

Before Hill's accusations added high drama to the proceedings, Thomas's confirmation hearings had already been contentious. After the Thomas nomination battle, it appeared that presidents had learned that their Supreme Court nominees would be more likely to be confirmed if the nominees were not perceived as ideologically extreme. Nominees appeared to have learned, following the examples of Bork and Thomas, that their confirmation would be more likely if they could avoid giving any indication of how they might vote on controversial issues.

—*Howard C. Ellis*

CROWN HEIGHTS CONFLICTS

August, 1991

The disturbances led to investigations at both the state and national levels. The Justice Department also conducted investigations of possible civil rights violations.

The Event: Racial unrest between Hasidic Jews and their immigrant neighbors
Place: Brooklyn, New York

Crown Heights, a racially mixed section of Brooklyn, New York, began to experience civil unrest in the late 1980's. Many of the residents are poor black immigrants from Caribbean countries and Lubavitchers. The latter are Orthodox (Hasidic) Jews who maintain a strong religious identity that is reflected in their dress and their insularity. These groups had been subjected to stereotyping and victimized by discrimination, from both within and without the Crown Heights community. African American leaders charged that the Lubavitchers received better treatment from local authorities than that accorded black residents, and Hasidic leaders countered that black anti-Semitism made Lubavitchers victims of street crimes and subject to continual harassment.

TRIGGERING THE VIOLENCE

The racial unrest erupted into full-scale rioting in the summer of 1991, on the heels of the accidental killing of a seven-year-old Guyanese American youth named Gavin Cato. On the evening of August 19, a car carrying the Lubavitcher Grand Rebbe and Menachem Schneerson, a Hasidic spiritual leader, ran a red light at the intersection of President Street and Utica Avenue, striking and killing Cato and injuring his cousin, Angela. As a crowd gathered at the scene, a private Jewish ambulance whisked away the Hasidic driver, Yosef Lifsh, and his two passengers. Their departure spurred an angry reaction, leading, three hours later, to the fatal stabbing of Yankel Rosenbaum, a visiting Hasidic professor from Australia, and the arrest of his alleged attacker, a sixteen-year-old Trinidadian American and Brooklyn resident, Lemrick Nelson, Jr.

In the predawn hours of August 20, after Rosenbaum's death at Kings County Hospital, protests escalated into mob violence, with African Americans and Hasidic Jews fighting with words, stones, and bottles, ignoring police efforts to stop the rioting. The violence continued through the next two days, fed by the rumor (later shown to be true) that the Hasidic driver, Lifsh, had left on a plane bound for Israel. Black leaders, including the Reverend Al Sharpton and Alton Maddox, demanded the arrest and return of Lifsh, and their followers rebuffed the efforts of New York mayor David Dinkins and police commissioner Lee Brown to restore peace, especially after learning that Nelson had been charged with second-degree murder in Rosenbaum's death. By August 24, rioting finally gave way to protest marches and an uneasy peace maintained by auxiliary police units that had been sent into Crown Heights to restore order.

In the months following the demonstrations, both groups complained that the police and city officials did little to solve the community's problems. In September, the Brooklyn grand jury refused to indict Lifsh in the death of Cato, angering the black citizens and their leaders. More unrest followed in October, 1992, when Nelson was acquitted of all charges in Rosenbaum's death. The Hasidic Jews protested and within a month filed a classaction suit against the city government on the grounds of unfair treatment in the 1991 riots.

The disturbances led to investigations at both the state and national levels. One major New York report issued in July, 1993, by Richard Girgenti, state director of criminal justice, was highly critical of both Mayor Dinkins and Commissioner Brown. The report, forwarded to the U.S.

Attorney General, also led to ongoing Justice Department investigations of possible civil rights violations.

—John W. Fiero

See also: Black Jews; "Black Manifesto"; Hawkins murder; Jews and African Americans

HARLINS MURDER

March 16, 1991

The verdict in this case angered African Americans in Los Angeles and made Korean businesses primary targets for theft and vandalism by African Americans.

The Event: Fatal shooting of a fifteen-year-old African American girl by a Korean business owner
Place: Los Angeles, California

After a dispute over a $1.79 bottle of orange juice, fifteen-year-old Latasha Harlins was shot and killed at the Empire Liquor Market Deli in South Central Los Angeles on March 16, 1991. A security camera recorded the African American teenager being shot in the back of the head by the market owner. The merchant, Soon Ja Du, a forty-nine-year-old Korean woman, was charged with murder. Because the shooting occurred only thirteen days after African American Rodney King was beaten by Los Angeles police, it aggravated racial and ethnic tensions in Los Angeles.

On March 26, 1991, Ja Du was found guilty of voluntary manslaughter, but Judge Karlan granted the defendant probation. This decision angered African Americans in Los Angeles and made Korean businesses primary targets for theft and vandalism by African Americans. In addition, the decision escalated the number of conflicts between African American and Asian youth in Los Angeles. Bitter feelings generated by the Harlins and Rodney King verdicts were unleashed during the Los Angeles riots of 1992.

—Alvin K. Benson

See also: Civil rights worker murders; King beating case; Koreans and African Americans; Los Angeles riots

POWERS V. OHIO

April 1, 1991

The Supreme Court held that prosecutors cannot use peremptory challenges to exclude African Americans from juries in criminal trials.

The Case: U.S. Supreme Court ruling on race discrimination and jury composition

Justice Anthony M. Kennedy wrote the opinion for the 7-2 majority, holding that prosecutors cannot attempt to pack the jury with jurors racially satisfactory to themselves by using peremptory challenges in jury selection in criminal cases. Kennedy held that this was true even if the accused and the excluded juror were of the same race. The past practice of allowing the use of peremptory challenges affected not only the defendant's right to a fair trial but also the excluded juror's right to participate in the administration of justice. The defendant further was entitled to raise the excluded juror's right at trial. Dissenting, Justice Antonin Scalia argued that this decision was illogical, freeing a guilty defendant based on the fact that some other person's abstract right to participate in the judicial process was denied.

—Richard L. Wilson

See also: *Batson v. Kentucky; Edmonson v. Leesville Concrete Company; Moore v. Dempsey; Norris v. Alabama; Strauder v. West Virginia; Williams v. Mississippi*

THOMAS-HILL HEARINGS

October, 1991

The hearings sparked intense national debate over issues of racism, sexism, and political gamesmanship. The public humiliation suffered by both Clarence Hill and Anita Thomas opened debate on the nature and fairness of the Senate confirmation process.

The Event: Confirmation hearings of Supreme Court nominee Clarence Thomas, in which Anita Hill made charges of sexual harassment against Thomas

After the resignation of Supreme Court associate justice Thurgood Marshall, the first African American to serve on the Court, President George Bush sought to fill the vacancy with another African American. Marshall, however, had been a leading advocate of the Civil Rights movement and the last staunchly liberal Supreme Court justice from the Earl Warren court era. Bush's nominee, Clarence Thomas, was his predecessor's political and philosophical opposite.

A 1974 Yale Law School graduate, Thomas possessed a distinguished resume, including the chairmanship of the Equal Employment Opportunity Commission (EEOC) from 1982 to 1990and service as a judge on the United States Court of Appeals for the District of Columbia Circuit from 1990 to 1991 . He was also one of a number of black intellectuals who challenged the merits of affirmative action. Critics, such as Nan Aaron--the founder and President of Alliance for Justice-- and members of the congress, respectively, charged that his tenure at the EEOC had been marked by a reluctance to pursue civil rights complaints, and his judicial record demonstrated his willingness to throw out many of the liberal decisions of the earlier Supreme Court. These were political concerns, however, in a political climate that favored Thomas's views, and no charge of unethical conduct stood up under investigation.

In 1991, Anita Hill, a law professor at the University of Oklahoma and former aide to Judge Thomas at United States Department of Education and EEOC, submitted a confidential statement to the Senate Judiciary Committee, claiming Thomas sexually harassed her when she worked under him ten years earlier. The committee did not pursue the allegations after the FBI investigated the claims and came up with an " inconclusive" report. However, Hill was summoned to testify on live television watched by 20 million people before the

Clarence Thomas, Associate Justice of the Supreme Court of the United States by Steve Petteway

unable to prevent the degeneration of the televised proceedings into a quasi-judicial brawl.

Thomas's characterization of the second hearing as a "high-tech lynching" provoked the greatest reaction from the African American community, outraging many African Americans with the implication that African Americans themselves and their liberal white allies were figuratively lynching, in Thomas' words, an "uppity" black because of his conservativism. The viciousness of the attacks on Hill, for feminists, seemed to illustrate perfectly the very reason most victims of sexual harassment do not bring charges against their harassers.

Thomas, though confirmed, began his service on the Supreme Court tainted by Hill's accusation. Judiciary hearings operate without standards of evidence or the rules that govern court proceedings. Biden's committee could not determine the truth of the matter but could merely vote based on their impression of Thomas's character and the political desirability of seating him on the Court.

—*Janet Alice Long*

See also: Marshall's appointment to the Supreme Court; Politics and government

U.S. CONGRESS STRENGTHENS EQUAL OPPORTUNITY LAWS

November 7, 1991

With passage of the Civil Rights Act of 1991, Congress restored equal opportunity law to its status before 1989, the year in which several U.S. Supreme Court decisions weakened two decades of legal precedents.

Also known as: Civil Rights Act of 1991; U.S. Statutes at Large 105 Stat. 1071; Public Law 102-166

Locale: Washington, D.C.

Categories: Civil rights and liberties; laws, acts, and legal history

KEY FIGURES

George H. W. Bush (b. 1924), president of the United States, 1989-1993

John Danforth (b. 1936), U.S. senator from Missouri

Ted Kennedy (b. 1932), U.S. senator from Massachusetts

SUMMARY OF EVENT

The Civil Rights Act of 1991 has been described as among the most sweeping civil rights laws to be passed by Congress. In response to several adverse decisions by the U.S. Supreme Court, Senators Ted Kennedy, a Democrat, and John Danforth, a Republican, jointly sponsored the Civil Rights Act of 1991, which was drafted with the objective of overturning these decisions. President George H. W. Bush, who had vetoed a similar bill in 1990, signed the bill into law in 1991. Through congressional hearings, Congress concluded that additional remedies under federal law were needed to deter unlawful harassment and intentional discrimination in the workplace; decisions of the U.S. Supreme Court had weakened the effectiveness of federal civil rights protection; and legislation was necessary to provide additional protection against unlawful discrimination in employment. The expressed purpose of the Civil Rights Act of 1991 was to restore the state of discrimination law to what it had been before 1989, the year in which a conservative Supreme Court issued several decisions that seriously threatened the enforceability of

equal opportunity laws. The act further expanded the scope of coverage of relevant civil rights statutes to include individuals or plaintiffs who sued under the Age Discrimination Act (ADA) or the Rehabilitation Act of 1973, and granted coverage to federal employees of Congress and employees of U.S. companies located in foreign countries. Title VII of the Civil Rights Act of 1964 had made it unlawful to discriminate in employment because of race, ethnicity, color, sex, or religion. The primary issue facing judicial bodies empowered to adjudicate claims of discrimination was to define what employment practices violated Title VII and other antidiscrimination laws. Traditionally, employers screened potential employees by the use of general intelligence and aptitude tests, wordof- mouth recruiting, and other subjective criteria that disproportionately excluded minorities from employment and promotion or had disparate impacts on their possibilities of employment or promotion.

In *Griggs v. Duke Power Company* (1971), which is considered the most important decision in the evolution of equal employment opportunity law, the Supreme Court had articulated the major principle that invalidated general intelligence tests and other criteria that had the effect of excluding minorities, regardless of the intent of the employer. The Court stated that if any criteria had a disparate impact on the protected group, the criteria were unlawful and could be sustained only if they were related to the job and necessary for business. The burden of proof to rebut the claim shifted to the employer once the possibility of discrimination had been shown through statistical or other evidence.

In 1989, the Supreme Court issued several decisions that reversed the *Griggs* burden-of-proof standard and several other major legal principles governing unlawful discrimination. In *Wards Cove Packing Company v. Atonio*, the Supreme Court changed the *Griggs* standard by holding that employees not only must show that they were disparately and discriminatorily affected but also must prove that the employer could have employed alternate ways with less disparate impact. In *Price Waterhouse v. Hopkins*, the Court held that even after the employer has been found guilty of unlawful discrimination, it could still escape liability by showing that the employee would have been dismissed or treated differently for another nondiscriminatory reason. These changes made it significantly more difficult for plaintiffs to prevail in suits.

Significance

The Civil Rights Act of 1991 restored the *Griggs* principle. It also reversed the *Price Waterhouse* decision, stipulating that an unlawful practice is established when the complaining party demonstrates that race, color, religion, or national origin was a motivating factor for any employment practice, even though other factors also motivated the decision.

In *Patterson v. McLean Credit Union* (1989) the Supreme Court severely limited section 1981 of the Civil Rights Act of 1866 when it held that the act covered only unlawful discrimination with regard to race and national origin at the time of hiring. Acts of discrimination that occurred after hiring were no longer illegal under the Civil Rights Act of 1866. The Civil Rights Act of 1991 reversed this decision by prohibiting pre- and postemployment discrimination.

In *Lorance v. AT&T Technologies* (1989) the Supreme Court upheld the dismissal of discrimination charges by female employees who charged that the implementation of a new seniority system discriminated against them. This decision established the principle that although women had been adversely affected by a new seniority policy, their complaint was barred because the statute of limitations had expired. The Supreme Court ruled that the timing began at the time of the policy change and not when the women became aware of the discriminatory effects of the policy. This reasoning was criticized on the grounds that an individual often may not know the discriminatory impact of the policy change until long after the statute of limitations for filing has passed. The Civil Rights Act of 1991 restored the legal principle that the statute of limitations begins when the individual becomes aware of the discrimination. Many municipalities have entered into consent decrees that grant relief to minority employees to avoid lengthy and costly litigations. Such consent decrees may adversely affect the interests of white male employees. However, all parties affected by the decree are notified and given an opportunity to intervene to protect the interests of their members. Once the consent decree

has been approved by the court, it cannot be challenged in the future.

In *Martin v. Wilks* (1989) the Supreme Court established a new principle. It allowed new white firefighters who were not a party to the original consent decree and judgment to reopen the decision. Had this new principle been allowed to stand, it would have threatened the validity of hundreds of consent decrees in the United States. The Civil Rights Act of 1991 reversed this decision. The act precluded any later challenge by a present employee, former employee, or applicant to a consent decree granting affirmative rights to minority employees. Several major differences existed between section 1981 of the Civil Rights Act of 1866 and other equal opportunity laws with respect to remedies available to plaintiffs. Whereas a plaintiff had a right to a jury trial and compensatory and punitive damages under section 1981 of the 1866 act, plaintiffs who sued under Title VII, the ADA, and the Rehabilitation Act had no right to a jury trial and could only seek compensatory damages. The Civil Rights Acts of 1991 expanded these rights accorded to plaintiffs under section 1981 to plaintiffs who were subjected to intentional discrimination under Title VII, the ADA, and the Rehabilitation Act.

Another notable limitation in the equal opportunity law was the absence of protection from discrimination for federal employees and U.S. citizens working in U.S. firms overseas. The Civil Rights Act of 1991 extended the right to sue to federal employees in the legislative and executive branches under Title VII, ADA, and the Rehabilitation Act. One exception was made to the definition of unlawful practices: that party affiliation and political compatibility may not be attacked as unfair employment practices. Furthermore, the act extended coverage to U.S. employees employed in foreign lands by U.S. firms. Civil service examinations are required for most jobs and promotions in the public sector. Applicants are supposed to be chosen based on competitive scores earned. It has been charged, however, that these tests are biased in favor of white men in particular and white applicants and employees in general. Generally, a higher proportion of whites will score higher than members of minority groups. To ensure that a larger number of minorities will be hired and promoted, the scores are adjusted for minorities such that some minorities with lower scores occasionally may be selected over whites with higher scores. This adjustment of test scores, which is referred to as race norming, emerged as a contentious issue in the United States. The Civil Rights Act of 1991 expressly prohibits compensatory adjustments to test scores in employment based upon race or other protected characteristics.

—Richard Hudson

See also: U.S. Supreme Court Bans Discrimination in Hiring; U.S. Congress Mandates Equal Employment Opportunity; U.S. Congress Bans Literacy Tests for Voting; U.S. Supreme Court Rules on Affirmative Action Programs; U.S. Supreme Court Upholds Goals, Not Quotas, to Remedy Discrimination.

KING BEATING CASE

1991-1994

Violent race riots occurred after a California court acquitted the police officers involved in the Rodney King beating. The riots affected areas throughout Los Angeles but particularly devastated parts of impoverished South Central Los Angeles.

The Event: Arrest and beating by police of Rodney King, a black man, that sparked a major investigation of police brutality in Los Angeles

Following a high-speed chase along a Los Angeles highway that ended just after midnight on March 3, 1991, California Highway Patrol officers Timothy Singer and Melanie Singer stopped driver Rodney Glen King and his two passengers, Bryant Allen and Freddie Helms, for questioning. More than twenty Los Angeles Police Department (LAPD) officers soon arrived on the scene in Los Angeles's Lake View Terrace neighborhood. Police sergeant Stacey Koon, assisted by officers Theodore Briseno, Laurence Powell, and Timothy Wind, took over the investigation. The police quickly subdued and handcuffed Allen and Helms without incident. Their encounter with King, however, caused a controversy with far-reaching legal and social consequences.

KING'S ARREST

According to the four white police officers who arrested King, a black man, King refused at first to leave the car and then resisted arrest with such vigor that the officers considered it necessary to apply two jolts from a Taser electric stun gun, fifty-six blows with aluminum batons, and six kicks (primarily from Briseno) to subdue King before they successfully handcuffed and cordcuffed King to restrain his arms and legs. The event probably would have gone unnoticed had not George Holliday, an amateur cameraman who witnessed the incident, videotaped the arrest and sold the tape to a local television station news program. The videotape became the crucial piece of evidence that the state of California used to charge the four LAPD arresting officers with criminal assault and that a federal grand jury subsequently used to charge the officers with civil rights violations.

Broadcast of Holliday's tape on national news programs elicited several responses from the LAPD. On March 6, 1991, the LAPD released King from custody and admitted that officers failed to prove that King had resisted arrest. On March 7, Los Angeles police chief Daryl Gates announced that he would investigate King's arrest and, if the investigation warranted it, would pursue criminal assault charges against the arresting officers. On March 14, a Los Angeles County grand jury indicted Sergeant Koon and officers Briseno, Powell, and Wind for criminal assault, and they subsequently pleaded not guilty.

INVESTIGATION OF POLICE BRUTALITY

Overwhelming public sympathy for King following the national broadcast of Holliday's videotape prompted Los Angeles mayor Thomas Bradley to investigate charges that instances of police brutality motivated by racism were commonplace during LAPD arrest operations. On April 1, 1991, Mayor Bradley appointed a nonpartisan commission, headed by Warren Christopher (who had formerly served as President Jimmy Carter's deputy secretary of state), to study the LAPD's past record of complaints regarding police misconduct. On April 2, Mayor Bradley called on Police Chief Gates, who had served on the LAPD since 1949 and had been police chief since 1978, to resign. In May, the LAPD suspended Sergeant Koon and officers Briseno and Powell without pay and dismissed officer Wind, a rookie without tenure, pending the outcome of their criminal trial. King then filed a civil rights lawsuit against the city of Los Angeles.

Several significant developments occurred as the officers awaited trial. On July 9, 1991, the Christopher Commission released the results of its investigation and its recommendations to the five-member Los Angeles Police Commission. The Police Commission employed the police chief and was responsible for the management of the LAPD. The Christopher Commission found that the LAPD, composed of 67.8 percent white officers in 1991, suffered from a "siege mentality" in a city where 63 percent of the population were people of color. The commission also found that a small but significant proportion of officers repeatedly used excessive force when making arrests and that the LAPD did not punish those officers when citizens filed complaints. Finally, the commission recommended measures to exert more control over the LAPD's operations, including limiting the police chief's tenure to a five-year term, renewable by the Police Commission for one additional term only. After the release of the Christopher Commission report, Police Chief Gates announced his retirement, effective April, 1992 (which he later amended to July, 1992). On July 23, 1991, a California court of appeal granted the police defendants' request for a change of venue for the upcoming criminal trial.

THE STATE CRIMINAL TRIAL

The trial of the four officers began on March 4, 1992, in the new venue—the primarily white community of Simi Valley in Ventura County. The jury who heard the state of California's case against the four officers consisted of ten whites, one Latino, and one Asian. The officers' defense lawyers presented Holliday's videotape broken down into a series of individual still pictures. They asked the jury to judge whether excessive force—that is, force that was not warranted by King's "aggressive" actions—was employed at any single moment during the arrest. Referring often to the "thin blue line" that protected society from the "likes of Rodney King," the defense built a case that justified the police officers' actions. King's lawyer, Steven Lerman, a personal injury specialist, advised King not to testify at the trial out of concern that King's "confused and frightened" state of mind since the beating might impair his memory of events and discredit his testimony. The Simi Valley

jury acquitted the four officers of all charges of criminal assault, with the exception of one count against officer Powell on which the jury was deadlocked.

The acquittal of the four police officers on April 29, 1992, ignited widespread and destructive riots led by poor and angry black Angelenos. The riots affected areas throughout Los Angeles but particularly devastated parts of impoverished South Central Los Angeles. Fifty-three people died during the riots, which raged until May 2, and more than one billion dollars' worth of property was damaged. There had long been friction between Los Angeles's neighboring Korean and black communities, and the Korean American community bore the brunt of the rioters' destructive attacks.

THE FEDERAL CIVIL RIGHTS TRIAL

On August 5, 1992, a federal grand jury indicted the four officers for violating King's civil rights. The grand jury charged Sergeant Koon with violating the Fourteenth Amendment, which obligated Koon, as the officer in charge of the arrest, to protect King while he was in police custody. Officers Briseno, Powell, and Wind were charged with violating the Fourth Amendment in using more force than necessary, and using that excessive force willfully, when they arrested King. King testified during the federal trial. On April 17, 1993, a jury of nine whites, two African Americans, and one Latino found Koon and Powell guilty and Briseno and Wind not guilty. On August 4, 1993, Koon and Powell were sentenced to two-and-one-half-year prison terms. In May, 1994, a Los Angeles jury awarded King $3.8 million in compensatory damages in his civil rights lawsuit against the city, but on June 1, 1994, the jury denied King's request for additional punitive damages.

Karen Garner

See also: Harlins murder; Koreans and African Americans; Los Angeles riots; Miami riots; MOVE bombing; Race riots of the twentieth century; Simpson murder trial

LOS ANGELES RIOTS

April 29-May 1, 1992

Verdicts of not guilty in the trial of four police officers accused of police brutality revealed the wide gap between African Americans' and Euro-Americans' *views of the criminal justice system and sparked the worst rioting the city of Los Angeles had experienced up to that time.*

Locale: Los Angeles, California
Category: Wars, uprisings, and civil unrest

KEY FIGURES

Rodney King (b. 1965), African American who was the subject of a videotaped beating by Los Angeles police

Stacey Koon (b. 1950), Los Angeles police sergeant involved in the beating of Rodney King

Daryl F. Gates (b. 1926), chief of the Los Angeles Police Department

Reginald Denny (b. 1953), white truck driver severely beaten by African Americans during the early hours of the riots

Damian Williams (b. 1973), African American charged with participating in the beating of Reginald Denny

SUMMARY OF EVENT

Before the Rodney King beating on March 3, 1991, many in the Los Angeles community believed that the Los Angeles Police Department (LAPD) had demonstrated a pattern of excessive force, particularly against members of minority groups. One significant example was Operation Hammer, begun in 1989, during which the LAPD allegedly rounded up African Americans and Hispanics without any reasonable suspicion that they had committed any crime, simply because of the way the suspects looked and because the police wanted to avert the threat of gang violence. As a result, the chief of the LAPD, Daryl F. Gates, was despised by many in the African American community. The videotape of Rodney King's beating by members of the LAPD, therefore, came as no surprise to the African American community of Los Angeles. It merely confirmed what they already thought: that police use of excessive force against minorities was a common practice.

The videotape of King's beating, recorded by private citizen George Holliday in the morning hours of March 3, 1991, was eighty-one seconds in duration. The footage from the tape that was seen throughout the United States on television news programs showed King, a six-foot, three-inch African American weighing 225 pounds, prone on the ground, sustaining blows to his head, neck, kidney area, and legs from four policemen, who were kicking and smashing at him with their truncheons. Also present, but not in full view on the videotape, were nineteen other police officers surrounding the four who were administering the beating. In addition, onlookers—not seen on the tape—were pleading that the beating stop. The police paid no attention to them. As a result of the beating, King sustained eleven fractures to his skull, a crushed cheekbone, a broken ankle, internal injuries, a burn on his chest, and some brain damage.

Television viewers also did not see what preceded the beating. During the evening, King had consumed the equivalent of a case of beer (it was later determined that his blood alcohol level was twice the legal limit for operation of a vehicle). He was on parole at the time, and he ran the risk of landing back in jail if caught speeding. The police, led by Stacey Koon, started to pursue King because his car was seen to be exceeding the speed limit. The chase through the streets of Los Angeles escalated to one hundred miles per hour at one point, before the police were able to stop King and force him out of his car. Television viewers did not see King fighting with the police at that point, even standing up after being stunned twice with a Taser (electroshock weapon). Those who saw the videotape saw only the prone body of an African American man being assaulted repeatedly by white police officers.

The four officers seen delivering the blows to King on the videotape, including Koon, were charged with the beating at the end of March, 1991, in Los Angeles. Their attorneys moved for a change of venue for the trial, which was granted, and in the spring of 1992 the trial took place in Simi Valley, a suburban town an hour's drive north of Los Angeles. The town was home to a large proportion of LAPD officers and retirees and was dominated by law-and-order conservatives.

Six men and six women, none of whom was African American, made up the jury. According to those who were present, the prosecution presented a weak and diffuse case. The defense, however, was strong. Defense attorneys played the videotape in slow motion over and over until its effects became trivialized. The defense also emphasized how King presented a threat to the police. Koon testified about King's "Hulk-like strength and how he groaned like a wounded animal," conjuring up for the jury the image of police representing the "thin blue line" that protects the forces of civilization from the savagery represented by King. Among the jurors, many of whom had likely settled in Simi Valley to get away from the alleged evils and crime of the inner city, the message resonated. After thirty-two hours of deliberation, the jury acquitted the four officers on April 29, 1992. The verdicts were announced on television at 2:50 p.m.

At 4:00 that afternoon, in South Central Los Angeles, five African American gang members went to get some malt liquor at the Payless Liquor Store near the intersection of Florence and Normandie avenues. They started to take it without paying, and the store owner's son tried to stop them. One of the gang members smashed the son on the head with a bottle and allegedly said, "This is for Rodney King." The other gang members hurled the bottles they held through the store windows while the owner pressed the alarm for the police. By the time two officers arrived in response, the suspects were gone.

At 5:30 p.m., at the corner of Florence and Normandie, eight black men wielding baseball bats started breaking the car windows of passing motorists. Eighteen police cars and thirty-five officers from the LAPD sped to the area. They arrested three suspects and then left at 5:45. In the next hour, the crowd attacking cars grew to some two hundred people. One of the victims was Reginald Denny, a white truck driver, who was pulled from his truck and beaten by African Americans, including Damian Williams, with a fire extinguisher. The police did not return.

Chief Gates had left police headquarters at 6:30 to attend a fund-raising event in the affluent suburb of Brentwood. By 7:30, the crowd at Florence and Normandie had started lighting fires. An hour later, the LAPD finally returned to the area and began trying to disperse the crowd.

By that time, the fires, rioting, and looting had spread to other parts of the city. As the riots continued for two more days, local television news crews flooded the airwaves with helicopter views of hundreds of fires throughout the city and normally law-abiding citizens looting stores. On Friday, May 1, 1992, Rodney King appeared on television to appeal for calm with the plea, "Can we all get along?" By the end of that day, the violence was over.

SIGNIFICANCE

The acquital of the four officers charged with assaulting Rodney King reinforced the perceptions of many that the American criminal justice system treats whites and African Americans differently. Some observers, however, have argued that the riots were less the result of racial tensions than of persistent localized disparities between economic and social classes.

By the time the riots ended in Los Angeles on May 1, 1992, fifty-eight people had died, more than twelve thousand people had been arrested, and property damage was estimated to be as high as $1 billion. In addition, similar uprisings had started in Atlanta, Las Vegas, Minneapolis, New York, Omaha, and Seattle. The 1992 riots in Los Angeles caused more damage and spread across a wider area than did any incidents of urban unrest in the city during the 1960's.

In part as a result of the criticism he received for his handling of the riots and his role in fostering the police culture that had contributed to them, Gates resigned from the LAPD in late 1992. He was replaced by an African American chief of police, Willie L. Williams. Koon and one of the other officers originally charged with beating King, Laurence Powell, were tried and convicted in federal court of violating King's civil rights. King won a civil suit against the city of Los Angeles and was awarded $3.8 million.

—*Jennifer Eastman*

See also: Rioters Protest Miami Police Brutality.

R.A.V. v. City of St. Paul
June 22, 1992

The Case: U.S. Supreme Court ruling on hate crime and free expression

This holding, invalidating an ordinance which made it a crime to burn a cross to harass African Americans, demonstrates how the Supreme Court affords a preferred status to First Amendment free speech, even reprehensible speech.

During the early morning hours of June 21, 1990, "R.A.V."—an unnamed seventeen-year-old, self-

described as a white supremacist—and several other teenagers burned a makeshift wooden cross on the front lawn of the only African American family in their St. Paul, Minnesota, neighborhood. They were prosecuted for disorderly conduct in juvenile court under the city's "bias-motivated crime ordinance," which prohibited cross burning along with other symbolic displays that "one knows" or should know would arouse "anger, alarm or resentment in others on the basis of race, color, creed, religion, or gender."

The state trial court ruled that this ordinance was unconstitutionally overbroad because it indiscriminately prohibited protected First Amendment speech as well as unprotected activity. The Supreme Court of Minnesota reversed the lower court's decision and upheld the ordinance, which it interpreted to prohibit only unprotected "fighting words," face-to-face insults which are likely to cause the person to whom the words are addressed to attack the speaker physically.

The U.S. Supreme Court ruled unanimously in favor of R.A.V. and invalidated the ordinance, but the justices did not agree in their reasoning. Stating that they found the cross burning reprehensible, Justice Antonin Scalia, writing for the majority, nevertheless concluded that the ordinance was unconstitutional because it criminalized only specified "fighting words" based on the content of the hate message and, consequently, the government was choosing sides. He noted that the ordinance would prohibit a sign that attacked Catholics but would not prohibit a second sign that attacked those who displayed such an anti-Catholic bias.

Four justices concurred in the ruling of unconstitutionality, but Justice Byron White's opinion sharply criticized the majority opinion for going too far to protect racist speech. He reasoned that the ordinance was overbroad because it made it a crime to cause another person offense, hurt feelings, or resentment and because these harms could be caused by protected First Amendment speech. Justices Harry Blackmun and John Paul Stevens also wrote separate opinions complaining that hate speech did not deserve constitutional protection.

This holding calls into question numerous similar state laws designed to protect women and members of minorities from harassment and discrimination. Some of these individuals and groups may still invoke longstanding federal civil rights statutes, however, which carry severe criminal penalties of fines and imprisonment. In 1993, *R.A.V.*'s significance was called into question by the *Wisconsin v. Mitchell* decision upholding a state statute that increased a sentence for a crime of violence if the defendant targeted the victim because of the victim's race or other specified status.

See also: Church bombings; Church burnings; *Wisconsin v. Mitchell*

WISCONSIN V. MITCHELL

June 11, 1993

The Supreme Court upheld the constitutionality of a state law that increased the sentence for a crime in which the defendant intentionally selected the victim on the basis of race, national origin, religion, sexual orientation, or similar characteristics.

The Case: U.S. Supreme Court ruling on freedom of speech

Following a showing of the 1988 film *Mississippi Burning*, several African American men and boys congregated at an apartment complex to talk about the film. After a discussion of a scene in the film in which a young African American boy is beaten by a white man, the accused, Todd Mitchell, asked those who joined him outside if they were ready to go after a white man.

Walking on the opposite side of the street and saying nothing, fourteen-year-old Gregory Riddick approached the complex. Mitchell selected three individuals from the group to go after Riddick. The victim was beaten, and his tennis shoes were stolen.

In a Kenosha, Wisconsin, trial court, Mitchell was convicted as a party to the crime of aggravated battery. By Wisconsin law, this crime carried a maximum prison sentence of two years. Mitchell's sentence was extended to four years, however, under a state statute commonly known as the "hate crimes" statute. This statute provided for sentence extensions if it could be determined that the victim was selected because of his or her race, religion, color, disability, sexual orientation, national origin, or ancestry.

Mitchell appealed his conviction and the extended sentence. His conviction was upheld by the court of appeals, but the Supreme Court of Wisconsin reversed the decision of the appellate court. Wisconsin's Supreme Court held that the "hate crimes" statute violated the defendant's First Amendment protection for freedom of speech because it was unconstitutionally overbroad and punished only what the state legislature found to be offensive. Moreover, the state supreme court believed that this statute would have a "chilling effect" on a citizen's freedom of speech; that is, a citizen would fear reprisal for actions that might follow the utterance of prejudiced or biased speech.

The U.S. Supreme Court reversed the state court's decision. Chief Justice William H. Rehnquist wrote the opinion in this unanimous decision. The Court held that Mitchell's First Amendment rights to free speech had not been violated.

The Court pointed out that the statute was not aimed at speech but at conduct, which is not protected by the First Amendment. The Court also addressed the concern about the "chilling effect" of the statute, finding that

such would not be the case and that the state supreme court's hypothesis was far too speculative to be entertained. This decision indicates that the U.S. Supreme Court appears ready to uphold legislation designed to enhance punishment for criminal acts based on bigotry and bias without making bigoted or biased speech itself a crime.

—*Donna Addkison Simmons*

See also *R.A.V. v. City of St. Paul*

SHAW V. RENO
June 28, 1993

By calling for close scrutiny of a predominantly black congressional district whose shape it considered "bizarre," the Supreme Court in Shaw v. Reno *struck a blow against the practice of drawing district boundaries to create "majority-minority" electoral districts.*

The Case: U.S. Supreme Court ruling on gerrymandering

After the 1990 census, the state legislature of North Carolina began the task of "reapportionment," or redrawing its electoral districts. Although about 22 percent of the state's population was African American, no African Americans had been elected to Congress for almost a century. To remedy this, and ostensibly to meet provisions of the Voting Rights Act, the legislature created two majority-nonwhite districts. In order to avoid disturbing incumbents' districts, the legislature drew one of the two districts largely along an interstate highway, snaking 160 miles through the north-central part of the state. The resulting district was 53 percent black.

Five voters filed suit against the reapportionment plan, objecting that the race-based district violated their right to participate in a nonracial electoral process. The case reached the Supreme Court, whose 5–4 majority instructed the lower courts to reconsider the constitutionality of such a district in the light of its "bizarre" shape and its "uncomfortable resemblance to political apartheid." In essence, the majority expressed its concern about the practice of creating districts on the basis of race and of establishing contorted geographical boundaries. The coupling of the two practices presumably could result in districts that patently violated the

Constitution's equal protection clause, unless a compelling state interest could be demonstrated.

When the *Shaw* case was subsequently returned to North Carolina, a federal panel upheld the reapportionment plan after finding that the state did indeed have a compelling interest in complying with the Voting Rights Act. Nevertheless, the Supreme Court's *Shaw* decision has been the basis for other important decisions concerning racially defined districts. In 1994, for example, a majority-black district in Louisiana was rejected by a federal district court invoking *Shaw*. The court expressed particular concern that the district was intentionally created on the basis of the voters' race. More significant, in 1995 the U.S. Supreme Court extended *Shaw*'s admonitions about racial reapportionment to argue that voters' rights are violated whenever "race was the predominant factor motivating the legislature's decision to place a significant number of voters within or without a particular district," irrespective of shape.

Shaw served as a watershed in the contest between advocates of racial representation and those who champion a "color-blind" electoral system. It came at a time when various racial issues that had for years remained largely outside sharp political debate—affirmative action, welfare reform, and so forth—had been thrust into the center stage of American political discourse. Although *Shaw* by no means resolved these debates, it helped to delineate the battle lines.

—*Steve D. Boilard*

See also: *Shaw v. Hunt*; Voting Rights Act of 1965

ADARAND CONSTRUCTORS V. PEÑA

June 12, 1995

In this decision, the U.S. Supreme Court held that broad affirmative action programs involving employment and contracts were unconstitutional but preserved the applicability of affirmative action to specific and limited circumstances of discrimination.

The Case: U.S. Supreme Court ruling on affirmative action

Randy Pech, a white contractor in Colorado Springs, Colorado, submitted the lowest bid for a federal road-repair project. The contract, however, was awarded to a company owned by a Latino man because of a 1987 law requiring that the Department of Transportation award at least 10 percent of its funds to companies owned by women or members of minority groups. Pech took his complaint to the courts. The case was decided by the Supreme Court at a time when criticism of affirmative action had become widespread both among the public and in Congress. In addition, the makeup of the Court itself had changed since the last federal affirmative action case in 1990; notably, Thurgood Marshall, a staunch liberal, had retired and been replaced by another African American jurist, Clarence Thomas, a conservative.

Overturning previous decisions offering support of federal affirmative action, on June 12, 1995, the Court voted 5 to 4 that the type of affirmative action program involved in the case was unconstitutional. In an opinion written by Justice Sandra Day O'Connor, the Supreme Court stated that the Constitution protects individuals but was not intended to offer special protections to groups. Treating "any person unequally because of his or her race" causes the person to suffer an injury that is not acceptable under the Constitution's guarantee of equal protection under the law. The law can treat people differently because of race "only for the most compelling reasons," and racial classifications by government agencies are "inherently suspect and presumptively invalid." The Court did say, however, that affirmative action programs could be acceptable to remedy specific, provable cases of discrimination.

The decision severely undercut all federal affirmative action programs, most notably those involving jobs or contracts required to go to members of minority groups ("minority setasides"). In addition, federal law at the time of Adarand required firms that did more than fifty thousand dollars of business a year with the federal government and had more than fifty employees to have a written affirmative action policy, which meant that the Adarand decision could affect the policies of nearly all major employers in the United States. Reaction to the decision was strong and immediate. A leader of the Anti-Defamation League called it a "sea change" in the law. Many civil rights leaders protested the decision and urged the government not to abolish all affirmative action efforts. Conservative Republican leaders in Congress, in contrast, vowed to pass legislation to eliminate all racial preferences in federal hiring and contracting.

—*McCrea Adams*

See also: Affirmative action; *Bakke* case; Emancipation Proclamation; *Fullilove v. Klutznick*; *Griggs v. Duke Power Company*; Thirteenth Amendment; *United Steelworkers of America v. Weber*

O. J. SIMPSON TRIAL

January 24-October 3, 1995

O. J. Simpson was one of America's most famous celebrities when he went on trial for the murder of his former wife and one of her acquaintances. The trial featured virtually uninterrupted news coverage and analysis, frequent melodrama, and strong racial undercurrents, and raised far-reaching questions about violence against women and the role of racism in the American legal system.

Also known as: Trial of the Century
Locale: Los Angeles, California
Category: Crime and scandal

KEY FIGURES
O. J. Simpson (b. 1947), former professional football player and popular actor

Nicole Brown Simpson (1959-1994), former wife of O. J. Simpson

Ronald Goldman (1968-1994), acquaintance of Nicole Brown Simpson

Johnnie Cochran (1937-2005), prominent California defense attorney

Marcia Clark (b. 1953), Los Angeles assistant district attorney

Mark Fuhrman (b. 1952), Los Angeles police detective

Lance Ito (b. 1950), Los Angeles Superior Court judge

Kato Kaelin (b. 1959), resident at O. J. Simpson's guest house

SUMMARY OF EVENT

O. J. Simpson, a former athlete who had won the Heisman Trophy as a college football player and had been a National Football League all-pro running back, had made a successful transition to film acting by the mid-1990's. On the night of June 12, 1994, Simpson's former wife, Nicole Brown Simpson, was murdered

outside her home, along with an acquaintance, Ronald Goldman. Goldman had stopped by to return a pair of glasses that Nicole Brown Simpson had left that evening at the restaurant where he worked. Two years earlier, Brown Simpson and Simpson had ended their sevenyear marriage after numerous allegations of domestic violence, although they still shared custody of their two children and occasionally spent time together.

Evidence discovered at the scene of the murders and later at O. J. Simpson's home quickly implicated Simpson, and five days later, a warrant was issued for his arrest. He fled in a Ford Bronco driven by his friend Al Cowlings and led police on a slow sixty-mile chase through Los Angeles, threatening suicide before returning home and eventually surrendering.

On January 24, 1995, Simpson went on trial in Los Angeles for two counts of murder. His personal attorney, Robert Shapiro, assembled a team of prominent attorneys from across the nation, including F. Lee Bailey, a personal friend of Shapiro and at the time perhaps the most famous attorney in the United States; outspoken Harvard professor Alan Dershowitz; Barry Scheck, DNA expert and codirector of the Innocence Project; and Johnnie Cochran, a flamboyant and highly respected personal injury lawyer whose charisma would give the trial its most memorable moments. After opening statements, prosecutors Marcia Clark and Christopher Darden began building a long and complex case against

Simpson based on a time line of the murders and Simpson's movements during that period, DNA evidence left at the crime scene, and a pair of leather gloves that appeared to tie Simpson to the murders.

The time line was established largely through the testimonies of Rosa Lopez, a domestic worker for a Simpson neighbor who at one point in the trial fled the country to avoid testifying; Allan Park, a limousine driver who arrived to take Simpson to the airport at about the time of the crime and could get no answer on the home's intercom; and Kato Kaelin, a guest in Simpson's guesthouse who had hamburgers with Simpson early in the evening and later heard a strange noise outside his window close to where a bloody glove was found. In early March, Los Angeles police detective Mark Fuhrman testified that he had found the glove behind Simpson's home and that it matched another found at the crime scene, but Bailey's cross-examination of Fuhrman focused instead on Fuhrman's frequent use of a racial epithet. Fuhrman denied having used the word in the previous ten years. Two months later, on June 15, prosecutor Darden suddenly asked Simpson to try on the gloves, a move that backfired when Simpson struggled to pull the gloves on before finally announcing that they did not fit.

DNA evidence discovered in blood samples placed Simpson at the scene of the murders and indicated that Goldman's blood had somehow found its way into Simpson's car. In late July, however, a forensic toxicologist working for the defense testified to finding a preservative in the blood samples, suggesting that the samples had not actually been collected at the scene and allowing the defense to argue that police had planted Simpson's blood at the scene and on the gloves. Earlier in the trial, Scheck had forced a prosecution witness from the Los Angeles Police Department to admit that procedural errors had indeed been made, so when, in late August and early September, the defense presented a series of witnesses testifying that Fuhrman had in fact used racial epithets several times in the previous ten years, the defense argument that police had planted evidence against Simpson seemed to become more convincing.

During his closing argument, Cochran drove home the theory with the jury by repeatedly using the refrain, "If it doesn't fit, you must acquit." Complicating the Fuhrman episode, several audiotapes Fuhrman had made with a pair of authors who had interviewed him as background for a book revealed that Fuhrman had insulted Judge Lance Ito's wife, a police captain in the

Los Angeles Police Department. The prosecution attempted unsuccessfully to remove Ito from the bench, but by that point, the trial had become so infused with petty issues—jury strikes, bickering among the attorneys, Fuhrman's disappearance from the trial after pleading the Fifth Amendment—that the motion to remove Ito quickly passed.

The jury began deliberating on the morning of October 3 and soon called for a review of Park's testimony. Then suddenly, less than four hours after they had begun deliberations, they announced that they had reached a verdict. The next day, with as many as 100 million people watching on television or listening on radio, Simpson was declared "not guilty."

SIGNIFICANCE

In the wake of the media frenzy and the trial's frequent melodrama, the trial not only posed serious questions about justice in America but also appeared at times to be a parody of a trial. The jury went on strike when three deputies who had accompanied them on trips were reassigned, the parade of eccentric witnesses and grandstanding attorneys blurred the lines between entertainment and news, and the gavel-to-gavel television coverage made celebrities of many of the participants, several of whom made millions of dollars from books and media appearances. Throughout the trial and after, Simpson's own celebrity status prompted accusations that he was, according to some, receiving preferential treatment or, for others, being subjected to overly aggressive prosecution.

Perceptions of Simpson's guilt or innocence differed dramatically between white Americans and black Americans, both during the trial as well as after the verdict. Whites considered the evidence convincing and overwhelming, but blacks generally dismissed both physical evidence and witness testimony as tainted by investigative error or police misconduct. The fact that Simpson was black and his victims were white only magnified the racial overtones, and with memories still fresh of the videotaped beating of Rodney King four years earlier by Los Angeles police officers who were later exonerated, the issue of race would emerge again and again throughout the trial.

If It Doesn't Fit . . .

In his closing statement at the criminal trial of O. J. Simpson, lead defense attorney Johnnie Cochran appealed to the jury's sense of racial injustice and distrust of the police investigation:

The Defendant, Mr. Orenthal James Simpson, is now afforded an opportunity to argue the case, if you will, but I'm not going to argue with you, ladies and gentlemen. What I'm going to do is to try and discuss the reasonable inferences which I feel can be drawn from this evidence. . . .

From the very first orders issued by the LAPD so-called brass, they were more concerned with their own images, the publicity that might be generated from this case than they were in doing professional police work. . . . Because of their bungling, they ignored the obvious clues. . . . We think if they had done their job as we have done, Mr. Simpson would have been eliminated early on. . . .

And so as we look then at the time line and the importance of this timeline, I want you to remember these words. Like the defining moment in this trial, the day Mr. Darden asked Mr. Simpson to try on those gloves and the gloves didn't fit, remember these words; if it doesn't fit, you must acquit. . . .

And when you are back there deliberating on this case, you're never going to be ever able to reconcile this time line and the fact there's no blood back there. . . . They don't have any mountain or ocean of evidence.

It's not so because they say so. That's just rhetoric. We this afternoon are talking about the facts. And so it doesn't make any sense. It just doesn't fit. If it doesn't fit, you must acquit. . . . Then we come, before we end the day, to Detective Mark Fuhrman.

This man is an unspeakable disgrace. He's been unmasked for the whole world for what he is. . . . And they put him on the stand and you saw it. You saw it. It was sickening. . . . Then Bailey says: "Have you used that word, referring to the 'n' word, in the past ten years? . . . I want you to assume that perhaps at some time since 1985 or '86, you addressed a member of the African American race as a Nigger. Is it possible that you have forgotten that act on your part?" . . .

Let's remember this man. . . . Why did they then all try to cover for this man Fuhrman? . . . This man could have been off the force long ago if they had done their job, but they didn't do their job. People looked the other way. People didn't have the courage. One of the things that has made this country so great is people's willingness to stand up and say that is wrong.

I'm not going to be part of it. I'm not going to be part of the cover-up. That is what I'm asking you to do. Stop this cover-up. Stop this cover-up. If you don't stop it, then who? Do you think the police department is going to stop it? Do you think the D.A.'s office is going to stop it? Do you think we can stop it by ourselves? It has to be stopped by you.

Just over a year after he was found not guilty in the criminal trial, Simpson was sued in civil court by Goldman's family for Goldman's wrongful death. On February 4, 1997, after only a four-month trial, the jury brought back a $33.5 million judgment against Simpson. Soon afterward, Simpson moved to Florida, where the laws protected many of his assets. For years following the judgment, he avoided paying the award.

—*Devon Boan*

See also: Los Angeles Riots.

FARRAKHAN LEADS THE MILLION MAN MARCH

October 16, 1995

Nation of Islam leader Louis Farrakhan organized and led a massive march of African American men in Washington, D.C., with the aim of changing public and private perceptions of African American males. The event resulted in critical discussions within the African American community and placed Farrakhan in a prominent and powerful leadership role.

Locale: Washington, D.C.

Categories: Religion, theology, and ethics; social issues and reform

KEY FIGURES
Louis Farrakhan (b. 1933), leader of the Nation of Islam
Benjamin Chavis (b. 1948), former executive director of the National Association for the Advancement of Colored People

The Million Man March, Washington, D.C., October 1995

SUMMARY OF EVENT

In 1995, more than 50 percent of the individuals incarcerated in the United States were African American men, yet African Americans made up only 12 percent of the nation's population. There were more African American men unemployed and underemployed than attending college, and the numbers registered to vote were even lower. Moreover, the black and white races in the United States were more divided than unified. Feelings in the African American community were still raw after the acquittal of Los Angeles police officers who were videotaped beating black motorist Rodney King a few years earlier. The subsequent riots in Los Angeles in 1992 and the acquittal of former professional football player O. J. Simpson for the murder of his ex-wife, Nicole Brown Simpson, and her friend Ronald Goldman gave evidence of a serious racial divide in the country. In addition, popular culture was feeding negative perceptions of African Americans, particularly males, through films, television programs, and music that highlighted violence and illegal drug activity among members of this group.

Minister Louis Farrakhan, the impassioned leader of the Nation of Islam religious organization, used the unrest of African Americans and negative images of African American males specifically as an impetus to call for one million African American men to join in a march to the Lincoln Memorial in Washington, D.C., on October 16, 1995. Farrakhan called the event a holy day for African American men to reconnect with themselves, their families, one another, and the African American community.

The Million Man March would encourage African American men to take their rightful place in their communities as fathers, leaders, and providers. The event, which Farrakhan organized in cooperation with the Reverend Benjamin Chavis, former executive director of the National Association for the Advancement of Colored People (NAACP), and approximately three hundred local community organizations, became the stimulus for public and private discussion of many issues related to the African American community and race relations in the United States.

The mission statement of the Million Man March required African American men to repent or atone for their "sins" against themselves and humanity. The purpose of the march was to emphasize the need for African American men to be accountable and responsible while taking primary steps toward self-sufficiency in their personal, social, political, and economic lives. The march brought together young and old, rich and poor, professionals and unemployed.

Speakers at the event included a number of popular and politically prominent African American men, among them Kweisi Mfume, former U.S. congressman from Maryland and president of the NAACP; the Reverend Jesse Jackson, founder of the Rainbow/PUSH Coalition; actor and entertainer Bill Cosby; former professional baseball player Reggie Jackson; and scholar Cornel West.

Farrakhan spoke for more than two hours, during which he asked participants to recite a long pledge to engage in civic, social, political, cultural, and religious activities.

Famed poet Maya Angelou also participated in the official program, although the Million Man March was exclusively for African American men—women and men of other races were not invited. Several women spoke at the event, but African American women in general were encouraged to participate only in supporting, background roles. It was suggested that African American women should stay home and support the men by making the day a "holy day." In addition, all African Americans who did not attend the march were asked to avoid spending any money that day, to demonstrate the economic power of African Americans as a group. Many African American women did attend the event to show their support, but others adamantly objected to the gender divide it imposed.

The organizers intended the march to be nondenominational and nonpolitical; nevertheless, debates quickly arose concerning the reception, treatment, role, and participation in the march of Christians, Jews, and others who were not adherents of the Nation of Islam, as well as homosexuals and women, who were excluded. Moreover, the participation of Farrakhan, a man known for rhetoric that was often considered sexist and racist, added to the debates surrounding the event. Before, during, and after the Million Man March, observers pointed out the need in the African American community for further discussion and action concerning the gender divide, religious differences and mutual respect, economic self-empowerment, and political and social involvement and advancement.

In regard to Farrakhan's participation, many found it difficult to separate the message from the messenger. The often politically incendiary and radical rhetoric of the Nation of Islam leader tended to separate him and others from the idealistic and positive goals of the march.

Another widespread sentiment, however, was that although the controversial Farrakhan originated the idea for the march, the event's goals superseded his personality and rhetoric. Still, many condemned the march as a separatist event that served what they believed were sexist, patriarchal, and even racist motives on the part of Farrakhan.

Another controversy that followed the march concerned the numbers of people in attendance. The National Park Service originally estimated the crowd gathered in the nation's capital at 400,000, whereas the Nation of Islam's estimate was closer to 2 million. Some charged that the low "official" estimates of the size of the crowd reflected attempts by the political establishment to minimize the event's importance. Later review of panoramic photographs of the event led to some consensus that the number was actually around 835,000. This was not the only area where there was a lack of agreement, as responses to the Million Man March varied widely within and outside the African American community.

SIGNIFICANCE

It is believed that one result of the Million Man March was that thousands of African American men registered to vote and participated in the 1996 elections. Also, according to the National Association of Black Social Workers, adoption rates of African American children by African Americans increased after the march. Membership in national African American organizations such as the NAACP, the Southern Christian Leadership Conference, and the Nation of Islam grew significantly after the march as well. Many individuals who had been concerned about the march or even opposed to it because of the often controversial and heated rhetoric of Louis Farrakhan later saw the overall impact of the event as positive, representing a welcome renewal for African Americans.

The organization and implementation of the Million Man March demonstrated the political and social impact that one person can have on the United States and within the African American community. Farrakhan gained additional public prominence from his role in organizing the march, and his success in creating an event aimed at encouraging the empowerment, self-determination, and self-sufficiency of African American men demonstrated the Nation of Islam leader's influence and power.

The march clearly highlighted the state of race relations in the United States in the 1990's, showing the divisions that existed within the African American

---

Farrakhan's Million Man Speech

On October 16, 1995, Louis Farrakhan addressed his audience at the Million Man March, held in Washington, D.C. Farrakhan urged blacks to join organizations that seek to uplift the people:

So, my beloved brothers and sisters, here's what we would like you to do. Everyone of you, my dear brothers, when you go home, here's what I want you to do. We must belong to some organization that is working for, and in the interests of, the uplift and the liberation of our people. Go back, join the NAACP if you want to, join the Urban League, join the All African People's Revolutionary Party, join us, join the Nation of Islam, join PUSH, join the Congress of Racial Equality, join SCLC, the Southern Christian Leadership Conference.

But we must become a totally organized people and the only way we can do that is to become a part of some organization that is working for the uplift of our people. . . . I know that the NAACP did not officially endorse this march.

Neither did the Urban League. But, so what? So what? Many of the members are here anyway. . . . These are our brothers and we're not going to stop reaching out for them simply because we feel there was a misunderstanding. We still want to talk to our brothers because we cannot let artificial barriers divide us. . . . No, we must continue to reach out for those that have condemned this, and make them to see that this was not evil, it was not intended for evil, it intended for good. Now, brothers, moral and spiritual renewal is a necessity. Every one of you must go back home and join some church, synagogue or temple or mosque that is teaching spiritual and moral uplift. I want you, brothers, there's no men in the church, in the mosque. The men are in the streets, and we got to get back to the houses of God.

---

community as well as the division between white and African Americans. The event renewed debates surrounding questions that had been asked for years in the United States: What is the nature of the roles of African American women and African American men? Is there a composite leader for the African American community? Among African Americans, whose voices are heard most and whose are heard least? Who is responsible for racism in the United States? Will African Americans and white Americans ever truly be treated as equals?

The Million Man March demonstrated to all Americans that a large group of African American men can congregate together in a peaceful manner for a positive purpose. Although the ultimate goals of the march were not met in the decade following—given that the numbers of African American men incarcerated, unemployed, underemployed, and without housing did not decrease significantly—the event did encourage discussion around the country on the many issues that Farrakhan proposed to address concerning the empowerment of African Americans.

—*Khadijah O. Miller*

See also: U.S. Supreme Court Endorses Busing to End School Segregation; Jackson Becomes the First Major Black Candidate for U.S. President.

SHAW V. HUNT

June 13, 1996

In this decision, the Supreme Court held that the equal protection clause of the Fourteenth Amendment prohibits the drawing of irregularly shaped congressional districts designed to produce electoral majorities of racial and ethnic minorities.

The Case: U.S. Supreme Court ruling on gerrymandering to create "majority-minority" districts

One of the purposes of the Voting Rights Act of 1982 was to protect members of racial and ethnic minorities from vote dilution. After the census of 1990, the Department of Justice interpreted the act to mean that legislatures must adopt reapportionment plans that included, whenever possible, congressional districts with heavy concentrations of racial and ethnic minorities. Some of the resulting race-conscious districts were spread out and highly irregular in shape. In the election of 1992, these new districts helped elect an unprecedented number of African Americans to Congress.

In North Carolina, there were two race-based districts, with one following a narrow strip of land for 160 miles. Ruth Shaw and other white voters of North Carolina filed suit, claiming that these two voting districts violated their rights under the equal protection clause. In *Shaw v. Reno* (1993), the Supreme Court directed the federal district court to reconsider the reapportionment plan according to the strict scrutiny standard. This decision, often called *Shaw I*, clearly indicated that a majority of the justices did not approve of racial gerrymandering. The lower court, nevertheless, approved the districts.

In *Shaw v. Hunt* (also known as *Shaw II*), the Supreme Court reversed the lower court's judgment. Speaking for a majority of five, Chief Justice William H. Rehnquist noted that any law that classifies citizens on the basis of race is constitutionally suspect and concluded that the drawing of the two contested districts had not been narrowly tailored to further a compelling state interest. He insisted that the state's interest in remedying the effects of past or present racial discrimination must be justified by an "identified past discrimination" rather than simply a generalized assertion of such discrimination. Also, he argued that the Justice Department's policy of maximizing majority-black districts was not authorized by the Voting Rights Act, which said nothing about subordinating the traditional districting factors of compactness, contiguity, and respect for political subdivisions. Justice John Paul Stevens wrote a strong dissent, arguing that the white plaintiffs' claims of harm were "rooted in speculative and stereotypical assumptions."

In two closely related decisions, *Bush v. Vera* (1996) and *Abrams v. Johnson* (1997), the Court struck down race-based congressional districts in Texas and Georgia respectively. Each of these decisions was decided by a 5–4 vote, which meant that a future change in Court personnel could result in a different judgment about the controversial issue of racial gerrymandering.

—*Thomas Tandy Lewis updated by Patrica A. McDaniel*

See also: Gerrymandering; *Shaw v. Reno*; Voting Rights Act of 1975

TIGER WOODS BECOMES WORLD'S TOP-RATED GOLFER

June 15, 1997

After turning professional in 1996, Tiger Woods quickly came to dominate the sport of golf. In 1997, he won the Masters Tournament, his first major tournament as a professional, and became the youngest player up to that time to achieve the top spot in the Official World Golf Ranking.

Locale: United States
Category: Sports

KEY FIGURES

Tiger Woods (b. 1975), American professional golfer
Earl Woods (1932-2006), father of Tiger Woods

SUMMARY OF EVENT

When Tiger Woods exploded onto the professional golf scene in 1996 he had already experienced notable successes in golf. He won his first golf tournament at the age of eight, and at fifteen he became the youngest golfer up to that time to win the U.S. Junior National Championship.

He went on to become the first African American and the youngest golfer to win the U.S. Amateur Golf Championship, a tournament he then won three years in a row. In 1996, he became the first African American to earn a PGA (Professional Golfers' Association) Tour card since Adrian Stills in 1985. On his way to winning his first major professional tournament, the Masters, in April, 1997, at twenty-one years of age, Woods shattered several PGA records. His score of 270 over four rounds was the lowest in the history of the Masters, and his twelve-stroke victory over the second-place finisher was the greatest winning margin since 1862. Not long after his Masters win, on June 15, 1997, Tiger Woods became the youngest professional golfer ever to take the number one spot in the Official World Golf Ranking.

Woods's phenomenal success drew a great deal of media attention. In 1997, television coverage of the Masters included sixty-six of his sixty-nine final-round shots and earned the Columbia Broadcasting System (CBS) record television ratings for a Masters final. After Woods joined the PGA Tour in 1996, hundreds of millions of new dollars began to flow into the sport of professional golf, including increases in television contracts. Prize money on the PGA Tour in 1996, the year Woods turned pro, added up to a little more than $69 million. In contrast, by 2001 the total purse had escalated to $180 million. As the most recognized athlete in the world, Woods brought more people out to the tournaments and created more media coverage.

In addition to raising the financial status of professional golf, Woods transformed the public image of the sport, taking golf's long history as a decadent pastime for white people and turning it inside out. As Tim Finchem, commissioner of the PGA Tour, noted, Woods's impact came not only from his skill but also from his persona and the dignified way he carried himself.

In December, 1996, several months after Woods left Stanford University to become a professional golfer, an article in *Sports Illustrated* quoted his father, Earl Woods, as claiming that his son was qualified through his ethnicity to do more than any other man in history to change the course of humanity. According to the elder Woods, Tiger's heritage—which includes Thai, Chinese, American Indian, and European as well as African forebears—placed him in a position to stimulate new interest in the concept of the United States as a melting pot.

Building on the interest in Tiger Woods, stories about mixed-race children and racially mixed marriages proliferated in the mass media. Woods, however, was somewhat reluctant to make public statements about issues of race and ethnicity. He frowned on being referred to as African American because he felt that such categorization neglected his Asian mother. For the most part, he seemed inclined to concentrate on golf and let others speak on behalf of race relations. He did, however, always find time to devote to helping disadvantaged youth, both on and off the golf course. To that end, he and his father established the Tiger Woods Foundation in 1996.

SIGNIFICANCE

Tiger Woods's success and popularity had major impacts on the sport of golf, which had long stood as a potent symbol of exclusion and racial intolerance. Although golf is still overwhelmingly a sport played and watched by white people, surveys have shown that from 1996 to 2003, the number of African Americans who identified themselves as avid fans of professional golf rose 380 percent.

In the same period, the percentage of African American golfers doubled. By 2003, approximately five hundred golf programs were operating in urban, inner-city areas in the United States, compared with just eighty-five such programs in 1994.

Woods attracted interest to the sport of golf in the United States and around the world, among adults and children of all ethnic groups who previously had no interest in the sport. The country-club mystique of golf began to disappear as the sport became democratized and more affordable, with an increasing proportion of new courses open to the public (in 2003, 90 percent of new golf courses built in the United States were public courses).

In addition, Woods's example of commitment to a relentless work ethic in the gym and on the practice range brought a new level of physical fitness and dedication to the realm of professional golf. The game's equipment revolution around the end of the twentieth century was also fueled in part by the desire among lesser players

to catch up to Woods. His mile-long drives were a major contributor to an obsession with distance off the tee, which led many golf courses, including Augusta National, to redesign golf holes to allow for greater length.

Woods's influence and success continued into the twenty-first century. In 2000, his fifteen-stroke victory at the U.S. Open at Pebble Beach made Woods the first golfer since Ben Hogan in 1953 to win three major tournaments in a year. In April, 2001, Woods became the first golfer to hold all four majors titles at once, although not in the same year, when he again captured the Masters title. This feat became known as the "Tiger slam."

—*Mary McElroy*

See also: Robinson Becomes Baseball's First African American Manager.

MILLION WOMAN MARCH

October 25, 1997

The second in a series of African American activist marches in the late 1990's, the Million Woman March targeted empowerment and unity in the African American community.

The Event: Gathering together of hundreds of thousands of black women from all over the world
Place: Philadelphia, Pennsylvania

The Million Woman March took place on October 25, 1997, in Philadelphia, Pennsylvania. Organized by Philé Chionesu, the owner of an African artifacts store in Philadelphia, and Asia Coney, president of the Tasker Tenant Improvement Council in Philadelphia, the march created a network of African American women community activists. These women took on positions of leadership such as national cochair and regional coordinator in order to rally African American women to demonstrate their commitment to solving the problems that faced African Americans at the end of the twentieth century.

Although the march was not organized through a religious organization, it was inspired by the October 16, 1995, Million Man March organized by the Muslim minister Louis Farrakhan of the Nation of Islam. Philadelphia was selected as the destination because it is where the Declaration of Independence was signed.

Organizers wanted African American women to make their own declaration of independence from poverty, discrimination, enslavement, and abuse. The march used grassroots organization and publicity, relying on word of mouth, the Internet, and black media sources instead of corporate sponsorship and mainstream television and print media.

Two years earlier, many African American women had supported the Million Man March, deferring to Farrakhan's request that women refrain from attending the march to avoid unnecessary distraction. However, many African American women were eager to have their turn to demonstrate their commitment to bettering the lives of black people, and the Million Woman March provided just such an opportunity.

A DAY FOR WOMEN

A complete program of events was designed to reinforce the motto of the October 25 march: Great Grandmother Taught Grandmother. Grandmother Taught Mother. Mother Taught Me. I Will Teach You. The march began with a 6 a.m. spiritual ceremony at Penn's Landing, a site on the waterfront of the Delaware River regarded as sacred by some African Americans because it is where Africans were bought and sold after reaching the colony of Philadelphia. Accompanied by the traditional rhythms of an African drum procession, participants marched two miles from Penn's Landing to the steps of the Philadelphia Museum of Art.

The Million Woman March addressed a wide variety of themes and issues, including sisterhood, positive relationships with men, domestic violence, women's health, incarceration of women, family, independent African American schools, leadership, global human rights, and the Central Intelligence Agency's possible role in crack cocaine trafficking in the inner cities. The march's mission statement highlighted these concerns, as well as a reaffirmation of women's roles as mothers, as nurturers, and as protectors of life. The march also addressed the African American woman's role in rebuilding deteriorated African American neighborhoods.

The seven-hour-long official program featured a diverse range of prominent black women in fields ranging from politics to religion, to music and the arts, and to activism. These speakers included Congresswoman Maxine Waters; Ilyassah and Camilla Shabazz, daughters of 1960's activist Malcolm X; actress Jada Pinkett; rapper and social activist Sister Souljah; singer-songwriter Faith Evans; Afeni Shakur, the mother of hip-hop artist Tupac Shakur; Pam and Ramona Africa of Philadelphia's MOVE organization; and Khadijah Farrakhan, wife of Louis Farrakhan. South African political activist Winnie Mandela gave the keynote address. Her international fame as the politically active former wife of South African president Nelson Mandela lent an air of internationalism to the march and added to its significance. Not all march participants were black women: Bettye Mae Jumper of the Native American Tribal Council gave the program's prayer of unity. Organizers estimated that 2.1 million people convened in Philadelphia to support the march. Philadelphia police estimates range from 300,000 to one million attendees.

CONSEQUENCES

Many participants attended the march because they wanted to become a part of history. Women also attended the event to meet new people, exchange ideas, network, and see the faces of the hundreds of thousands of women whose daily lives are occupied with solving problems that affect the African American community. It is difficult to measure the exact impact of the march in real terms, but it is likely that the march at least served as a symbol to the world that African American women are leaders who are actively concerned with the progress of their communities. March leaders hoped that the image of hundreds of thousands of African American women gathered together to express their political power sent a positive message to the world that helped eliminate negative stereotypes of African American women. They also hoped it would heighten awareness of the difficulties of battling both sexism and racism.

The utility of march events such as the Million Woman March is the subject of debate. Critics question whether the money spent on travel, hotels, and souvenirs and the time involved in planning and attending the event could be put toward more tangible gains. For example, officials from the Philadelphia Convention and Visitors Bureau said that the march generated $21.7 million dollars for the city. What would happen, they ask, if the participants donated the equivalent of these expenses toward an African American social, political, educational, or economic cause instead of marching? The most consistent criticism is that it is difficult for a march to produce concrete achievements.

The Internet has provided one of the best means for maintaining the spirit of the Million Woman March and the networks it generated. African American women created forums, newsletters, and other opportunities for discussion of the march. In addition, African American women supported similar events such as the African American-centered 1998 Million Youth March in Harlem, New York; the unified, multiracial Million Mom March held in May, 2000, inWashington, D.C.; and the Nation of Islam sponsored Million Family March in Washington, D.C., held in October, 2000.

—*Christel N. Temple*

See also: Birmingham March; Colored Women's League; Combahee River Collective; Million Man March; Nation of Islam; National Association of Colored Women; National Black Women's Political Leadership Caucus; Poor People's March on Washington; Selma-Montgomery march.

FARMER V. RAMSAY

1998, 2002

White student Rob Farmer contends he was denied admission to the University of Maryland School of Medicine on the basis of race, with admissions favoring less qualified minority candidates over Farmer. The case is one of a number of cases since 1978 challenging affirmative action in hiring and school admission.

Identification: Court case brought against the University of Maryland School of Medicine alleging that the school's affirmative action policies violated student rights.

The concept of "affirmative action," resulted from President John F. Kennedy's executive order 10925, issued March 6, 1961, which included a provision that U.S. government contractors should "...take affirmative action to ensure that applicants are employed, and employees are treated during employment, without regard to their race, creed, color, or national origin." Essentially, affirmative action refers to processes taken to redress past discrimination or to prevent present or future discrimination. Opponents of affirmative action have argued that the implementation of affirmative action policies is fundamentally unfair in that employers and other institutions choosing among candidates have been encouraged to favor minority individuals over equally qualified or more qualified non-minority candidates. However, supporters argue that such programs are necessary to combat institutionalized racism that prohibits individuals of racial minority from achieving the same opportunities as non-minorities. In addition, it has been argued that affirmative action helped to build a diverse educational environment and workforce, which in turn leads to institutional innovation and enhanced cultural sensitivity. However, because affirmative action policies can lead to institutions and employers favoring minority candidates, non-minority students and prospective employees have repeatedly challenged affirmative action policies as unconstitutional.

In the 1978 case *Regents of the University of California v. Bakke*, the U.S. Supreme Court ruled that the use of "racial quotas" in college admissions was unconstitutional, as such quotas violated the Equal Protection Clause of the Fourteenth Amendment to the U.S. Constitution, guaranteeing equal protection under the law. According to the ruling, an employer or school admissions organization cannot require admissions officials to recruit certain numbers of candidates from specific minority groups. However, the supreme court also ruled that race can lawfully be considered as one of several factors when making admissions or hiring decisions. The courts found further that admission institutions may consider race or ethnicity as a factor affecting a candidate's contribution to the diversity of the institution as a reason to consider race or ethnicity when evaluating admissions. One of the most important results of the case was the court's recognition that affirmative action programs necessarily involved discrimination but that such discrimination was justified by compelling interests as long as such programs were "narrowly tailored" to harm as few people as possible. In subsequent cases, the Supreme Court has upheld the rights of universities and employers to consider race in the admissions and/or hiring process, but has ruled that certain methods of considering race are unconstitutional.

In 1998, prospective medical student Rob Farmer brought suit against the University of Maryland School of Medicine, claiming that he had been rejected for admission because of reverse discrimination. Farmer alleged that he would have been accepted, had he been a member of an "under-represented" minority group, which includes African Americans, American Indians, and Latino Americans. The University of Maryland School of Medicine denied all charges and claimed that the school's admissions process was constitutional and that the race or ethnicity of the applicant was one of many factors considered when evaluating students. The university alleged further that Farmer's rejection was based on a poor application. The university's admission process was explained in court as a highly competitive process, with the university admitting only 6 percent of applicants. In 1995, the year that Farmer first applied for admission, the university received 4400 applications, with only 140 spaces available for students.

In a 1998 interview with *The Baltimore Sun*, Farmer said, "If your family is involved in crime, you can get into med school with a 2.5 [grade-point average], but if you're a white guy and all you've tried to do is work hard and be honest, you can't get in." Farmer, who grew up poor, but graduated cum laude from the University of Colorado in 1991 with degrees in English and advertising, eventually began working as an emergency medical technician and decided to go to medical school. Taking pre-med classes at Towson University while working in construction, Farmer admittedly obtained a low score on the Medical College Admissions Test (MCAT), and was turned down by the University of Maryland in 1995. However, Farmer then participated in a summer study program offered by the university for disadvantaged students and, after finishing the course and retaking his tests, ranked in the top 25 percent of national students. Farmer argued that his scores placed him at or above many students accepted for admissions that year. Though Farmer applied for admission three times, in 1994, 1995, and 1996, his 1994 application was admittedly poor, and Farmer did not contest the school's decision to reject that year's application. Towson University, where Farmer completed his pre-med qualifying classes, refused to recommend him in his 1996 application, with Towson's Pre-Medical Committee stating they had "serious reservations" the prevented them from issuing a recommendation. Farmer's 1995 application, which was his strongest bid for a position, and had a qualified recommendation from Towson, was the focus of his suit.

The University of Maryland School of Medicine's Advanced Pre-Medical Development Program, which Farmer attended prior to his 1995 application, offers MCAT preparation and counseling to minority and/or financially disadvantaged applicants. Despite increasing his MCAT scores after completing the program, Hermoine Hicks, Director of Recruitment for the university, argued that, due to specific aspects of Farmer's application, the committee voted 14-0 against offering Farmer an interview. Hicks argued that the decision to reject Farmer was not based on race, but instead on a variety of factors including his relatively low GPA at Towson (where Farmer earned a 2.8 for a C-average), his employment history, and his personal statements, in which Farmer expressed negative views about doctors and the medical profession in general. In addition, the letter of recommendation from Towson University, listed him as "recommended with reservation," which is the fourth of

five recommendation categories ranging from "highly recommended" to "not recommended."

During the trial, Farmer challenged the university to demonstrate that African American candidates with similar applications to his had also been rejected. The university responded by demonstrating that numerous African American students with records similar and even more favorable than Farmer's had been denied interviews. Farmer also presented expert testimony evaluating his GPA, test scores, and overall application against other students who were accepted and rejected. In 2001, a federal judge dismissed the suit, arguing that Farmer's claims lacked legal merit and finding no evidence to support a claim of discrimination against the plaintiff or to suggest that the University of Maryland School of Medicine had used an unconstitutional "quota system." Farmer appealed the verdict, which was rejected by the Fourth Circuit Court of Appeals on August 3rd, 2002.

Of the legal challenges brought against institutions and employers using affirmative action policies since the 1970s, Farmer's challenge was neither strong nor compelling and the ruling against him was not considered controversial given Farmer's failure to demonstrate any evidence of discrimination or racial bias. The case did, however, uphold the right of the university to consider race and ethnicity in admissions, a controversial issue that has since been subject to additional legal challenges. Farmer's legal challenge came at a time when states were considering banning affirmative action, including the widely publicized 1996 California law that banned affirmative-action programs in state employment and public universities. Supporters of affirmative action believe that such programs are still needed to address historical patterns of institutional racism and discrimination and to promote future diversity in the U.S. workforce.

—*Micah Issitt*

WILLIAMS SISTERS MEET IN HISTORIC TENNIS FINAL
March 28, 1999

When Venus Williams defeated her sister Serena Williams in the final match of the Lipton Championships, the event marked the first time two sisters had faced each other in the finals of a major tennis tournament

in more than a century and drew increased attention to women's professional tennis.

Locale: Key Biscayne, Florida
Category: Sports

KEY FIGURES

Venus Williams (b. 1980), American tennis player
Serena Williams (b. 1981), American tennis player
Richard Williams (b. 1951), father and coach of Venus and Serena Williams

SUMMARY OF EVENT

In 1999, sisters Venus and Serena Williams were up-and-coming tennis stars who had each won a few Women's Tennis Association (WTA) tournaments. Tennis fans had speculated for months whether the siblings would one day meet each other in the final match of a WTA event. Such confrontations were indeed rare. Three sets of brothers had faced each other in tennis finals in the recent past: Gene Mayer defeated Sandy Mayer in 1981, Emilio Sánchez defeated Javier Sánchez in 1987, and John McEnroe defeated Patrick McEnroe in 1991. The only meeting of two sisters in a tennis final, however, had occurred 115 years earlier, in 1884, when Maud Watson defeated Lillian Watson in the most prestigious tennis tournament of all, Wimbledon. On March 28, 1999, the anticipated showdown between the Williams sisters finally occurred at the Lipton Championships in Key Biscayne, Florida.

Venus and Serena Williams were raised to be tennis champions. The African American sisters were born to Richard and Oracene (Price) Williams fifteen months apart—Venus on June 17, 1980, and Serena on September 26, 1981. The girls grew up in Compton, California, in a modest, middle-class home. Unlike many tennis players, the Williams sisters did not grow up playing the game at country clubs—their parents could not afford such luxuries.

Legend has it that Richard Williams decided to teach his two daughters how to play tennis so that they would grow up to have good incomes. He supposedly became inspired while watching a women's tennis match on television, noting the size of the winner's check. Consequently, he took the girls to the Compton city courts when they were just toddlers and encouraged them to hit hundreds of tennis balls every day. Both sisters were natural athletes, and they enjoyed the game tremendously from the beginning. Richard Williams, with no formal training in the sport, became his daughters' primary coach.

Venus Williams was the more talented of the two as they grew up and began entering junior tournaments. Although Serena also had great success early on, almost everyone in tennis circles in Southern California pegged Venus as a star in the making. Serena, observers believed, would be a good, solid player, but Venus would be exceptional. Many newspaper articles in the early 1990's touted Venus as someone destined to be a champion.

She declared herself a professional in 1994; Serena followed in 1995. Both sisters were strong and athletic. At six feet, one inch tall, Venus used her long legs and arms to track down and return balls that smaller or slower players would have missed. Serena grew to be five feet, eleven inches, but was more muscular and powerful than her sibling. Both developed serves that were several miles an hour faster than those their opponents could produce. Likewise, they were excellent at returning balls hit to them—playing from the baseline (the back of the court) and outslugging their challengers. Both, too, could come to the net and offer lobs and drop shots to their rivals.

When the sisters began as professionals, Venus was consistently rated ahead of Serena. At the beginning of the Lipton Championships, for example, Venus was ranked sixth in the world and Serena was seventeenth. Venus had won four singles championships; Serena had won two. The sisters, who were best friends and roommates, had also won two doubles titles playing together.

In 1998, they had also accomplished a unique feat: Each had won two mixed doubles championships in tennis's four "grand slam" events. The most important tennis tournaments for men and women alike are the national "opens" of Australia, France, Great Britain, and the United States. The British championship is commonly known as Wimbledon, the name of the London suburb where the event is staged. These four tournaments are the only ones known to tennis aficionados as "major" or "grand slam" contests. These tournaments are also among the very few tennis events held each year when men and women play together; each features (in addition to men's and women's singles and doubles titles) a mixed doubles category, in which each team consists of one woman and one man. In 1998, Venus and her mixed doubles partner, Justin Gimelstob, won the Australian Open and the French Open. Serena and Max Mirnyi then teamed up to win Wimbledon and the U.S. Open in the same year.

Despite these successes, the Williams sisters were still teenagers who had only begun to show the world what they could do on a tennis court when they met for their first showdown in a final match in March, 1999. Venus blitzed her sister in the first set, 6-1. Serena bounced back in the second, winning 6-4. The match remained even through the first eight games of the decisive set, but Venus won the last two games to take the set 6-4 and the match by the score of 6-1, 4-6, 6-4. The historic confrontation took almost two hours and was witnessed by fourteen thousand fans in the stadium and by millions more on television.

SIGNIFICANCE

This first all-Williams final set the stage for much more intrafamily tennis drama in future years. The Williams sisters faced each other again in several tennis finals in the early twenty-first century, usually in major tournaments.

At first, Venus was the dominant sibling—as she had been at the Lipton Championships in 1999. For example, Venus defeated Serena in the 2001 U.S. Open final. By the time that match was played in August, 2001, the sisters had helped to make women's tennis so popular that the contest was broadcast at night to make it available to a larger television audience. This marked the first time that a women's tennis final was telecast in such a time slot.

Venus and Serena Williams brought a new level of excitement to women's professional tennis and influenced the game significantly with their style of play. Almost every observer of the history of women's tennis has agreed that the power and athleticism that the Williams sisters displayed transformed the game, as, in response to the Williams style of play, many other women players began incorporating more muscle-building workouts into their training.

—Roger D. Hardaway

COLIN POWELL NAMED SIXTY-FIFTH SECRETARY OF STATE

November 2000

Diplomat and military leader

Powell was named the sixty-fifth secretary of state of the United States by President George W. Bush in November, 2000. Powell was the first African American named to this important post. He previously served as national security adviser and chairman of the Joint Chiefs of Staff, the highest military position in the U.S. Department of Defense. A professional soldier for thirty-five years, Powell retired from the military in 1993 as a four-star general.

Born: April 5, 1937; New York, New York
Also known as: Colin Luther Powell
Areas of achievement: Diplomacy; Government and politics; Military

EARLY LIFE

The second child and only son of Luther Powell and Maud Ariel McKoy Powell, Colin Luther Powell was born in 1937 in New York. His father was a gardener and a building superintendent, and his mother was a seamstress. When Powell was six, his family moved to the Bronx. Powell's maternal grandmother, Alice McKoy, took care of Powell and his older sister, Marilyn, while their parents were working. As the family's situation improved, the household moved to Queens, where Powell ran track and played basketball at Morris High

Official portrait of Colin L. Powell as the Secretary of State of the United States of America. Taken in January 2001, by Department of State of the United States of America

School. Two months before his seventeenth birthday, thanks to an accelerated program, Powell graduated and soon enrolled at City College of New York (CCNY), where he joined the Reserve Officers' Training Corps (ROTC). Powell enjoyed the ROTC, and he joined an elite precision drill team, the Pershing Rifles. Although hewas an average student at CCNY, Powell excelled at his ROTC coursework, dedicating his weekends and free hours to practice. The military's discipline, structure, and camaraderie appealed to Powell. A geology major who had originally pursued an engineering degree, Powell graduated from CCNY in 1958 with a B.S. degree and the honor of distinguished military graduate. He was commissioned as a second lieutenant in the U.S. Army. Powell's basic training was in Fort Benning, Georgia, and he was soon posted overseas to the Third Armored Division in West Germany. At the end of his first year, Powell was promoted to first lieutenant. After his twoyear tour of duty, Powell was sent to Fort Devens, near Boston. By 1961, he had completed his required three years of ROTC service, and he was at a crossroads .With little hesitation, Powell committed to a career in the Army.

Powell met Alma Vivian Johnson, a native of Birmingham, Alabama, on a blind date, and they formed a friendship that culminated in marriage on August 25, 1962. Shortly after the wedding, Powell was sent to Fort Bragg, North Carolina, for training as a military adviser and then on to South Vietnam for a two-year tour of duty. Now holding the rank of captain, Powell was wounded in Vietnam when he stepped on a punji stake, a sharp stick designed by the Viet Cong to hobble soldiers. Powell was awarded a Purple Heart, and later that year he received a Bronze Star. He returned to Vietnam as a major in 1968 with the Twenty-third Infantry Division. During that year, he was injured during a helicopter crash, and he received a Soldier's Medal for bravery in helping to rescue men from the burning wreckage. After his second tour in Vietnam, Powell returned to the United States and enrolled in graduate school at George Washington University in Washington, D.C., where he earned a master's degree in business administration in 1971. In July of 1971, Powell was assigned to the Pentagon, where he worked in the office of the assistant vice chief of staff of the Army.

LIFE'S WORK

Powell was named a White House Fellow in 1972-1973 and assigned to the Office of Management and Budget (OMB). The OMB was headed by Caspar Weinberger, who later became President Ronald Reagan's secretary of defense, and Frank C. Carlucci, later Reagan's national security adviser. Powell soon took an assignment at Camp Casey in South Korea. When he returned to the United States in 1974, he was assigned to the Pentagon once more, where he took classes in the National War College. In early 1976, Powell was promoted to full colonel. As Powell alternated stints in Washington with service abroad, his family grew. The Powells had three children, Michael, Linda, and Annemarie. Powell took command of the Second Brigade of the 101st Airborne Division at Fort Campbell, Kentucky, where he remained until 1977. Once again, he was called back to Washington, this time to serve in the office of the secretary of defense in President Jimmy Carter's administration. In June, 1979, Powell was promoted to brigadier general, and for a brief time he was the administrative secretary to Charles Duncan, the secretary of energy under Carter.

The early 1980's found Powell out West, first at Fort Carson, Colorado, and then as deputy commander of Fort Leavenworth, Kansas. In June, 1983, Powell was promoted to major general and returned to Washington to serve in the Reagan administration as military assistant to Weinberger. In this capacity, he aided in the plans for the invasion of Grenada and the air strike on Libya. In 1986, Powell was named commander of the Fifth Corps in Frankfurt, West Germany, where he commanded seventy-five thousand troops. In early 1987, he returned to Washington to serve as deputy assistant to President George H.W. Bush for national security affairs. In April, 1989, Powell was promoted to general and was picked by Bush to be the chairman of the Joint Chiefs of Staff. At the relatively young age of fifty-two, Powell became only the third general since World War II to be promoted to the four-star rank without ever being a divisional commander; the other two were Dwight D. Eisenhower and Alexander Haig.

As chair of the Joint Chiefs, Powell's mission was to support General Norman Schwarzkopf in the Persian Gulf War. The short duration of the war, which ended with Iraq's withdrawal from Kuwait, was the result of overwhelming force and a large international contingent of soldiers. This strategy of fighting wars became known as the Powell Doctrine. After his retirement from the military, Powell eventually declared himself a Republican and began to campaign for Republican candidates in 1995. A political moderate, Powell published his autobiography, *My American Journey*, in 1995, and opinion polls showed him to be one of the most popular public figures in the political arena. Although he was sought after as a candidate for either the presidency or the vice presidency, Powell said that he was not interested in becoming president. In 2000, President George W. Bush picked Powell to be his secretary of state, and the U.S. Senate voted unanimously to confirm him.

In the wake of the September 11, 2001, attacks, the Bush administration declared a global war on terror and adopted a preemptive-strike policy that viewed states that supported terrorists as enemies on par with the terrorists themselves. High on the list of states supporting terrorism, according to the Bush administration, was Saddam Hussein's Iraq. After invading Afghanistan, the White House switched its emphasis and efforts to Iraq. In order to garner international support for this invasion, it was necessary to prove Iraq held weapons of mass destruction. In early February, 2003, Powell went before the United Nations Security Council to argue in favor of military action in Iraq. Armed with defense intelligence that was later found to be faulty, Powell presented his case. Citing various Iraqi defectors and information supplied by the Central Intelligence Agency, Powell said, "There can be no doubt that Saddam Hussein has biological weapons and the capability to rapidly produce more, many more." This statement helped build international support for the invasion of Iraq. In a 2005 interview with journalist Barbara Walters, Powell said of his role in the Iraq war, "It will always be a part of my record. It was painful. It's painful now."

SIGNIFICANCE

A trailblazer, Powell has held numerous positions of power in the United States military and government. A career soldier who got his start in the ROTC, Powell was the first African American and the youngest man ever to serve as chairman of the Joint Chiefs of Staff, the first African American to serve as national security adviser, and the first African American to serve as secretary of state. Powell oversaw Operation Desert Shield and Operation Desert Storm during President George

---

Powell and the 2008 Presidential Election

Although he did not seek the presidency for himself, Colin Powell was in a position to influence the outcome of the 2008 presidential election. Although public-approval ratings for President George W. Bush had plummeted, Powell maintained a reputation as a good soldier who had carried out orders for the White House, misguided though the orders might have been. He was seen as separate from the policy makers in the Bush administration. Eight years earlier, in the 2000 presidential election, Powell had supported Arizona's John McCain in the Republican primaries against Bush. As it became clear that Bush would become the party's choice, Powell threw his support behind the Texas Republican and was seen as a clear choice for a top spot in the new administration. As the Bush presidency evolved in the wake of the September 11, 2001, terrorist attacks on the United States, Powell's moderate views seemed to run counter to Vice President Dick Cheney's and Defense Secretary Donald Rumsfeld's hawkish attitudes. Once Bush's first term ended, Powell left the administration. Early in the 2008 presidential campaign, Powell again supported McCain. However, as the general election approached and McCain faced Democratic candidate Barack Obama, Powell's support for McCain began to waver, especially after McCain's selection of Alaska's governor, Sarah Palin, as his running mate. On October 18, 2009, in a *Meet the Press* interview, Powell announced his support for Obama, whom he called a "transformational figure."

H.W. Bush's administration. President Bill Clinton presented him with the Presidential Medal of Freedom with Distinction, the country's highest civilian award. In 1997, Powell founded the youth organization America's Promise Alliance.

—*Randy L. Abbott*

AFRICAN AMERICAN'S DNA TESTING

Founded 2003

Genetic DNA testing is the process of providing DNA, via skin cells or saliva, to determine one's maternal and paternal lineages back to Africa, and well as one's admixture composition – the percentages of one's ancestral countries or regional origins.

Identification (definition): Autosomal and Admixture genetic DNA testing is opening up a world of Ancestry for African-Americans around the world.

Locale: International

Categories: DNA Testing, Ancestry,

KEY FIGURES:

Rick Kittles (1976–) and *Gina Paige* arefounders of African Ancestry DNA service.

Dr. Henry Louis Gates (1950–) Keyser, West Virginia, scholarship; social issues; social sciences, and host of *Finding Your Roots* PBS Show (since 2012)

Alondra Nelson (1968–) author of *The Social Life of DNA: Race, Reparations, and Reconciliation After the Genome*

Deadria Farmer-Paellmann (1968–) uncovered major corporations that benefited directly from pre-Civil War slavery.

During the Atlantic Slave Trade, some 20,000,000 Africans were removed from their native land, countries, communities, and families, in chains, without any information identifying their origins nor relationships to their family, tribes, or country. This process separated Africans and theirs ancestors (from the Motherland) and descendants, across the Diaspora, as well as their lineages.

Dr. Rick Kittles, a geneticist, and Dr. Gina Paige founded the African Ancestry company to provide African-Americans with autosomal (direct line) maternal and paternal, as well as admixture DNA testing services which would allow them to trace their on lineage back to the Motherland – Africa, through both their maternal and paternal lines, as well as the percentages of their ancestry from countries around the world. Their vision was to support the African Diaspora in improving their cultural, spiritual, emotional, mental, physical, and economic well-being by learning from whence they came, and re-connecting to their ancestral roots, before their ancestors enslavement, based upon a growing database of 30,000 indigenous African people's DNA samples, from well over 400 groups, dating back more than 500 years, that live in the current day regions which had the greatest roles with regards to the Atlanta Slave Trade.

Tests that are offered include the maternal (MatriClan) mtDNA, the paternal (PatriClan) Y Chromosome, and the Admixture test. The process involves scraping cells from one's inner cheek, or providing a saliva sample. Upon receiving the results from a test, through genetic structural signature matches, a person learns not only the specific countries that they come from, but their ethnic groups as well. The company guarantees statistically probability matches of ninety percent or better.

Autosomal (direct line) DNA testing, along with additional truths being uncovered through the efforts of various African-American scholars, and individual history researchers, offer descendants of Mother Africa, and the world, the opportunity to understand that Afuruka (Africa's original name) began long before the enslavement of her people. It has been most beneficial in supporting family historians with tracing the origins and path of their enslaved ancestors whose information is often difficult to locate prior to the 1860s, due to the original African names being changed to a master's surname, no names being listed in the census prior to the Emancipation Proclamation, and the 1870 census, especially those who were previously relegated to existing according to the 1890s One Drop Rule, by being labeled mulatto, mustefin, quadroon, or octoroon.

African-American DNA has also been used as a case for reparations. After many years of enslavement, Reconstruction, Jim Crow, policies restricting access to the American dream – life, liberty, and the pursuit of happiness, many have sought reparations for the Nadir that their ancestors, and they themselves have experienced. Deadria Farmer-Paellman researched and uncovered evidence that major corporations in America's wealth is directly tied to pre-Civil War enslavement of Africans, Mulattos, and Negro people. Her research, and subsequent challenge to these corporations, led the state of California to require other insurers to search their archives for what was known as slave policies. Slave policies insured the lives of slaves, for the benefit of their masters. So far, sixty companies – banks, insurance companies, textile makers, and various estates - have been identified as having profited directly from the enslavement of African-Americans, and their ancestors.

Sadly, to date there have been no reparations made, and only rhetorical or no apologies.

Alondra Nelson, author of *The Social Life of DNA: Race, Reparations, and Reconciliations After the Genome*, says that genetic DNA testing, for family history research, has begun a multi-billion industry. By 2014, more than one million people have offered up samples to learn where they come from, find their birth parents (adoptees), and learn about their families medical profiles. Various privately owned companies—www. AfricanAncestry.com, www.23AndMe.com, www. Ancestry.com,ww.familytreedna.com, and https:// genographic.nationalgeographic.com—offer African-Americans, and people around the world access to information that might otherwise have gone lost forever.

More and more, people of the African Diaspora are joining various genealogy groups—Afrigeneas, African American Genealogy Forum, Out Black Ancestry Facebook group, and their local and national Genealogical societies. Additionally, more shows, such as PBS' "Finding Your Roots," are offering people interested in their heritage the opportunity to learn how the process is done, both through document research and the use of DNA.

—Patricia A. McDaniel

See also: Dr. Henry Louis Gates hosts first episode of *Finding Your Roots*; The One Drop Rule; African

GRATZ V. BOLLINGER
2003

The 2003 U.S. Supreme Court Case of Gratz v Bollinger was an affirmative action case in which the court decided that the University of Michigan's method of taking race and ethnicity into account when considering applicants to the university was unconstitutional. The case was one of two Supreme Court cases decided that year that established new legal precedents for college and university affirmative action policies.

Identification: One of two important Supreme Court cases of 2003 dealing with the issue of affirmative action in university admissions decisions.

The Supreme Court case, *Gratz v Bollinger*, began when white students Jennifer Gratz and Patrick Hamacher were rejected for admission to the University of Michigan in 1995 and 1997 respectively. The Center for Individual Rights (CIR), a non-profit law firm that has focused on representing non-minority students challenging controversial affirmative action policies, contacted Gratz and Hamacher and offered to represent them bringing suit against the university for reverse discrimination. The CIR filed a suit in 1997, specifically accusing the University and former university presidents James Duderstadt and Lee Bollinger, of violating the equal protection clause of the Fourteen Amendment guaranteeing equal protection regardless of race or ethnicity, which has been interpreted as a ban on racial or ethnic discrimination.

During the trial, it was explained that the University of Michigan had adopted an affirmative action policy that ranked applicants on a point system with a maximum of 100 points. Individuals of under-represented minorities, African Americans, American Indians, and Latinos, received an automatic 20-points based solely on their racial or ethnic categorization. During the course of the case, it was argued that defendant Jennifer Gratz did not have standing to sue the university because she applied before the controversial point system was introduced. The case progressed through the courts and was pending appeal in the Sixth Circuit courts when the Supreme Court agreed to hear the case, having also heard similar arguments in the case of *Grutter v. Bollinger* that same year. The University of Michigan defended the use of race and ethnicity as admissions criteria, and cited statistics indicating that in 1995, the year that Gratz was rejected for admission, 1,400 non-minority students with lower GPA's and test scores than Gratz were admitted, while 2,000 non-minority students with higher test scores and GPAs were rejected. The university used their admission statistics to argue that race and ethnicity were not, therefore, the only reason that Gratz and co-plaintiff Hamacher were rejected for admission.

While the justices were split 6-3 on the issue, the court ruled in favor of the plaintiffs, with Chief Justice Rehnquist writing the majority opinion on the case. The majority opinion hinged on several key considerations, first, that the bureaucratic approach the university had conceived for ranking individuals based on ethnicity and race was inconsistent with providing applicants with providing each student with individual consideration. The court argued that an applicant's capability to contribute to the diversity of the student body needed to be considered on a case-by-case basis, rather than through a fixed, automatic system. Further, the ruling establishes a legal precedent requiring institutions that wish to use affirmative action criteria to use individual evaluation of numerous factors, rather than reducing the contribution of race or ethnicity to simplify the process.

The Gratz decision has consequences for institutions receiving thousands of annual applications that have attempted to simplify the consideration of diversity in the application process. The court's ruling further reinforced the Supreme Court ruling in *California v Bakke* (1978), which states that affirmative action programs must be "narrowly tailored" in order to hurt a few people as possible. Further, the ruling holds that consideration of an applicant's contributions to diversity must also allow universities and other intuitions to consider other aspects of an applicant's history, including socioeconomic status, religion, and general cultural background. In essence, the ruling in the Gratz case rejects a systematized consideration of race in favor of a more nuanced, individualized system in which race is one of numerous factors that can legally be considered when assessing an applicant's potential contributions to the diversity of the institution. While the case forced the University of Michigan to stop using a "point system" for considering race, the case also upheld affirmative action programs in general, with the majority ruling that race and ethnicity were still appropriate and important qualities for consideration towards the goal of fostering diversity in higher education and subsequently the U.S. workforce. The *Gratz v. Bollinger* case attracted more than 100 amicus briefs, with the U.S. Justice Department filing a brief on behalf of the plaintiffs while numerous corporations filed briefs in defense of the university, arguing for the benefit of cultivating more diverse classes of graduates to take part in the nation's industries.

—Micah Issitt

GRUTTER V. BOLLINGER

2003

Grutter v. Bollinger *was one of two Supreme Court cases decided in 2003 that helped to determine the constitutionality of considering of race and ethnicity in university and college admissions. The case upheld the right of institutions to consider race and ethnicity as long as consideration of those factors was part of a holistic process that attempted to assess an individual's potential contributions to the diversity of the institution.*

Identification: One of two U.S. Supreme Court cases in 2003 dealing with the legality of affirmative action in university and college admissions systems.

Barbara Grutter, a graduate from University of Michigan, returned to school at 43-years-old, hoping for a career change to become a health care attorney. In 1996, she applied for admission to the University of Michigan Law School, holding a 3.81 GPA from her previous undergraduate education, and scoring a 161 on LSAT examinations, placing her in the 86th percentile of all applicants. Grutter was rejected for admission and later learned that minority students with lower test scores had been admitted. She was approached by the Center for Individual Rights (CIR), a non-profit law firm that has been prominent in trying to strike down affirmative action policies as discriminatory, and decided to file suit against the university for "reverse discrimination."

In the case, Grutter argued that the University of Michigan Law School's admission policies violated the Fourteenth Amendment clause guaranteeing equal protection under the law, which has been used in the courts to prohibit racial prejudice in hiring, school admissions, and government programs. The university countered by arguing that admissions policies were created to foster a "critical mass" of underrepresented racial and ethnic minorities, specifically African Americans, Latinos, and American Indians, as a way to increase the school's overall diversity and to help make the university inviting to students of various ethnic and racial backgrounds. The plaintiffs did not argue against the benefit of creating a diverse school body, and numerous amicus briefs were filed by corporations arguing that promoting diversity was important to creating a more innovative, culturally sensitive, and diverse workforce.

Grutter won her case in District Court, which found the University of Michigan admissions policy to be unlawful. The case was appealed to the Sixth Circuit Court of Appeals, where the court reversed the decision, citing the Supreme Court decision of *California v Bakke* (1978), in which the court determined that race could be one of several factors that colleges and universities could use to determine admissions policies, but ruled that racial quota systems, in which an institution sets aside a specific number of positions for minority candidates, are unconstitutional. The 1978 court ruled that affirmative action programs must be "narrowly tailored" to harm as few people as possible. Therefore, the Grutter case became an investigation of whether the University of Michigan Law School's affirmative action policies were sufficiently "narrow" in application. The Supreme Court agreed to hear the case in 2003, and counsel presented arguments on April 1st, 2003.

As the first Supreme Court case dealing with Affirmative Action since the court upheld affirmative action in = *California v. Bakke*, public interest in the case was high and the courts agreed to release case documents and statements to the public. In a split decision on June 23, 2003, the Supreme Court upheld affirmative action, voting 5-4 that the university could legally consider race and ethnicity when making admissions decisions. However, in the related case of *Gratz v Bollinger*, also decided on June 23, 2003, the court ruled that the University of Michigan's use of a "point system" that automatically awarded 20 (out of 100) points to underrepresented minorities, was unconstitutional because the system substituted institutional simplicity for individual consideration and was therefore not narrowly tailored to harm the fewest number of applicants.

Justice Sandra Day O'Connor cast the deciding vote in the Grutter case, and, in her majority opinion wrote that affirmative action was still needed, but that she and the court in general hoped that the need for such policies would disappear over the next 25 years. The majority opinion further argued that although race-conscious policies could be seen to violate Fourteenth Amendment protections, the university's reasons for considering race were sufficiently compelling. Taken together with the *Gratz* case, the Supreme Court's rulings upheld the idea that affirmative action was still necessary and legal, but that such programs had to employ an individual, case-by-case strategy, with race or ethnicity being one factor in the institution's overall consideration process. The case was considered one of the most important civil rights cases in recent history and was widely considered a qualified victory for affirmative action and the idea that promoting cultural diversity is an appropriate and sufficient reason to consider race in admissions. The ruling in the case can similarly be applied to consideration of race in hiring policies.

—*Micah Issitt*

BARACK OBAMA

November 2008

The first African American elected president of the United States, Obama has also worked as a lawyer, community organizer, legislator, author, and law school professor. He was awarded the Nobel Peace Prize in 2009.

President of the United States
Born: August 4, 1961; Honolulu, Hawaii
Also known as: Barack Hussein Obama
Areas of achievement: Diplomacy; Government and politics

EARLY LIFE

Barack Hussein Obama (bah-RAHK hoo-SAYN oh-BAH-mah) was born in Honolulu, Hawaii, on August 4, 1961. His mother was Stanley Ann Dunham, an American born and raised in Kansas, and his father was Barack Obama, Sr., a Kenyan of the Luo-speaking people. Obama's parents were married on February 2, 1961, while students at the University of Hawaii, but divorced in 1964. His mother subsequently married Lolo Soetero, an Indonesian, and went with him and her son to live in Jakarta, Indonesia, in 1967. After completing a graduate degree at Harvard University, the elder Obama returned to Kenya and saw his son only one more time, in 1971. He died in a road accident in 1982. From the remarriages of his parents, Obama has several half brothers and half sisters. From 1967 to 1971, Obama studied at public and parochial grade schools in Jakarta. He returned to Honolulu for the rest of his primary education and

U.S. President Barack Obama's official photograph in the Oval Office on 6 December 2012.

graduated from high school in 1979. His favorite sport became basketball. He lived with his maternal grandparents, who had moved to Hawaii from their home in Kansas. His mother lived with him from 1972 to 1977, then returned to Indonesia to pursue her anthropological research. She died of cancer in 1995 in Hawaii.

The individuals most influential in forming Obama's character were his mother and grandmother, both of whom were born and raised in small-town Kansas and valued family, work, and plain speaking. As a youth, he experimented with drugs, a decision for which he later expressed regret. Obama began his college career at Occidental College in Los Angeles in 1979, before transferring two years later to Columbia University in New York. At Columbia, he earned a degree in political science and international relations in 1983. He remained in New York until 1985, when he moved to Chicago to work as a community organizer on the city's South Side. After a two-month tour of Europe and Africa in mid-1988, he entered Harvard Law School and became the first African American to serve as president of the *Harvard Law Review*. After graduating from Harvard, Obama returned to Chicago to practice civil rights law and teach constitutional law at the University of

Chicago Law School. He emerged as not only a community organizer but also a community leader. In 1992, he married fellow Harvard Law graduate Michelle Robinson. They had two daughters, Malia in 1998 and Natasha (better known as Sasha) in 2001. Obama's introspective memoir, *Dreams from My Father: A Story of Race and Inheritance* (1995), became a best seller. He began to contemplate a political career.

LIFE'S WORK

Although Obama considered running for mayor of Chicago, his strongest community roots were in the area of south Chicago that formed the Thirteenth District of the Illinois state senate. In March of 1996, he won the Democratic Party nomination for the district unopposed. He carried the November 5 election with more than 80 percent of the vote. Obama won reelection in 1998, this time for a four-year term, obtaining just under 90 percent of the vote. In 2002, he won another four-year term, running unopposed. Although he breezed through the state senate elections, Obama was defeated in a 2000 bid for the Illinois First Congressional District seat, losing the Democratic primary by a wide margin to the incumbent congressman, Bobby Rush.

In the Illinois senate, Obama introduced or supported legislation that reformed the state's welfare system, provided tax relief for low-income families, and supported labor interests. Democrats won control of the senate in 2003, and Obama was named chairman of the Health and Human Services Committee. With more power to shape and pass legislation, he moved to improve health care for children, standardize access to health care statewide, and monitor hospital quality. He also responded to labor demands related to equal pay, overtime, and protection of whistleblowers. He addressed police issues related to domestic violence, racial profiling, and evidence-gathering in potential capital punishment cases. He was noted for his bipartisan approach to writing and supporting legislation. In 2002, Obama began considering a future run for a U.S. Senate seat and engaged Chicago political strategist David Axelrod for his campaign. Sweeping through the 2004 spring primary, he won a solid majority for the nomination. He further enhanced his rising political profile by giving a charismatic address that summer to the Democratic National Convention. In the November election, Obama trounced his conservative Republican opponent, Alan Keyes, a last-minute substitute for a previous Republican candidate who had resigned amid a marriage scandal.

Obama's position in the U.S. Senate provided him a national and international stage on which to act. With Republican senator Richard Lugar, he sponsored the Lugar-Obama Nuclear Proliferation Act of 2007 to reduce conventional weapons of warfare. He also teamed with Republican senator Tom Coburn to produce the Federal Funding Accountability and Transparency Act of 2006 that created a Web site, USAspending.gov, to enhance transparency in government finance. Obama also supported legislation for campaign finance reform, energy efficiency, and children's health insurance. A member of the Committee on Foreign Relations, he traveled to Europe, the Middle East, and Africa. Obama next set his sights on the Democratic presidential nomination, announcing his candidacy at the beginning of 2007. His opposition to the Iraq War and support of health care reform, as well as his skills as an orator, quickly placed him among the front-runners. His main opponent became Senator Hillary Clinton of New York, who emphasized Obama's lack of experience and expressed doubts that his rhetoric could be turned into tangible action. By June, after a protracted primary campaign, Obama had edged past Clinton to achieve the necessary majority of delegates for the nomination. At the Democratic National Convention in August, Obama selected Senator Joseph Biden of Delaware as his running mate.

Obama's Democratic ticket ran against a Republican duo of Senator John McCain of Arizona and Alaska governor Sarah Palin. McCain and Palin presented themselves as "mavericks," while Obama and Biden championed "change you can believe in." Obama continued his highly successful fund-raising campaign, rejecting both official public funding and lobbyist support. Opting for private funding, much of which came in small amounts from individual donors, he accumulated well over half a billion dollars, an unprecedented amount to raise privately. His campaigns also made innovative use of the Internet. He took part in three televised debates with McCain and was generally judged to have won them all. Further weakening the McCain campaign was its association with the presidency of George W. Bush, whose popularity sank under the weight of a major economic crisis and unpopular wars in Iraq and Afghanistan. In the final weeks of the 2008 campaign, opinion polls showed the Obama-Biden ticket leading McCain-Palin by a significant margin.

For the general election on November 4, voter turnout was estimated at over 60 percent, relatively high by modern American standards. More than 130 million

Youth in Indonesia and Hawaii

Barack Obama was born in Honolulu, Hawaii, and spent most of his youth there. However, from 1967 to 1971, he lived in Jakarta, Indonesia, with his mother and Indonesian stepfather. The family lived in the upscale Menteng district, a residential subdivision of the city. It was a product of early twentieth century urban planning, combining elements of Dutch and native Indonesian domestic architectural styles, intended for Europeans residing in the former Dutch colony. Obama attended fourth grade at Besuki Public School. The school was established during the colonial administration for children of the Dutch and upper-class Indonesians. The next year, Obama continued his elementary education at a Roman Catholic parochial school, St. Francis Assisi. His mother supplemented his formal education with lessons on African American history and English. From his years in Jakarta, Obama acquired a conversational command of the Indonesian language. His parentage and childhood made him one of the most culturally cosmopolitan individuals ever to enter the American presidency.

votes were cast, with nearly 70 million (53 percent) going to Obama. Electoral College results were 365 to 173 in favor of the Democratic ticket, which ran strongest in the populous states of the East Coast, West Coast, and upper Midwest. The Republican ticket claimed nearly 60 million votes (47 percent), prevailing in the South, Southwest, and lower Midwest. The Democratic Party also won overwhelming majorities in both houses of Congress. At a victory rally on the night of his election, Obama addressed a massive crowd in downtown Chicago's Grant Park, where forty years earlier police and protesters had clashed in one of the most turbulent Democratic conventions in history. Until his inauguration on January 20, 2009, Obama and his transition team worked with the outgoing Bush administration to deal with the mounting global financial and economic collapse. Obama took office as the United States' first African American president amid a vast array of economic, social, and international challenges. He was awarded the Nobel Peace Prize that year in recognition of his "efforts to strengthen international diplomacy and cooperation between peoples." The award stirred controversy, since America remained heavily involved in two wars, and the Nobel committee was criticized by some for acting prematurely to honor a president mere months into his term. The committee, however, argued that Obama had "captured the world's attention and given its people hope for a better future."

SIGNIFICANCE

Although the Obama presidency faced unprecedented, paralyzing dilemmas, its mere existence was a major milestone in American history. In his November 4,

2008, victory speech in Grant Park, Obama proclaimed that his ascension to the presidency had proved that "America is a place where all things are possible." His campaign emphasized "change" and "hope" as its main themes, and his election symbolized for many Americans the changing of long-held racial attitudes and hope for a more unified future.

—*Edward A. Riedinger*

BLACK CHURCH AND THE LGBT COMMUNITY

2012

The Black Church, or African American church, has been an important part of the African American community since before the Civil War and was an essential focal point for the Civil Rights Movement. However, because many African American churches practice a socially-conservative form of Christianity, Black Churches have not historically supported LGBT rights or the movement for gay marriage.

Identification: The relationship between the LGBT community and African American Christian churches.

The adoption of Christianity among African slaves in the United States was a complex process that often involved the "creolization" of European Christian traditions, blending elements of native African spirituality with the spiritual traditions of white congregations. During the abolition movement, congregations of African American Christians played an important role in organizing members of the community. After the abolition of slavery, as states adopted segregation laws, a plethora of new Black Churches formed across the nation. Having long served as a platform for social outreach, providing food for the poor and education for African American children, the churches of the post-slavery era were also essential to the development of the Civil Rights Movement. Martin Luther King Jr.'s Southern Christian Leadership Conference, for instance, was organized through congregations in African American churches. Throughout the existence of the African American church, the church has been a focal point in the formation of black communities, and an epicenter for social and civil rights.

For a variety of reasons, sociologists have found that African American churches tend to support a conservative form of Christianity that often includes a literal interpretation of biblical scripture. The tendency to interpret scripture literally has places African American churches and African American Christians at odds with the LGBT community. According to some biblical interpretations, the Apostle Paul's letter to the Romans [1: 26-32], which portrays homosexuality as a perversion, can be taken as a spiritual condemnation of homosexuality. Thus, many in the African American church community have taken a spiritual stance against homosexuality, LGBT rights, and the recent effort to legalize LGBT marriage. In 2012, when both President Barack Obama and the National Association for the Advancement of Colored People (NAACP) announced their support for same-sex marriage as a civil right, the opposition to LGBT rights within Black Churches became the subject of intense debate within the African American community.

While African American church members are overwhelmingly opposed to LGBT rights, historians studying the issue have shown that both closeted and openly LGBT individuals have played an important role in African American churches for generations. The church choir, for instance, has long served as an important haven for LGBT members of the community who face discrimination because of their sexual orientation, and LGBT musicians and singers have played a major role in the development of gospel and other types of African American spiritual music. In this way, the Black Chruch presents a paradox, being both one of the most tolerant places for LGBT African Americans, while also encouraging homophobia within the African American community as a whole by spreading the idea that same-sex intimacy is a sin against spiritual principles. Some members of the LGBT community have described the African American church's approach to the issue as an unofficial "don't ask, don't tell" policy. Writing in a 2015 issue of *The Advocate*, Pastor Mitchell Jones argues that the church's approach to homosexuality, encouraging LGBT individuals to remain in the closet and pray to avoid sexual urges, is an important factor in the high rates of HIV in the African American community, citing research indicating that 6-in-10 gay and bisexual African American men will be HIV positive by 40-years-old.

While African American churches have been slow to embrace LGBT rights, some prominent representatives, such as celebrity preacher Al Sharpton, have called for African Americans to embrace diversity and express tolerance towards members of the LGBT community. In the 2015 documentary, *Holler if You Hear Me: Black and Gay in the Church*, filmmaker Clay Cane uses interviews with African American members of both the churches and the LGBT community to promote the idea that black churches should embrace LGBT rights. Cane argues that the African American church serves as a "second family" for many members of the congregation and an important focal point of African American communities, and argues that the issue is important because LGBT individuals should not be forced to decide between expressing their sexuality and leaving the surrogate family of their church.

—Micah Issitt

HENRY LOUIS GATES, JR. HOSTS FIRST EPISODE OF *FINDING YOUR ROOTS*
March 25, 2012

Gates is best known as a major exponent and promoter of African and African American literature. His groundbreaking work to win recognition and acceptance of both genres established him as an important literary critic and teacher. Gates raised awareness of the important contributions of African and African American writers and drew attention to many forms of racism, including intellectual racism. Educator Henry Louis Gates Jr. has hosted several PBS series that examine U.S. history. In "Finding Your Roots," the Harvard professor continues his quest to "get into the DNA of American culture." In each episode, celebrities view ancestral histories, sometimes learn of connections to famous/infamous people, discover secrets and share the emotional experience with viewers. Analyzing genetic code, DNA diagnosticians trace bloodlines and occasionally debunk long-held beliefs.

Born: September 16, 1950; Keyser, West Virginia
Areas of achievement: Education; Scholarship; Social issues; Social sciences

EARLY LIFE
Henry Louis Gates, Jr., was born on September 16, 1950, to Pauline Augusta Coleman, a housekeeper, and Henry Louis Gates, Sr., a paper millworker. Gates spent his earliest years in Piedmont, West Virginia, in the Allegheny Mountains. He graduated from high school in 1968, a few weeks after leading a school boycott on the day of the funeral of Martin Luther King, Jr. His mother fought depression during his early years, and Gates devoted himself to religion, but turned away from it during the 1960's.

While playing touch football at the age of fourteen, Gates was injured. Although a physician at first thought his pain was psychosomatic, Gates later was found to have fractured a portion of his hip. As a result of the injury, he developed a condition known as slipped epiphysis and a right leg two inches shorter than his left. He wore an elevated shoe and used a cane to walk. In 2001, his hip joint was replaced surgically. After briefly attending Potomac State College, Gates was awarded an Andrew W. Mellon Scholarship in 1973 to enroll at Yale University, where he finished his baccalaureate degree summa cum laude in history. He then received a Ford Foundation Fellowship to study for a doctorate at Cambridge University, where at Clare College he was mentored by several scholars, notably Wole Soyinka, the Nigerian writer who acquainted him with African literature. Soyinka became the first black African to receive a Nobel Prize in Literature in 1986.

When Gates returned to Yale in 1975, he spent a month in law school but decided to look for other pursuits. Soon after, he got a job as a secretary in Yale's African American studies department. In 1976, he was hired as lecturer in African American studies and was promised an assistant professorship when his doctoral dissertation at Cambridge University was completed. In 1979, he received his doctorate and married Sharon Lynn Adams. They went on to have two daughters and later divorced.

In 1979, Gates was appointed as assistant professor in the English and African American Studies departments at Yale. In 1984, he was promoted to associate professor and applied for tenure. When he was denied tenure, he left Yale for Cornell University, where he taught from 1985 to 1989. Gates next taught at Duke University from 1989 to 1991. He moved to Harvard in 1991 as professor of English and as the second and only black member of the African American studies department, a department that he chaired until 2006. He is director of Harvard's W. E. B. Du Bois Institute for African and African American Research.

LIFE'S WORK

Gates is foremost a scholar who brought African literature to the attention of theworld. When he learned that Soyinka had been denied a position at Cambridge University because African literature was perceived as worthy of only anthropological or sociological consideration, Gates embarked on a quest to disprove that view among scholars of English literature.

Gates's major scholarly works, *Black Literature and Literary Theory* (1983) and *The Signifying Monkey: Towards a Theory of Afro-American Criticism* (1988), sought to define a distinctly black cultural aesthetic. He has explicated how the African American experience, unknown to those outside the culture, shaped black literature in the United States. His analysis of the works of African American writers shows how the themes of earlier writers were incorporated into the work of later writers but with different meanings in a kind of wordplay, similar to way the word "bad" can mean "good" in certain contexts. Gates's publications have received mixed reviews from scholars outside the African American mainstream. He responded that African and African American literatures have their own standards and should not be judged from a Eurocentric perspective. Gates also commented on how fellow academics harbor forms of racism in their criticisms and scholarship. He drew negative reactions from Eurocentric scholars and black separatists alike. He also sparked debate within the African American community when he urged black youths not to aspire to be athletes but to aim for other professions.

The intellectual discussion generated by Gates's views has resulted in much scholarly output. He is the author and editor (and frequently coauthor or coeditor) of more than thirty publications. His books have sought to bring less well-known writers to wider attention and to reinterpret the work of better-known writers in new contexts. In 1980, Gates launched the Black Periodical Literature Project, which sought to unearth African American literature that had been forgotten over the years. In 1983, for example, he discovered that Harriet E.Wilson, author of the novel *Our Nig* (1859), was not white (as had been believed) but was instead America's first black female novelist.

Gates also launched a genealogy project so that African Americans could trace their ancestry. As a result, he discovered that he was half European and half Yoruba, one of the major ethnic groups in Nigeria, and that he was descended from John Redman, a free African American who fought in the Revolutionary War. The project spawned three documentaries and a book, *In Search of Our Roots: How Nineteen Extraordinary African Americans Reclaimed Their Past* (2009).

Gates served as host, narrator, and scriptwriter of several documentaries. He was responsible for *From Great Zimbabwe to Kilimatinde* (1996), *The Two Nations of Black America* (1998), *Leaving Eldridge Cleaver* (1999), *America Beyond the Color Line* (2004), and *Looking for Lincoln* (2009). Perhaps the most notable is *Wonders of the African World* (1999), based on findings by scholars who traveled to twelve African countries for a year to find hitherto forgotten and venerable civilizations as well as traces of the slave trade.

Another major accomplishment was Gates's publication (with coeditor Kwame Anthony Appiah) of *Africana: The Encyclopedia of the African and African American Experience* (1999). Fulfilling W. E. B. Du Bois's dream of creating an African American equivalent to the *Encyclopedia Britannica*, *Africana*was completed with help from Microsoft president Bill Gates, who provided one million dollars toward the project. The encyclopedia's first edition contained five volumes, more than thirty-five hundred entries encompassing the history of African and the African diaspora in the Western Hemisphere, and a CD-ROM. A Web site was later developed to update the encyclopedia until its second edition was issued in 2005. In 1997, *Time* magazine listed Gates among the twenty-five most influential Americans. In 1998, he received the National Humanities Medal, and in 2000, the National Association for the Advancement of Colored People (NAACP) gave him the Image Award for Outstanding Literary Work, Non-fiction, for *Wonders of the African World*. In 2006, Gates was inducted into the Sons of the American Revolution in honor of his link to Redman, the Revolutionary War soldier. That year, he was appointed to the Alphonse Fletcher, Jr., University Professor at Harvard University. He also served as chair of the Fletcher Foundation.

In 2008, Gates cofounded and became editor-in-chief of *The Root*, an online magazine published by *The Washington Post* and aimed at African American readers. He also is a member of the governing boards of the Aspen Institute, Brookings Institution, Stanford University's Center for the Institute for Advanced Study in the Behavioral Sciences, the Legal Defense Fund of the NAACP, and the New York Public Library.

SIGNIFICANCE

Gates helped to establish African and African American literature within the multicultural mainstream of literature as a whole. He brought greater acceptance and attention to African American scholarship and spoke out against racism in America on many occasions. In 1981, the MacArthur Foundation awarded him a five-year "genius" grant of $150,000, recognizing him as a gifted scholar and enabling him to devote attention to intellectual pursuits. By 2010, he had received some fifty honorary degrees and numerous academic honors and social action awards. For *The Signifying Monkey*, Gates won the American Book Award in 1989. In 2002, the National Endowment for the Humanities conferred its highest honor on Gates by inviting him to deliver the annual Jefferson Lecture.

—*Michael Haas, updated by Patricia A McDaniel*

Gates, the Policeman, and President Obama

While Henry Louis Gates, Jr.'s scholarly contributions are revered within the academic world, he also is well known for highlighting instances of racism as a public intellectual. Barack Obama, who later became president of the United States, knew him in that role while he was a student at Harvard Law School. On July 16, 2009, when Gates returned from an exhausting out-of town trip to his residence in Cambridge, Massachusetts, he had difficulty gaining entry to his home. His keys jammed in the lock, so his driver helped him open the door. A neighbor, suspecting foul play, summoned the police, who arrived after Gates was already inside.

Gates was surprised that police officers would question his right to be in his own house. His irritation and offense led to a confrontation in which Gates was arrested on a charge of disorderly conduct. President Obama, when asked about the incident, came to Gates's defense and criticized the arresting officer, Sergeant James Crowley. Crowley responded publicly, defending his actions and denying that racism or racial profiling had triggered the incident. Ultimately, the charge against Gates was dropped, and Obama invited Gates and Crowley to the White House for an informal but highly publicized meeting, at which they were joined by Vice President Joe Biden. These widely reported developments provoked a national discussion on race relations.

BLACK LIVES MATTER

2013

Black Lives Matter (BLM) is an international activist movement, originating in the African-American community, that campaigns against violence and systemic racism toward black people. BLM regularly holds protests against police killings of black people and broader issues of racial profiling, police brutality, and perceived racial inequality in the United States criminal justice system. In 2013, the movement began with the use of the hashtag #BlackLivesMatter on social media, after the acquittal of George Zimmerman in the shooting death of African- American teen Trayvon Martin. Black Lives Matter became nationally recognized for its street demonstrations following the 2014 deaths of two African Americans: Michael Brown, resulting in protests and unrest in Ferguson, and Eric Garner in New York City.

Since the Ferguson protests, participants in the movement have demonstrated against the deaths of numerous other African Americans by police actions or while in

Protest march in response to the Jamar Clark shooting, Minneapolis, Minnesota

police custody. In the summer of 2015, Black Lives Matter activists became involved in the 2016 United States presidential election. The originators of the hashtag and call to action, Alicia Garza, Patrisse Cullors, and Opal Tometi, expanded their project into a national network of over 30 local chapters between 2014 and 2016. The overall Black Lives Matter movement, however, is a decentralized network and has no formal hierarchy.

Black Lives Matter has also been criticized. Some black civil rights leaders have criticized the tactics of BLM. Some critics accuse Black Lives Matter of being antipolice, and question the statistics provided by BLM activists regarding the rate at which black people are killed by police. Other criticisms include: BLM's lack of focus on intra-racial violence, allegations of racism and sexism, and criticism of the policy statements laid out by the Movement for Black Lives.

There have been many reactions to the Black Lives Matter movement. The U.S. population's perception of Black Lives Matter varies considerably by race. The phrase "All Lives Matter" sprang up as a response to the Black Lives Matter movement. However, "All Lives Matter" has been criticized for dismissing or misunderstanding the message of "Black Lives Matter". Following the shooting of two police officers in Ferguson, the hashtag Blue Lives Matter was created by supporters of the police.

FOUNDING

The movement was co-founded by three black community organizers: Alicia Garza, Patrisse Cullors, and Opal Tometi. Garza, Cullors and Tometi met through "Black Organizing for Leadership & Dignity" (BOLD), a national organization that trains community organizers. They began to question how they were going to respond to what they saw as the devaluation of black lives after Zimmerman's acquittal. Garza wrote a Facebook post titled "A Love Note to Black People" in which she said: "Our Lives Matter, Black Lives Matter." Cullors replied: "#BlackLivesMatter." Tometi then added her support, and Black Lives Matter was born as an online campaign.

Since then, Black Lives Matter has organized thousands of protests and demonstrations. Expanding beyond street protests, BLM has expanded to activism on American college campuses, such as the 2015–16 University of Missouri protests.

BLM claims inspiration from the African-American Civil Rights Movement, the Black Power movement, the 1980s Black feminist movement, Pan-Africanism, the Anti- Apartheid Movement, hip hop, LGBTQ social movements, and Occupy Wall Street. Several media organizations have referred to BLM as "a new civil rights movement." Some of the protesters, however, actively distinguish themselves from the older generation of black leadership, such as Al Sharpton, by their aversion to middle-class traditions such as church involvement, Democratic Party loyalty, and respectability politics.

Notable Black Lives Matter activists include co-founder of the Seattle Black Lives Matter chapter Marissa Johnson, lawyer and president of the Minneapolis chapter of the NAACP Nekima Levy-Pounds, and writer Shaun King. In a September 2016 interview with W. Kamau Bell and Hari Kondabolu, King described himself as part of the broader Black Lives Matter movement and supportive of the formal organization Black Lives Matter, but not affiliated with the latter.

Black Lives Matter originally used social media—including hashtag activism—to reach thousands of people rapidly. Since then, Black Lives Matters has embraced a diversity of tactics. Black Lives Matter protest against police brutality in St. Paul, Minnesota

In 2014, the American Dialect Society chose #Black- LivesMatter as their word of the year. Yes! Magazine picked #BlackLivesMatter as one of the twelve hashtags that changed the world in 2014. Memes are also important in garnering support for the Black Lives Matter new social movement. Information communication technologies such as Facebook and Twitter spread memes and are important tools for garnering web support in hopes of producing a spillover effect into the offline world.

As of September 2016, the phrase "Black Lives Matter" has been tweeted over 30 million times, and Black Twitter has been credited with bringing international attention to the BLM movement. Using the hashtag #BlackLivesMatter has helped activists communicate the scale of their movement to the wider

online community and stand in solidarity amongst other participants. Dr. Khadijah White, a professor at Rutgers University, argues that BLM has ushered in a new era of black university student movements. The ease with which bystanders can record graphic videos of police violence and post them onto social media has driven activism all over the world.

On August 8, 2015, a speech by Democratic presidential candidate and civil rights activist Bernie Sanders was disrupted by a group from the Seattle Chapter of Black Lives Matter including chapter co-founder Marissa Johnson who walked onstage, seized the microphone from him and called his supporters racists and white supremacists. Sanders issued a platform in response. Nikki Stephens, the operator of a Facebook page called "Black Lives Matter: Seattle" issued an apology to Sanders' supporters, claiming these actions did not represent her understanding of BLM. She was then sent messages by members of the Seattle Chapter which she described as threatening, and was forced to change the name of her group to "Black in Seattle". The founders of Black Lives Matter stated that they had not issued an apology. In August 2015, the Democratic National Committee passed a resolution supporting Black Lives Matter.

In November 2015, a BLM protester was physically assaulted at a Donald Trump rally in Birmingham, Alabama. In response, Trump said, "maybe he should have been roughed up because it was absolutely disgusting what he was doing." Trump had previously threatened to fight any Black Lives Matter protesters if they attempted to speak at one of his events.

In March 2016, Black Lives Matter helped organize the 2016 Donald Trump Chicago rally protest that forced Trump to cancel the event. Four individuals were arrested and charged in the incident. Two were "charged with felony aggravated battery to a police officer and resisting arrest", one was "charged with two misdemeanor counts of resisting and obstructing a peace officer", and the fourth "was charged with one misdemeanor count of resisting and obstructing a peace officer". A CBS reporter was one of those arrested outside the rally. He was charged with resisting arrest.

FERGUSON EFFECT

Sam Dotson, chief of the St. Louis Police Department, coined the term "Ferguson effect" to describe what he believed was a change in enforcement behavior following the shooting of Michael Brown and subsequent unrest. According to Dotson, his officers were less active in enforcing the law because they were afraid they might be charged with breaking the law. FBI Director James Comey suggested that the Black Lives Matter movement is partly leading to a national rise in crime rates because police officers have pulled back from doing their jobs. A study published by the Justice Department, said there was an increase in homicides in 56 large cities over the course of 2015, and examined the "Ferguson effect" as one of three plausible explanations.

Other researchers have looked for this "Ferguson effect" in the rise in crime rates and failed to find evidence for it on a national level. A report over the increased homicide rate in St. Louis concluded there was an "absence of credible and comprehensive evidence" for the Ferguson Effect being responsible for that city's homicide increase.

MOYNIHAN REPORT REVISITED

June 13, 2013

The controversial 1965 report from labor secretary Daniel Moynihan explored the causes of African American poverty and concluded that the erosion of the African American nuclear family was a primary contributing factor. A 2013 report from the Urban Institute reexamined the state of African American families and evaluated the nation's progress in addressing African American poverty.

Identification: Study revisiting the famous Daniel Moynihan report on poverty among African American communities.

In 1965, Ph.D. sociologist and assistant secretary of the U.S. Department of Labor, Daniel Patrick Moynihan released a report entitled The Negro Family: The Case for National Action, more typically known as the "Moynihan report," which examined poverty in African American communities and recommended government mobilization and new policies to address the issue. Moynihan's report found that poverty in African American communities arose from a variety of factors, including availability of jobs, crime, and educational outcomes, but saw the disintegration of the nuclear family in African American communities as the preeminent factor. Moynihan cited statistics on the disproportionate number of fatherless African American households and argued that a lack of paternal authority, responsibility, and guidance was one of the most important factors in a self-perpetuating cycle of poverty. Since the release of the report, Moynihan's hypothesis has been celebrated as an important call for action, and alternatively maligned as an example of white patriarchal attitudes about the nature of poverty.

In a June 2013 report from the Urban Institute, authors Kenneth Braswell, Gregory Acs, Elaine Sorensen, and Margery Austin Turner find that although the gradual integration of African Americans into the U.S. educational system and workforce has resulted in a large and more affluent African American middle class, African American communities still suffer from many of the same problems that Moynihan identified in his report. As in the 1965 report, researchers found a higher incidence of poverty for African Americans, a higher unemployment rate, and a far higher share of children being raised in single parent families. The researchers identify numerous social and sociological factors, including persistent unemployment, public school systems that do not offer vocational training, and prejudice in the justice system, with courts and police continuing to target African American men disproportionately, as important factors contributing to the high poverty rate. Given what the authors characterize as a disappointing level of progress since the original Moynihan report, the authors recommend changes to state and federal programs in an effort to enhance economic mobility for African Americans living at or near the poverty level. The report also raises the need for significant justice department reform, as the targeting of African American men by police, and the subsequent disproportionate number of African Americans incarcerated in U.S. prisons, has become an important element in the cycles of joblessness, poverty, and single parent households in the African American community.

—Micah Issitt

THE NATIONAL GREAT BLACKS IN WAX MUSEUM

October 15, 2016

The first ever wax museum, in the nation to exhibit the strength, struggles, and triumphs of African Americans, and African American history, both then, and now.

Identification (definition): A wax museum, in Baltimore, MD, dedicated to sharing the truth of the African-American history and heritage with people all around the world.

Locale: Originally located on Saratoga Street, yet later re-established in an expanded location on East North Avenue, Baltimore, MD.

The National Great Blacks in Wax Museum is the first ever Black History wax museum, both in Baltimore, MD and in our nation. This non-profit organization was founded by Dr. Elmer P. Martin and Dr. Joanne M. Martin in 1983. It began with a commitment to their dream, $6,000 of their own savings, which was originally earmarked for their first home, yet used to purchase their first four wax figures, which they exhibited whenever and wherever possible, and their desire to instill in African-Americans the importance of knowing their own history. Within three years, they had garnered a small Baltimore storefront museum and a total of 21 wax figures. Their vision and focus has been one of a commitment to studying, preserving, and sharing the truth about the history of African Americans. What makes their museum unique is in how they have accomplished all of their objectives through the creation of life-sized, and life-like, wax figures of prominent African-Americans, from throughout the Diaspora, that emphasize both historical and current-day experiences within the global African American community.

The objectives of this wax museum are to reveal little known, and more often neglected, facts about the history of African-Americans. Drs. Elmer and Joanne Martin intend to motivate African-American youth to desire, aspire to, and realize greater achievement in their own lives, by exposing them to great leaders from around the world, as their role models, eliminate all myths regarding racial inferiority or superiority as a way to improve race relations, and collaborate with and support other charitable non-profit organizations that are focused on improving the social and economic status of African-Americans, worldwide.

The original site of the museum was on Saratoga Street. Within 1200 square feet of space, the museum was housed at this location for two years. During that time, more than 2,000 local, city, and county schools toured the museum, in 1984, during Black History month. By 1985, that number had grown to 2,500. Visitors have traveled from as far as Japan, along with other visitors and tour groups from around the nation, to learn about the history of African-Americans via this unique totally accessible museum experience. By years end, the Martins realized that their Saratoga Street site was no longer able to accommodate the growing number of visitors and tour groups; and thus, they sought funding and a building to expand upon their vision of bringing the African-American experience to all. Since it's founding, and subsequent move to the east side of Baltimore, patronage to the museum has more than quadrupled.

In 1985, and thanks to a bill sponsored by Senator Clarence Blount, the Martins were awarded a $100,000 matching grant. Upon receiving this grant, they closed the Saratoga Street location, spear-headed a campaign to raise the additional matching $100,000, established a Board of Trustees, and begin seeking out a larger museum space. Between 1985 and 1987, they the City of Baltimore awarded the museum $300,000 in grants and loans, along with an unused fire station, on East North Avenue, for use with further development and expansion. Along with a Victorian mansion and two former apartment buildings they gained 30,000 feet of office and exhibit space. By this time, they had over 100 wax figures and scenes, with a full sized slave ship model exhibit depicting the 400 year African-American history of the Middle Passage / Atlantic Slave Trade, including the horrific conditions they experienced.

The National Great Blacks in Wax Museum has received numerous awards and press, since their inception, for opportunities for people around the world to learn about the authentic experience of the African Diaspora, and for the numerous opportunities they offer young at-risk youth to learn about, and serve at, the museum, from an early age. As they grow older, these youth go on to take on various volunteer and internship positions, while simultaneously realizing along the way that they have found a safe haven within their community, for a better understanding of the truth of who they are and where their history began, as a foundation for where they desire to go in their own lives.

—Patricia A McDaniel

UNARMED BLACK KILLINGS BY WHITES IN THE TWENTY-FIRST CENTURY

2000-present

OVERVIEW

The twenty-first century began with the lingering memory of the unjustified killing of New York City's Amadou Diallo, an unarmed twenty-three-year-old black male who matched the profile of a rape suspect. Unarmed, he was met with a barrage of bullets when he pulled his wallet from a pocket to show identification. An epidemic of unarmed blacks being killed has captured both national and international media attention in recent years as increasing numbers of unarmed black males and females are killed by whites, whose actions are usually met with impunity.

Racial profiling has played a major role in identifying those blacks alleged to be suspects or criminals. Aside from their fashion styles of wearing baggy, drooped pants, hoodie sweatshirts, head scarves, or long dreads or braids that can be easily refashioned or changed, their black skin color, the primary badge used in racial profiling, cannot be refashioned nor changed. The ongoing trend of whites killing unarmed blacks triggered new conversations that now reexamines the entire legacy of unarmed black killings, liking this to slave killings, lynchings, and a new type of genocide directed at the black community with the belief that black lives do not matter in the United States.

Slavery Era: African American slaves represented the first body of unarmed blacks to be killed by whites. Slaves were the chattel property of their masters who had sole priority in deciding the treatment of their human property. Local lawmakers gave slave owners the freedom to control, punish, reward, or dispose of their human property without legal recourse. Slave masters, therefore, created separate laws called slave codes to create nothing short of total subjection and obedience from their slaves. They sold, disciplined, and determined the fate of their slaves as they wanted, replete with rules for them to follow and punishments, if they did not. Physical punishments included being whipped, branded, castrated, having noses or ears slit, and death. Nonphysical punishments included no reading or writing; carrying written passes if they left; and wearing a heavy livery around their necks to prevent them from running away. While white patrollers were allowed to go on any plantation or enter a slave cabin to retrieve runaway slaves for rewards, they, however, were not free to punish or harm the property of another. If so,

they were sued for destruction or loss of property. In the end, the legal right was in place for a white master and his white overseers, with permission, to mercilessly whip, abuse, or kill an unarmed black person.

Reconstruction Era: During the Civil War started when the Emancipation Proclamation was passed to free slaves in all the rebelling states, this was not the beginning of the end for abusing unarmed blacks. Once blacks were freed, the value of their lives diminished, as they were no longer the protected property of whites. For those freedmen leaving their plantations when they learned that President Lincoln had freed them, the majority left or ran away from their masters in search of Union military camps. Upon the freed peoples' arrival, most white Northern Union soldiers met them with a cold reception and little to no southern hospitality. As the black contraband increased in numbers in Union camps, the soldiers had their own solutions for reducing these numbers. They were either sent them back to their masters; were forbidden to enter their camps; or allowed their former masters to enter the camps to retrieve their slave property themselves. As the contraband numbers continued to grow, Union soldiers hired them as laborers, as military personnel, or made them prisoners.

The transition from slavery to freedom was not easy for African Americans. Some planters brutally restrained their slaves from leaving once they were legally freed. White patrollers, the same poorer whites who made a living searching for runaway slaves, now focused their energies on forcing freed blacks back to their former masters' plantations or farms. In doing so, many unarmed freed blacks died as they resisted attempts to return them to their former masters. At the end of the Civil War, it was not unusual to find dead bodies of murdered blacks alongside or near rural dirt roads, highways, and bypaths. Hospital records revealed blacks being treated for broken skulls, cracked bones, and knife wounds.

The rebuilding of the South during Reconstruction marked a new beginning of unforeseen white cruelty and physical torture aimed at unarmed African Americans. Southern whites imposed rules called black Codes to restrict the movement and lives of the newly freed African Americans. Black codes included laws that made it illegal for blacks to bear any type of arms and thus keeping them legally unarmed to protect themselves.

In addition, they were prohibited from serving on juries; serving in political offices; and being unemployed, where they would be forced to work indefinitely as apprentices for designated whites. If blacks violated any of these codes, they were faced with paying fines, incarceration, or both and were visited by vigilante groups, such as the Ku Klux Klan or the Red Shirts, or experienced some form of violent physical intimidation.

Post-Reconstruction Era: The 1896 *Plessy V Ferguson* Supreme Court ruling legitimized separating blacks from whites in all social aspects of life- economically, legally, politically, culturally, and so forth. With the support of the Supreme Court, whites generated a series of laws referred to as "jim crow* laws" that dictated every facet of black life including where they should live; who they should marry; where they should work; or how they should act, dress, or approach whites. De jure laws were the established legal laws that banned interracial schooling, marriages, or employment and de facto laws formulated the black behavior etiquette around whites such as no

eye or body contact when talking; entering white residences through the back door; or not disputing the word of a white person. The jim crow era represented the beginning of the most violent white on black unarmed killings, which were generally called lynchings. The era of lynching unarmed blacks began during the eve of the Reconstruction Era in 1865 and continued for over one hundred years. It is this era of lynching history that is being compared today by modern scholars, activists, and blacks who have lost unarmed friends and relatives to white killings to the ongoing killings of twenty-first century unarmed blacks.

TWENTIETH CENTURY VIOLENCE AGAINST AFRICAN AMERICANS

In the early twentieth century, the vast majority of blacks continued to live in the Southern region of the U.S. The late nineteenth century up through the mid-twentieth century came to be known as the jim crow era with the majority of blacks living in the jim crow South. During this time, blacks lived in constant fear of their lives. Although slavery had ended, they still did not have control over how they lived or how they wanted to live unless they migrated to the far northeastern or far western regions of the U.S. where there were less restrictions placed on them. Poverty and family, however, kept the majority of blacks living in the South and having to live under the restrictions of jim

crow segregation. Whether it was the wrath felt from an individual white or the violence from the white Knights of the KKK or the Red Shirts, the majority of Southern African Americans lived in fear of their lives and their relatives and neighbors.

Black fear in the South was unending. The chance of being the next victim to be brutally lynched, whether privately or publicly with white children, women, and men onlookers, was a reality. Digital archives such as the "Charles Chestnutt Digital Archive" of Berea College or the extensive archives of "Digital History" from the University of Houston revealed Census Bureau statistics that recorded an estimated 4,743 lynchings between 1882 and 1968. Most lynchings occurred in the South which would accounted for the fear held by Southern blacks, with others taking place in the Midwest and West. Most were African American males and others included children and women. A small minority of non-blacks who were lynched included immigrants who were culturally and religiously different, like the Chinese, Italian, and Jewish people, or white Americans deemed too helpful or sympathetic towards blacks.

Organizations like the National Association for the Advancement of Colored People (NAACP) formed anti-lynching components to expose this southern horror to the public and fought to get black protection by trying to get federal laws passed by introducing legislation like the "Dyer Anti-Lynching Bill." On the other hand, individual activists like Ida B. Wells-Barnett dedicated their lives to traveling around the world to call attention to the treatment and fear of blacks living under this cloud of violence. Southern whites using extreme violence to kill unarmed blacks continued during most of the twentieth century. Southern whites refused to accept increasing economic and job competition from blacks; growing black prosperity as a result of educational attainment; increasing black political participation; and black youths' increasing fearlessness and attitudes of non-deference towards white authority.

The criminal justice system was another means where African American life was devalued. For example, the "convict leasing system" was another system of violence where whites killed large numbers of unarmed blacks. The convict leasing system emerged during slavery where planters sometimes leased out their slaves to companies or the government as cheap labor to build railroads, work in mining, or on plantations. When slavery ended, the leasing system continued but now with black convicts being used as a captured labor force. African Americans were arrested for frivolous infractions and sent to prison or reform schools if too young to serve indefinite lengths of time. Prisons and reformatories for delinquent boys, in turn, leased out its convicts to work for private industries and businesses, in coal mining industries, or for plantations owned by wealthy white families, all generating humongous income for the leasing State. This income was used to build more prisons, maintain and sustain the costs of these prisons, and keep costs to a small minimum from the overall State budget. These leased black convicts died at high rates from being severely beaten, tortured to death, or shot by white prison guards and wardens, furthering a history of unarmed blacks being killed by whites who continued to do so unpunished. The convict leasing system ended around 1928 but was eventually was transformed into the "chain gang" system, where black prisoners were chained together to work alongside roadways. Although the black chain gang system phased out during the Great Depression era so that unemployed people could do those jobs, it did resurface again in the 1990s. Though criticisms of being chained appeared degrading, humiliating, and demeaning, the chain gang system did not continue the history of killing these unarmed black convicts.

*According to Webster dictionary's, a proper noun is the name of a "real person, a place, or organization," and in light of that explanation, jim crow cannot a proper noun. Jim crow is a common noun, an adjective, and a social term ingrained in bias that simply means segregating inferior black people from superior white people.

TWENTY-FIRST CENTURY UNARMED SHOOTINGS

Unarmed black females, as well as males, also are victims of white violence. On August 27, 2016, a white male from Ohio, Mathew Desha, fatally shot Deborah Pearl after their cars collided in a car accident. Desha was at fault in the accident when he ran a red light and his car plunged into Pearl's moving vehicle. When they both emerged unharmed from their vehicles to check the damage, an armed Desha shot several rounds of bullets that killed the older black woman, Pearl, without cause. Like killings in the twenty-first century reflected a continuance of white violence directed at unarmed African Americans. In earlier incident in 2013, a young Renisha McBride was gunned down by Theodore Wafer on his porch in the early morning hours in Dearborn Heights, Detroit when she sought help after her car was in an accident. In Charleston, South Carolina, Dylann Roof blindsided a church bible study by mass firing upon

them in 2015, killing nine unarmed blacks where five included women.

Aside from unarmed black females, the increased killings of unarmed black male youth under 25 years old had reached such a high level of occurrence until U.S. President Barak Obama offered his major criticisms regarding the increased murders of unarmed blacks. For example, on May 2012, an elderly John Spooner left his home to confront his 13-year-old neighbor, Darius Simmons, about moving the trash while his mother looked on. Spooner shot the youth in the chest and as he fled, fired off another shot. Young Simmons collapsed to his death as his mother witnessed his killing. Two months later, another youth, Trayvon Martin, was shot to death in July 2012. His killing sparked even more rage in the U.S. when his shooter, neighborhood watch resident George Zimmerman, was found not guilty due to self-defense. This decision shocked many in the U.S., re-energizing discussion on the role black racial profiling played in killing of unarmed blacks, in general, and black youth, in particular. Accusations of black fashion such as the dark hoodie sweatshirt worn by Trayvon Martin provoked whites into killing blacks they perceived as thugs, thieves, hoodlums, and criminal suspects. When three black community activists-- Alicia Garza, Patrisse Cullors, and Opal Tometi tweeted out #BlackLivesMatter after Zimmerman's acquittal, they went on to co-found Black Lives Matter, a movement now international that calls attention to racial profiling, police brutality, and racial injustice in the U.S. criminal system.

A similar neighborhood watch killing occurred August 2016 when a Raleigh, North Carolina Chad Copley, fired shots from inside his garage across the street at some young black partygoers he called "hoodlums," killing 20 year old Kouren-Rodney Bernard Thomas. His mother emphasized that her son was not only a hoodlum but the clothing he wore that night did not include baggy pants, a head rag, nor a hoodie. One nonsensical, unjustified shooting occurred on November 9, 2012 in Lonoke County, Arkansas. Earnest Hoskins, twenty-one years old, was the only African American attending a lunch meeting with his boss and four other coworkers. For an unknown reason, his boss Chris Reynolds pulled out a gun, shot him in the presence of the others, and was sentenced for manslaughter with the possibility of being released with good behavior after a few years. Whether the shooters were convicted or acquitted, the fact remained that another unarmed black male or female life was taken as if it did not matter.

The most controversial unarmed killings are those done by law enforcement agents. Today, thousands of unarmed citizens of all races, gender, and ages have been killed by police officers around the country. In particular, unarmed blacks are being killed by other blacks and minorities serving in law enforcement, as seen in cases where these unarmed victims were killed by blacks or minorities, including Freddie Gray, twenty-five, of Baltimore killed by six officers on April 12, 2015, with three being African American male and female officers—Cesar R. Goodson, Jr., Sgt. Alicia D. White, and William G. Porter. Another case concerns Sean Bell, twenty-three, of New York City who was killed by black Police Officer Gescard Isnora on November 25, 2006, as well as the case of Shem Walker, forty-nine, of New York City, who was killed by a black undercover agent whose name remains anonymous.

Aside from the elderly and very young, some victims were also special needs as with the autistic victim, Steven Eugene Washington, twenty-seven, of Los Angeles who was gunned down by two Hispanic officers—Allan Corrales and George Diego; a schizophrenic, Dontre Hamilton, shot fourteen times after being patted down from sleeping on a park bench; and a special needs individual, Ezell Ford, who was stopped for no reason and killed by an Asian police officer, Sharlton Wampler, and a Hispanic police pfficer, Antonio Villegas. Others with health issues have died suddenly while being taken into police custody following the use of excessive physical force, such as thirty-six-year-old Dante Parker of San Bernardino County, California in August 2012, who suffered from respiratory issues and thirty-seven-year-old Tanisha N. Anderson of Cleveland, Ohio, in November 2014, who suffered from mental illness. One woman, fifty-seven-year-old Alberta Spruill of New York City, died from a heart attack on May 16, 2003, when the police accidently raided the wrong home by kicking in her door using a concussion grenade and handcuffing her. Two hours later she passed away at a hospital; ultimately, her family received a $1.6 million settlement by the City of New York. More recently, foty-three-year-old Carlos Alcisof New York City also died from a heart attack in New York City when policemen mistakenly raided his home in search of a cell phone thief; his family was awarded $10 million from New York City and the New York Police Department as part of a wrongful death settlement.

By far, however, white law enforcement agents did the majority of unarmed blacks killed in the twenty-first century, and most of these occurrences were the result of racial profiling and mistaken identity. The topic of unarmed black killings by white policeman has surfaced to being one of the most searched on the worldwide web. Reactions to these unarmed black killings by policeman have led to nationwide protests, federal criticisms of the escalation, and formation of organizations including *Black Lives Matter*. Congress instructed the Attorney General in 1994 to "compile and publish annual statistics on police use of excessive" on everyone—regardless of race, ethnicity, gender, or age. Databases kept by the *Bureau of Justice Statistics* in addition to major newspaper outlets like *The Washington Post* and *The Guardian* have documented records for both the twentieth and twenty-first centuries.

Ample research has been done on the topic of police killings of unarmed minorities and non-minorities in the U.S. In particular, more research and scholarship has been specifically generated on the topic of police shootings of unarmed blacks. The August 2014 police killing of unarmed 18-year-old Michael Brown in Ferguson, Missouri, led to citywide rioting and looting in response to the killing of an unarmed black male. The riots came to be known as the "Ferguson Unrest." When videos surfaced showing the victim with his hands up in the air, the slogan "Hands Up, Don't Shoot" became one of several chants heard at Black Lives Matter protest rallies through the U.S.

Even children are not exempted from these shootings as in the case of thirteen-year-old Andy Lopez from Santa Rosa, California, killed on October 22, 2013, when policemen mistook his pellet gun for a real gun and opened fire on him as he walked through a vacant lot. One year later, in November 2014, twelve-year-old Tamir Rice of Cleveland, Ohio, was shot by a policeman while playing with his bb gun at a nearby park, devastating his parents and shocking the nation once again. When Freddie Gray of Baltimore, Maryland, died in April 2015 after suffering body trauma and falling into a coma while being transported in a police van, that event, like the event in Ferguson led to widespread rioting in Baltimore City.

As the names continue to be added to the unarmed black death list, constantly growing each month, and with many of those deaths related to racial profiling and mistaken identity, so does the mounting criticism against law enforcement's use of unjustified, excessive force. Vigilante groups as well as individuals have emerged with a vengeance to retaliate against anyone working as law enforcement officer, even though the majority of officers do not engage in excessive force and unjustified shootings. As a result, police officers find themselves being stalked, profiled, and targeted to be victims of shootings and violence. Some officers now live in a state of fear as they try to continue their work and fulfill their to protect others.

Below is a list of black unarmed victims killed by white violence.

SAMPLE LIST OF UNARMED BLACKS KILLED BY WHITES CIVILIANS AND POLICEMAN: 2000-2016

2000:

Malcolm Ferguson, 23, Bronx, New York, on March 1, 2000, Ferguson. although not a suspect nor guilty of any crime, was shot by an undercover cop when five drug undercover cops wearing hoodies saw Ferguson in the hallway. When Ferguson retreated up a stairway, officers chased him. Louis Rivera shot Ferguson in the head at close range and he died at the scene.

Patrick Dorismond, 26, of New York City, New York, March 16, 2000. While standing outside of a lounge, Dorismond and a friend were approached by an undercover policeman man seeking to buy marijuana. A scuffle occurred and, Dorismond was shot in the chest by the undercover cop, Anthony Vasquez. Vasquez was acquitted but the Dorismond's family was awarded $2.25 million by New York City in a wrongful death settlement.

Ronald Beasley, 36, Dellwood, Missouri, June 12, 2000. Killed in a parking lot drug bust

Earl Murray, 36, Dellwood, Missouri, June 12, 2000. Killed in a parking lot drug bust

Prince Jones, 25, Fairfax County, Virginia, September 1, 2000. Killed as a result of mistaken identity

2001:

Timothy Thomas, 19, Cincinnati, Ohio, on April 7, 2001, after being chased on foot by Officer Stephen Roach. During the month leading up to his death, Thomas was stopped as often as twice a day for the same violations. On the night of his death, he was spotted by an off duty officer who called in backup. Thomas saw the officers approaching and ran into a nearby alley. Roach shot Thomas when he thought he was reaching for a gun. Later investigation revealed that Thomas was attempting to pull up his pants rather than reach for a gun.

2003:

Orlando Barlow, 28, Las Vegas, Nevada, February 28, 2003. Killed while surrendering.

Kendra James, 21, Portland, Oregon, May 5, 2003. Killed during a traffic stop

Ousmane Zongo, 43, New York City, New York, May 22, 2003. Zonga, unarmed, was shot five times, twice in the back, by undercover officer Bryan Conroy. Zongo worked a storage facility repairing and restoring art and artifacts. The facility, raided for housing counterfeit CDs, was being guarded by Conroy Zongo was startled by Conroy, out of uniform and with a gun drawn. Conroy testified he shot Zongo when he lunged at him. Conroy was found guilty of a negligent killing for failrure to follow protocol and reveal his badge. Zongo's family, living Burkina Faso, Africa, received $3 million from New York City in a wrongful death settlement.

Alberta Spruill, 57, New York, New York, May 16, 2003. Mistaken identity caused death from heart attack

2004:

Timothy Stansbury, 19, New York City, New York, January 24, 2004. Stansbury was working at McDonald's and planning on attending community college. Stansbury and other tenants in his building routinely exited the building through the roof door and walked across the roof to cross over to the adjoining building.

On January 24, Stansbury and two of his friends did this as they were heading to a birthday party. Officer Richard S. Neri, Jr., a housing authority policeman on patrol on the roof, was startled when the door opened. He shot the unarmed teenager in the chest. Stansbury's family was paid $2 million by New York City in a wrongful death settlement.

2005:

Danziger Bridge Shootings, New Orleans, Louisiana, September 5, 2005, six days after the Katrina Hurricane devastated the city. Several out-of-uniform New Orleans police officers, including Sgt. Kenneth Bowen, Sgt. Robert Gisevius, Officer Anthony Villavaso, and Officer Robert Faulcon, lined up at the Danzier Bridge and shot at moving African American targets. Seventeen-year-old James Brissette and forty-year-old Ronald Madison were shot and killed. Four other African Americans were wounded but survived. A federal judge sentenced them to terms ranging from six to sixty-five years on April 4, 2012. Their sentences were reduced on April 20, 2016, from a retrial based on prosecutorial misconduct

Ronald Madison, 40, New Orleans, Louisiana, September 4, 2005. Mentally disabled man shot in the back

James Brisette, 17, New Orleans, Louisiana, September 4, 2005. Developmentally disabled man shot when he ran away

Henry Glover, 31, New Orleans, Louisiana, September 25, 2005. Glover was taken to a police substation in the Algiers Strip Mall by William Tanner. Later investigations revealed that Glover had been shot by a police officer, David Warren. Warren left him unattended to die and another policeman, Officer Gregory McRae, staged a fiery car accident and claimed that was how Glover lost his life. The coroner was unable to determine the shooting as the cause of the death and initially ruled it "accidental" and later as "undetermined." Warren was eventually acquitted on all counts of shooting the unarmed Glover. McRae was sentenced to 17 years for burning the body and is currently awaiting a retrial to appeal the decision.

2006:

Sean Bell, 23, New York, New York, November 25, 2006. Killed as he drove away

Kathryn Johnston, 92, Atlanta, Georgia, November 21, 2006. Killed in a botched drug raid

2007:

DeAunta "Tae Tae" Terrel Farrow, 12, of West Memphis, Tennessee, June 22, 2007. Farrow was carrying his toy gun to his cousin's home. Police Officer Erik Sammis and his partner, Jimmy Evans, spotted the boys and approached them with guns pointed. Sammis fired off two shots before learning that the gun was a toy. Sammis, who has been allegedly described as having a history of using excessive force and brutality, was not indicted on any charges but did resign from the force.

2008:

Tarika Wilson, 26, of Lima, Ohio, January 4, 2008. A SWAT team raid broke into her home in search of her companion, Anthony Terry, a suspected drug dealer. Wilson was killed while holding her 4-month-old son, himself shot in the shoulder and hand by Sgt. Joseph Chavalia. Although the undercover investigation revealed that Terry was not dealing drugs out of the home, it was thought that the address was his stash house. Based on a recent traffic stop when Wilson was driving Terry's car, it was believed that she stayed at a different address. Office Chavalia was acquitted of all charges of negligence.

2009:

Oscar Grant, 22, Oakland, California, January 1, 2009. Shot by BART Officer Johannes Mehserle at the Fruitvale Bay Area Rapid Transit (BART) station while detained following a brawl. Grant was handcuffed and lying on his stomach, was informed of his arrest by Officer Johannes Mehserle. Grant attempted to stand up in protest but was slammed against a wall and his head kneed to the wall. Officer Mehserle threatened "to taze" Grant instead shot him in the back as he lay prone on the platform. The story of the shooting was the basis of the movie, *Fruitvale Station*. Meheserle was sentenced to two years in the Los Angeles County jails and released after 11 months. Grant's mother and daughter were paid a total of $2.8 million in 2011 by BART in a wrongful death settlement.

Shem Walker, 49, New York, New York, July 11, 2009. Killed trying to eject a stranger (plain clothes cop) sitting on his mother's stoop

Victor Steen, 17, Pensacola, Florida, October 9, 2009. Steen was hit and dragged by a police cruiser after being tazed by Police officer Jerard Ard. Policies were changed to state that police vehicles may pursue suspectsbut must maintain specific vehicular distances to ensure the safety of cyclists and pedestrians. Steen's mother was paid $500,000 by Pensacola City in a wrongful death settlement.

Kiwane Carrington, 15, Champaign, Illinois, October 9, 2009. Killed during an arrest for suspected breaking and entering. According to Officer Daniel Norbits, Carrington was reaching in and out of his pocket. Norbits assumed he had a weapon and, therefore, grabbed his arm. As Carrington attempted to get out of Norbits' grip, Norbits said the gun went off and shot Carrington. Norbits was suspended for 30 days and the Carrington family was paid $470,000 from Champaign City in a wrongful death settlement.

2010:

Aaron Campbell, 25, Portland Oregon, on January 29, 2010. Campbell, depressed and suffering from suicidal tendencies, was a threat to himself but not others. When his fiancé called the police to come to talk to him, he cooperated and allowed his children to leave the house. When asked to come outside, Campbell did so. Policeman shot him with beanbag pellets when he refused to raise his hands in the air. After he ran to take cover behind his vehicle, Officer Frashour fired his rifle shooting an unarmed Campbell in the back, killing him. Although Frashour was fired, he was later reinstated. Campbell's family was paid a total of $1.2 million by the City of Portland in a wrongful death settlement.

Steven Eugene Washington, 27, Los Angeles, California, March 20, 2010. Developmentally disabled man shot while walking down the street

Aiyana Stanley-Jones, 7, Detroit, Michigan, May 16, 2010. Killed when wrong house was raided

Danroy "DJ" Henry, 20, Easton, Massachusetts, killed in Thornwood, New York, October 17, 2010. Henry, a Pace University football was killed in the parking lot of Finnegan's Grill in Thornwood. Police Officer Ronald Gagnon approached Henry and knocked on the window. Henry was driving away when his car struck the officer at the window as well as another approaching policeman, Officer Aaron Hess. Hess ended up on the hood of the car as Henry continued to drive. At this point, Hess and another officer fired into the car. Henry and a passenger, Cox, were both shot, and Henry later died at the hospital. The Henry's parents were paid a $6 million wrongful death settlement by New York.

Derrick Jones, 37, Oakland, California, November 8, 2010. Killed while running from the cops

2011:

Reginald Doucet, 25, of Los Angeles, California, January 14, 2011. Reginald Doucet refused to pay his cab fare. The driver informed Doucet he would have to leave some type of collateral behind before going to retrieve the cab fare. An angry Doucet disrobed to use his clothing as collateral. When the police officers arrived, a fight ensued and Officer Goff shot him the leg and as Doucet fell to the ground, Goff shot him again in the neck, which proved fatal. An eyewitness reported it was the policemanwho was the aggressor. While an earlier hearing exonerated the policemen from any wrongdoing, further examination supported the argument that the fatal shot to Doucet occurred after he was already grounded by the first shot to the leg The family of Reginald Doucet has filed a recent wrongful death lawsuit against the Los Angeles Police Department.

Raheim Brown, 20, Oakland, California, January 22, 2011. Killed during physical struggle

Kenneth Harding, 19, San Francisco, California, July 16, 2011. Killed while running from the cops

Alonzo Ashley, 29, Denver, Colorado, July 18, 2011. Died from being Tasered

James Craig Anderson, 49, Jackson, Mississippi, June 26, 2011. Killed as a result of a hate crime. Anderson's mother and siblings filed a wrongful death lawsuit against the seven members of the group who were participants in his death.

Kenneth Chamberlain, 68, White Plains, New York, November 19, 2011. Chamberlain's medical alert device was accidently set off and the police arrived. Chamberlain told the alert team that he did not need assistance. The policeman continued to enter the home and attempted to use the Taser and shot beanbags Chamberlain. Police Officer Anthony Carelli claimed that Chamberlain came after him with the butcher knife and, therefore, he shot him. The family of Kenneth Chamberlain is currently suing Westchester County in a wrongful death lawsuit for $21 million dollars.

2012:

Ramarley Graham, 18, Bronx, New York, February 2, 2012. Shot in the chest when attempting to flush a small bag of marijuana down the toilet. Officer Haste claimed that Graham reached for a gun from his waistband. An unarmed Graham died from the shootings and Haste was acquitted of manslaughter charges. The family of Ramarley Graham was paid a total of $3.9 million by the New York City in a wrongful death settlement

Sgt. Manuel Loggins, Jr., 31, Orange County, California, February 7, 2012. Killed when approached by the police for non-confrontational mental issues

Trayvon Martin, 17, Sanford, Florida, February 26, 2012. Trayvon Martin was returning to his mother's apartemnt from a neighborhood convenient store, talking on his cell phone. Zimmerman called the policeman to report a suspicious black male and was advised not to follow the suspect, but continued to follow him. Martin eventually took notice of Zimmerman told his friend on the phone that he was uncomfortable. When a physical struggle ensued between the two, Zimmerman shot unarmed Martin. Zimmerman argued self-defense during a trial. The jury found Zimmerman innocent. Zimmerman showed no remorse and even attempted to auction off the gun that killed young Martin online to the highest bidder. In 2015, the U.S. Justice Department decided not to file civil rights violation charges against George Zimmerman since there was not enough evidence to prove that Zimmerman violated Martin's civil rights.

Raymond Allen, 34, Galveston, Texas, February 27, 2012. Died after being tasered

Dante Price, 25, Dayton, Ohio, March 1, 2012. Killed while driving away from cops

Nehemiah Dillard, 29, Gainesville, Florida, March 5, 2012. Died after being tasered

Wendell Allen, 20, New Orleans, Louisiana, March 7, 2012. Killed during execution of a search warrant

Shereese Francis, 30, New York, New York, March 15, 2012. Killed from excessive restraints used

Rekia Boyd, 22, Chicago, Illinois, March 21, 2012. Killed when cellphone mistaken for gun

Kendrec McDade, 19, Pasadena, California, March 24, 2012. Killed while being pursued for a theft. After a thorough investigation, it was found that McDade was never armed with a gun, did not participate in the theft, and the 911 caller, Carillo, had admitted that he lied about them having guns in order to get law enforcement involved quicker. Carillo served jail time on charges of false reporting and falsely reporting an emergency when it was not. McDade's parents were paid a total of $1 million by the City of Pasadena in a wrongful death settlement.

Ervin Jefferson, 18, Atlanta, Georgia, March 24, 2012. Killed during verbal confrontation

Tamon Robinson, 27, New York, New York, April 18, 2012. Killed while running away form cops

Sharmel Edwards, 49, Las Vegas, Nevada, April 21, 2012. Killed while exiting the car after being chased

Shantel Davis, 23, New York, New York, June 14, 2012. Killed in car while listening to loud music

Alesia Thomas, 35, Los Angeles, California, July 22, 2012. Died in squad car en route to jail

Chavis Carter, 21, Jonesboro, Arkansas, July 29, 2012. Died in squad car en route to jail

Reynaldo Cuevas, 20, New York, New York, September 7, 2012. Killed while fleeing his own robbers

Malissa Williams, 30, Cleveland, Ohio, November 29, 2012. Killed in a mistaken car chase

Timothy Russell, 43, Cleveland, Ohio, November 29, 2012. Killed in a mistaken car chase

Darnisha Harris, 16, Breaux Bridge, Louisiana, December 2, 2012. Killed while driving erratically

Shelly Frey, 27, Houston, Texas, December 6, 2012. Killed while driving away from cops

Johnnie Kamahi Warren, 43, Dotham, Alabama, December 10, 2012. Died after being tasered

2013:

Kimani Gray, 16, New York, New York, March 9, 2013. Killed when questioning him

Deion Fludd, 17, New York, New York, May 5, 2013. Killed by train from police chase

Larry Eugene Jackson, Jr., 32, Austin, Texas, July 26, 2013. Killed while being chased

Carlos Alcis, 43, New York, New York, August 15, 2013. Died from mistaken police raid

Jonathan Ferrell, 24, killed in Charlotte, North Carolina, o September 14, 2013. Mistaken as a prowler when he sought help following a car accident Ferrell was shot ten times by police and died on the scence. Police Office Randall Kerrick was charged with using excessive force but was acquitted. Ferrell's family was paid $2.25 million by the City of Charlotte in a wrongful death settlement.

Miriam Carey, 34, Washington, D.C., October 3, 2013. Carey drove her car through a white House restricted checkpoint and drove up to 80mph down Pennsylvania Avenue. She was shot five times from behind during the chase and killed. Her mother Idella Carey, and her sister, Valarie Carey, argue there was a cover up of details that blocked pertinent information needed for them to pursue a proper lawsuit.

Andy Lopez, 13, Santa Rosa, California, October 22, 2013. Killed while playing with pellet gun

2014:

Jordan Baker, 26, of Houston, Texas, January 16, 2014. Killed as a result of racial profiling.

McKenzie Cochran, 25, Southfield, Michigan, January 28, 2014. Died from choke hold

Yvette Smith, 47, Bastrop, Texas, February 16, 2014. Yvette Smith called 911 when a fight broke out and Deputy Daniel Willis responded to the call. By the time he arrived, the fight had ended. When Smith opened, Deputy Willis shouted "Police!" but within seconds, he fired his gun twice, hitting Smith. She later died in the hospital. Willis initially reported that she was armed but later retracted his story and was indicted for murder. Yvette Smith's family was paid $1.22 million by Bastrop County in 2015 in a wrongful death settlement.

Victor White III, 22, Iberia Parish, Louisiana, March 22, 2014. Shot while handcuffed in police cruiser

Dontre Hamilton, 31, of Milwaukee, Wisconsin, April 30, 2014. Shot during a pat-down attempt.

Eric Garner, 43, New York City, New York, July 14, 2014. Caught the attention of the world with his words, "I can't breathe." When Police Officers Justin Damico and Daniel Pantaleo confronted Garner and he resisted, Pantaleo placed him in a chokehold. He pleaded over and over that he could not breathe. Garner lost consciousness and no one gave him mouth-to-mouth resuscitation while they waited for an ambulance. The coroner ruled Garner's death a homicide from the illegal chokehold and chest compression.. Eric Garner's family was paid $5.9 million by New York City in a wrongful death settlement.

Tyree Woodson, 38, Baltimore, Maryland, August 2, 2014. Shot while in custody in police station

John Crawford III, 22, Dayton, Ohio, August 5, 2014. Crawford picked up a bb gun from the sporting goods section of a store. A customer notified the police of a man with a gun said to be pointing it at people and children; the customer later recanted. According to the dispatched officers, they ordered Crawford to lie on the floor and when he did not comply, he was shot in the torso and arm. The store video captured Crawford talking on the phone and, from his mother's perspective, the offers gave no time for him to comply before shooting. The officers were not charged for the killings and the family is set to pursue a wrongful death lawsuit during the early part of 2017.

Michael Brown, 18, Ferguson, Missouri, August 9, 2014. When Police Officer Darren Wilson received a call about a theft, he spotted two black males matching the description walking down the street and confronted the pair. After a physical altercation occurred between Brown and Wilson, the youth fled. Wilson pursued Brown. As Brown walked towards Wilson, Wilson fired ten rounds, six of which hit Brown. The chant, "Hands Up, Don't Shoot" became one of the slogans of Black Lives Matter. Officer Darren Wilson was not indicted but the Department of Justice found the Ferguson Police Department guilty of practicing discrimination against African Americans. Ferguson experienced rioting, looting, vandalism, arson, shooting, as well as peaceful protests. The Ferguson Unrest occurred again the anniversary year of Michael Brown's death. His family filed a $20 million wrongful death lawsuit in August 2016.

Ezell Ford, 25, Florence, California, August 12, 2014. Killed while being questioned

Dante Parker, 36, Victorville, California, August 12, 2014. Died from being Tasered

Kajieme Powell, 25, St. Louis, Missouri, August 19, 2014. Mentally ill individual shot when acting erratically. Video revealed that Powell's hands were by his side and that he was not brandishing any weapon. Criticisms levied against the policemen included them using a Taser or shooting him in the leg as alternative force to subdue an upset Powell rather than using deadly excessive force within 15 seconds of their arrival. The officers were not charged with any wrongdoing but followed the correct protocol. Powell's family filed a wrongful lawsuit against the shooting officers and the Chief of Police Sam Dotson of St. Louis in October 2014.

Tanisha Anderson, 37, f Cleveland, Ohio, November 13, 2014. Mentally ill person suffered death ruled a homicide from sudden death due to the prone physical constraint during an arrest for disturbing the peace. Anderson's family has filed an unspecified wrongful death suit against Officers Scott Aldridge and Bryan Myers in 2015.

Akai Gurley, 28, Brooklyn, New York, November 20, 2014: mistakenly killed in stairwell

Tamir Rice, 12, Cleveland, Ohio, November 22, 2014. Killed following a call from a concerned citizen that described a black male at the park with a gun. According to Officers Timothy Loehmann and Frank Garmback, they observed a black male sitting under the pavilion with a gun lying on the table. When the police called for him to put his hands up, the suspect, instead, reached to pull the gun out of his waistband. Loehmann fired twice at Rice; the fatal bullet hitt him in his torso. Neither responding officer attended to Rice's wounds but two other law enforcement agents who arrived later applied first aid to the child until the ambulance arrived to transport him to the hospital where he died the next day. Rice's family received a $6 million dollar wrongful death settlement from the City of Cleveland in 2016.

Rumain Brisbon, 34, Phoenix, Arizona, December 2, 2014. Killed as a result of mistaken identy following a tip that a drug deal was to occur inside a car that matched description of Brisbon's black Cadillac SUV. Officer Mark Rine demanded that Brisbon show his hands. Brisbon did not comply and when Rine drew his weapon, Brisbon ran on foot to a nearby apartment. Inside the apartment, Rine assumed Brisbon was reaching for a gun in his pocket and shot him twice. Witnesses said Rine attempted to engage Brisbon physically and once apprehended, Brisbon had both hands up while laying on the floor of the apartment. Officer Rine was exonerated from any wrongdoing and the family filed a $65 million lawsuit against the City of Phoenix in May 2015.

Jerame Reid, 36, Bridgeton, New Jersey, December 30, 2014: mentally disturbed man killed when approached

2015:

Freddie Gray, 25, Baltimore, Maryland, April 12, 2015. Gray was taken down during a police chase in process called the "leg lace." The two arresting officers pinned Gray down. Gray complained to the officers that he could not breathe and asked for an inhaler that he did not receive. Gray was transported to Baker Street where police shackled him and filled out the necessary paper work. During transport to lockup, Gray fell into a coma and was hospitalized. He died a week later from spinal cord injuries. Major rioting and followed the killing of an unarmed black. The Office of Baltimore City's State Attorney, Marilyn Mosby, called for the arrest of the six policeman involved including three whites and three blacks, one black officer being a female. All six officers were exonerated in July 2016. The City of Baltimore paid the family of Freddie Gray a $6.4 million wrongful death settlement in September 2015.

Tony Robinson, 19, Madison, Wisconsin, March 6, 2015. Killed during an altercation

Philip White, 32, Vineland, New Jersey, March 31, 2015. Died of respiratory distress enroute to hospital

Eric Harris, 44, Tulsa, Oklahoma, April 2, 2015. Killed while being chased

Walter Scott, 50, North Charleston, South Carolina, April 4, 2015. Scott driving with a broken car taillight when Police Officer Michael T. Slaeger pulled him over. Scott, fearing arrest for outstanding warrants, starting running to avoid going to jail Slaeger took off running behind him and attempted to use his stun gun. Scott struggled to take it from him broke away to run again, Slaeger fired eight shots in his direction, shooting an unarmed Scott in the back as he ran. When a private citizen's recording surfaced and contradicted Slaeger's account of events, he was charged and arrested for murder. The family of Walter Scott was paid a $6.5 million wrongful death settlement from the City of Charleston.

Artago Damon Howard, 36, Union County, Arkansas, January 8, 2015. Killed during altercation

Jeremy Lett, 28, Tallahassee Florida, February 5, 2015. Killed during altercation

Lavall Hall, 25, Miami Gardens, Florida, February 15, 2015: mentally ill man shot during chase

Thomas Allen, 34, Wellston, Missouri, March 1, 2015. Killed during a traffic stop

Charly Leundeu Keunang, 43, Los Angeles, California, March 1, 2015: homeless man killed in altercation

Naeschylus Vinzant, 37, Aurora, Colorado, March 6, 2015. Killed during arrest

Anthony Hill, 27, DeKalb County, Georgia, March 9, 1929. Mentally ill man kill during confrontation

Bobby Gross, 35, Washington DC, March 12, 2015. Killed being in an unauthorized area of train tunnel

Brandon Jones, 18, Cleveland, Ohio, March 19, 2015. Killed after being apprehended

Frank Shepard, 41, Houston, Texas, April 15, 2015. Killed after high speed chase

William Chapman, 18, Portsmouth, Virginia, April 22, 2015. Killed in Wal-Mart parking lot while being apprehended for shoplifting

David Felix, 24, New York City, New York, April 25, 2015. Killed while running from the cop

Kris Jackson, 22, South Lake Tahoe, California, June 15, 2015. Killed while running from the cop

Spencer McCain, 41, Owings Mills, Maryland, June 25, 2015. Killed during a domestic violence call to his home

Victor Emanuel Larosa, 23, Jacksonville, Florida, July 3, 2015. Killed while running from the cop

Salvado Ellswood, 36, Plantation, Florida, July 12, 2015. Killed during altercation

Albert Joseph Davis, 23, Orlando, Florida, July 17, 2015. Killed during the arrest

Darrius Steward, 19, Memphis, Tennessee, July 17, 2015. Killed during altercation with cop

Samuel DuBose, 45, Cincinnati, Ohio, July 19, 2015. Killed during a traffic stop

Christian Taylor, 19, Arlington, Texas, August 7, 2015. Killed breaking into a car dealership

2016:

Antronie Scott, 36, San Antonio, Texas, February 4, 2016. Killed during warrant stop

Wendell Celestine Jr, 37, Antioch, California, February 5, 2016. Died while in custody

Randy Nelson, 49, Athens, Alabama, February 8, 2016. Died after being Tased

David Joseph, 17, Auston, Texas, February 8, 2016. Killed while being confronted

Dyzhawn Perkins, 19, Arvonia, Virginia, February 13, 2016. Killed during confrontation

Calin Roquemore, 23, Beckville, Texas, February 24, 2016. Killed running away from cop

Christopher Davis, 21, East Troy, Wisconsin, February 24, 2016: shot was sitting in the front seat of a car during drug bust

Peter Gaines, 35, Houston, Texas, March 12, 2016: drug-agitated man killed during confrontation

Marco Loud, 20, Houston, Texas, March 12, 2016: drug-agitated man killed during altercation

Torrey Lamar Robinson, 35, Port Richey, Florida, March 19, 2016. Died after being Tased

Darius Robinson, 41, Anadarko, Oklahoma, April 4, 2016. Killed while in custody in jail

Kevin Hicks, 44, Indianapolis, Indiana, April 5, 2016. Killed during altercation

Demarcus Semer, 23, Fort Pierce, Florida, April 23, 2016. Killed during a traffic stop.

Ashtian Barnes, 24, Houston, Texas, April 28, 2016. Killed during a traffic stop

Willie Tillman, 33, Fayetteville, Arkansas, May 9, 2016. Killed during a traffic stop

Vernell Bing Jr, 22, Jacksonville, Florida, May 23, 2016. Shot after a high speed chase

Ollie Brooks, 64, 2016, Tulsa, Oklahoma, May 28, 2016. Died after pepper spray and Tase-related heart failure

Devonte Gates, 21, East St Louis, Illinois, May 26, 2016. Unarmed murder suspect killed during arrest

Doll Pierre-Louis, 24, Miami Gardens, Florida, May 25, 2016. Killed during a traffic stop

Antwun Shumpert, 37, Topelo, Mississippi, June 18, 2016. Killed after running from a traffic stop

Clarence Howard, 25, Palm Bay, Florida, June 19, 2016. Killed by off-duty cop in a road rage confrontation

Delrawn Small, 37, Brooklyn, New York, July 4, 2016. Killed by off-duty cop in a road rage confrontation

Alton Sterling, 37, Baton Rouge, Louisiana, July 5, 2016: CD street peddler killed after altercation with cops

Philando Castile, 32, Falcon Heights, Minnesota, July 6, 2016. Killed during a traffic stop

Kouren-Rodney Bernard Thomas, 20, Raleigh, North Carolina, August 7, 2016. Killed by neighborhood watch person shooting at hoodlums

—*Kibibi V. Mack-Shelton, PhD*

Appendixes

Notable Figures in African American History

Abernathy, Ralph David (1926-1990): Christian minister and civil rights activist. Abernathy was a close friend of Martin Luther King, Jr., when both took Baptist pastorates in Montgomery, Alabama, around 1951. He helped to coordinate the Montgomery bus boycott in 1955 and to organize the Southern Christian Leadership Conference (SCLC) in 1957. After King's assassination, he became president of the SCLC (1968-1977). In 1977, he ran unsuccessfully for Congress. The year before he died, he published a controversial autobiography, *And the Walls Came Tumbling Down* (1989), which included details of King's extramarital affairs.

Ali, Muhammad (1942-2016): Professional boxing champion. Born Cassius Marcellus Clay, Jr., Ali started boxing at an early age in Louisville, Kentucky, and won an Olympic gold medal as a light-heavyweight in 1960. In 1964, he converted to the Black Muslim religion and changed his name from Clay to Ali. He won the world heavyweight boxing championship four times (1964, 1967, 1974, 1978). He was stripped of his title when he refused induction into the U.S. Army in 1967, but the U.S. Supreme Court reversed the draft evasion conviction in 1971. Ali became a symbol of black pride during the 1960's and remained an icon into the twenty-first century.

Allen, Richard (1760-1831): Founder of the African Methodist Episcopal Church. After gaining his freedom from slavery when he was twenty-one, Allen became the first African American ordained by the Methodist Society but was denied the right to worship at a predominantly white church in Philadelphia, so he founded his own church, which was later granted legal independence from the white church. In 1830, Allen led the first meeting of what would become the Negro Convention Movement.

Anderson, Marian (1897-1993): Contralto. Raised in Philadelphia, Anderson studied music from an early age and earned an international reputation while performing throughout Europe during the 1930's. On her return to the United States, her stature was immense; however, she became the focus of an embarrassing incident in 1939, when the Daughters of the American Revolution refused her permission to sing in Philadelphia's Constitution Hall because she was black. When first Lady Eleanor Roosevelt learned of the matter, she arranged for Anderson to perform on the steps of the Lincoln Memorial in Washington, D.C. The incident immortalized Anderson as a symbol of African American oppression. Anderson continued performing until 1965 and earned a long list of distinctions.

Angelou, Maya (1928-2014): Novelist, poet. Born Marguerite Johnson, Angelou worked as a nightclub singer in New York and San Francisco, as an editor for the English-language *Arab Observer* in Cairo, Egypt, and as a teacher of music and drama in Ghana. She became a national figure with the publication of the first volume of her autobiography, *I Know Why the Caged Bird Sings* (1970), which detailed her experiences with southern racism and sexual abuse. She was nominated for an Emmy Award for her performance as Nyo Boto in the television series *Roots* (1977). In 1993, she was invited to read her poem "On the Pulse of Morning" at the inauguration of President Bill Clinton.

Asante, Molefi Kete (1942-): Scholar. Born Arthur Lee Smith, Jr., he legally changed his name in 1975. After receiving a doctoral degree in communications from the University of California at Los Angeles (UCLA) in 1968, he taught at Purdue, UCLA, the State University of New York, Howard University, and Temple University and was named director of the Center for Afro-American Studies at UCLA. His more than two dozen books include *Afrocentricity: The Theory of Social Change* (1980), *African Culture: The Rhythms of Unity* (1985), and *The Historical and Cultural Atlas of African-Americans* (1991). He was also a founding editor of the *Journal of Black Studies*.

Baker, Josephine (1903-1986): Civil rights activist. After graduating as valedictorian with a bachelor's degree from Shaw Boarding School in 1927, she moved to New York City, where she became deeply involved with progressive politics. In 1931, she became director of the Young Negroes Cooperative League, which provided reasonably priced food to its members during the Depression. She also worked with the literacy program of the Works Progress Administration. During the 1940's, she set up and directed branch offices of the National Association for the Advancement of Colored People. She moved to Atlanta, Georgia, to work with the Southern Christian Leadership Conference in 1958 and was an unofficial adviser to the Student Nonviolent Coordinating Committee during the 1960's. She also helped organize the Mississippi Freedom Democratic Party and raised money for freedom fighters in Rhodesia (Zimbabwe) and South Africa. (Not to be confused with the singer Josephine Baker, 1903-1975).

Baldwin, James Arthur (1924-1987): Author and playwright. Baldwin has often been praised for his ability to make readers feel the destructive power of racial prejudice on both black and white people. His books include two autobiographical works, *Notes of a Native Son* (1955) and *Nobody Knows My Name* (1961); several powerful novels, including *Go Tell It on the Mountain* (1953), *Another Country* (1962), and *Just Above My Head* (1979); and a number of plays, including *Blues for Mister Charlie* (1964) and *The Amen Corner* (1964). He spent the final years of his life in France, where he was made commander of the Legion of Honor, France's highest civilian honor.

Baraka, Amiri (1934-2014): Poet and playwright. Born LeRoi Jones, Baraka founded *Yugen* magazine and Totem Press in 1958 and the Black Arts Repertory Theater in 1964. He achieved fame with his honest treatment of racism in plays such as *Dutchman* (1964), *The Slave* (1966), and *Four Revolutionary Plays* (1968). He was also a leading spokesperson for the Black Power movement in Newark, New Jersey, where he headed the activist Temple of Kawaida. In 1972, he chaired the National Black Political Convention.

Bethune, Mary McLeod (1875-1955): Educator. After teaching at various schools in Georgia and Florida, Bethune founded the Daytona Educational and Industrial School for Negro Girls in 1904 and McLeod Hospital in 1911. In 1922, her Daytona school merged with the Cookman Institute to become Bethune-Cookman College, of which she served as president until 1942. During the 1920's, she served on conferences under Herbert Hoover. She also served as director of the Division of Negro Affairs of the National Youth Administration (1936-1944), was special assistant to the secretary of war during World War II, and was a special adviser on minority affairs to President Franklin D. Roosevelt (1935-1944). Bethune also played important roles in the National Urban League, National Association for the Advancement of Colored People, and the National Council of Negro Women.

Bond, Julian (1940-2015): Georgia politician and civil rights activist. Astudent founder of the Committee on Appeal for Human Rights, Bond attracted the attention of Martin Luther King, Jr., and helped found the Student Nonviolent Coordinating Committee, of which he was the first director of communications (1961-1966). A Democrat, he was elected to the Georgia house of representatives (1965-1975) and the Georgia senate (1975-1987). He helped found the Southern Poverty Law Center in 1971, served as president of the Atlanta branch of the National Association for the Advancement of Colored People (NAACP; 1974-1989), and became chairman of the NAACP in 1998. Bond also hosted the television program *America's Black Forum* and narrated the Public Broadcasting Service civil rights series *Eyes on the Prize*.

Bradley, Thomas (1917-1998): California politician. Bradley held various positions with the Los Angeles Police Department from 1940 to 1961 and earned a law degree in the 1950's. In 1963, he became the first African American elected to the Los Angeles City Council and was also the first African American elected the city's mayor in 1973, despite the fact that African Americans constituted a small minority of the city's voters. While serving four terms as mayor, he also ran for governor of California twice (1982, 1986). Bradley also was a founding member of the Black Achievers Committee of the National Association for the Advancement of Colored People.

Braun, Carol Moseley (1947-): Illinois politician. Braun was an assistant U.S. attorney for the northern district of Illinois (1973-1977) and served as an Illinois state representative (1979-1987), in which position she established a reputation as an ardent supporter of civil rights legislation. After serving as Cook County recorder of deeds (1987-1993), she became the first African American woman to be elected to the U.S. Senate, in which she served one term (1993-1999).

Brooke, Edward W. (1919-2015): Massachusetts politician and former state attorney general who, in 1966, became the first African American elected to a full term in the U.S. Senate since Reconstruction. A liberal Democrat, Brooke was reelected in 1972. After losing his bid for a third term in 1978, he returned to practicing law and became a lobbyist in Washington, D.C.

Brown, H. Rap (1943-): Civil rights activist. Brown became leader of the Student Nonviolent Coordinating Committee in 1967. The following year he was charged with inciting a riot in Cambridge, Maryland, and was convicted of carrying a gun across state lines. In 1969, he published *Die Nigger Die* (1969) while serving a prison term for a robbery conviction. After converting to Islam, he changed his name to Jamil Abdullah Al-Amin and became the leader of Community Mosque in Atlanta, Georgia.

Brown, John (1800-1859): White abolitionist. Brown joined antislavery forces in Kansas in 1855 and murdered five proslavery advocates in 1856 in retaliation for a previous massacre. After establishing a plan for a slave refuge state, he led a band that seized the federal arsenal at Harpers Ferry, Virginia, in 1859, hoping to incite a slave insurrection. Convicted of treason and hanged, he later became an icon of the abolitionist movement.

Bruce, Blanche Kelso (1841-1898): Mississippi politician. Born a slave, Bruce built a fortune as a plantation owner after the Civil War and served in various local and state positions in Mississippi during Reconstruction. He was a U.S. senator from Mississippi (1875-1881), and became the first African American to serve a full term in the Senate. He was also a staunch defender of black, Chinese, and American Indian rights. After Reconstruction, he worked with the U.S. register of the treasury (1881-1889, 1895-1898) and as recorder of deeds for the District of Columbia (1889-1895).

Bunche, Ralph (1904-1971): Diplomat and scholar. A former head of the political science department of Howard University, Bunche served as senior social analyst for the Office of the Coordinator of Information in African and Far Eastern Affairs and with the African section of the Office of Strategic Services during World War II. Recognized as an expert on colonial affairs, he joined the U.S. State Department in 1944 and served as delegate or adviser to nine international conferences over the next four years. After serving as chief assistant on the United Nations Palestine Commission, he became the first African American to receive the Nobel Peace Prize in 1950, for his role in the Arab-Israeli cease-fire of 1948-1949. Bunche also served as U.N. undersecretary of Special Political Affairs (1957-1967) and undersecretary general of the United Nations (1968-1971).

Carmichael, Stokely (1941-1998): Trinidad-born political activist. After attending Howard University, Carmichael became an accomplished organizer for the Student Nonviolent Coordinating Committee (SNCC) of which he was elected chair in 1966. He popularized the phrase "black power" and became known for radical positions that led to his expulsion from SNCC in 1968. He joined the Black Panther Party in 1968, but resigned the following year and moved to Guinea in West Africa, where he became a supporter of Pan-Africanism. In 1978, he changed his name to Kwame Toure, in honor of the West African nationalist leaders Sékou Touré and Kwame Nkrumah.

Chavis, Benjamin (1948-): Civil rights activist. After training as a theologian, Chavis became a civil rights organizer for the Southern Christian Leadership Conference and the United Church of Christ. In 1971, he was indicted as one of the Wilmington Ten for the firebombing of a store in Wilmington, Delaware. He was convicted but was granted parole, and his conviction was reversed in 1980. Five years later, he was appointed executive director of the Commission for Racial Justice, and he served as executive director of the National Association for the Advancement of Colored People (1993-1994)—a position fromwhich he was forced to resign because of a financial scandal. In 1995, he served as national director of the Million Man March.

Chisholm, Shirley (1924-2005): New York Democratic politician. After an early career in child care and education, Chisholm was elected New York State assemblywoman in 1964. In 1969, she became the first African American woman elected to the U.S. House of Representatives, where she served until 1983. She also cofounded the National Political Congress of Black Women. Her autobiography is titled *Unbossed and Unbought* (1970).

Cleaver, Eldridge (1935-1998): Civil rights activist. After serving a prison sentence from 1958 to 1966, Cleaver joined the Black Panther Party and became one of the most vocal proponents of the doctrine of black power. His memoir *Soul on Ice* (1968) became one of the most powerful statements of that movement. After becoming involved in a 1968 shooting, Cleaver fled to Algeria. He returned to the United States in 1975 and espoused more conservative views.

Cone, James (1938-): Theologian. A faculty member at Union Theological Seminary since 1969, Cone provided a systematic case for divine support of the black liberation struggle in the United States and elsewhere. His many books include *Black Theology and Black Power* (1969), *For My People: Black Theology and the Black Church* (1984), and *Martin and Malcolm and America: A Dream or a Nightmare?* (1991).

Cosby, Bill (1937-): Actor and comedian. By the mid-1960's, Cosby was playing top nightclubs with his comedy routine and regularly appearing on television. In 1965, he became the first African American star of a prime-time television series, *I Spy*, for which he won Emmy Awards (1965-1968). Throughout the 1970's, he appeared in films and television shows and in Las Vegas, Reno, and Tahoe nightclubs. His television sitcom *The Cosby Show* (1985-1992) presented upper-middle-class black family life to mainstream American audiences and was the top-rated show of its time. Cosby also earned five Grammy Awards and wrote *Fatherhood* (1986) and *Time Flies* (1987). A quiet but forceful advocate of African American education, Cosby donated twenty million dollars to Spellman College in 1988. In 2004, Cosby received national attention for his outspoken criticisms of the values and parenting skills of many low-income African Americans, whom he accused of neglecting their responsibilities as parents by raising their children to think of themselves as victims of racism.

Crummell, Alexander (1819-1898): Christian minister and author. After earning a degree at Cambridge University in England, Crummell served as professor of mental and moral science at the College of Liberia (1853-1873) in West Africa and was minister of St. Luke's Protestant Episcopal Church in Washington, D.C. (1876-1898). In 1897, he helped found the American Negro Academy. His many books include *Future of Africa* (1862) and *Africa and America* (1892).

Davis, Angela (1944-): Political activist and scholar. After an extensive education at Brandeis University, the Sorbonne, and the University of Frankfurt, Davis took a teaching job at the University of California at Los Angeles (UCLA). In 1969, she joined the Communist Party. She later became involved with the Black Panther Party. After being implicated in a courtroom shooting in 1970, she went underground but eventually was arrested. However, she was acquitted on all charges in 1972. She later became co-chair of the National Alliance Against Racism and Political Repression. Her books include *If They Come in the Morning* (1971), *Women, Race, and Class* (1983), and *Women, Culture, and Politics* (1989).

Davis, Benjamin O., Jr. (1912-2002): Career military officer. The son of Brigadier General Benjamin Davis, Sr., the younger Davis became the second African American general in the U.S. military and the first in the U.S. Air Force in 1954. During World War II, he was a decorated pilot and squadron commander of the Tuskegee Airmen. In 1965, President Lyndon B. Johnson promoted him to the rank of lieutenant general, in which capacity he served as chief of staff of U.S. forces in Korea.

Davis, Benjamin O., Sr. (1877-1970): Career army officer. Davis served in the Spanish-American War and in the all-black Ninth Cavalry. In 1940, he became the first African American to reach the rank of general in the regular army, when President Franklin D. Roosevelt promoted him to brigadier general. Davis retired from military service in 1948.

Delany, Martin Robison (1812-1885): Doctor, author, and abolitionist. Born a slave in what later became West Virginia, Delany fled north when his masters discovered that he could read. He edited the abolitionist newspapers *The Mystery* and *The North Star*. Disappointed with the treatment of blacks in the United States, he recommended founding an African American colony in Africa or South America. In 1863, he was commissioned the first black major in the U.S. Army. He later published *Principal of Ethnology: The Origin of Races and Color* (1879).

Douglass, Frederick (c. 1817-1895): Abolitionist and journalist. The most prominent African American of his time, Douglass escaped from slavery in 1838 and fled north. A brilliant orator, he became famous as an agent of the Massachusetts Anti- Slavery Society during the 1840's. After publishing *Narrative of the Life of Frederick Douglass* (1845), he lectured in England and Ireland (1845-1847), earning enough money to purchase his freedom, thereby ending status as a fugitive slave. Douglass founded and served as coeditor of *The North Star*, 1847-1860 (*Frederick Douglass's Paper* from 1851) and came to oppose the radical abolitionism of William Lloyd Garrison and John Brown. After the Civil War, he held several federal government positions. He was U.S. marshal for the District of Columbia (1877-1881); recorder of deeds for the District of Columbia (1881-1886), and U.S. minister to Haiti (1889-1891).

Du Bois, W. E. B. (1868-1963): Civil rights activist, scholar, and author. The leader of the Niagara Movement (1905-1909), Du Bois helped found the National Association for the Advancement of Colored People (NAACP) in 1909 and acted as the association's director of publications and editor of *The Crisis* (1909-1934). He was also a professor of sociology at Atlanta University (1932-1944) and served as head of the special research department of the NAACP (1944-1948). Dissatisfied with the pace of social change in the United States, he joined the Communist Party and emigrated to Ghana in West Africa in 1961 to become editor in chief of the Pan-Africanist *Encyclopedia Africana*, sponsored by Ghanaian president Kwame Nkrumah. His numerous books include *The Souls of Black Folk* (1903), *The Negro* (1915), *The Gift of Black Folk* (1924), *Color and Democracy* (1945), *The World and Africa* (1947), and the *Black Flame* trilogy (1957-1961).

Eisenhower, Dwight D. (1890-1969): Thirty-fourth president of the United States (1953-1961). A moderate Republican, Eisenhower appointed California governor Earl Warren chief justice of the United States during his first year in office. He expected Warren to behave as a political conservative and was consequently surprised by Warren's social activism, especially after Warren guided the Court to a unanimous ruling in the *Brown v. Board of Education* case in 1954. During the Little Rock crisis three years later, Eisenhower reluctantly sent federal troops into Arkansas to enforce school desegregation. During that same year, 1957, he appointed the federal Civil Rights Commission, which was required by the Civil Rights Act of 1957.

Evers, Medgar (1925-1963): Civil rights activist. Appointed Mississippi field secretary of the National Association for the Advancement of Colored People in 1954, Evers fought for enforcement of school integration and advocated the right of African Americans to vote and the boycotting of merchants who discriminated against them. His murder in 1963 made him one of the first martyrs of the Civil Rights movement.

Farmer, James (1920-1999): Civil rights leader. One of the organizers of the Congress of Racial Equality (CORE), in 1942, Farmer arranged the first successful sit-in demonstration, at a Chicago restaurant the following year. He later also served as program director of the National Association for the Advancement of Colored People (1959-1961), and he introduced the tactic of the Freedom Ride in 1961 to test principles of desegregation. Farmer left CORE in 1966 and was appointed assistant secretary of Health, Education, andWelfare in 1969. In 1976, he became associate director of the Coalition of American Public Employees.

Farrakhan, Louis (1933-): Muslim cleric. Born Louis Eugene Walcott, Farrakhan joined the Nation of Islam during the 1950's. He denounced Malcolm X after the latter's split with Elijah Muhammad and succeeded Malcolm as leader of New York's Harlem mosque. Farrakhan left the Nation of Islam after it began accepting white members during the mid-1970's and founded a rival organization that was later known by the same name. In 1984, he supported Jesse Jackson in the presidential campaign, marking a turning point in Black Muslim political involvement. In 1995, he and Benjamin Chavis organized the Million Man March.

Forten, James (1766-1842): Abolitionist and entrepreneur. Born of free parents in Philadelphia, Forten served aboard a privateer during the American Revolution, during which he was captured and held prisoner for seven months. While he was in England, he became acquainted with abolitionist philosophy. By 1798, he owned a prosperous maritime company. He became active in the abolitionist movement during the 1830's and joined the American Anti-Slavery Society. He also helped raise funds for William Lloyd Garrison's newspaper *The Liberator* and founded the American Moral Reform Society.

Fortune, T. Thomas (1856-1928): Journalist and editor. Fortune worked in various positions for the *New York Sun* during the late 1870's and early 1880's. In 1883, he founded the *New York Age*, which became the leading black journal of opinion in the United States. Fortune crusaded against school segregation and joined Booker T. Washington in organizing the National Negro Business League in 1900. Fortune coined the term "Afro-American" as a substitute for "Negro" in the New York press.

Gandhi, Mohandas K. (1869-1948): Indian nationalist leader who had an indirect but strong influence on the American Civil Rights movement. After going to South Africa to practice law, Gandhi became a leader of the Indian civil rights struggle in Natal. While there, he developed the philosophy of nonviolent direct action to force political change that he later introduced to the independence struggle in his native India. Gandhi's philosophy was a powerful influence on the nonviolent strategies of the American Civil Rights movement, and it particularly influenced the philosophy of Martin Luther King, Jr.

Garrison, William Lloyd (1805-1879): Abolitionist who published *The Liberator* from 1831 to 1865. He founded the American Anti-Slavery Society in 1833 and was its president from 1843 to 1865. Garrison opposed the Compromise of 1850 and encouraged the separation of the northern and southern states. After the Civil War, he campaigned against mistreatment of Native Americans and in favor of women's suffrage.

Garvey, Marcus (1887-1940): Jamaican-born black nationalist leader. Two years after founding the Universal Negro Improvement Association (UNIA) in 1914, Garvey came to the United States, where he founded UNIA branches in cities throughout the northern states. At UNIA's first convention in New York City in 1920, he outlined a plan for the establishment of an African nation-state for American blacks. He preached racial pride through civil rights and economic selfsufficiency. After being convicted of fraud in 1925, he was sent to a federal prison, but his sentence was commuted by President Calvin Coolidge, and he was deported back to Jamaica in 1927. He continued to be active in progressive politics but his influence on developments in the United States waned greatly.

Gordy, Berry, Jr. (1929-): Songwriter and music producer. Gordy served with the U.S. Army in the Korean War. After a number of failed or unsatisfying jobs in Detroit, Michigan, he began writing hit songs with the help of his sister Gwen Gordy and Billy Davis. In 1959, he formed Motown Record Corporation and a number of related businesses. By the mid-1960's, Gordy had brought black soul music to mainstream American audiences with highly polished performances by artists such as the Supremes, Smokey Robinson, the Four Tops, the Marvelettes, Marvin Gaye, the Jackson Five, Lionel Richie, and Stevie Wonder. He was inducted into the Rock and Roll Hall of Fame in 1988.

Grace, Charles Emmanuel "Sweet Daddy" (1881-1960): Religious leader. Born Marcelino Manoel de Graca in the Cape Verde Islands, Grace established the United House of Prayer for All People during the early 1920's.

His ministerial style was rooted in faith healing and speaking in tongues. Products such as "Daddy Grace" coffee, tea, and creams were believed to have healing powers. By 1960, Grace's church claimed 25,000 adherents in 375 congregations.

Graves, Earl (1935-): Publisher and editor. Graves served in the U.S. Army as an officer in the Green Berets (1957-1960) and was an administrative assistant to Robert F. Kennedy (1964- 1968). In 1970, he launched *Black Enterprise* to provide African Americans with practical help for succeeding in business. By the late 1990's, the magazine had a subscription base of more than 300,000. Graves also wrote *How to Succeed in Business Without Being White* (1997).

Haley, Alex (1921-1992): Journalist and author. Haley got into journalism while serving in the U.S. Coast Guard (1952-1959). He later interviewed Malcolm X for *Playboy* magazine—an assignment that led to his first book, *The Autobiography of Malcolm X* (1965). He then spent a dozen years researching his family history, leading to publication of the novel *Roots* (1976), based on the life of a West African man named Kunta Kinte who was sent to North America in slavery. Haley's book led to a twelve-hour television series, hundreds of interviews and articles, instructional packets and tapes, and sparked intense interest in genealogy and history among both black and white Americans.

Hamer, Fannie Lou (1917-1977): Civil rights activist. After forty years of working on the same plantation, Hamer lost her job when she tried to vote. She then began working with the Student Nonviolent Coordinating Committee. She helped register black voters and helped form the Mississippi Freedom Democratic Party, for which she spoke eloquently in favor of seating black delegates to the Democratic National Convention in 1964. Hamer herself became one of the first delegates to the Democratic convention in 1968. She founded Freedom Farms Corporation in 1969 and toured and spoke widely on behalf of civil rights legislation.

Hayes, Rutherford B. (1822-1893): Nineteenth president of the United States (1877-1881). Though an ardent Radical Republican early in the Reconstruction era, Hayes moderated his views and as president ended that era by withdrawing military support for Republican state governments in the South. The end of Reconstruction left African Americans in the South at the mercy of resentful white politicians, who enacted discriminatory legislation and effectively disfranchised black voters.

Hill, Anita (1956-): Professor of law. Hill was a relatively unknown instructor at the University of Oklahoma when she gained national attention during Senate confirmation hearings for U.S. Supreme Court justice nominee Clarence Thomas in 1991. At that time, she charged that she had been sexually harassed when working for Thomas at the Equal Employment Opportunities Commission in the early 1980's. Afterward, she withstood attempts by some lawmakers to have the University of Oklahoma Law School fire her and spoke widely around the country throughout the 1990's in favor of civil rights and women's rights.

Hooks, Benjamin (1925-2010): Lawyer, preacher, and civil rights leader. Hooks was the first African American to serve as a judge in a criminal court in Tennessee's Shelby County. He also served as executive director of the National Association for the Advancement of Colored People (1977-1992). In that capacity, he vigorously promoted integration, pro-African foreign policy, and progressive employment legislation.

Howard, Oliver Otis (1830-1909): U.S. Army officer. Howard entered the Army in 1854 and fought in the Civil War, during which he was promoted to brigadier general in 1861. After the war, he served as a commissioner for the Bureau of Refugees, Freedmen, and Abandoned Lands (1865-1874) and as founder and first president of Howard University (1869-1874). After returning to the Army, he commanded the federal campaign against Chief Joseph of the Nez Perce Indians in the Northwest in 1877 and was superintendent at West Point (1881-1882). Howard was considered one of the few "humanitarian" generals who campaigned on behalf of Indian rights.

Hughes, Langston (1902-1967): Writer and poet. After dropping out of Columbia University, Hughes wrote poetry and worked as a cabin boy on a freighter, on which he sailed to Africa. He was later a major figure in the 1920's

Harlem Renaissance. His essay "The Negro Writer and the Racial Mountain" (1926) established an early ethic of black pride. He wrote in many fields, including poetry (*The Weary Blues*, 1926; *Fine Clothes to the Jew*, 1927; *Shakespeare in Harlem*, 1942; *Montage of a Dream Deferred*, 1951); librettos (*Street Scene*, 1947); plays (*Mulatto*, 1935); and autobiography (*The Big Sea*, 1940; *I Wonder as I Wander*, 1956).

Innis, Roy (1934-): Civil rights leader. Innis joined the Congress of Racial Equality (CORE) in 1963 and became its national director in 1968. He also founded the Harlem Commonwealth Council, which was designed to promote black businesses. Controversy over his involvement in recruiting black Vietnam War veterans to fight in Angola's civil war and charges that he misappropriated funds led to important defections from CORE, which became largely inactive in the 1980's.

Jackson, Jesse (1941-): Civil rights activist, Baptist minister, and politician. Jackson joined the Southern Christian Leadership Conference (SCLC) in 1965 and served as the executive director of its Operation Breadbasket program (1967-1971). He also founded Operation PUSH (People United to Save Humanity) in 1971. His PUSH-EXCEL program for encouraging young students to improve academically received funding from the administration of U.S. president Jimmy Carter. Jackson campaigned for the Democratic nomination for president of the United States in 1984 and 1988. In the latter campaign, he finished a strong second to Michael Dukakis, who lost to George Bush in the November election. His candidacy demonstrated the possibility of an African American eventually being elected president. Afterward, he continued to press for child care, health care reform, housing reform, and statehood for the predominantly African American District of Columbia.

Johnson, Andrew (1808-1875): Seventeenth president of the United States. A Tennessee politician, Johnson became one of the rare southerners in the Union government when he was elected vice president in 1864. Abraham Lincoln's assassination shortly after the conclusion of the CivilWar suddenly elevated Johnson to the presidency and gave him responsibility for overseeing the postwar reconstruction of the South. However, his inclination to be lenient toward the South pitted him against the Congress, which was dominated by Radical Republicans who subjected him to impeachment and wrested away control of Reconstruction policy. Johnson narrowly survived his impeachment trial and eventually left office under a cloud. However, he later enjoyed some vindication when he was reelected to the Senate.

Johnson, Jack (1878-1946): Boxer. The first black heavyweight boxing champion of the world (1908-1915), Jackson became the center of racial controversy as the public called for Jim Jeffries, the white former champion, to come out of retirement to defeat him. Johnson beat Jeffries in 1910 but remained a target of racist attacks through the rest of his life, which Howard Sackler later dramatized in a play, *The Great White Hope* (1967).

Johnson, James Weldon (1871-1938): Poet, diplomat, and civil rights leader. As a young man, Johnson was known principally as a lyricist for popular songs, including "Lift Every Voice and Sing" (1899). He later served as U.S. consul in Puerto Cabello, Venezuela (1906-1909), and in Corinto, Nicaragua (1909-1912). From 1920 to 1930, he was executive secretary of the National Association for the Advancement of Colored People (1920-1930). Johnson's many books include *The Autobiography of an Ex-Colored Man* (1912), *The Book of American Negro Poetry* (1922), *God's Trombones* (1927), and *Negro Americans, What Now* (1934).

Johnson, John H. (1918-2005): Publisher who addressed the need for mainstream black publications with the establishment of *The Negro Digest* (1942) and *Ebony* (1945). Johnson was also a member of the advisory council of the Harvard Graduate School of Business and a director of the Chamber of Commerce of the United States.

Johnson, Lyndon B. (1908-1973): Thirty-sixth president of the United States (1963-1969). A native Texan, Johnson began his political career as state administrator and served in the National Youth Administration (1935-1937). In 1936, he was elected to the House of Representatives as a Democrat. In 1949, he moved from the House to the Senate, in which he became majority leader in 1955-1961. After attempting to win the Democratic nomination for president in 1960, he joined the Democratic ticket under John F. Kennedy and was elected vice president. On Kennedy's assassination in 1963, Johnson became president. Despite his conservative southern background, he became a champion of progressive social programs and articulated what he called the "Great Society." Under his leadership, Congress passed the Civil Rights Act of 1964 and the Voting Rights Act of 1965, which were designed to ensure that African Americans received their full civil rights. Johnson also established the Department of Housing and Urban Development and made Thurgood Marshall the first black Supreme Court justice in 1967.

Jones, Absalom (1746-1818): Protestant cleric. In 1794, Jones became the first leader of St. Thomas African Episcopal Church. One year later, he was ordained the first African American Protestant Episcopal priest in the United States.

Jordan, Vernon (1935-): Lawyer and civil rights leader. Jordan was field secretary for the Georgia branch of the National Association for the Advancement of Colored People (1962-1964). He also served as director of the Voter Education Project of the Southern Regional Council (1964-1968), was executive director of the United Negro College Fund (1970-1972), and executive director of the National Urban League (1972-1981). In 1992, Jordan became a political confidante of President Bill Clinton.

Kennedy, John F. (1917-1963): Thirty-fifth president of the United States (1961-1963). After graduating from Harvard in 1940, Kennedy served as a naval officer during World War II. A Democrat, he was elected a Massachusetts representative to Congress in 1947. After three terms in the House of Representatives (1947-1953), he was elected to the Senate (1953-1960). In 1960, he became the first Roman Catholic elected president of the United States. As president, he established the Peace Corps and the Alliance for Progress in Latin America. An outspoken advocate of civil rights for African Americans, he federalized the Alabama national guard to ensure integration of the state's schools in 1963. His efforts to persuade Congress to pass major civil rights legislation were interrupted by his assassination in late 1963, but his goal was realized by his successor, Lyndon B. Johnson.

Kennedy, Robert F. (1925-1968): Politician and lawyer. In 1960, Kennedy managed the presidential campaign of his brother, John F. Kennedy, who made him attorney general of the United States (1961-1964). In that capacity, he was an ardent supporter of civil rights. In 1964, he was elected to the U.S. Senate from his adopted state of New York. He continued to champion civil rights and was mounting a serious challenge for the Democratic nomination for the presidency in 1968 until he was assassinated the same night that he won the California primary. Kennedy's books include *The Enemy Within* (1960), *Just Friends and Brave Enemies* (1962), and *To Seek a Newer World* (1967).

King, Martin Luther, Jr. (1929-1968): Civil rights activist and Baptist minister. King earned a doctoral degree from Crozer Theological Seminary in Rochester, New York, in 1955. Afterward, he accepted the pastorate of the Dexter Avenue Baptist Church in Montgomery, Alabama. In 1956, he helped organize the Montgomery bus boycott, which led to the founding of the Southern Christian Leadership Conference, of which he served as first president. Meanwhile, he was also a co-pastor of Ebenezer Baptist Church in Atlanta (1960-1968). Through the remainder of his life, he was acknowledged as the primary leader of the Civil Rights movement and personally directed many of its campaigns. Some of these led to his arrest. While serving a jail sentence in Birmingham, Alabama, where he was arrested while protesting segregation and unfair hiring practices in 1963, he wrote his classic "Letter from Birmingham Jail." That same year, he delivered his "I Have a Dream" speech during the historic March on Washington. *Time* magazine named him "Man of the Year" in 1963; the following year, he was awarded the Nobel Peace Prize. Around that same time, he began to speak out forcefully against the Vietnam War and urban poverty, causing many black leaders to question his tactics in the civil rights struggle. He was assassinated in Memphis, Tennessee, in 1968. His January birthday was later made a federal holiday.

King, Rodney (1966-2012): California motorist who was severely beaten by Los Angeles police officers in 1991. Caught on a videotape made by a bystander and broadcast nationwide, his beating became a *cause célèbre* and the focus of a criminal trial of the four officers charged with beating him. After a predominantly white jury acquitted the officers in April, 1992, Los Angeles erupted in riots that killed fifty-eight people and caused $1 billion in property damage.

Lee, Spike (1957-): Filmmaker. While attending New York University's Institute of Film and Television, Lee won the Student Award presented by the Academy of Motion Picture Arts and Sciences for *Joe's Bed-Sty Barbershop: We Cut Heads* (1982). His controversial films, highlighting past and present struggles of African Americans in a land of alien values, include *She's Gotta Have It* (1986), *Do the Right Thing* (1989), *Mo' Better Blues* (1990), *Malcolm X* (1992), and *He Got Game* (1998).

Lincoln, Abraham (1809-1865): Sixteenth president of the United States (1861-1865). After a boyhood on pioneer farms in the Midwest, Lincoln was elected to the Illinois state legislature in 1834. While representing Illinois in the House of Representatives (1847-1849), he spoke out against the Mexican War. In 1858, he was defeated in his bid for a seat in the U.S. Senate but established his position against slavery during his famous debates with Stephen A. Douglas during the campaign. In 1860, his election as president of the United States accelerated the movement toward secession by southern states that led to the Civil War, which dominated his presidency. Because of his dedication to preserving the Union, his attitude toward abolishing slavery was equivocal. Nevertheless, he is remembered as the "Great Emancipator" because of his issuance of the Emancipation Proclamation in early 1863. Aimed only at U.S. states and territories then in rebellion against the United States, that declaration freed no slaves but did make abolition a northern goal in the Civil War. At the conclusion of the war, Lincoln was about to face the challenge of developing a Reconstruction policy for the defeated Confederacy but was assassinated by a disgruntled southerner, John Wilkes Booth.

Locke, Alain (1886-1954): Philosopher and writer. After studying at Harvard University, Oxford University, and the University of Berlin, Locke served on the faculty at Howard University (1912-1953). He celebrated black cultural contributions in works such as *The New Negro: An Interpretation* (1925) and a special issue of the journal *Survey Graphic*, which announced the arrival of a "Harlem Renaissance" and published work by Langston Hughes, Zora Neale Hurston, and W. E. B. Du Bois. Locke also wrote or edited *Race Contacts and Inter-Racial Relations* (1916), *Opportunity* (an annual review of the state of black writing), *Negro Art: Past and Present* (1936), and *The Negro and His Music* (1940).

Lowery, Joseph E. (1924-): Cleric and civil rights leader. The pastor of the Warren Street Church in Birmingham, Alabama (1952-1961), Lowery was one of the cofounders of the Southern Negro Leaders Conference, which evolved into the Southern Christian Leadership Conference (SCLC) in 1957, and served as its first vice president under Martin Luther King, Jr. He became president of the SCLC in 1977 and pastor of Cascade United Methodist Church in Atlanta, Georgia, in 1986.

McKay, Claude (1889-1948): Jamaican-born poet, novelist, and essayist. A key figure in the Harlem Renaissance, McKay is noted for his poetry about his experiences with American racism. His poetry volumes include *Constab Ballads* (1912), *Songs of Jamaica* (1912), and *Harlem Shadows* (1922)—which established his reputation as a major Harlem Renaissance figure. McKay's fiction includes the short stories of *Gingertown* (1932) and the novels *Home to Harlem* (1928), *Banjo: A Story Without a Plot* (1929), and *Banana Bottom* (1933). He also published an autobiography, *A Long Way from Home* (1937), and the nonfiction *Harlem: Negro Metropolis* (1940).

McKissick, Floyd (1922-1991): Lawyer and civil rights leader. After suing the University of North Carolina at Chapel Hill for admission to its law school, he became the first African American to earn a degree there. He was later the head of the Congress of Racial Equality (1966-1968). From 1968 to 1980, he worked unsuccessfully to establish a new and self-sufficient community in Warren County, North Carolina, known as Soul City.

Malcolm X (1925-1965): Black nationalist leader. Malcolm was born Malcolm Little in a Nebraska family that was committed to Marcus Garvey's United Negro Improvement Association. After his father's murder by white racists, he left school and went to New York, where he was convicted of burglary. While in prison, he converted to the Nation of Islam. A brilliant speaker, he began making provocative, anti-white statements, for which he was expelled from the Nation of Islam by Elijah Muhammad. He then formed the Organization of Afro-American Unity and Muslim Mosque Inc. in 1964. After undertaking a pilgrimage to Mecca, he converted to orthodox Islam, changed his name to El-Hajj Malik El-Shabazz, and moderated his political and social views. In 1965, he was shot to death by Black Muslims. He was the author, with Alex Haley, of *The Autobiography of Malcolm X* (1965).

Marshall, Thurgood (1908-1993): Lawyer, civil rights activist, and jurist. Marshall served as chief legal counsel for the National Association for the Advancement of Colored People (1938-1961) and played a key role in the landmark *Brown v. Board of Education* case (1954), in which the U.S. Supreme Court overturned the "separate but equal" doctrine in public education. Marshall won twenty-nine of the thirty-two cases that he argued before the Supreme Court. He later became a federal circuit court judge (1961-1967) and was appointed the first African American justice on the U.S. Supreme Court (1967-1991).

Meredith, James (1933-): Civil rights activist. Meredith became the first African American to attend the University of Mississippi in 1962. His admission to the university generated riots and the stationing of federal troops on the campus. In 1966, while leading a march to encourage black voter registration, he was shot by a sniper but recovered. That same year, he wrote *Three Years in Mississippi* (1966).

Morrison, Toni (1931-): Writer. Born Chloe Anthony Wofford, Morrison has incorporated African and African American folklore, legend, and mythology into her novels. Her works also contain many autobiographical references. Her novel *Beloved* (1987), which examines the brutality of American slavery, won the Pulitzer Prize in fiction in 1988 and was made into a motion picture in 1998. In 1993, Morrison became the first African American to win the Nobel Prize in Literature. Her books include *The Bluest Eye* (1970), *Sula* (1974), *Song of Solomon* (1977), *Tar Baby* (1981), and *Jazz* (1992).

Muhammad, Elijah (1897-1975): Religious and black nationalist leader. Born Elijah Poole to a former slave, Muhammad became chief assistant to W. D. Fard, the founder of the Lost-Found Nation of Islam, in 1930. Upon Fard's mysterious disappearance in 1934, he succeeded to leadership of the Nation of Islam. In that capacity, he preached racial segregation, black integrity, and the need for economic independence from whites. His support for Japan in World War II and the conviction of three members of the Nation of Islam for the assassination of Malcolm X in 1965 led to unfavorable press coverage, but his movement continued to grow, especially among the underemployed of the major cities.

Newton, Huey P. (1942-1989): Black activist. In 1966, Newton was the cofounder, with Bobby Seale, of the Black Panther Party for Self-Defense, which became a major force in California politics. The following year, he was convicted of manslaughter in the killing of an Oakland police officer, but his conviction was later overturned. In 1977, he helped elect Lionel Wilson as the first black mayor of Oakland. After frequently being in legal trouble throughout the 1970's and 1980's, he was killed by a drug dealer in 1989.

Owens, Jesse (1913-1980): Track and field athlete. One of the first great all-around track and field athletes, Owens earned four gold medals at the 1936 Berlin Olympics (100- and 200-meter races, 400-meter relay, broad jump). He became internationally famous in that Olympiad when German leader Adolf Hitler refused to present Owens his gold medals. Owens later traveled and spoke widely on the value of sports in breaking down racial barriers.

Parks, Rosa (1913-2005): Civil rights activist. While serving as secretary of the Montgomery, Alabama, chapter of the National Association for the Advancement of Colored People during the 1950's, Parks was arrested and fined for refusing to give up her seat to a white passenger on a Montgomery, Alabama, bus. Her arrest sparked a 382-day citywide bus boycott aimed at desegregating public transportation. White harassment eventually led Parks and her family to move to Detroit, Michigan, where she worked in the office of Congressman John Conyers and continued to campaign for civil rights.

Patterson, Frederick D. (1901-1988): Educator. A faculty member and later president of Tuskegee Institute, Patterson was also chairman of the R. R. Moton Memorial Institute. In 1944, he organized the United Negro College Fund to aid historically black colleges and universities.

Payne, Daniel Alexander (1811-1893): Educator, abolitionist, and cleric. Born in South Carolina to free black parents, Patterson opened a school for black students in Charleston in 1829. After his school was closed by an act of the South Carolina legislature, he traveled north to study and delivered powerful abolitionist speeches throughout the 1840's and 1850's. In 1852, he was elected a bishop of the African Methodist Episcopal Church. In 1863, he bought Wilberforce University from the Methodist Episcopal Church and devoted the rest of his life to developing the university and overseeing missionary endeavors. His writings include *Recollections of Seventy Years* (1888) and *History of the African Methodist Episcopal Church* (1891).

Powell, Adam Clayton, Jr. (1908-1972): New York City politician. Instrumental in securing better treatment for African Americans in Harlem during the Depression of the 1930's, Powell succeeded his father as pastor of the Abyssinian Baptist Church in 1936. He also served in various New York government posts until 1944, when he was elected to the U.S. House of Representatives (1945-1967, 1969-1971). While a congressman, he sponsored more than fifty pieces of social legislation, many aimed at ending discrimination against minorities. In 1960, he became chairman of the House Committee on Education and Labor. In 1967, he was censured in the House and unseated for misuse of public funds but was readmitted the following year.

Powell, Colin (1937-): Military leader and government official. Born in New York City to Jamaican immigrants, Powell joined the U.S. Army and served two tours of duty in the Vietnam War. He later served as a military assistant to the secretary of defense (1983) and as national security adviser to President Ronald Reagan (1987-1989). Under President George Bush, he served as chairman of the joint chiefs of staff (1989- 1993)—a position that made him the highest-ranking African American officer in military history, as well as the highest-ranking officer in the United States at the time. In that position, he gained international recognition for his role in conducting the Persian Gulf War (1991). His popularity and vocal support for personal responsibility made him an attractive political candidate after he left the military. He addressed the 1996 Republican National Convention in San Diego, heightening rumors that he might one day run for high office, but he declined to seek office. After George W. Bush was elected president in 2000, Powell became U.S. secretary of state. He distinguished himself as a voice of moderation through the new military conflicts in which the United States became involved but resigned his cabinet post after Bush's reelection in 2004. He was succeeded as secretary of state by Condoleezza Rice.

Randolph, A. Philip (1889-1979): Labor leader and civil rights activist. Randolph is remembered as a key figure in the racial integration of American labor. In 1925, he began a successful fight to have the Brotherhood of Sleeping Car Porters recognized as an agent in negotiation with the Pullman Company. His actions led to Pullman's signing a contract with the porters in 1937. In 1941, Randolph was instrumental in persuading President Franklin D. Roosevelt to sign Executive Order 8802, which banned discrimination in employment by companies with defense contracts. Randolph's threat to organize a black boycott of the military draft in 1948 helped persuade President Harry S. Truman to sign Executive Order 9981, which ended racial segregation in the armed forces. Randolph was a symbolic and unifying force when he acted as chairman and provided opening remarks for the 1963 March on Washington. In 1968, he retired as president of the Brotherhood of Sleeping Car Porters.

Rice, Condoleezza (1954-): Educator and foreign policy expert. From 1989 to 1991, Rice served as a director of Soviet and East European Affairs with the National Security Council. She also served as a strategic adviser to the Joint Chiefs of Staff. In 1990, President George Bush appointed her his assistant for national security affairs, and during that same year, Rice sat at the bargaining table when Bush met Soviet premier Mikhail Gorbachev in Malta. After the Bush administration left office in 1993, Rice became provost at Stanford University; she was the first African American chief academic officer and budget officer at the university and one of the highest-ranking black college administrators in the entire nation. In 2001, newly elected President George W. Bush appointed Rice his national security adviser. During her four years in that office, Rice was considered to be one of the most influential members of the Bush administration. In 2005, after Bush was reelected, he appointed Rice to succeed Colin Powell as secretary of state.

Robeson, Paul (1898-1976): Singer and actor. The son of a runaway slave, Robeson earned a law degree at Columbia University and became a successful stage actor after being discovered by playwright Eugene O'Neill during the 1920's. His performance in O'Neill's *The Emperor Jones* (1923) led to a successful singing career. Active in national and international civil and human rights campaigns, Robeson spoke out vigorously for the independence of Europe's African colonies. His trips to the Soviet Union and other associations with communists led to the revocation of his passport in 1950 and a decline in his career. He regained his passport after an eight-year legal battle in 1958 and then moved to London, where he lived until 1963. His published autobiography is *Here I Stand* (1958).

Robinson, Jackie (1919-1972): Baseball player; after a stellar career at the University of California at Los Angeles (UCLA), Robinson left in his junior year to play professional football for the Los Angeles Bulldogs. After serving as a lieutenant in the U.S. Army during World War II, he played professional baseball with the Kansas City Monarchs of the Negro American League. In 1947, he became the first black player in modern Major League Baseball history. During his ten-year career with the Brooklyn Dodgers, he won many honors on the field, while responding to hostility from other players and fans with grace. His success paved the way for the expansion of opportunities for black athletes in all professional sports. He was inducted into the Baseball Hall of Fame in 1962.

Roosevelt, Franklin D. (1882-1945): Thirty-second president of the United States (1933-1945). During his three-plus terms in office, Roosevelt led the nation through the Great Depression and most of World War II and was seen as a supporter of civil rights for African Americans. He appointed more than two dozen African Americans to federal offices, and those appointees formed an unofficial Black Cabinet. In 1941, Roosevelt signed Executive Order 8802, which prohibited discrimination on the basis of race or color in the defense industry and armed forces. Roosevelt eased restrictions on opportunities for African Americans in the government and the military services but left the decision to order full desegregation of the military to his successor, Harry S. Truman.

Rustin, Bayard (1910-1987): Civil rights leader. During the Depression, Rustin organized the Young Communist League (1936-1941). Afterward, he worked with James Farmer on the Chicago Committee of Racial Equality, which developed into the Congress of Racial Equality. He was later a founding member of the Southern Christian Leadership Conference. In 1963, he served as organizational coordinator of the March on Washington, after which he became executive director of the A. Philip Randolph Institute (1964-1979). In 1975, he founded the Organization for Black Americans to Support Israel.

Scott, Dred (1795-1858): Missouri slave whose struggle to win his freedom led to one of the most infamous rulings in U.S. Supreme Court history. During the 1850's, he sued for his freedom on the grounds that because he had accompanied his master into the free state of Illinois he should no longer be considered a slave. After going through Missouri's courts, his case reached the U.S. Supreme Court in 1857. In its *Scott v. Sandford* decision, the Court ruled that Scott, as a slave, was not a legal citizen and therefore had no standing before the courts. Scott himself was eventually freed by his owner shortly before his death the following year, but the Supreme Court's ruling in the case defined slaves as noncitizens. It would not be until ratification of the Fourteenth Amendment to the U.S. Constitution in 1868 that African Americans were legally considered citizens.

Seale, Bobby (1936-): Black activist. Seale was cofounder, with Huey P. Newton, of the Black Panther Party for Self- Defense in 1966. In 1971, he was tried for the kidnapping and killing of a suspected police informant, but his case ended in a mistrial. Disenchanted with revolutionary politics, Seale left the Panthers in 1974. His writings include *Seize the Time: The Story of the Black Panther Party* (1970) and *A Lonely Rage: The Autobiography of Bobby Seale* (1978).

Sharpton, Al (1954-): Christian cleric and social activist. After gaining prominence for his Pentecostal preaching in Brooklyn, Sharpton became active in the Civil Rights movement. He served as youth director of Jesse Jackson's Operation Breadbasket. He also briefly served as a bodyguard for singer James Brown and worked with fight promoter

Don King. In 1971, Sharpton founded the National Youth Movement (later renamed the United African Movement). Apolitically controversial figure whose motives have often been questioned, Sharpton has been involved in many high-profile racial incidents in New York City, including the Bernhard Goetz murder trial in 1984, the Howard Beach killing in 1986, the Tawana Brawley affair in 1987, and the Bensonhurst killing in 1989. In 2004, he campaigned for the Democratic nomination for the presidency and earned some credibility as a mainstream politician.

Stevens, Thaddeus (1792-1868): Radical Republican politician, abolitionist, and advocate of African American civil rights. As a Pennsylvania congressman (1849-1853, 1859-1868), Stevens opposed fugitive slave laws; led the Radical Republican plan for Reconstruction after the Civil War, and was instrumental in framing the Fourteenth Amendment to the U.S. Constitution (1868). He was also one of the leaders in Congress's impeachment of President Andrew Johnson.

Thomas, Clarence (1948-): Second African American associate justice on the U.S. Supreme Court (1992-). After being appointed to the Court by President George Bush in 1991, Thomas had to endure a difficult confirmation battle in the Senate that was highlighted by the testimony of his former aide Anita F. Hill, who accused him of sexual harassment. Thomas remained a controversial justice because of his refusal to support positions many believed were essential to African American well-being.

Till, Emmett (1941-1955): Lynching victim. A Chicago teenager, Till was killed by white racists while visiting relatives in Mississippi. His murder helped call national attention to the virulence of racism in the South, and the speedy acquittal, by an all-white jury, of his accused murderers revealed the failings of the justice system. In 2004, the U.S. Justice Department announced that it was reopening its investigation into Till's murder.

Truman, Harry S. (1884-1972): Thirty-third president of the United States (1945-1953). After rising from the vice presidency to the presidency on the death of Franklin D. Roosevelt early in the latter's fourth term, Truman became the first U.S. president to call openly for civil rights legislation to improve the social and political condition of African Americans. In 1946, he appointed the President's Committee on Civil Rights, which the following year issued a report titled *To Secure These Rights*. In 1948, Truman completed the work begun by his predecessor by banning racial segregation in the armed forces with Executive Order 9981.

Truth, Sojourner (c. 1797-1883): Abolitionist. Born into slavery as Isabella Baumfree, Truth was freed by the New York State Emancipation Act in 1827. Afterward, she preached and lectured widely to abolitionist audiences, adopting the symbolic name Sojourner Truth in 1843. During the Civil War, she raised money for soldiers and runaway slaves and served as councilor with the National Freedmen's Relief Association. She dictated her autobiography, *The Narrative of Sojourner Truth* (1850).

Tubman, Harriet (c. 1820-1913): Abolitionist. Born Araminta Ross in Maryland, Tubman escaped from slavery in 1848. Afterward, she helped rescue more than three hundred slaves in nineteen forays along the Underground Railroad. She also helped John Brown recruit men for his raid on Harpers Ferry in 1858. After 1860, she spoke widely on emancipation and women's rights. During the Civil War, she served as nurse and spy for the Union army and was later buried with military honors.

Turner, Henry McNeal (1834-1915): Religious leader. Born to free parents in South Carolina, Turner was tutored by lawyers for whom he worked as a janitor. In 1853, he became a preacher in the Methodist Episcopal Church South. Five years later, he switched his affiliation and preached for African Methodist Episcopal churches in Baltimore and Washington, D.C. (1858- 1863). During the Civil War, he served as chaplain to the First U.S. Colored Troops. After the war, he was elected a Georgia State representative (1868-1869, 1870). In 1880, he was elected a bishop of the African Methodist Episcopal Church. After campaigning for full voting rights for African Americans, he advocated a return to Africa when the federal civil rights laws were overturned by the U.S. Supreme Court in 1883. His proclamation that "God is a Negro" anticipated modern black theology.

Turner, Nat (1800-1831): Slave rebellion leader. A Virginia slave, Turner planned and led the bloodiest slave revolt in U.S. history in Virginia's Southampton County in 1831. More than sixty slaves and free blacks rose up against white landowners and killed at least fifty-five people, including women and children. All the rebels were eventually killed or executed. Turner himself was caught and tried and hanged. Although his revolt was an isolated event in a remote part of Virginia, it had a profound impact on white southerners, who responded with more repressive laws and a wave of lynchings.

Walker, Alice (1944-): Writer and poet. Walker's works deal principally with the experiences of black women living in a racist and sexist society. Her early books were critically acclaimed, but she did not become widely popular until publishing her third novel, *The Color Purple* (1982), which won a Pulitzer Prize in fiction and was adapted to film in 1985. Walker has also been a champion of the works of Zora Neale Hurston. Walker has published in several genres, including poetry: *Once* (1968) and *Revolutionary Petunias and Other Poems* (1973); novels: *The Third Life of Grange Copeland* (1970), *Meridian* (1976), and *Possessing the Secret of Joy* (1992); short stories: "In Love and Trouble" (1973) and "You Can't Keep a Good Woman Down" (1976); and criticism: *A Zora Neale Hurston Reader* (1980).

Warren, Earl (1891-1974): Former governor of California whom President Dwight D. Eisenhower appointed chief justice of the United States in 1953. Warren took office at a moment when the Court was facing new challenges to lower court rulings on school segregation. Under Warren's strong leadership, the Court reached a unanimous decision in the landmark *Brown v. Board of Education* (1954) case that outlawed desegregation in public schools and paved the way for new civil rights legislation and additional progressive Supreme Court rulings. Warren himself is remembered for destroying the "separate but equal" doctrine by declaring that "in the field of public education the doctrine of 'separate but equal' has no place. Separate educational facilities are inherently unequal."

Washington, Booker T. (1856-1915): Educator. Born a slave in Virginia, Washington became committed to the idea that education would raise African Americans to equality. After teaching Native Americans at the Hampton Institute (1879-1881), he founded the Tuskegee Normal and Industrial Institute in 1881 and served as its president through the rest of his life. He also cofounded the National Negro Business League in 1900. He advised Presidents William Howard Taft and Theodore Roosevelt on racial issues and promoted what has been called the "Atlanta Compromise,"—the doctrine of African Americans accepting segregation in return for greater economic opportunities. His conservative racial views appealed to many white Americans who feared more radical change but were opposed by other African American leaders, including W. E. B. Du Bois. Washington's autobiography, *Up from Slavery* (1901), became one of the most widely read books by African Americans during the early twentieth century.

Wells-Barnett, Ida B. (1862-1931): Journalist. Wells-Barnett was editor and part owner of the black newspaper *Memphis Free Speech*. Her vigorous campaigns against lynching led to a mob attack on her newspaper's offices. With Frederick Douglass and Ferdinand L. Barnett, Wells-Barnett wrote "The Reason Why the Colored American Is Not in the World's Columbian Exposition" (1893). She also published the anti-lynching pamphlet "Red Record" (1895) and defended W. E. B. Du Bois's criticisms of Booker T. Washington in the former's *The Souls of Black Folk* (1903). In 1909, she helped Du Bois found the National Association for the Advancement of Colored People.

White, Walter (1893-1955): Civil rights leader. The executive secretary of the National Association for the Advancement of Colored People from 1931 to 1955, White was an energetic and outspoken advocate of African American rights. He was also a fervent campaigner against lynching and fought a long and fruitless campaign for passage of a federal anti-lynching law. His writings include two fictional accounts of lynchings and a report on African American service in World War II.

Wilder, L. Douglas (1931-): Virginia politician. A decorated Korean War veteran, Wilder became a successful Virginia trial lawyer and was an officer in the National Urban League during the Civil Rights movement. In 1969, he became the first African American elected to the Virginia senate since Reconstruction. In 1985 he was elected lieutenant governor; four years later, he was elected governor—the first African American elected governor of any U.S. state.

Wilkins, Roy (1901-1981): Journalist and civil rights leader. Wilkins was on the staff of the Kansas City *Call* (1923-1931). He served as assistant executive secretary of the National Association for the Advancement of Colored People (NAACP) from 1931 to 1955, when he became the organization's executive secretary. He remained in the latter position until 1964 and then became the NAACP's executive director (1965-1977). He was also chairman of the Leadership Conference on Civil Rights. Wilkins was the editor of *The Crisis* from 1934 to 1949.

Woodson, Carter (1875-1950): Scholar. Often known as the "Father of Modern Black History," Woodson formed the Association for the Study of Negro Life and History (later the Association for the Study of Afro-American Life and History) in 1915. A year later, that body established the *Journal of Negro History*. Woodson also founded Associated Publishers in 1920 and the *Negro History Bulletin* in 1921. Woodson is credited with creating Negro History Week, which later expanded into Black History Month. His many books include *The Education of the Negro Prior to 1861* (1915); *The Negro in Our History* (1922), *The Miseducation of the Negro* (1933), and *African Heroes and Heroines* (1939).

Wright, Richard (1908-1960): Novelist. Wright used personal experiences from his Mississippi youth to dramatize the brutal effects of racism in such books as *Uncle Tom's Children*, which won the Best Work of Fiction by a Works Progress Administration writer in 1938; *Native Son* (1940); and the largely autobiographical *Black Boy* (1945). A member of the Communist Party from 1933 to 1944, he moved to Paris in 1946. There he continued writing. His later books include *The Outsider* (1953), *Black Power* (1954), *White Man Listen* (1957), and *Eight Men* (1961). *American Hunger* (1977) is a continuation of his autobiography.

Young, Andrew (1932-): Civil rights activist, politician, and diplomat. An aide and confidant of Martin Luther King, Jr., during the early 1960's, Young was executive vice president of the Southern Christian Leadership Conference in 1967. During the 1970's, he entered Georgia state politics. He served as a Georgia state representative (1973-1977) and was mayor of Atlanta (1981-1989). In between, he was made U.S. ambassador to the United Nations (1977-1979) by President Jimmy Carter, a former governor of Georgia. Young also chaired the Atlanta Committee for the 1996 Olympic Games.

Young, Whitney (1921-1971): Educator and civil rights leader. Young was executive director of the St. Paul chapter of the Minnesota Urban League (1950-1954); dean of Atlanta University School of Social Work (1954-1961); and executive director of the National Urban League (1961-1971). During the 1960's, he called for a "domestic Marshall Plan" to end black poverty and helped President Lyndon B. Johnson craft his War on Poverty. In 1969, he received the Medal of Freedom. His writings include *To Be Equal* (1964) and *Beyond Racism* (1969).

LIST OF CONTRIBUTORS

McCrea Adams
Independent Scholar

Mary Welek Atwell
Radford University

Barbara Bair
Library of Congress

Carl L. Bankston III
Tulane University

Bernice McNair Barnett
University of Illinois at Urbana

Paul Barton-Kriese
Indiana University

Alvin K. Benson
Utah Valley State College

S. Carol Berg
College of St. Benedict

Milton Berman
University of Rochester

Cynthia A. Bily
Adrian College

Steve D. Boilard
Independent Scholar

James J. Bolner
Louisiana State University, Baton Rouge

Aubrey W. Bonnett
State University of New York, Old Westbury

J. Quinn Brisben
Independent Scholar

Michael H. Burchett
Limestone College

Byron D. Cannon
University of Utah

Glenn Canyon
Independent Scholar

Sharon Carson
University of North Dakota

Erica Childs
Fordham University

John G. Clark
University of Kansas

Thomas Clarkin
University of Texas

Robert Cole
Utah State University

William H. Coogan
University of Southern Maine

Tom Cook
Wayne State College

William J. Cooper, Jr.
Louisiana State University, Baton Rouge

Stephen Cresswell
West Virginia Wesleyan College

Laura A. Croghan
College of William and Mary

Edward R. Crowther
Adams State College

Gilbert Morris Cuthbertson
Rice University

Richard V. Damms
Mississippi State University

Sudipta Das
Southern University at New Orleans

Jane Davis
Fordham University

Theresa R. Doggart
University of Tennessee, Chattanooga

Davison M. Douglas
William and Mary Law School

Paul E. Doutrich
York College of Pennsylvania

Jennifer Eastman
Clark University

Robert P. Ellis
Worcester State College

Daryl R. Fair
College of New Jersey

John W. Fiero
University of Southwestern Louisiana

Brian L. Fife
Ball State University

Alan M. Fisher
California State University, Dominguez Hills

John C. Gardner
Louisiana State University, Baton Rouge

Karen Garner
University of Texas at Austin

Phyllis B. Gerstenfeld
California State University, Stanislaus

Richard A. Glenn
Millersville University

Robert F. Gorman
Southwest Texas State University

Lewis L. Gould
University of Texas at Austin

William H. Green
University of Missouri, Columbia

Jimmie F. Gross
Armstrong State College

Michael Haas
University of Hawaii at Manoa

Pamela D. Haldeman
Mount St. Mary's College

Irwin Halfond
McKendree College

Roger D. Hardaway
Northwestern Oklahoma State University
Claude Hargrove
Fayetteville State University
Keith Harper
Mississippi College
Katy Jean Harriger
Wake Forest University
William M. Harris, Sr.
Jackson State University
Stanley Harrold
South Carolina State University
James Hayes-Bohanan
University of Arizona
John Hill
Clafin University
Ronald W. Howard
Mississippi College
Micah Issitt
Independent Scholar
John Jacob
Northwestern University
Robert Jacobs
Central Washington University
Ron Jacobs
University of Vermont
Duncan R. Jamieson
Ashland University
Robert L. Jenkins
Mississippi State University
K. Sue Jewell
Ohio State University
Sagirah Jones
Independent Scholar
Mabel Khawaja
Hampton University
Kathleen Odell Korgen
William Paterson University
Beth Kraig
Pacific Lutheran University
Jeri Kurtzleben
University of Northern Iowa
M. Bahati Kuumba
Buffalo State College
Linda Rochell Lane
Tuskegee University
Eleanor A. LaPointe
Ocean County College
Sharon L. Larson

University of Nebraska at Lincoln
Abraham D. Lavender
Florida International University
Jama Lazerow
Wheelock College
Thomas Tandy Lewis
Anoka-Ramsey Community College
Matthew Lindstrom
Siena College
Janet Alice Long
Independent Scholar
Anne C. Loveland
Louisiana State University, Baton Rouge
William C. Lowe
Mount St. Clare College
Robert D. Lukens
University of Delaware
Siobhan McCabe
Siena College
Patricia McDaniel
Independent Scholar
Grace McEntee
Appalachian State University
Robert E. McFarland
North Georgia College
Susan Mackey-Kallis
Villanova University
Kibibi Mack-Shelton
Claflin University
Paul D. Mageli
Independent Scholar
Jonathan Markovitz
University of California, San Diego
Chogollah Maroufi
California State University, Los Angeles
Thomas D. Matijasic
Prestonsburg Community College
DaVaughn Miller
Clafin University
Joseph A. Melusky
Saint Francis College
Beth A. Messner

Ball State University
Gregg L. Michel
University of Virginia
William V. Moore
College of Charleston
Echol Nix
Clafin Univeristy
Charles H. O'Brien
Western Illinois University
Eileen O'Brien
University of Florida
Anita Okoye
Independent Scholar
Max C. E. Orezzoli
Florida International University
William Osborne
Florida International University
Jason Pasch
Independent Scholar
Craig S. Pascoe
University of Tennessee, Knoxville
Darryl Paulson
University of South Florida
Thomas R. Peake
King College
William E. Pemberton
University of Wisconsin, La Crosse
Marilyn Elizabeth Perry
Independent Scholar
Doris F. Pierce
Purdue University
Mark A. Plummer
Illinois State University
Marjorie Podolsky
Penn State University, Erie
David L. Porter
William Penn College
John Powell
Penn State University, Erie
Steven J. Ramold
University of Nebraska at Lincoln
R. Kent Rasmussen
Independent Scholar
E. A. Reed
Baylor University

Douglas W. Richmond
University of Texas, Arlington

Barbara Roos
Grand Valley State University

Courtney B. Ross
Louisiana State University, Baton Rouge

Irene Struthers Rush
Independent Scholar

Dorothy C. Salem
Cleveland State University
Cuyahoga Community College

Lisa M. Sardinia
Pacific University

Elizabeth D. Schafer
Independent Scholar

Larry Schweikart
University of Dayton

Terry L. Seip
Louisiana State University, Baton Rouge

R. Baird Shuman
University of Illinois, Urbana-Champaign

Donald C. Simmons, Jr.
Mississippi Humanities Council

Donna Addkison Simmons
Independent Scholar

James Smallwood
Oklahoma State University

Christopher E. Smith
University of Akron

Ira Smolensky
Monmouth College

Mary Ellen Snodgrass
Independent Scholar

David L. Sterling
University of Cincinnati

Leslie Stricker
Park College

Robert Sullivan
Independent Scholar

Kathryn Silva
Clafin University

James Tackach
Roger Williams University

Vanessa Tait
University of California, Santa Cruz

Harold D. Tallant
Georgetown College

G. Thomas Taylor
University of Maine

Emily Teipe
Fullerton College

Christel N. Temple
University of Maryland

Nancy Conn Terjesen
Kent State University

Vincent Michael Thur
Wenatchee Valley College

Leslie V. Tischauser
Prairie State College

Brian G. Tobin
Lassen College

Mfanya D. Tryman
Mississippi State University

Annita Marie Ward
Salem-Teikyo University

Elwood David Watson
East Tennessee State University

William L. Waugh, Jr.
Georgia State University

Donald V. Weatherman
Arkansas College

Richard Whitworth
Ball State University

Lou Falkner Williams
Kansas State University

Harry L. Wilson
Roanoke College

Richard L. Wilson
University of Tennessee, Chattanooga

Thomas Winter
University of Cincinnati

Michael Witkoski
Independent Scholar

Trudi D. Witonsky
University of Wisconsin, Madison

C. A. Wolski
Independent Scholar

Gene Redding Wynne, Jr.
Tri-County Technical College

Clifton K. Yearley
State University of New York, Buffalo

Time Line of African American History

Year	Event
1619	First Africans are brought to the colony of Virginia as indentured servants.
1641	Massachusetts Bay Colony recognizes the legality of slavery.
1662	Virginia legislature rules that children of unions of slave and free parents are slave or free according to their mothers' status.
1664	Maryland enacts the first law outlawing marriage between white women and black men.
1688	Pennsylvania Mennonites protest slavery.
1691	Virginia law restricts manumissions to prevent the growth of a free black class.
1712	Slave revolt in New York results in the execution of twenty-one slaves and the suicides of six others.
1723	Virginia denies African Americans the right to vote.
1739	South Carolina slaves rise up in Stono Rebellion (September 9).
1775	First abolitionist organization in the United States, the Pennsylvania Society for the Abolition of Slavery, is formed (April 14).
1784	First African American Masonic lodge is founded in Boston.
1786	Underground Railroad is started.
1787	The U.S. Constitution drafted in Philadelphia does not mention slavery by name but contains several clauses alluding to the existence of slaves and the slave trade.
1787	Free African Society is founded in Pennsylvania.
1787	Northwest Ordinance, governing the organization of the Northwest Territories, disallows slavery in the territories (July 13).
1793	Virginia outlaws entry of free African Americans into the state.
1793	Federal Fugitive Slave Act requires the return of escaped slaves to their owners.
1793	Invention of the cotton gin encourages the spread of slavery in the South.
1808	Federal government bans importation of slaves into the United States, but illegal importation continues.
1816	American Colonization Society is founded.
1816	African Methodist Episcopal Church is founded (April 9).
1820	Congress enacts the Missouri Compromise, under which Missouri is admitted to the Union as a slave state, Maine is admitted as a free state, and slavery is prohibited in the remaining territories north of Missouri's southern boundary (March 3).
1821	African Methodist Episcopal Zion Church is founded.

1827	First African American newspaper, *Freedman's Journal*, begins.
1831	Nat Turner leads major slave insurrection in Virginia.
1831	Abolitionist William Lloyd Garrison begins publishing *The Liberator* (January 1).
1832	New England Anti-Slavery Society is organized.
1833	American Anti-Slavery Society is founded (December).
1839	Slaves being transported aboard the Spanish ship *Amistad* revolt and take control of the ship.
1841	Supreme Court's decision in *Groves v. Slaughter* holds that an amendment to Mississippi's state constitution that bans bringing slaves into the state for sale is not valid in the absence of legislation to enforce it (March 10).
1843	Sojourner Truth begins giving abolitionist lectures.
1847	Frederick Douglass publishes *The North Star* in Rochester, New York.
1850	Congress passes new Fugitive Slave Act to facilitate the return of slaves who flee from the South to the North.
1850	Compromise of 1850 allows for California's admission to the Union as a nonslave state (September 20).
1852	Harriet Beecher Stowe publishes *Uncle Tom's Cabin*, a novel that attacks slavery.
1853	National Council of Colored People is founded in Rochester, New York (July 6).
1854	Congress passes the Kansas-Nebraska Act, a compromise between pro- and antislavery positions (May 30).
mid-1850's	Free-soil and proslavery factions fighting in Kansas—a period known in history as "Bleeding Kansas."
1857	Ashmun Institute (later Lincoln University) is founded in Pennsylvania (January 1).
1857	Supreme Court's *Scott v. Sandford* decision declares that slaves are not citizens of the United States and that the Missouri Compromise is unconstitutional (March 6-7).
1859	Capture of the slave ship *Clotilde* ends the delivery of slaves to the United States from abroad.
1859	Abolitionist John Brown is hanged after his October raid on the federal arsenal at Harpers Ferry, Virginia (December 2).
1861	Armed fighting in the Civil War begins (April).
1861	Congress passes first Confiscation Act to confiscate all property, including slaves, used in the Confederate war effort (August).
1862	Congress's second Confiscation Act declares that seized slaves will not be returned to their Confederate owners and will later be freed (July).
1863	President Abraham Lincoln issues the Emancipation Proclamation, declaring slaves in states still in rebellion against the Union to be free (January 1).
1863	Draft riots erupt in New York City after the federal government enacts its first military conscription act (July).
1865	As southern states begin to enforce black codes, which severely limit liberties of newly freed African Americans, Radical Republicans in Congress began planning Reconstruction policies.
1865	Federal government creates the Freedmen's Bureau to assist African Americans make the transition from slavery to freedom (March 3).
1865	Civil War ends with Confederate commander Robert E. Lee's formal surrender at Appomatox (April 9).
1865	Ratification of the Thirteenth Amendment to the U.S. Constitution prohibits slavery or other involuntary servitude (December 18).

1866	Ku Klux Klan is founded in Tennessee.
1866	Congress enacts the Civil Rights Act of 1866, declaring that persons born in the United States are, without regard to race, citizens of the United States entitled to equal protection of the law (April 9).
1868	Ratification of the Fourteenth Amendment grants citizenship to all persons born in the United States, without regard to race, and requires states to accord individuals equal protection of the law and due process of the law (July).
1870	Ratification of the Fifteenth Amendment guarantees the right to vote without regard to race, color, or previous condition of servitude (February).
1871	Congress enacts the Ku Klux Klan Act in an attempt to restrain the violence perpetrated by the organization.
1873	White terrorists kill more than sixty African Americans in Colfax, Mississippi (April 13).
1875	Congress enacts the Civil Rights Act of 1875, prohibiting racial discrimination in transportation, hotels, inns, theaters, and places of public amusement (March 1).
1875	Angry white mob kills more than twenty African Americans in Clinton, Mississippi (September 4-6).
1876	Supreme Court's decision in *United States v. Cruikshank* limits the authority of the federal government to protect the civil rights of African Americans. (March 27).
1876	Racially divisive fighting erupts between Republicans and Democrats during the months leading up to the presidential election in Charleston, South Carolina (September-November).
1877	Compromise of 1877 awards the presidency to Rutherford B. Hayes in return for a Republican promise to withdraw the last Union troops from the South, thus ending Reconstruction (January).
1880	Supreme Court's decision in *Strauder v. West Virginia* holds that excluding African Americans from juries is a violation of the Fourteenth Amendment's equal protection clause (March 1).
1881	Booker T. Washington founds the Tuskegee Institute.
1883	Supreme Court's *Civil Rights* cases ruling declares the Civil Rights Act of 1875 unconstitutional (October 15).
1884	*Ex parte Yarbrough* is the Supreme Court's only nineteenth century decision that allows the federal government to enforce the Fifteenth Amendment by punishing private individuals for obstructing a citizen's right to vote (March 3).
1890	Supreme Court's decision in *Louisville, New Orleans, and Texas Railway Company v. Mississippi* upholds Mississippi law requiring segregated accommodations on railroads (March 3).
1892	Colored Women's League is founded in Washington, D.C. (June).
1895	Booker T. Washington offers his Atlanta Compromise in an address delivered at the Atlanta Exposition (September 18).
1896	National Association of Colored Women is founded.
1896	Supreme Court's *Plessy v. Ferguson* decision establishes the separate but equal doctrine by holding that a legally mandated provision for separate railway cars for whites and blacks does not violate the equal protection clause (May 18).
1899	In its *Cumming v. Richmond County Board of Education* decision, the Supreme Court refuses to enforce the "equal" stipulation in the separate but equal doctrine governing segregated schools (December 18).
1904	W. E. B. Du Bois articulates the concept of the "Talented Tenth."
1905	Niagara Movement, predecessor of the National Association for the Advancement of Colored People, is organized with the help of W. E. B. Du Bois.
1906	Troop of African American soldiers are unfairly blamed for a shooting incident in Brownsville, Texas (August 13).

1910-1930's.	More than one million African Americans move from the South to northern states in the Great Migration
1910	National Association for the Advancement of Colored People (NAACP) is founded (May).
1911	National Urban League is organized to protect the rights of African Americans who migrate to northern cities from the South (September 29).
1915	Supreme Court's *Guinn v. United States* decision invalidates state voter literacy requirements intended to prevent African Americans from voting (June 21).
1916	Marcus Garvey arrives in the United States from Jamaica and becomes a leading advocate of black nationalism.
1917	Jamaican immigrant Marcus Garvey founds the first North American branch of his Universal Negro Improvement Association in New York City (May).
1917	Supreme Court's *Buchanan v. Warley* decision strikes down state laws mandating racial segregation in housing (November 5).
1920's-1935	Harlem Renaissance sees a flowering of black culture and racial pride.
1925	Brotherhood of Sleeping Car Porters is founded.
1927	Supreme Court's *Nixon v. Herndon* decision finds unconstitutional the exclusion of blacks from voting in state Democratic primaries (March 7).
1929	L. C. Dyer introduces antilynching bill in Congress.
1930	Wallace Fard founds the Nation of Islam in Detroit, Michigan.
1931	Trial of the Scottsboro Nine begins in Alabama.
1932-1972	U.S. Public Health Service conducts long-term study at Tuskegee, Alabama, of African American men afflicted with syphilis who think they are receiving treatment for their condition.
1935	Mary McLeod Bethune founds the National Council of Negro Women.
1935	Supreme Court's decision in *Grovey v. Townsend* accepts the right of political parties to exclude African Americans from voting in primaries (April 1).
1938	Supreme Court's *Missouri ex rel. Gaines v. Canada* decision holds that refusal of a state to allow African Americans to attend a state's only public law school violates the equal protection clause (December 12).
1939	NAACP creates the Legal Defense and Educational Fund to oppose racially discriminatory laws, and Thurgood Marshall takes charge of these efforts.
1939	Contralto Marian Anderson performs from the steps of Washington, D.C.'s Lincoln Memorial (January 2).
1941	In response to A. Philip Randolph's call for African Americans to march on Washington to protest racial discrimination in the armed forces, defense industries, and federal employment generally, President Franklin D. Roosevelt issues Executive Order 8802, which temporarily establishes the Fair Employment Practices Committee (June 25).
1941	United States enters World War II after Japan's surprise attack on Pearl Harbor (December 8).
1942-1946	Black pilots who train for service in the U.S. Army Air Forces at Tuskegee, Alabama, become known as the Tuskegee Airmen.
1942	James Farmer and students at the University of Chicago establish the Congress of Racial Equality (CORE; June).
1943	First sit-in demonstrations protesting segregation in Chicago (May-June).
1944	Supreme Court's *Smith v. Allwright* decision finds that exclusion of African Americans from participation in party primaries violates the Constitution (April 3).

1944	United Negro College Fund is founded (April 25).
1946	President Harry S. Truman issues an executive order establishing the President's Committee on Civil Rights (December 5).
1947	Jackie Robinson becomes the first African American in modern times to play Major League Baseball.
1947	Journey of Reconciliation attracts national attention to the civil rights work of the Congress of Racial Equality (April 9-23).
1948	Supreme Court's *Shelley v. Kraemer* decision holds that the Constitution prevents state courts from enforcing racially restrictive real estate covenants (May 3).
1948	President Harry S. Truman signs Executive Order 9981 prohibiting racial discrimination in the armed forces and other federal employment (July 26).
1950	Supreme Court's *Sweatt v. Painter* decision holds that Texas's attempt to establish a separate law school for blacks rather than admit black applicants to the University of Texas Law School violates the equal protection clause. On the same day, the Court's decision in *McLaurin v. Oklahoma State Regents for Higher Education* overrules Oklahoma's policy of maintaining segregated programs for African Americans in a public university graduate school (June 5).
1953	Supreme Court's decision in *Terry v. Adams* outlaws white primaries (May 4).
1954	Supreme Court's *Brown v. Board of Education* decision finds that racial segregation in public schools violates the equal protection clause (May 17).
1954	First White Citizens' Councils form, in reaction to *Brown v. Board of Education* (summer).
1955	Supreme Court issues a second opinion in the *Brown v. Board of Education* case (*Brown II*), requiring desegregation of public schools "with all deliberate speed."
1955	Rosa Parks's defiance of segregated seating rules on a Montgomery, Alabama, bus touches off a year-long bus boycott.
1955	Fifteen-year-old African American Emmett Till is murdered in Mississippi after allegedly flirting with a white woman; a jury ultimately acquits two white men charged with his murder (August 28).
1956	Most southern members of Congress sign the "Southern Manifesto" denouncing the Supreme Court's *Brown v. Board of Education* decision (March 12).
1957	Martin Luther King, Jr., and other African American leaders found the Southern Christian Leadership Conference (SCLC).
1957	Congress passes the first civil rights act since Reconstruction, banning discrimination in public places based on race, color, religion, or national origin.
1957	After Arkansas's governor uses National Guard troops to block African American children from entering Little Rock's Central High School, President Dwight D. Eisenhower federalizes the guard and mobilizes additional federal armed forces to ensure that the school is peacefully integrated (September).
1958	President Dwight D. Eisenhower meets with national African American leaders in the Summit Meeting of National Negro Leaders (June).
1958	Supreme Court's decision in *Cooper v. Aaron* directs that fear of violence is not an acceptable excuse for delaying school desegregation (September 12).
1960	Supreme Court's decision in *Gomillion v. Lightfoot* strikes down gerrymandering in Tuskegee, Alabama.
1960	Student sit-ins begin at lunch counters in Greensboro, North Carolina (February-July).
1960	Student Nonviolent Coordinating Committee (SNCC) is founded (April).
1960	Congress passes the Civil Rights Act of 1960, which expands protections of voting rights (May 6).

1961	President John F. Kennedy issues an executive order that establishes the Equal Employment Opportunity Commission and requires businesses with government contracts to take "affirmative action" in the equal treatment of employees.
1961	Freedom rides sponsored by CORE test the ban on segregation in interstate buses; riders are beaten, and a bus is burned in Birmingham, Alabama (May-August).
1962	President John F. Kennedy signs an executive order banning racial discrimination in federally financed housing.
1962	Voter registration drives begin in southern states under the direction of the Council of Federated Organizations (COFO).
1962	James Meredith enrolls in the University of Mississippi over the defiant protests of Governor Ross R. Barnett and in the face of mob violence.
1963	Birmingham March to protest segregation is sponsored by the SCLC (April 4-May 7).
1963	First African Liberation Day is celebrated (May 25).
1963	Medgar W. Evers, the field secretary for the Mississippi NAACP, is assassinated (June 12).
1963	March on Washington is sponsored by civil rights, labor, and religious organizations; featured speaker Martin Luther King, Jr., delivers his "I Have a Dream" speech (August 28).
1963	Four African American girls are killed when a bomb explodes at the Sixteenth Street Baptist Church in Birmingham, Alabama (September 15).
1964	Council of Federated Organizations (COFO), a group of associated civil rights groups, organizes the Freedom Summer project to register African Americans to vote in Mississippi.
1964	Mississippi Freedom Democratic Party is founded in Jackson, Mississippi.
1964	Ratification of the Twenty-fourth Amendment prohibits poll taxes in federal elections (January 23).
1964	Civil rights workers James Chaney, Michael Schwerner, and Andrew Goodman are murdered near Philadelphia, Mississippi (June).
1964	Congress passes the Civil Rights Act of 1964, which prohibits racial, religious, sexual, and other forms of discrimination in a variety of contexts (July 2).
1964	Supreme Court's *Heart of Atlanta Motel v. United States* decision upholds the power of Congress to prohibit racial discrimination in privately owned hotels and inns (December 14).
1965	Moynihan Report attempts to explain the high levels of poverty in African American communities.
1965	Malcolm X is assassinated in New York City (February 21).
1965	Martin Luther King, Jr., leads a march from Selma to Montgomery, Alabama, to protest voting discrimination (March).
1965	Congress passes the Voting Rights Act.
1965	Watts riot flares in Los Angeles (August).
1966	Stokely Carmichael takes over leadership of SNCC and coins the phrase "Black Power" to advocate more militant responses to continued racial discrimination.
1966	Supreme Court's decision in *Harper v. Virginia Board of Elections* outlaws poll taxes (March 24).
1966	Black Panther Party is organized in Oakland, California, by Bobby Seale and Huey P. Newton (October).
1967	Summer race riots disrupt more than thirty northern cities.
1967	Supreme Court's *Loving v. Virginia* decision holds that a state law barring interracial marriages is unconstitutional.
1967	President Lyndon Johnson appoints Thurgood Marshall to the U.S. Supreme Court (June 13).

1968	Republic of New Africa is founded in Detroit, Michigan.
1968	Kerner Commission (National Advisory Committee on Civil Disorders) releases its report concerning urban riots, claiming as key reasons white racism and increasing racial and economic stratification (February).
1968	Campus police in Orangeburg, South Carolina, kill three African American students (February 8).
1968	Martin Luther King, Jr., is assassinated in Memphis, Tennessee, a few days after leading a protest march for striking sanitation workers (April 4).
1968	Congress passes the Civil Rights Act of 1968, which prohibits discrimination in the sale and rental of housing and in home financing (April 11).
1968	Poor People's March on Washington attempts to broaden the Civil Rights movement into a nonracial national campaign to reduce poverty (April 28-May 13).
1968	Supreme Court's *Green v. County School Board of Kent County* decision finds that a "freedom of choice" plan adopted by a Virginia school district does not satisfy its obligation to desegregate its schools (May 27).
1968	Supreme Court's *Jones v. Alfred H. Mayer Co.* decision finds that Congress has the power to prohibit racial discrimination in housing sales (June 17).
1968	Shirley Chisholm of New York is the first African American woman elected to Congress (November 5).
1969	Supreme Court's *Alexander v. Holmes County Board of Education* decision requires southern school boards to desegregate their schools immediately.
1969	Militant black leaders issue "Black Manifesto," calling for white churches and synagogues to pay reparations to African Americans for the hardships of slavery (April 26).
1969	League of Revolutionary Black Workers is founded in Detroit, Michigan (June).
1970	Black members of Congress form the Congressional Black Caucus.
1971	National Black Women's Political Leadership Caucus is founded.
1971	In *Griggs v. Duke Power Company*, the Supreme Court bans non-job-related tests that might unfairly screen minorities (March 8).
1971	Supreme Court's *Swann v. Charlotte-Mecklenburg Board of Education* decision authorizes busing to desegregate the school district (April 20).
1971	Supreme Court's *Griffin v. Breckenridge* decision upholds a federal law punishing racially motivated assaults on public highways (June 7).
1972	Congress passes Equal Employment Opportunity Act, which prohibits government agencies and educational institutions from discriminating in hiring, firing, promotion, compensation, and admission to training programs (March 13).
1973	Supreme Court's decision in *Keyes v. Denver School District No. 1*, its first school desegregation case involving a major city outside the South, holds that a district-wide busing plan is an appropriate remedy for rectifying deliberately segregated schools (June 21).
1974	Combahee River Collective is founded.
1974	In *Milliken v. Bradley*, the Supreme Court holds that federal judges may not order the busing of students across school district lines (July 25).
1975	Supreme Court's *Albemarle Paper Company v. Moody* rules that employers guilty of racial discrimination in screening tests must compensate harmed employees with back pay.
1975	Congress passes the Voting Rights Act of 1975, which abolishes the use of literacy tests for voters (August 6).
1976	Alex Haley publishes *Roots*.

1976	Supreme Court's *Washington v. Davis* decision holds that laws having a disproportionately burdensome effect on racial minorities are not subject to the same rigorous review as laws purposefully discriminating on grounds of race (June 7).
1978	Supreme Court's *Bakke* case decision rules against the use of quotas to achieve racial balance in colleges and universities but allows an applicant's race to be considered in the admissions process.
1979	Supreme Court's *United Steel Workers of America v. Weber* decision upholds the ability of private employers to adopt affirmative action plans (June 27).
1980	Race riots leave eighteen people dead in Miami after four Miami police officers are acquitted of charges of beating a black insurance executive to death (May 17-23).
1980	In *Fullilove v. Klutznick*, the Supreme Court upholds minority set-aside contracts established by Congress for federal programs (July 2).
1983	Jesse Jackson founds the Rainbow Coalition.
1985	Philadelphia city government bombs a residential neighborhood to evict MOVE squatters (May 13).
1986	Supreme Court's *Batson v. Kentucky* decision holds that a prosecutor's attempt to disqualify possible jurors because of their race violates the equal protection clause of the Fourteenth Amendment.
1986	Holiday honoring Martin Luther King, Jr., is celebrated officially for the first time.
1987	National Coalition of Blacks for Reparations in America is founded.
1987	Three white teenagers are convicted of manslaughter following a racially motivated attack on three black men in the Howard Beach section of New York City a year earlier.
1987	Supreme Court's *McCleskey v. Kemp* decision holds that mere proof of a racially disproportionate impact of death penalty sentences on African Americans does not violate the Constitution (April 22).
1988	Fair Housing Amendments Act establishes a procedure for imposing fines for those found guilty of housing discrimination based on race, color, sex, religion, or national origin.
1988	Jesse Jackson runs a strong second in the race for the Democratic nomination for the presidency.
1988	Congress passes the Civil Rights Restoration Act, restricting federal funding to institutions that discriminate on the basis of race, gender, disability or age, reversing a 1984 Supreme Court decision that narrowed the scope of federal antidiscrimination laws (March 22).
1989	Supreme Court's *Richmond v. J. A. Croson, Co.* decision holds that state and local affirmative action programs must be subject to "strict scrutiny," a constitutional standard requiring the most compelling government justifications.
1989	Following a 1988 federal court ruling that Mississippi judicial districts must be redrawn, voters elect five black trial court judges.
1989	In *Martin v. Wilks*, the Supreme Court allows white firefighters in Birmingham, Alabama, to challenge a 1981 court-approved affirmative action program designed to increase minority representation and promotion (June 12).
1989	Black honor student Yusuf Hawkins is killed in the predominantly Italian Brooklyn neighborhood of Bensonhurst when he and three friends are assaulted by about thirty white men (August 23).
1989	Douglas Wilder is the first African American to be elected a state governor—in Virginia—in U.S. history (November 7).
1990	Milwaukee, Wisconsin, school board votes to open two schools for blacks utilizing a special curriculum focusing on black culture and featuring programs designed to develop self-esteem and personal responsibility.
1990	President George Bush vetoes the Civil Rights Act, which would have overturned five recent Supreme Court rulings making it more difficult to win discrimination lawsuits against employers.

1990	Under a new law, the Justice Department begins collecting statistics on hate crimes in order to determine if changes in federal law are needed.
1990	Black activists boycott Korean American supermarkets in Brooklyn following charges that a black customer had been assaulted in one of the stores.
1991	President George Bush signs the Civil Rights Bill, making it easier for employees to sue employers for discrimination, but only after changes are made to a vetoed 1990 bill that might have created racial quotas.
1991	Clarence Thomas succeeds Thurgood Marshall as the second black Supreme Court justice, despite protests from civil rights groups decrying his opposition to affirmative action programs and busing for school desegregation.
1991	National Civil Rights Museum, dedicated to the 1950's and 1960's struggle for racial equality in the United States, is opened in Memphis, Tennessee.
1991	Studies by the Urban Institute find that hiring and housing discrimination against blacks is "widespread and entrenched."
1991	Killing of a young Guyanese immigrant by a Jewish driver leads to the retaliatory murder of an Australian scholar by black youths and prompts four days of rioting in Brooklyn's Crown Heights neighborhood.
1991	Los Angeles police officers beat Rodney King after stopping him for a driving violation in an incident caught on videotape by a bystander (March 3).
1991	Supreme Court's decision in *Powers v. Ohio* holds that prosecutors cannot use peremptory challenges to exclude African Americans from criminal trial juries (April 1).
1991	Supreme Court's decision in *Edmonson v. Leesville Concrete Company* extends an earlier ruling to rule that potential jurors may not be peremptorily excluded from civil trials on the basis of their race (June 3).
1991	Congress passes the Civil Rights Act of 1991, which outlaws employment discrimination (November 21).
1992	U.S. Department of Education determines that the admissions policy of the University of California at Berkeley's law school violates the Civil Rights Act of 1964 by comparing prospective candidates only against others in their own racial group.
1992	In *United States v. Fordice*, the Supreme Court rules that remnants of segregation remain in the Mississippi system of higher education and that positive steps must be taken to remedy such segregation.
1992	Four Los Angeles police officers are acquitted of charges stemming from the 1991 beating of Rodney King, touching off five days of rioting in Los Angeles that result in more than fifty deaths and $1 billion in property damage (April 29).
1992	In *R.A.V. v. City of St. Paul*, the Supreme Court unanimously rules that a St. Paul, Minnesota, law making the use of racist language a criminal offense is a violation of First Amendment guarantees of free speech (June 22).
1993	Los Angeles police officers Stacey Koon and Laurence Powell are sentenced to prison for violating the civil rights of Rodney King in a 1991 beating incident.
1993	In *Wisconsin v. Mitchell*, the Supreme Court rules that states can punish racially motivated crimes more harshly than similar crimes not motivated by bias (June 11).
1994	Seventy-three-year-old white supremacist Byron De La Beckwith is convicted of the 1963 murder of civil rights leader Medgar Evers and is sentenced to life in prison.
1994	Flagstar Company agrees to pay $45.7 million in a classaction settlement stemming from 4,300 racial bias complaints against its Denny's restaurant chain.

1994	Federal jury orders the city of Los Angeles to pay Rodney King $3.8 million in damages stemming from his 1991 beating by white police officers.
1995	Delegates to the annual convention of Southern Baptists, the nation's largest Protestant denomination, pass a resolution denouncing racism and apologizing for "historic acts of evil such as slavery."
1995	Supreme Court's *Adarand Constructors v. Peña* decision requires that in federal contracts based on affirmative action, set-asides are valid only when those benefiting have suffered actual discrimination in the past.
1995	Maryland Democratic representative Kweisi Mfume becomes chief executive of the NAACP following longstanding controversies over improper financial practices of former directors William F. Gibson, Benjamin Chavis, and Benjamin L. Hooks.
1995	O. J. Simpson's acquittal of the 1994 murder of his wife and a companion divides the country along racial lines (October 3).
1995	Approximately 700,000 people, mostly African American men, attend Louis Farrakhan's Million Man March, a Washington, D.C., rally highlighting male family responsibilities and addressing problems plaguing the black community in America (October 16).
1996	California voters approve Proposition 209, designed to end all forms of affirmative action in "the operation of public employment, public education, or public contracting."
1996	Wave of church burnings begins sweeping the South.
1996	U.S. Fifth Circuit Court of Appeals rules, in *Hopwood v. Texas*, that the University of Texas Law School may not consider race as a factor in its admissions process.
1996	President Bill Clinton signs the Church Arson Prevention Act, making destruction of religious property "on the basis of race, color, or ethnicity" a federal crime.
1996	Texaco Incorporated agrees to pay $176.1 million to settle a discrimination suit filed on behalf of 1,500 current and former black employees.
1996	Oakland, California, school board determines that the English dialect spoken by many African Americans is a separate language (Ebonics) based upon West African roots, thus qualifying for federal funds approved for bilingual education.
1997	National Church Arson Task Force, appointed by President Clinton in 1996, reports that racism was only one of many factors contributing to more than four hundred church fires that had been set during the 1990's.
1997	President Bill Clinton launches a year-long debate on race relations in America by appointing black historian John Hope Franklin to lead a panel consisting of three whites, two blacks, one Hispanic, and one Korean American.
1997	Winnie Madikizela-Mandela speaks at the Million Woman March, a Philadelphia rally organized to unify African American women against common community and family problems (October 25).
1999	Mistaken killing of an African immigrant by New York City police provokes public outrage.
1999	African American farmers win a lawsuit against the U.S. Department of Agriculture for discriminating against them in awarding loans in the past.
2000	Coca-Cola Company agrees to pay $192.5 million to settle a discrimination suit filed on behalf of an estimated 2,000 black employees.
2000	South Carolina's legislature votes to remove the Confederate flag from the statehouse in response to protests and boycotting efforts launched by the NAACP.
2001	Newly elected president George W. Bush makes Colin Powell the first African American secretary of state.

2002	Slavery Reparations Coordinating Committee reveals plans to sue corporations that have profited from slavery.
2003	Supreme Court's *Grutter v. Bollinger* decision holds that race can be used as a standard in school admissions.
2004	Kweisi Mfume resigns as chief executive officer of the NAACP.
2004	U.S. Justice Department announces that it is reopening its investigation into the 1955 murder of Emmett Till in Mississippi.
2005	Total African American population is about 36 million people.
2005	Condolezza Rice succeeds Colin Powell as U.S. secretary of state and becomes the first African American woman to hold that post.
2006	In *Parents v. Seattle* and *Meredith v. Jefferson*, affirmative action suffers a setback when a bitterly divided court rules, 5 to 4, that programs in Seattle and Louisville, Ky., which tried to maintain diversity in schools by considering race when assigning students to schools, are unconstitutional
2009	Barak Obama becomes 44th president of the United States
2013	Black Lives Matter (#BlackLivesMatter) is formed
2014	On Aug. 9, Michael Brown, an unarmed 18-year-old was shot and killed in Ferguson, Mo., by Darren Wilson. On Nov. 24, the grand jury decision not to indict Wilson was announced, sparking protests in Ferguson and cities across the U.S., including Chicago, Los Angeles, New York, and Boston.
2015	The 114th Congress includes 46 black members in the House of Representatives and two in the Senate.

BIBLIOGRAPHY

GENERAL REFERENCE

Allen, Bonnie. *We Are Overcome: Thoughts on Being Black in America*. New York: Crown, 1995.

America, Richard F. *Paying the Social Debt: What White America Owes Black America*. Westport, Conn.: Praeger, 1993.

Armour, Jody David. *Negrophobia and Reasonable Racism: The Hidden Costs of Being Black in America*. New York: New York University Press, 1997.

Asante, Molefi Kete. *The Afrocentric Idea*. Philadelphia: Temple University Press, 1987.

_____. *Afrocentricity*. Trenton, N.J.: Africa World Press, 1988.

Berry, Mary Frances, and John Blassingame. *Long Memory: The Black Experience in America*. New York: Oxford University Press, 1982.

Blauner, Bob. *Black Lives, White Lives: Three Decades of Race Relations in America*. Berkeley: University of California Press, 1989.

Boxill, Bernard R. *Blacks and Social Justice*. Totowa, N.J.: Rowman & Allanheld, 1984.

Brooks, Roy L. *Rethinking the American Race Problem*. Berkeley: University of California Press, 1990.

Broussard, Albert S. *Black San Francisco: The Struggle for Racial Equality in the West, 1900-1954*. Lawrence: University Press of Kansas, 1993.

Brown, Tony. *Black Lies, White Lies: The Truth According to Tony Brown*. New York: Wm. C. Morrow, 1995.

Clark, Kenneth B. *Dark Ghetto: Dilemmas of Social Power*. New York: Harper & Row, 1965.

Cleaver, Eldridge. *Soul on Ice*. New York: McGraw-Hill, 1968.

Coleman, Jonathan. *Long Way to Go: Black and White in America*. New York: Atlantic Monthly Press, 1997.

Collier, Peter, and David Horowitz. *The Race Card: White Guilt, Black Resentment, and the Assault on Truth and Justice*. Rocklin, Calif.: Prima Publishing, 1997.

Croucher, Sheila. *Imagining Miami*. Charlottesville: University Press of Virginia, 1997.

Cruse, Harold. *Plural but Equal: A Critical Study of Blacks and Minorities in America's Plural Society*. New York: William Morrow, 1987.

Davis-Adeshoté, Jeanette, et al. *Black Survival in White America: From Past History to the Next Century.* Orange, N.J.: Bryant and Dillon, 1995.

Dorman, James H., and Robert R. Jones. *The Afro-American Experience.* New York: Wiley, 1974.

Du Bois, W. E. B. *The Souls of Black Folk.* 1903. Reprint. New York: Vintage Books, 1990.

Dunn, Marvin. *Black Miami in the Twentieth Century.* Tallahassee: University of Florida Press, 1997.

Dvorak, Katharine L. *An African American Exodus.* Brooklyn, N.Y.: Carlson, 1991.

Gaillard, Frye. *The Dream Long Deferred.* Chapel Hill: University of North Carolina Press, 1988.

Goldschmid, Marcel L., ed. *Black Americans and White Racism: Theory and Research.* New York: Holt, Rinehart and Winston, 1970.

Gubar, Susan. *Racechanges: White Skin, Black Face in American Culture.* New York: Oxford University Press, 1997.

Guerrero, Ed. *Framing Blackness.* Philadelphia: Temple University Press, 1993.

Hacker, Andrew. *Two Nations: Black and White, Separate, Hostile, Unequal.* New York: Charles Scribner's Sons, 1992.

Johnson, Charles S. *The Negro in American Civilization: A Study of Negro Life and Race Relations in the Light of Social Research.* New York: Henry Holt, 1930.

Jordan, Winthrop D. *White over Black: American Attitudes Toward the Negro, 1550-1812.* 1968. Reprint. New York: W.W. Norton, 1995.

Keyes, Alan L. *Masters of the Dream: The Strength and Betrayal of Black America.* New York: William Morrow, 1995.

Long, Richard A. *African Americans: A Portrait.* New York: Crescent Books, 1993.

Lyman, Stanford M. *The Black American in Sociological Thought.* New York: Putnam, 1972.

McWilliams, Carey. *Brothers Under the Skin.* Rev. ed. Boston: Little, Brown, 1964.

Miller, Arthur G., ed. *In the Eye of the Beholder: Contemporary Issues in Stereotyping.* New York: Praeger, 1982.

Mills, Charles W. *Blackness Visible: Essays on Philosophy and Race.* Ithaca, N.Y.: Cornell University Press, 1998.

Munford, Clarence J. *Race and Reparations: A Black Perspective for the Twenty-first Century.* Trenton, N.J.: Africa World Press, 1996.

Myrdal, Gunnar. *An American Dilemma: The Negro Problem and American Democracy.* New York: Harper & Row, 1944. Reprint. New York: McGraw-Hill, 1964.

Nash, Gary B. *Forbidden Love: Secret History of Mixed Race America.* New York: H. Holt, 1999.

Parsons, Talcott, and Kenneth B. Clark, eds. *The Negro American.* Boston: Houghton Mifflin, 1966.

Pettigrew, Thomas F. *A Profile of the Negro American.* Princeton, N.J.: D. Van Nostrand, 1964.

Pieterse, Jan Nederveen. *White on Black.* New Haven, Conn.: Yale University Press, 1992.

Ploski, Harry A., and James Williams, eds. *The Negro Almanac: A Reference Work on the African American.* Detroit, Mich.: Gale Research, 1989.

Rosenblatt, Paul, Terri A. Karis, and Richard D. Powell. *Multiracial Couples: Black and White Voices.* Thousand Oaks, Calif.: Sage Publications, 1995.

Shipler, David K. *A Country of Strangers: Blacks and Whites in America.* New York: Knopf, 1997.

Sigelman, Lee, and Susan Welch. *Black Americans' Views of Racial Inequality.* Cambridge, England: Cambridge University Press, 1991.

Silberman, Charles E. *Crisis in Black and White.* New York: Vintage Books, 1964.

Smith, Lillian. *Killers of the Dream.* New York: W.W. Norton, 1949.

Steele, Shelby. *A Dream Deferred: The Second Betrayal of Black Freedom in America.* New York: HarperCollins, 1998.

Thernstrom, Stephan, and Abigail Thernstrom. *America in Black and White: One Nation Indivisible.* New York: Random House, 1997.

West, Cornell. *Race Matters.* New York: Random House, 1993.

_____. *Restoring Hope: Conversations on the Future of Black America.* Boston: Beacon Press, 1997.

Williamson, Joel. *New People: Miscegenation and Mulattoes in the United States.* Baton Rouge: Louisiana State University Press, 1995.

Wonkeryor, Edward Lama. *On Afrocentricity, Intercultural Communication, and Racism.* Lewiston, N.Y.: Edwin Mellin Press, 1998.

HISTORY

Anderson, Eric, and Alfred A. Moss, Jr., eds. *The Facts of Reconstruction: Essays in Honor of John Hope Franklin.* Baton Rouge: Louisiana State University Press, 1991.

Bell, Howard Holman. *A Survey of the Negro Convention Movement, 1830-1861.* New York: Arno Press, 1969.

Blight, David W. *Race and Reunion: The Civil War in American Memory*. Cambridge, Mass.: Belknap Press of Harvard University Press, 2001.

Bonnett, Aubrey W., and G. Llewellyn Watson, eds. *Emerging Perspectives on the Black Diaspora*. Lanham, Md.: University Press of America, 1990.

Brown, Richard H. *The Missouri Compromise: Political Statesmanship or Unwise Evasion?* Boston: D. C. Heath, 1964.

Carter, Dan T. *Scottsboro: A Tragedy of the American South*. Rev. ed. Baton Rouge: Louisiana State University Press, 1979.

_____. *When the War Was Over: The Failure of Self-Reconstruction in the South, 1865-1867*. Baton Rouge: Louisiana State University Press, 1985.

Chalmers, Allan Knight. *They Shall Be Free*. Garden City, N.Y.: Doubleday, 1951.

Collins, Bruce. *The Origins of America's Civil War*. New York: Holmes & Meier, 1981.

Conniff, Michael L., and Thomas J. Davis. *Africans in the Americas: A History of the Black Diaspora*. New York: St. Martin's Press, 1994.

Cox, LaWanda. *Lincoln and Black Freedom: A Study in Presidential Leadership*. Columbia: University of South Carolina Press, 1981.

Cox, LaWanda, and John H. Cox. *Politics, Principle, and Prejudice: Dilemma of Reconstruction America, 1865-1866*. New York: Free Press, 1963.

Cronon, E. David. *Black Moses: The Story of Marcus Garvey and the Universal Negro Improvement Association*. Madison: University of Wisconsin Press, 1955.

Crouch, Barry A. *The Freedmen's Bureau and Black Texans*. Austin: University of Texas Press, 1992.

Dykstra, Robert R. *Bright Radical Star: Black Freedom and White Supremacy on the Hawkeye Frontier*. Cambridge, Mass.: Harvard University Press, 1993.

Etcheson, Nicole. *Bleeding Kansas: Contested Liberty in the Civil War Era*. Lawrence: University Press of Kansas, 2004.

Foner, Eric. *Nothing But Freedom: Emancipation and Its Legacy*. Baton Rouge: Louisiana State University Press, 1983.

_____. *Reconstruction: America's Unfinished Revolution*. New York: Harper & Row, 1988.

Franklin, John Hope. *The Emancipation Proclamation*. Garden City, N.Y.: Doubleday, 1963.

_____. *Reconstruction: After the Civil War*. Chicago: University of Chicago Press, 1961.

Franklin, John Hope, and Alfred A. Moss, Jr. *From Slavery to Freedom: A History of African Americans*. 7th ed. New York: McGraw- Hill, 1994.

Frazier, Thomas R., ed. *Afro-American History: Primary Sources*. New York: Harcourt, Brace & World, 1970.

Garvey, Amy Jacques. *Garvey and Garveyism*. 1963. Reprint. New York: Collier, 1976.

Garvey, Marcus. *Philosophy and Opinions of Marcus Garvey*. Edited by Amy Jacques-Garvey, with new introduction by Robert A. Hill. New York: Atheneum, 1992.

Guelzo, Allen C. *Lincoln's Emancipation Proclamation: The End of Slavery in America*. New York: Simon & Schuster, 2004.

Hamilton, Holman. *Prologue to Conflict: The Crisis and Compromise of 1850*. New York: W. W. Norton, 1964.

Harlan, Louis R. *Booker T. Washington: The Making of a Black Leader, 1856-1901*. New York: Oxford University Press, 1972.

_____. *Booker T. Washington: The Wizard of Tuskegee, 1901- 1915*. New York: Oxford University Press, 1983.

_____. *Booker T. Washington in Perspective: Essays of Louis R. Harlan*. Edited by Raymond W. Smock. Jackson: University Press of Mississippi, 1988.

Hill, Robert A., and Barbara Bair, eds. *Marcus Garvey: Life and Lessons*. Berkeley: University of California Press, 1987.

Holt, Michael. *The Political Crisis of the 1850's*. New York: W. W. Norton, 1978.

Hornsby, Alton, Jr. *Chronology of African-American History*. Detroit, Mich.: Gale Research, 1991.

Keegan, Frank L. *Blacktown, U.S.A*. Boston: Little, Brown, 1971.

Kellogg, Charles Flint. *NAACP: A History of the National Association for the Advancement of Colored People*. Baltimore: Johns Hopkins University Press, 1964.

Kusmer, Kenneth L., ed. *Black Communities and Urban Development in America, 1720-1990*. New York: Garland, 1991.

Lanctot, Neil. *Negro League Baseball: The Rise and Ruin of a Black Institution*. Philadelphia: University of Pennsylvania Press, 2004.

Lasch-Quinn, Elisabeth. *Black Neighbors: Race and the Limits of Reform in the American Settlement House Movement, 1890-1945*.

Chapel Hill: University of North Carolina Press, 1993.

Leckie, William H. *The Buffalo Soldiers: A Narrative of the Negro Cavalry in the West*. Norman: University of Oklahoma Press, 1967.

Lemann, Nicholas. *The Promised Land: The Great Black Migration and How It Changed America*. New York: Alfred A. Knopf, 1991.

Lewis, David Levering. *W. E. B. Du Bois: Biography of a Race, 1868- 1919*. New York: Henry Holt, 1993.

Lewis, Rupert, and Maureen Warner-Lewis, eds. *Garvey: Africa, Europe, the Americas*. Kingston, Jamaica: Institute of Social and Economic Research, University of the West Indies, 1986.

Lofgren, Charles A. *The Plessy Case: A Legal-Historical Interpretation*. New York: Oxford University Press, 1987.

Lubiano, Wahneema, ed. *The House That Race Built: Black Americans, U.S. Terrain*. New York: Pantheon, 1997.

McPherson, James M. *The Battle Cry of Freedom: The Civil War Era*. Oxford, England: Oxford University Press, 1988.

_____. *The Negro in the Civil War*. New York: Vintage Books, 1965.

_____. *Ordeal by Fire: The Civil War and Reconstruction*. 2d ed. New York: McGraw-Hill, 1992.

_____. *The Struggle for Equality: Abolitionists and the Negro in the Civil War and Reconstruction*. Princeton, N.J.: Princeton University Press, 1964.

Magdol, Edward. *A Right to the Land: Essays on the Freedmen's Community*. Westport, Conn.: Greenwood Press, 1977.

Mathurin, Owen Charles. *Henry Sylvester Williams and the Origins of the Pan-African Movement, 1869-1911*. Westport, Conn.: Greenwood Press, 1976.

Meier, August. *Negro Thought in America, 1880-1915: Racial Ideologies in the Age of Booker T. Washington*. Ann Arbor: University of Michigan Press, 1988.

Miller, Loren. *The Petitioners: The Story of the Supreme Court of the United States and the Negro*. New York: Pantheon Books, 1966.

Moses, Wilson Jeremiah. *The Golden Age of Black Nationalism, 1850-1925*. New York: Oxford University Press, 1978.

Nieman, Donald G. *Promises to Keep: African-Americans and the Constitutional Order, 1776 to the Present*. New York: Oxford University Press, 1991.

Norris, Clarence, and Sybil D. Washington. *The Last of the Scottsboro Boys*. New York: Putnam, 1979.

Oates, Stephen B. *Our Fiery Trial: Abraham Lincoln, John Brown, and the Civil War Era*. Amherst: University of Massachusetts Press, 1979.

Ovington, Mary White, et al. *Black and White Sat Down Together: The Reminiscences of an NAACP Founder*. New York: Feminist Press of City University of New York, 1996.

Patterson, Haywood, and Earl Conrad. *Scottsboro Boy*. Garden City, N.Y.: Doubleday, 1950.

Quarles, Benjamin. *Lincoln and the Negro*. New York: Oxford University Press, 1962.

_____. *The Negro in the Civil War*. Boston: Little, Brown, 1953.

Rabinowitz, Howard N., and George W. Frederickson. *Race Relations in the Urban South, 1865-1890*. New York: Oxford University Press, 1996.

Rhym, Darren. *The NAACP*. Philadelphia: Chelsea House, 2002.

Richardson, Heather Cox. *The Death of Reconstruction: Race, Labor, and Politics in the Post-Civil War North, 1865-1901*. Cambridge, Mass.: Harvard University Press, 2001.

Rymer, Russ. *American Beach: A Saga of Race, Wealth, and Memory*. New York: HarperCollins, 1998.

Shropshire, Kenneth L., and Kellen Winslow. *In Black and White: Race and Sports in America*. New York: New York University Press, 1996.

Simon, Scott. *Jackie Robinson and the Integration of Baseball*. Hoboken, N.J.: J. Wiley & Sons, 2002.

Snyder, Brad. *Beyond the Shadow of the Senators: The Untold Story of the Homestead Grays and the Integration of Baseball*. Chicago: Contemporary Books, 2003.

Stampp, Kenneth, ed. *The Causes of the Civil War*. Rev. ed. Englewood Cliffs, N.J.: Prentice-Hall, 1974.

_____. *The Era of Reconstruction, 1865-1877*. New York: Alfred A. Knopf, 1965.

Tygiel, Jules. *Baseball's Great Experiment: Jackie Robinson and His Legacy*. New York: Vintage, 1984.

Van Deburg, William L., ed. *Modern Black Nationalism: From Marcus Garvey to Louis Farrakhan*. New York: New York University Press, 1997.

Walther, Eric H. *The Shattering of the Union: America in the 1850's*. Wilmington, Del.: Scholarly Resources, 2004.

Waugh, John C. *On the Brink of Civil War: The Compromise of 1850 and How It Changed the Course* of American History.Wilmington, Del.: Scholarly Resources, 2003.

Wood, Peter H. *Black Majority: Negroes in Colonial South Carolina from 1670 Through the Stono Rebellion*. New York: W.W. Norton, 1974.

AFFIRMATIVE ACTION

Anderson, Terry H. *The Pursuit of Fairness: A History of Affirmative Action*. New York: Oxford University Press, 2004.

Annals of the American Academy of Political and Social Science 523 (September, 1992). Special issue, Affirmative Action Revisited.

Ball, Howard. *The Bakke Case: Race, Education, and Affirmative Action*. Lawrence: University Press of Kansas, 2000.

Beckwith, Francis J., and Todd E. Jones, eds. *Affirmative Action: Social Justice or Reverse Discrimination?* Amherst, N.Y.: Prometheus, 1997.

Benokraitis, Nijole, and Joe R. Feagin. *Affirmative Action and Equal Opportunity: Action, Inaction, Reaction*. Boulder, Colo.: Westview Press, 1978.

Bolick, Clint. *The Affirmative Action Fraud: Can We Restore the American Civil Rights Vision?* Washington, D.C.: Cato Institute, 1996.

Bowen, William G., and Derek Bok. *The Shape of the River: Long- Term Consequences of Considering Race in College and University Admissions*. Princeton, N.J.: Princeton University Press, 1998.

Bowie, Norman E., ed. *Equal Opportunity*. Boulder, Colo.: Westview Press, 1988.

Burstein, Paul. "Affirmative Action, Jobs, and American Democracy: What Has Happened to the Quest for Equal Opportunity?" *Law and Society Review* 26, no. 4 (1992): 901-922.

Carter, Stephen L. *Reflections of an Affirmative Action Baby*. New York: Basic Books, 1992.

Cohen, Carl. *Naked Racial Preferences: The Case Against Affirmative Action*. Lanham, Md.: Madison Books, 1995.

Delgado, Richard. *The Coming Race War? And Other Apocalyptic Tales of America After Affirmative Action and Welfare*. New York: New York University Press, 1996.

Dworkin, Ronald. "What Did *Bakke* Really Decide?" In *A Matter of Principle*. Cambridge, Mass.: Harvard University Press, 1985.

Eastland, Terry. *Ending Affirmative Action: The Case for Colorblind Justice*. New York: Basic Books, 1996.

Edley, Christopher F., Jr. *Not All Black and White: Affirmative Action, Race, and American Values*. New York: Hill & Wang, 1996.

Ezorsky, Gertrude. *Racism and Justice: The Case for Affirmative Action*. Ithaca, N.Y.: Cornell University Press, 1991.

Fiscus, Ronald J. *The Constitutional Logic of Affirmative Action*. Durham, N.C.: Duke University Press, 1992.

Fullinwider, Robert. *The Reverse Discrimination Controversy*. Totowa, N.J.: Rowman and Littlefield, 1980.

Glazer, Nathan. *Affirmative Discrimination: Ethnic Inequality and Public Policy*. New York: Basic Books, 1975.

Gray, W. Robert. *The Four Faces of Affirmative Action: Fundamental Answers and Actions*. Westport, Conn.: Greenwood Press, 2001.

Greene, Kathanne W. *Affirmative Action and Principles of Justice*. New York: Greenwood Press, 1989.

Greenwalt, Kent. *Discrimination and Reverse Discrimination*. New York: Alfred A. Knopf, 1983.

Horne, Gerald. *Reversing Discrimination: The Case for Affirmative Action*. New York: International, 1992.

Jackson, Charles C. "Affirmative Action: Controversy and Retrenchment." *The Western Journal of Black Studies* 16, no. 4 (Winter, 1992). Jones, Augustus J. *Affirmative Talk, Affirmative Action: A Comparative Study of the Politics of Affirmative Action*. New York: Praeger, 1991.

Kahlenberg, Richard D. *The Remedy: Class, Race, and Affirmative Action*. New York: Basic Books, 1996.

Leonard, Jonathan. "The Federal Anti-Bias Effort." In *Essays on the Economics of Discrimination*, edited by Emily P. Hoffman. Kalamazoo, Mich.: W. E. Upjohn Institute, 1991.

Lerner, Robert, and Althea K. Nigai. *Racial Preferences in Undergraduate Enrollment at the University of California, Berkeley, 1993- 1995: A Preliminary Report*. Washington, D.C.: Center for Equal Opportunity, 1996.

Lynch, Frederick R. *The Diversity Machine: The Drive to Change the "White Male Workplace."* New York: Free Press, 1996.

McCormack, Wayne. *The "Bakke" Decision: Implications for Higher Education Admissions*. Washington, D.C.: American Council on Education and the Association of American Law Schools, 1978.

McWhirter, Darien A. *The End of Affirmative Action: Where Do We Go from Here?* New York: Carol Publishing Group, 1996.

Maguire, Daniel. *A Case for Affirmative Action.* Dubuque, Iowa: Shepherd, 1992.

Post, Robert, and Michael Paul Rogin, eds. *Race and Representation: Affirmative Action.* New York: Zone Books, 1998.

Pusser, Brian. *Burning Down the House: Politics, Governance, and Affirmative Action at the University of California.* Albany: State University of New York Press, 2004.

Roberts, Paul Craig, and Lawrence M. Stratton, Jr. *The New Color Line: How Quotas and Privilege Destroy Democracy.* Washington, D.C.: Regnery, 1995.

Rosenfeld, Michel. *Affirmative Action and Justice: A Philosophical and Constitutional Inquiry.* New Haven, Conn.: Yale University Press, 1991.

Sindler, Allan P. *Bakke, Defunis, and Minority Admissions: The Quest for Equal Opportunity.* New York: Longman, 1978.

Sowell, Thomas. *Preferential Policies: An International Perspective.* New York: William Morrow, 1990.

Steinberg, Stephen. *Turning Back: The Retreat from Racial Justice in American Thought and Policy.* Boston: Beacon Press, 1995.

Stohr, Greg. *A Black and White Case: How Affirmative Action Survived Its Greatest Legal Challenge.* Princeton: Bloomberg Press, 2004.

Swain, Carol M., ed. *Race Versus Class: The New Affirmative Action Debate.* Lanham, Md.: University Press of America, 1996.

Thernstrom, Abigail. *Whose Votes Count? Affirmative Action and Minority Voting Rights.* Cambridge, Mass.: Harvard University Press, 1987.

U.S. Commission on Civil Rights. *Affirmative Action in the 1980's: Dismantling the Process of Discrimination: A Statement of the United States Commission on Civil Rights.* Washington, D.C.: Author, 1981.

Urofsky, Melvin I. *A Conflict of Rights: The Supreme Court and Affirmative Action.* New York: Charles Scribner's Sons, 1991.

Wise, Tim J. *Affirmative Action: Racial Preference in Black and White.* New York: Routledge, 2005.

Zelnick, Bob. *Backfire: A Reporter's Look at Affirmative Action.* Chicago: Henry Regnery, 1996.

AFRICAN AMERICANS AND OTHER MINORITIES

Abelmann, Nancy, and John Lie. *Blue Dreams: Korean Americans and the Los Angeles Riots.* Cambridge, Mass.: Harvard University Press, 1995.

Adams, Maurianne, and John Bracey, eds. *Strangers and Neighbors: Relations Between Blacks and Jews in the United States.* Amherst: University of Massachusetts Press, 1999.

Berman, Paul, ed. *Blacks and Jews: Alliance and Arguments.* New York: Delacorte Press, 1994.

Bonnett, Aubrey W. *Institutional Adaptation of West Indian Immigrants to America.* Washington, D.C.: University Press of America, 1982.

Brock, Lisa, and Digna Castañeda Fuertes, eds. *Between Race and Empire: African-Americans and Cubans Before the Cuban Revolution.* Philadelphia: Temple University Press, 1998.

Collum, Danny Duncan. *Black and White Together: The Search for Common Ground.* Maryknoll, N.Y.: Orbis Books, 1996.

Daughtry, Herbert D., Sr. *No Monopoly on Suffering: Blacks and Jews in Crown Heights.* Trenton, N.J.: Africa World Press, 1997.

Diner, Hasia R. *In the Almost Promised Land: American Jews and Blacks, 1919-1935.* Westport, Conn.: Westview, 1977.

Forbes, Jack D. *Black Africans and Native Americans: Color, Race, and Caste in the Evolution of Red-Black Peoples.* Urbana: University of Illinois Press, 1993.

Halliburton, R., Jr. *Red over Black: Black Slavery Among the Cherokee Indians.* Westport, Conn.: Greenwood Press, 1977.

Helg, Aline. *Our Rightful Share: The Afro-Cuban Struggle for Equality, 1886-1912.* Chapel Hill: University of North Carolina Press, 1995.

Hentoff, Nat, ed. *Black Anti-Semitism and Jewish Racism.* New York: Richard W. Baron, 1969.

Hoover, Dwight W. *The Red and the Black.* Chicago: Rand McNally, 1976.

Joyce, Patrick D. *No Fire Next Time: Black-Korean Conflicts and the Future of America's Cities.* Ithaca, N.Y.: Cornell University Press, 2003.

Kasinitz, Philip. *Caribbean New York: Black Immigrants and the Politics of Race.* Ithaca, N.Y.: Cornell University Press, 1992.

Katz, William Loren. *Black Indians: A Hidden Heritage.* New York: Atheneum, 1986.

Kaufman, Jonathan. *Broken Alliance: The Turbulent Times Between Blacks and Jews in America.* New York: Scribner's, 1988.

Kim, Claire Jean. *Bitter Fruit: The Politics of Black-Korean Conflict in New York City.* New Haven: Yale University Press, 2000.

Kim, Kwang Chung, ed. *Koreans in the Hood: Conflict with African Americans.* Baltimore: Johns Hopkins University Press, 1999.

Laguerre, Michel S. *Diasporic Citizenship: Haitian Americans in Transnational America*. New York: St. Martin's Press, 1998.

Lerner, Michael, and Cornel West. *Jews and Blacks: Let the Healing Begin*. New York: G. P. Putnam's Sons, 1995.

Lieberson, Stanley. *A Piece of the Pie: Blacks and White Immigrants Since 1880*. Berkeley: University of California Press, 1980.

Littlefield, Daniel F., Jr. *Africans and Creeks: From the Colonial Period to the Civil War*. Westport, Conn.: Greenwood Press, 1979.

_____. *Africans and Seminoles: From Removal to Emancipation*. Westport, Conn.: Greenwood Press, 1978.

Melnick, Jeffrey. *Black-Jewish Relations on Trial: Leo Frank and Jim Conley in the New South*. Jackson: University Press of Mississippi, 2000.

Miller, Jake. *The Plight of Haitian Refugees*. New York: Praeger, 1984.

Min, Pyong Gap. *Caught in the Middle: Korean Merchants in America's Multiethnic Cities*. Berkeley: University of California Press, 1996.

Ownby, Ted, ed. *Black and White Cultural Interaction in the Antebellum South*. Jackson: University Press of Mississippi, 1993.

Palmer, Ransford W. *Pilgrims from the Sun: West Indian Migration to America*. New York: Twayne Publishers, 1995.

Phillips, William M., Jr. *An Unillustrious Alliance: The African American and Jewish American Communities*. Westport, Conn.: Greenwood Press, 1991.

Piatt, Bill, et al. *Black and Brown in America: The Case for Cooperation*. New York: New York University Press, 1997.

Salzman, Jack, and Cornel West, eds. *Struggles in the Promised Land: Towards a History of Black-Jewish Relations in the United States*. New York: Oxford University Press, 1997.

Schorsch, Jonathan. *Jews and Blacks in the Early Modern World*. New York: Cambridge University Press, 2004.

Stepick, Alex. *Haitian Refugees in the U.S.* London: Minority Rights Group, 1982.

_____. *Pride Against Prejudice: Haitians in the United States*. Boston: Allyn and Bacon, 1998.

Vickerman, Milton. *Crosscurrents: West Indian Immigrants and Race*. New York: Oxford University Press, 1998.

Waldinger, Roger. *Still the Promised City? African-Americans and the New Immigrants in Post-Industrial New York*. Cambridge, Mass.: Harvard University Press, 1996.

Waters, Mary C. *Black Identities: West Indian Immigrant Dreams and American Realities*. Cambridge, Mass.: Harvard University Press, 1999.

Watkins-Owens, Irma. *Blood Relations: Caribbean Immigrants and the Harlem Community, 1900-1930*. Bloomington: Indiana University Press, 1996.

Williams, Richard E. *Hierarchical Structures and Social Value: The Creation of Black and Irish Identities in the United States*. Cambridge, England: Cambridge University Press, 1990.

Zéphir, Flore. *The Haitian Americans*. Westport, Conn.: Greenwood Press, 2004.

CIVIL RIGHTS

Abernathy, Ralph. *And the Walls Came Tumbling Down*. New York: Harper & Row, 1989.

Ashmore, Harry S. *"Civil Rights and Wrongs": A Memoir of Race and Politics, 1944-1996*. Rev. and expanded ed. Columbia: University of South Carolina Press, 1997.

Bartley, Numan V. *The Rise of Massive Resistance: Race and Politics in the South During the 1950's*. Baton Rouge: Louisiana State University Press, 1969.

Bass, Patrik Henry. *Like a Mighty Stream: The March on Washington, August 28, 1963*. Philadelphia: Running Press, 2002.

Bates, Daisy. *The Long Shadow of Little Rock: A Memoir*. New York: David McKay, 1962.

Blaustein, Albert P., and Robert L. Zangrando, eds. *Civil Rights and the American Negro: A Documentary History*. New York: Trident Press, 1968.

Bloom, Jack D. *Class, Race, and the Civil Rights Movement*. Bloomington: Indiana University Press, 1987.

Blossom, Virgil T. *It Has Happened Here*. New York: Harper and Brothers, 1959.

Blumberg, Rhoda L. *Civil Rights: The 1960's Freedom Struggle*. Boston: Twayne, 1984.

Breitman, George, Herman Porter, and Baxter Smith. *The Assassination of Malcolm X*. New York: Pathfinder Press, 1976.

Burk, Robert Frederick. *The Eisenhower Administration and Black Civil Rights*. Knoxville: University of Tennessee Press, 1984.

Burns, W. Haywood. *The Voices of Negro Protest in America*. New York: Oxford University Press, 1963.

Carmichael, Stokely, and Charles V. Hamilton. *Black Power: The Politics of Liberation in America*. New York: Random House, 1967.

Carmichael, Stokely, with Ekwueme Michael Thelwell. *Ready for Revolution: The Life and Struggles of Stokely Carmichael (Kwame Ture)*. New York: Scribner, 2003.

Carson, Clayborne. *In Struggle: SNCC and the Black Awakening of the 1960's*. Cambridge: Mass.: Harvard University Press, 1981.

_____. *Malcolm X: The FBI Files*. New York: Carroll & Graff, 1991.

Carson, Clayborne, et al., eds. *Eyes on the Prize Civil Rights Reader: Documents, Speeches, and First-hand Accounts from the Black Freedom Struggle, 1954-1990*. New York: Penguin, 1991.

Chappell, David L. *Inside Agitators: White Southerners in the Civil Rights Movement*. Baltimore: Johns Hopkins University Press, 1994.

Chong, Dennis. *Collective Action and the Civil Rights Movement*. Chicago: University of Chicago Press, 1991.

Churchill, Ward, and Jim Vander Wall. *Agents of Repression: The FBI's Secret Wars Against the Black Panther Party and the American Indian Movement*. Boston: South End Press, 1988.

Clark, John Henrick, ed. *Malcolm X: The Man and His Times*. Trenton, N.J.: African World Press, 1990.

Cleaver, Kathleen, and George Katsiaficas, eds. *Liberation, Imagination, and the Black Panther Party: A New Look at the Panthers and Their Legacy*. New York: Routledge, 2001.

Collier-Thomas, Bettye, and V. P. Franklin, eds. *Sisters in the Struggle: African American Women in the Civil Rights-Black Power Movement*. New York: New York University Press, 2001.

Couto, Richard A. *Ain't Gonna Let Nobody Turn Me Round: The Pursuit of Racial Justice in the Rural South*. Philadelphia: Temple University Press, 1991.

Crawford, Vicki L., Jacqueline Anne Rouse, and Barbara Woods, eds. *Women in the Civil Rights Movement: Trailblazers and Torchbearers, 1941-1965*. Bloomington: Indiana University Press, 1993.

Dees, Morris. *The Gathering Storm*. New York: HarperCollins, 1996.

Dees, Morris, with Steve Fiffer. *A Season for Justice: The Life and Times of Civil Rights Lawyer Morris Dees*. New York: Maxwell Macmillan International, 1991.

D'Emilio, John. *The Civil Rights Struggle: Leaders in Profile*. New York: Facts On File, 1979.

Dierenfield, Bruce J. *The Civil Rights Movement*. New York: Pearson Longman, 2004.

Dittmer, John. *Local People: The Struggle for Civil Rights in Mississippi*. Urbana: University of Illinois Press, 1994.

Draper, Alan. *Conflict of Interests: Organized Labor and the Civil Rights Movement in the South, 1954-1968*. Ithaca, N.Y.: ILR Press, 1994.

Dunbar, Leslie W. *Minority Report: What Has Happened to Blacks, American Indians, and Other Minorities in the Eighties*. New York: Pantheon, 1984.

Early, Gerald L. *This Is Where I Came In: Black America in the 1960's*. Lincoln: University of Nebraska Press, 2003.

Farmer, James. *Freedom—When?* New York: Random House, 1965.

_____. *Lay Bare the Heart: The Autobiography of the Civil Rights Movement*. New York: New American Library, 1985.

Finch, Minnie. *The NAACP: Its Fight for Justice*. Metuchen, N.J.: Scarecrow Press, 1981.

Forman, James. *The Making of Black Revolutionaries*. 1972. 2d ed. Washington, D.C.: Open Hand, 1985.

Freyer, Tony. *The Little Rock Crisis: A Constitutional Interpretation*. Westport, Conn.: Greenwood Press, 1984.

Garrow, David J., ed. *We Shall Overcome: The Civil Rights Movement in the United States in the 1950's and 1960's*. 3 vols. Brooklyn, N.Y.: Carlson, 1989.

Graham, Hugh Davis. *The Civil Rights Era: Origins and Development of National Policy*. New York: Oxford University Press, 1990.

Harvey, James C. *Black Civil Rights During the Johnson Administration*. Jackson: University and College Press of Mississippi, 1973.

Higham, John, ed. *Civil Rights and Social Wrongs: Black-White Relations Since World War II*. University Park: Pennsylvania State University Press, 1997.

Hill, Herbert, and James E. Jones, Jr., eds. *Race in America: The Struggle for Equality*. Madison: University of Wisconsin Press, 1993.

Hill, Lance. *The Deacons for Defense: Armed Resistance and the Civil Rights Movement.* Chapel Hill: University of North Carolina Press, 2004.

Jonas, Gilbert. *Freedom's Sword: The NAACP and the Struggle Against Racism in America, 1909-1969.* Foreword by Julian Bond. New York: Routledge, 2005.

Jones, Charles E., ed. *The Black Panther Party (Reconsidered).* Baltimore: Black Classic Press, 1998.

Kosof, Anna. *The Civil Rights Movement and Its Legacy.* New York: Watts, 1989.

Lee, Taeku. *Mobilizing Public Opinion: Black Insurgency and Racial Attitudes in the Civil Rights Era.* Chicago: University of Chicago Press, 2002.

Levine, Daniel. *Bayard Rustin and the Civil Rights Movement.* New Brunswick, N.J.: Rutgers University Press, 2000.

Levy, Peter B. *The Civil Rights Movement.* Westport, Conn.: Greenwood Press, 1998.

Ling, Peter J., and Sharon Monteith, eds. *Gender and the Civil Rights Movement.* New Brunswick, N.J.: Rutgers University Press, 2004.

McClymer, John F., ed. *Mississippi Freedom Summer.* Belmont, Calif.: Thomson/Wadsworth, 2004.

McKissack, Pat, and Fredrick McKissack. *The Civil Rights Movement in America from 1865 to the Present.* 2d ed. Chicago: Children's Press, 1991.

McMillen, Neil R. *The Citizens' Council: Organized Resistance to the Second Reconstruction, 1954-1964.* Urbana: University of Illinois Press, 1971.

McWhorter, Diane. *Carry Me Home: Birmingham, Alabama, the Climactic Battle of the Civil Rights Revolution.* New York: Simon & Schuster, 2001.

Malcolm X. *By Any Means Necessary: Speeches, Interviews and a Letter by Malcolm X.* Edited by George Breitman. New York: Pathfinder, 1970.

Malcolm X with Alex Haley. *The Autobiography of Malcolm X.* New York: Ballantine Books, 1965.

Marsh, Charles. *God's Long Summer: Stories of Faith and Civil Rights.* Princeton, N.J.: Princeton University Press, 1997.

Meier, August, and Elliot Rudwick. *CORE: A Study in the Civil Rights Movement, 1942-1968.* Urbana: University of Illinois Press, 1975.

Meredith, James H. *Three Years in Mississippi.* Bloomington: Indiana University Press, 1966.

Meriwether, Louise. *Don't Ride the Bus on Mondays: The Rosa Parks Story.* Englewood Cliffs, N.J.: Prentice Hall, 1973.

Miller, Marilyn. *The Bridge at Selma.* Morristown, N.J.: Silver Burdett, 1985.

Morris, Aldon B. *The Origins of the Civil Rights Movement: Black Communities Organizing for Change.* New York: Free Press, 1984.

Newton, Huey P. *To Die for the People.* New York: Random House, 1972.

_____. *War Against the Panthers: A Study of Repression in America.* 1980. Reprint. New York: Harlem River Press, 1996.

Oppenheimer, Martin. *The Sit-In Movement of 1960.* Brooklyn, N.Y.: Carlson, 1989.

O'Reilly, Kenneth. *Racial Matters: The FBI's Secret File on Black America, 1960-1972.* New York: Free Press, 1989.

Powledge, Fred. *Free at Last? The Civil Rights Movement and the People Who Made It.* Boston: Little, Brown, 1991.

Price, Steven D., comp. *Civil Rights, 1967-68.* Vol. 2. New York: Facts On File, 1973.

Record, Wilson, and Jane Cassels Record, eds. *Little Rock, U.S.A.* San Francisco: Chandler, 1960.

Riches, William T. Martin. *The Civil Rights Movement: Struggle and Resistance.* New York: Palgrave Macmillan, 2004.

Robinson, Jo Ann Gibson. *The Montgomery Bus Boycott and the Women Who Started It: The Memoir of Jo Ann Gibson Robinson.* Knoxville: University of Tennessee Press, 1987.

Rothschild, Mary Aickin. *A Case of Black and White: Northern Volunteers and the Southern Freedom Summers, 1964-1965.* Westport, Conn.: Greenwood Press, 1982.

Sargent, Frederic O. *The Civil Rights Revolution: Events and Leaders, 1955-1968.* Foreword by Bill Maxwell. Jefferson, N.C.: McFarland & Co., 2004.

Seale, Bobby. *Seize the Time: The Story of the Black Panther Party and Huey P. Newton.* New York: Random House, 1968.

Sitkoff, Harvard. *The New Deal for Blacks: The Emergence of Civil Rights as a National Issue.* New York: Oxford University Press, 1978.

_____. *The Struggle for Black Equality, 1954-1980.* New York: Hill and Wang, 1993.

Weisbrot, Robert. *Freedom Bound: A History of America's Civil Rights Movement.* New York: W. W. Norton, 1990.

Wexler, Sanford. *The Civil Rights Movement: An Eyewitness History.* New York: Facts On File, 1993.

Williams, Juan. *Eyes on the Prize: America's Civil Rights Years, 1954-1965*. New York: Viking, 1987.

Young, Andrew. *An Easy Burden: The Civil Rights Movement and the Transformation of America*. New York: HarperCollins, 1996.

Zinn, Howard. *SNCC: The New Abolitionists*. Cambridge, Mass.: South End Press, 2002.

CIVIL RIGHTS LAW

Abernathy, Charles F. *Civil Rights and Constitutional Litigation: Cases and Materials*. 2d ed. St. Paul, Minn.: West, 1992.

Abernathy, M. Glenn. *Civil Liberties Under the Constitution*. 5th ed. Columbia: University of South Carolina Press, 1989.

Bardolph, Richard, ed. *The Civil Rights Record: Black Americans and the Law, 1849-1870*. New York: Thomas Crowell, 1970.

Bell, Derrick A., Jr. *Race, Racism, and American Law*. 2d ed. Boston: Little, Brown, 1980.

Berman, Daniel M. *A Bill Becomes a Law: Congress Enacts Civil Rights Legislation*. New York: Macmillan, 1966.

Berry, Mary Frances. *Black Resistance/White Law: A History of Constitutional Racism in America*. Rev. ed. New York: Penguin, 1994.

Curtis, Michael Kent. *No State Shall Abridge*. Durham, N.C.: Duke University Press, 1986.

Davidson, Chandler, and Bernard Grofman, eds. *Quiet Revolution in the South: The Impact of the Voting Rights Act, 1965-1990*. Princeton, N.J.: Princeton University Press, 1994.

Flagg, Barbara J. *Was Blind, but Now I See: White Race Consciousness and the Law*. New York: New York University Press, 1998.

Grofman, Bernard, and Chandler Davidson, eds. *Controversies in Minority Voting: The Voting Rights Act in Perspective*. Washington, D.C.: Brookings Institution, 1992.

Halpern, Steven C. *On the Limits of the Law: The Ironic Legacy of Title VI of the 1964 Civil Rights Act*. Baltimore: Johns Hopkins University Press, 1995.

Hoemann, George H. *What God Hath Wrought: The Embodiment of Freedom in the Thirteenth Amendment*. New York: Garland Press, 1987.

Hyman, Harold M., and William M. Wiecek. *Equal Justice Under Law: Constitutional Development, 1835-1875*. New York: Harper & Row, 1982.

Klarman, Michael J. *From Jim Crow to Civil Rights: The Supreme Court and the Struggle for Racial Equality*. New York: Oxford University Press, 2004.

Kull, Andrew. *The Color-Blind Constitution*. Cambridge, Mass.: Harvard University Press, 1992.

Labb, Ronald M., and Jonathan Lurie. *The Slaughterhouse Cases: Regulation, Reconstruction, and the Fourteenth Amendment*. Lawrence: University Press of Kansas, 2003.

Lively, Donald E. *The Constitution and Race*. New York: Praeger, 1992.

Nelson, William. *The Fourteenth Amendment*. Cambridge, Mass.: Harvard University Press, 1988.

Perry, Michael J. *We the People: The Fourteenth Amendment and the Supreme Court*. New York: Oxford University Press, 1999.

Reams, Bernard D., Jr., and Paul E. Wilson, eds. *Segregation and the Fourteenth Amendment in the States: A Survey of State Segregation Laws, 1865-1953, Prepared for United States Supreme Court in re Brown vs. Board of Education of Topeka*. Buffalo, N.Y.: W. S. Hein, 1975.

Roberts, Ronald S. *Clarence Thomas and the Tough Love Crowd: Counterfeit Heroes and Unhappy Truths*. New York: New York University Press, 1995.

Tsesis, Alexander. *The Thirteenth Amendment and American Freedom: A Legal History*. New York: New York University Press, 2004.

Tushnet, Mark V. *Making Civil Rights Law: Thurgood Marshall and the Supreme Court, 1936-1961*. New York: Oxford University Press, 1994.

U.S. Commission on Civil Rights. *The Voting Rights Act: Unfulfilled Goals*. Washington, D.C.: Government Printing Office, 1981.

Whalen, Charles, and Barbara Whalen. *The Longest Debate: A Legislative History of the 1964 Civil Rights Act*. Washington, D.C.: Seven Locks Press, 1985.

CRIME

Cole, David. *No Equal Justice: Race and Class in the American Criminal Justice System*. New York: New Press, 1999.

Free, Marvin, Jr. *African Americans and the Criminal Justice System*. New York: Garland, 1996.

Fukarai, Hirosaki, Edgar W. Butler, and Richard Krooth. *Race and the Jury: Racial Disenfranchisement and the Search for Justice*. New York: Plenum, 1993.

Gibbs, Jewelle Taylor. *Race and Justice: Rodney King and O.J. Simpson in a House Divided*. San Francisco: Jossey-Bass, 1996.

Hutchinson, Earl Ofari. *The Crisis in Black and Black.* Los Angeles: Middle Passage Press, 1998.

Kennedy, Randall. *Race, Crime, and the Law.* New York: Pantheon Books, 1997.

Khalifah, H. Khalif, ed. *Rodney King and the L.A. Rebellion: Analysis and Commentary by Thirteen Best-Selling Black Writers.* Hampton, Va.: U.B. & U.S. Communications Systems, 1992.

Owens, Tom, with Rod Browning. *Lying Eyes: The Truth Behind the Corruption and Brutality of the LAPD and the Beating of Rodney King.* New York: Thunder's Mouth Press, 1994.

Paul, Arnold, ed. *Black Americans and the Supreme Court Since Emancipation: Betrayal or Protection?* New York: Holt, Rinehart and Winston, 1972.

Pinderhughes, Howard. *Race in the Hood: Conflict and Violence Among Urban Youth.* Minneapolis: University of Minnesota Press, 1997.

DESEGREGATION

Armor, David J. *Forced Justice: School Desegregation and the Law.* New York: Oxford University Press, 1995.

Barnes, Catherine A. *Journey from Jim Crow: The Desegregation of Southern Transit.* New York: Columbia University Press, 1981.

Barrett, Russell H. *Integration at Ole Miss.* Chicago: Quadrangle Press, 1965.

Brooks, Roy L. *Integration or Separation? A Strategy for Racial Equality.* Cambridge, Mass.: Harvard University Press, 1996.

Clark, E. Culpepper. *The Schoolhouse Door: Segregation's Last Stand at the University of Alabama.* New York: Oxford University Press, 1993.

Cohodas, Nadine. *The Band Played Dixie: Race and the Liberal Conscience at Ole Miss.* New York: Free Press, 1997.

Hochschild, Jennifer L. *The New American Dilemma: Liberal Democracy and School Desegregation.* New Haven, Conn.: Yale University Press, 1984.

Hughes, Larry W., William M. Gordon, and Larry W. Hillman. *Desegregating American Schools.* New York: Longman, 1980.

Jacoby, Tamar. *Someone Else's House: America's Unfinished Struggle for Integration.* New York: Free Press, 1998.

Jones, Leon. *From Brown to Boston: Desegregation in Education, 1954-1974.* Metuchen, N.J.: Scarecrow Press, 1979.

Klein, Woody, ed. *Toward Humanity and Justice: The Writings of Kenneth B. Clark, Scholar of the 1954 "Brown v. Board of Education" Decision.* Foreword by John Hope Franklin. Westport, Conn.: Praeger, 2004.

Kluger, Richard. *Simple Justice: The History of "Brown v. Board of Education" and Black America's Struggle for Equality.* New York: Alfred A. Knopf, 1976.

Kohn, Howard. *We Had a Dream: A Tale of the Struggles for Integration in America.* New York: Simon & Schuster, 1998.

Loevy, Robert D. *To End All Segregation: The Politics of the Passage of the Civil Rights Act of 1964.* Lanham, Md.: University Press of America, 1990.

Metcalf, George R. *From Little Rock to Boston: The History of School Desegregation.* Westport, Conn.: Greenwood Press, 1983.

Molotch, Harvey. *Managed Integration: Dilemmas of Doing Good in the City.* Berkeley: University of California Press, 1972.

Patterson, Orlando. *The Ordeal of Integration: Progress and Resentment in America's "Racial" Crisis.* Washington: Civitas/Counterpoint, dist. by Publishers Group West, 1997.

Schwartz, Bernard. *Swann's Way: The School Busing Case and the Supreme Court.* New York: Oxford University Press, 1986.

Small, Stephen. *Racialized Barriers: The Black Experience in the United States and England in the 1980's.* London: Routledge, 1994.

Wicker, Tom. *Tragic Failure: Racial Integration in America.* New York: William Morrow, 1996.

Wilkinson, J. Harvie, III. *From "Brown" to "Bakke": The Supreme Court and School Integration: 1954-1978.* New York: Oxford University Press, 1979.

Wolters, Raymond. *The Burden of "Brown": Thirty Years of School Desegregation.* Knoxville: University of Tennessee Press, 1984.

Ziegler, Benjamin, ed. *Desegregation and the Supreme Court.* Boston: D. C. Heath, 1958.

ECONOMICS

Banner-Haley, Charles T. *The Fruits of Integration: Black Middle- Class Ideology and Culture, 1960-1990.* Jackson: University Press of Mississippi, 1994.

Becker, Gary S. *The Economics of Discrimination.* 2d ed. Chicago: University of Chicago Press, 1971.

Benjamin, Lois. *The Black Elite: Facing the Color Line in the Twilight of the Twentieth Century.* Chicago: Nelson-Hall, 1991.

Bonacich, Edna. "A Theory of Middleman Minorities." *American Sociological Review* 38 (October, 1973): 583-594.

Burman, Stephen. *The Black Progress Question: Explaining the African American Predicament*. Newbury Park, Calif.: Sage Publications, 1995.

Carnoy, Martin. *Faded Dreams: The Politics and Economics of Race in America*. New York: Cambridge University Press, 1994.

Farley, Reynolds. *Blacks and Whites: Narrowing the Gap?* Cambridge, Mass.: Harvard University Press, 1984.

Feagin, Joe R., and Melvin P. Sikes. *Living with Racism: The Black Middle Class Experience*. Boston: Beacon Press, 1994.

Franklin, Raymond S., and Solomon Resnik. *The Political Economy of Racism*. New York: Holt, Rinehart and Winston, 1973.

Frazier, E. Franklin. *Black Bourgeoisie*. Glencoe, Ill.: Free Press, 1957.

Gans, Herbert. *The Urban Villagers*. Rev. ed. New York: Free Press, 1982.

Jaynes, Gerald D., and Robin M. Williams, eds. *A Common Destiny: Blacks and American Society*. Washington, D.C.: National Academy Press, 1988.

Levitan, Sar A., William B. Johnston, and Robert Taggart. *Still a Dream: The Changing Status of Blacks Since 1960*. Cambridge, Mass.: Harvard University Press, 1975.

Lewis, W. Arthur. *Racial Conflict and Economic Development*. Cambridge, Mass.: Harvard University Press, 1985.

Light, Ivan. *Immigrant Entrepreneurs: Koreans in Los Angeles*. Berkeley: University of California Press, 1988.

Mandle, Jay R. *Not Slave, Not Free: The African American Economic Experience Since the Civil War*. Durham, N.C.: Duke University Press, 1992.

Oliver, Melvin L., and Thomas M. Shapiro. *Black Wealth, White Wealth: A New Perspective on Racial Inequality*. New York: Routledge, 1995.

Perlo, Victor. *Economics of Racism U.S.A.: Roots of Black Inequality*. 2d ed. New York: International Publishers, 1976.

Pinkney, Alphonso. *The Myth of Black Progress*. New York: Cambridge University Press, 1984.

Shapiro, Thomas M. *The Hidden Cost of Being African American: How Wealth Perpetuates Inequality*. New York: Oxford University Press, 2004.

Smith, James P., and Finis R. Welch. *Closing the Gap: Forty Years of Economic Progress for Blacks*. Santa Monica, Calif.: Rand Corporation, 1986.

Squires, Gregory D. *Capital and Communities in Black and White: The Intersections of Race, Class, and Uneven Development*. Albany: State University of New York Press, 1994.

Wilson, William Julius. *The Declining Significance of Race: Blacks and Changing American Institutions*. Chicago: University of Chicago Press, 1978.

EDUCATION

Atkinson, Pansye S. *Brown vs. Topeka—an African American's View: Desegregation and Miseducation*. Chicago: African American Images, 1993.

Barnett, Marqueritz R., ed. *Readings on Equal Education*. New York: AMS Press, 1984.

Bell, Derrick. *Silent Covenants: "Brown v. Board of Education" and the Unfulfilled Hopes for Racial Reform*. New York: Oxford University Press, 2004.

_____, ed. *Shades of Brown: New Perspectives on School Desegregation*. New York: Teachers College Press, 1980.

Bond, Horace Mann. *Education for Freedom: A History of Lincoln University*. Princeton, N.J.: Princeton University Press, 1976.

Brown, M. Christopher, II, and Kassie Freeman, eds. *Black Colleges: New Perspectives on Policy and Practice*. Westport, Conn.: Praeger, 2004.

Clotfelter, Charles T. *After "Brown": The Rise and Retreat of School Desegregation*. Princeton, N.J.: Princeton University Press, 2004.

Fairclough, Adam. *Teaching Equality: Black Schools in the Age of Jim Crow*. Athens: University of Georgia Press, 2001.

Feagin, Joe R., et al. *The Agony of Education: Black Students at White Colleges and Universities*. New York: Routledge, 1996.

Formisano, Ronald P. *Boston Against Busing: Race, Class, and Ethnicity in the 1960's and 1970's*. Chapel Hill: University of North Carolina Press, 1991.

Gill, Walter. *Issues in African American Education*. Nashville, Tenn.: One Horn Press, 1991.

Graglia, Lino A. *Disaster by Decree: The Supreme Court Decisions on Race and the Schools*. Ithaca, N.Y.: Cornell University Press, 1976.

Hill, Leven, ed. *Black American Colleges and Universities*. Detroit, Mich.: Gale Research, 1994.

Jones-Wilson, Faustine C. *The Encyclopedia of African American Education*. Westport, Conn.: Greenwood Press, 1996.

Kozol, Jonathan. *Death at an Early Age: The Destruction of the Hearts and Minds of Negro Children in the Boston Public Schools*. Boston: Houghton, Mifflin, 1967.

Lefkowitz, Mary. *Not Out of Africa: How Afrocentrism Became an Excuse to Teach Myth*. New York: Basic Books, 1996.

Margo, Robert A. *Race and Schooling in the South, 1880-1950: An Economic History*. Chicago: University of Chicago Press, 1990.

Mwadilitu, Mwalimi I. [Alexander E. Curtis]. *Richard Allen: The First Exemplar of African American Education*. New York: ECA Associates, 1985.

Ogletree, Charles J., Jr. *All Deliberate Speed: Reflections on the First Half Century of "Brown v. Board of Education."* New York: W.W. Norton & Co., 2004.

Roebuck, Julian, and Komanduri Murty. *Historically Black Colleges and Universities: Their Place in American Higher Education*. Westport, Conn.: Praeger, 1993.

Rossell, Christine H., and Willis D. Hawley, eds. *The Consequences of School Desegregation*. Philadelphia: Temple University Press, 1983.

Samuels, Albert L. *Is Separate Unequal? Black Colleges and the Challenge to Desegregation*. Lawrence: University Press of Kansas, 2004.

Williams, Juan, and Dwayne Ashley with Shawn Rhea. *I'll Find a Way or Make One: A Tribute to Historically Black Colleges and Universities*. New York: Amistad/HarperCollins, 2004.

Wollenberg, Charles. *All Deliberate Speed: Segregation and Exclusion in California Schools, 1855-1975*. Berkeley: University of California Press, 1976.

EMPLOYMENT AND LABOR

Blumrosen, Alfred. *Modern Law: The Law Transmission System and Equal Employment Opportunity*. Madison: University of Wisconsin Press, 1993.

Davis, George, and Glegg Watson. *Black Life in Corporate America: Swimming in the Mainstream*. New York: Doubleday, 1985.

Equal Employment Opportunity Act of 1972. Washington, D.C.: U.S. Government Printing Office, 1972.

Fernandez, John P., and Jules Davis. *Race, Gender, and Rhetoric: The True State of Race and Gender Relations in Corporate America*. New York: McGraw-Hill, 1999.

Hartigan, John A., and Alexandra K.Wigdor, eds. *Fairness in Employment Testing: Validity Generalizations, Minority Issues, and the General Aptitude Test Battery*. Washington, D.C.: National Academy Press, 1989.

Kent, Ronald C., et al. *Culture, Gender, Race, and U.S. Labor History*. Westport, Conn.: Greenwood Press, 1993.

Newman, Katherine S. *No Shame in My Game: The Working Poor in the Inner City*. New York: Knopf and the Russell Sage Foundation, 1999.

Practising Law Institute. *The Civil Rights Act of 1991: Its Impact on Employment Discrimination Litigation*. New York: Author, 1992.

Royster, Deirdre A. *Race and the Invisible Hand: How White Networks Exclude Black Men from Blue-Collar Jobs*. Berkeley: University of California Press, 2003.

Sedmak, Nancy J. *Primer on Equal Employment Opportunity*. 6th ed. Washington, D.C.: Bureau of National Affairs, 1994.

Shulman, Steven, and William Darity, Jr., eds. *The Question of Discrimination: Racial Inequality in the U.S. Labor Market*. Middletown, Conn.: Wesleyan University Press, 1989.

Singer, M. *Diversity-Based Hiring: An Introduction from Legal, Ethical, and Psychological Perspectives*. Brookfield, Vt.: Ashgate, 1993.

Stith, Anthony, and Tonya A. Martin, eds. *Breaking the Glass Ceiling: Racism and Sexism in Corporate America—the Myths, the Realities and the Solutions*. Orange, N.J.: Bryant & Dillon, 1996.

Turner, Margery Austin, Michael Fix, and Raymond J. Struyk. *Opportunities Denied: Discrimination in Hiring*. Washington, D.C.: Urban Institute, 1991.

Twomey, David. *Equal Employment Opportunity Law*. 2d ed. Cincinnati: South-Western Publishing, 1990.

U.S. Equal Employment Opportunity Commission. *EEOC Compliance Manual*. Chicago: Commerce Clearing House, 1995.

Wilson, William Julius. *When Work Disappears: The World of the New Urban Poor*. New York: Knopf, 1996.

FAMILY AND COMMUNITY

Billingsley, Andrew. *Black Families in White America*. Englewood Cliffs, N.J.: Prentice-Hall, 1968.

Blackwell, James. *The Black Community: Diversity and Unity*. New York: Harper & Row, 1975.

David, Jay, ed. *Growing Up Black: From Slave Days to the Present, Twenty-five African-Americans Reveal the Trials and Triumphs of Their Childhoods*. New York: Avon Books, 1992.

Frazier, Edward Franklin. *The Negro Family in the United States*. Chicago: University of Chicago Press, 1939.

Griffin, John Howard. *Black Like Me*. Boston: Houghton Mifflin, 1961.

Haizlip, Shirlee Taylor. *The Sweeter the Juice*. New York: Simon & Schuster, 1994.

Hamblin, Ken. *Pick a Better Country: An Unassuming Colored Guy Speaks His Mind About America*. New York: Simon & Schuster, 1996.

Hill, Robert, ed. *Research on the African-American Family: A Holistic Perspective*. Westport, Conn.: Auburn House, 1993.

Horton, James Oliver. *Free People of Color: Inside the African American Community*. Washington, D.C.: Smithsonian Institution Press, 1993.

Jewell, K. Sue. *Survival of the African American Family: The Institutional Impact of U.S. Social Policy*. Westport, Conn.: Praeger, 2003.

McAdoo, Harriette Pipes, ed. *Black Families*. 3d ed. Thousand Oaks, Calif.: Sage, 1997.

McCall, Nathan. *Makes Me Wanna Holler: A Young Black Man in America*. New York: Random House, 1994.

Page, Clarence. *Showing My Color: Impolite Essays on Race and Identity*. New York: HarperCollins, 1996.

Parks, Gordon. *Born Black*. Philadelphia: Lippincott, 1971.

Staples, Robert. *Black Families at the Crossroads*. San Francisco: Jossey-Bass, 1993.

Warner, Lee H. *Free Men in an Age of Servitude: Three Generations of a Black Family*. Lexington: University Press of Kentucky, 1992.

HATE AND WHITE SUPREMACY

Alexander, Charles C. *The Ku Klux Klan in the Southwest*. Norman: University of Oklahoma Press, 1995.

Almaguer, Tomás. *Racial Fault Lines: The Historical Origins of White Supremacy in California*. Berkeley: University of California Press, 1994.

Baird, Robert M., and Stuart E. Rosenbaum, eds. *Bigotry, Prejudice and Hatred: Definitions, Causes, and Solutions*. Buffalo, N.Y.: Prometheus Books, 1992.

Bennett, Lerone, Jr. *Confrontation: Black and White*. Baltimore: Penguin, 1966.

Boesel, David, and Peter H. Rossi, eds. *Cities Under Siege: An Anatomy of the Ghetto Riots, 1964-1968*. New York: Basic Books, 1971.

Bridges, Tyler. *The Rise of David Duke*. Jackson: University Press of Mississippi, 1994.

Brundage, W. Fitzhugh. *Lynching in the New South: Georgia and Virginia, 1880-1930*. Urbana: University of Illinois Press, 1993.

_____, ed. *Under Sentence of Death: Lynching in the South*. Chapel Hill: University of North Carolina Press, 1997.

Button, James W. *Black Violence: Political Impact of the 1960's Riots*. Princeton, N.J.: Princeton University Press, 1978.

Cannon, Lou. *Official Negligence: How Rodney King and the Riots Changes Los Angeles and the LAPD*. New York: Times Books, 1998.

Capeci, Dominic J., Jr. *The Harlem Riot of 1943*. Philadelphia: Temple University Press, 1977.

Chalmers, David M. *Hooded Americanism: The First Century of the Ku Klux Klan*. 3d ed. Durham, N.C.: Duke University Press, 1987.

Cobbs, Elizabeth H., and Petric J. Smith. *Long Time Coming: An Insider's Story of the Birmingham Church Bombing That Rocked the World*. Birmingham, Ala.: Crane Hill, 1994.

Connery, Robert, ed. *Urban Riots*. New York: Vintage Books, 1969.

Daniels, Jessie. *White Lies: Race, Class, Gender and Sexuality in White Supremacist Discourse*. New York: Routledge, 1997.

Davis, Daryl. *Klan-Destine Relationships: A Black Man's Odyssey in the Ku Klux Klan*. Far Hills, N.J.: New Horizon Press, 1998.

Dray, Philip. *At the Hands of Persons Unknown: The Lynching of Black America*. New York: Random House, 2002.

Feagin, Joe R., and Harlan Hahn. *Ghetto Revolts*. New York: Macmillan, 1973.

Feldberg, Michael. *The Philadelphia Riots of 1844: A Study of Ethnic Conflict*. Westport, Conn.: Greenwood Press, 1975.

Fine, Sidney. *Violence in the Model City: The Cavanaugh Administration, Race Relations and the Detroit Riot of 1967*. Ann Arbor: University of Michigan Press, 1989.

Finkelman, Paul, ed. *Lynching, Racial Violence, and Law*. New York: Garland, 1992.

Frederickson, George M. *White Supremacy: A Comparative Study in American and South African History*. New York: Oxford University Press, 1980.

Gale, Dennis E. *Understanding Urban Unrest: From Reverend King to Rodney King*. Newbury Park, Calif.: Sage Publications, 1996.

Gates, Henry Louis, Jr., ed. *Speaking of Race, Speaking of Sex: Hate Speech, Civil Rights, and Civil Liberties*. New York: New York University Press, 1994.

Ginzburg, Ralph. *100 Years of Lynchings*. Baltimore: Black Classic Press, 1997.

Gooding-Williams, Robert, ed. *Reading Rodney King/ Reading Urban Uprising*. New York: Routledge, 1993.

Grimshaw, Allen D. *Racial Violence in the United States*. Chicago: Aldine Publishing, 1969.

Horne, Gerald. *Fire This Time: The Watts Uprising and the 1960's*. Charlottesville: University Press of Virginia, 1995.

Howard, Walter T. *Lynchings: Extralegal Violence in Florida During the 1930's*. London: Susquehanna University Press, 1995.

Kennedy, Stetson. *I Rode with the Ku Klux Klan: The Klan Unmasked*. Gainesville: University Presses of Florida, 1990.

Kotlowitz, Alex. *The Other Side of the River: A Story of Two Towns, a Death, and America's Dilemma*. New York: Nan A. Talese, 1998.

Kronenwetter, Michael. *United They Hate: White Supremacist Groups in America*. New York: Walker, 1992.

Lee, Alfred McClung. *Race Riot, Detroit 1943*. 1943. Reprint. New York: Octagon Books, 1968.

Levin, Jack, and Jack McDevitt. *Hate Crimes: The Rising Tide of Bigotry and Bloodshed*. New York: Plenum Press, 1993.

Los Angeles Times editors. *Understanding the Riots: Los Angeles Before and After the Rodney King Case*. Los Angeles: Los Angeles Times, 1992.

McGovern, James R. *Anatomy of a Lynching: The Killing of Claude Neal*. Baton Rouge: Louisiana State University Press, 1982.

MacLean, Nancy. *Behind the Mask of Chivalry: The Making of the Second Ku Klux Klan*. New York: Oxford University Press, 1994.

Madhubuti, Haki R., ed. *Why L.A. Happened: Implications of the '92 Los Angeles Rebellion*. Chicago: Third World Press, 1993.

Markovitz, Jonathan. *Legacies of Lynching: Racial Violence and Memory*. Minneapolis: University of Minnesota Press, 2004.

National Advisory Commission on Civil Disorders [Kerner Commission]. *Report*. New York: Bantam, 1968.

Pinkney, Alphonso. *Lest We Forget: White Hate Crimes, Howard Beach, and Other Racial Atrocities*. Chicago: Third World Press, 1994.

Porter, Bruce, and Marvin Dunn. *The Miami Riot of 1980: Crossing the Bounds*. Lexington, Mass.: D. C. Heath, 1984.

Raper, Arthur. *The Tragedy of Lynching*. New York: Arno Press, 1969.

Ridgeway, James. *Blood in the Face: The Ku Klux Klan, Aryan Nations, Nazi Skinheads, and the Rise of a New White Culture*. Rev. ed. New York: Thunder's Mouth Press, 1995.

Ruiz, Jim. *The Black Hood of the Ku Klux Klan*. San Francisco: Austin & Winfield, 1998.

Sears, David O., and John B. McConahay. *The Politics of Violence: The New Urban Blacks and the Watts Riot*. Boston: Houghton Mifflin, 1973.

Smith, John David, ed. *Disfranchisement Proposals and the Ku Klux Klan*. New York: Garland, 1993.

Southern Poverty Law Center, comp. *The Ku Klux Klan: A History of Racism and Violence*. 4th ed. Montgomery, Ala.: Klanwatch, 1991.

Stanton, Bill. *Klanwatch: Bringing the Ku Klux Klan to Justice*. New York: Weidenfeld, 1991.

Tolnay, Stewart E., and E. M. Beck. *A Festival of Violence: An Analysis of Southern Lynchings, 1882-1930*. Urbana: University of Illinois Press, 1995.

Trelease, Allen W. *White Terror: The Ku Klux Klan Conspiracy and the Southern Reconstruction*. Baton Rouge: Louisiana State University Press, 1995.

Turner, John. *The Ku Klux Klan: A History of Racism and Violence*. Montgomery, Ala.: Southern Poverty Law Center, 1982.

Wade, Wyn Craig. *The Fiery Cross: The Ku Klux Klan in America*. New York: Simon & Schuster, 1987.

Zangrando, Robert. *The NAACP Crusade Against Lynching, 1909- 1950*. Philadelphia: Temple University Press, 1980.

HOUSING

Bullard, Charles, J. Eugene Grigsby III, and Charles Lee, eds. *Residential Apartheid: The American Legacy*. Los Angeles: UCLA Center for Afro-American Studies, 1994.

Ellen, Ingrid Gould. *Sharing America's Neighborhoods: The Prospects for Stable Racial Integration*. Cambridge, Mass.: Harvard University Press, 2000.

Haar, Charles M. *Suburbs Under Siege: Race, Space, and Audacious Judges*. Princeton, N.J.: Princeton University Press, 1996.

Harrison, M. L. *Housing, "Race," Social Policy, and Empowerment*. Brookfield: Avebury, 1995.

Kirp, David L., John Dwyer, and Larry Rosenthal. *Our Town: Race, Housing, and the Soul of Suburbia*. New Brunswick, N.J.: Rutgers University Press, 1996.

Kushner, James A. *Fair Housing: Discrimination in Real Estate, Community Development, and Revitalization*. New York: McGraw- Hill, 1983.

Metcalf, Georg. *Fair Housing Comes of Age*. New York: Greenwood Press, 1988.

Schwemm, Robert G., ed. *The Fair Housing Act After Twenty Years*. New Haven, Conn.: Yale Law School, 1989.

Yinger, John. *Closed Doors, Opportunities Lost: The Continuing Costs of Housing Discrimination*. New York: Russell Sage Foundation, 1995.

MARTIN LUTHER KING, JR.

Ansbro, John J. *Martin Luther King, Jr.: The Making of a Mind*. Maryknoll, N.Y.: Orbis Books, 1982.

Branch, Taylor. *Parting the Waters: America in the King Years, 1954- 1963*. New York: Simon & Schuster, 1988.

_____. *Pillar of Fire: America in the King Years, 1963-65*.
New York: Simon & Schuster, 1998.

Burns, Stewart. *To the Mountaintop: Martin Luther King, Jr.'s Sacred Mission to Save America, 1955- 1968*. New York: Harper San- Francisco, 2004.

Clark, Kenneth B., ed. *The Negro Protest: James Baldwin, Malcolm X, Martin Luther King Talk with Kenneth B. Clark*. Boston: Beacon Press, 1963.

Colaiaco, James A. *Martin Luther King, Jr.: Apostle of Militant Nonviolence*. New York: St. Martin's Press, 1988.

Fairclough, Adam. *Martin Luther King, Jr.* Athens: University of Georgia Press, 1990.

_____. *To Redeem the Soul of America: The Southern Christian Leadership Conference and Martin Luther King, Jr.* Athens: University of Georgia Press, 1987.

Frady, Marshall. *Martin Luther King, Jr.* New York: Penguin Group, 2002.

Frank, Gerold. *An American Death: The True Story of the Assassination of Dr. Martin Luther King, Jr.* Garden City, N.Y.: Doubleday, 1972.

Garrow, David J. *Bearing the Cross: Martin Luther King, Jr., and the Southern Christian Leadership Conference*. New York: William Morrow, 1986.

_____. *Protest at Selma: Martin Luther King, Jr., and the Voting Rights Act of 1965*. New Haven, Conn.: Yale University Press, 1978.

Hanigan, James P. *Martin Luther King, Jr., and the Foundations of Nonviolence*. Lanham, Md.: University Press of America, 1984.

Hansen, Drew D. *The Dream: Martin Luther King, Jr., and the Speech That Inspired a Nation*. New York: Ecco, 2003.

King, Martin Luther, Jr. *Stride Toward Freedom: The Montgomery Story*. New York: Harper & Row, 1958.

Kotz, Nick. *Judgment Days: Lyndon Baines Johnson, Martin Luther King, Jr., and the Laws That Changed America*. Boston: Houghton Mifflin, 2005.

Lewis, David L. *King: A Critical Biography*. New York: Praeger, 1970.

Ling, Peter J. *Martin Luther King, Jr.* New York: Routledge, 2002.

McPhee, Penelope, and Flip Schulke. *King Remembered*. New York: Pocket Books, 1986.

Oates, Stephen B. *Let the Trumpet Sound: The Life of Martin Luther King, Jr.* New York: Harper & Row, 1982.

Peake, Thomas R. *Keeping the Dream Alive: A History of the Southern Christian Leadership Conference from King to the Nineteen- Eighties*. New York: Peter Lang, 1987.

Sunnemark, Fredrik. *Ring Out Freedom! The Voice of Martin Luther King, Jr., and the Making of the Civil Rights Movement*. Bloomington: Indiana University Press, 2004.

Ward, Brian, and Tony Badger. *The Making of Martin Luther King and the Civil Rights Movement*. New York: New York University Press, 1996.

THE MEDIA

Bogle, Donald. *Blacks in American Films and Television*. New York: Garland Publishing, 1988.

_____. *Bright Boulevards, Bold Dreams: The Story of Black Hollywood*. New York: One World Ballantine Books, 2005.

_____. *Primetime Blues: African Americans on Network Television*. New York: Farrar, Straus and Giroux, 2001.

_____. *Toms, Coons, Mulattoes, Mammies, and Bucks*. New York: Continuum, 1992.

Campbell, Christopher P. *Race, Myth, and the News.* Thousand Oaks, Calif.: Sage Publications, 1995.

Center for Integration and Improvement of Journalism. *News Watch: A Critical Look at People of Color.* San Francisco: San Francisco State University Press, 1994.

Chideya, Farai. *Don't Believe the Hype: Fighting Cultural Misinformation About African Americans.* New York: Plume, 1995.

Cripps, Thomas. *Slow Fade to Black: The Negro in American Film, 1900-1942.* New York: Oxford University Press, 1993.

_____. *Making Movies Black: The Hollywood Message Movie from World War II to the Civil Rights Era.* New York: Oxford University Press, 1993.

Dennis, Everette E., and Edward C. Pease, eds. *The Media in Black and White.* New Brunswick, N.J.: Transaction, 1997.

Gabriel, John. *Whitewash: Racialized Politics and the Media.* New York: Routledge, 1998.

Gates, Henry Louis, Jr. *The Signifying Monkey: A Theory of Afro-American Literary Criticism.* New York: Oxford University Press, 1988.

Gershoni, Yekutiel. *Africans on African-Americans: The Creation and Uses of an African-American Myth.* New York: New York University Press, 1997.

Hill, George, Lorraine Raglin, and Chas Floyd Johnson. *Black Women in Television.* New York: Garland Publishing, 1990.

Hutchinson, Janis Faye, ed. *Cultural Portrayals of African Americans: Creating an Ethnic/Racial Identity.* Westport, Conn.: Bergin & Garvey, 1997.

Lhamon, W. T., Jr. *Raising Cain: Blackface Performance from Jim Crow to Hip Hop.* Cambridge, England: Cambridge University Press, 1998.

Lusane, Clarence. *Race in the Global Era: African Americans at the Millennium.* Boston: South End Press, 1997.

Mintz, Sidney W., and Richard Price. *The Birth of African-American Culture.* Boston: Beacon Press, 1992.

Rocchio, Vincent F. *Reel Racism: Confronting Hollywood's Construction of Afro-American Culture.* Boulder, Colo.: Westview Press, 2000.

Ross, Karen. *Black and White Media: Black Images in Popular Film and Television.* Cambridge, Mass.: Polity Press, 1996.

Torres, Sasha, ed. *Living Color: Race and Television in the United States.* Durham, N.C.: Duke University Press, 1998.

Tyler, Bruce Michael. *From Harlem to Hollywood: The Struggle for Racial and Cultural Democracy, 1920-1943.* New York: Garland, 1992.

MILITARY

Bogart, Leo. *Social Research and Desegregation of the United States Army.* Chicago: Markham, 1969.

Brandt, Nat. *Harlem at War: The Black Experience in WWII.* Syracuse, N.Y.: Syracuse University Press, 1996.

Dalifiume, Richard. *Desegregation of the U.S. Armed Forces: Fighting on Two Fronts, 1939-1953.* Columbia: University of Missouri Press, 1969.

Mershon, Sherie, and Steven L. Schlossman. *Foxholes and Color Lines: Desegregating the U.S. Armed Forces.* Baltimore: Johns Hopkins University Press, 1998.

Moskos, Charles C. *All That We Can Be: Black Leadership and Racial Integration the Army Way.* New York: Basic Books, 1996.

Nalty, Bernard C. *Strength for the Fight: A History of Black Americans in the Military.* New York: Free Press, 1986.

Stillman, Richard. *Integraton of the Negro in the U.S. Armed Forces.* New York: Frederick A. Praeger, 1968.

U.S. Department of Defense. Office of the Deputy Assistant Secretary of Defense for Civilian Personnel Policy/Equal Opportunity. *Black Americans in Defense of Our Nation.* Washington, D.C.: Government Printing Office, 1991.

POLITICS

Conti, Joseph G., and Brad Stetson. *Challenging the Civil Rights Establishment: Profiles of a New Black Vanguard.* Westport, Conn.: Praeger, 1993.

Cross, Theodore. *The Black Power Imperative: Racial Inequality and the Politics of Nonviolence.* New York: Faulkner, 1984.

Dawson, Michael C. *Behind the Mule: Race and Class in African-American Politics.* Princeton, N.J.: Princeton University Press, 1994.

Faryna, Stan, Brad Stetson, and Joseph G. Conti, eds. *Black and Right: The New Bold Voice of Black Conservatives in America.* Westport, Conn.: Greenwood, 1997.

Gilroy, Paul, and Houston A. Baker. *There Ain't No Black in the Union Jack: The Cultural Politics of Race and Nation.* Chicago: Chicago University Press, 1991.

Ginzberg, Eli, and Alfred S. Eichner. *Troublesome Presence: Democracy and Black Americans*. New Brunswick, N.J.: Transaction, 1993.

Hahn, Steven. *A Nation Under Our Feet: Black Political Struggles in the Rural South, from Slavery to the Great Migration*. Cambridge, Mass.: Belknap Press of Harvard University Press, 2003.

Hine, Darlene Clark. *Black Victory: The Rise and Fall of the White Primary in Texas*. Millwood, N.Y.: KTO Press, 1979.

Jewell, K. Sue. *From Mammy to Miss America and Beyond: Cultural Images and the Shaping of U.S. Social Policy*. New York: Routledge, 1993.

Lawson, Steven F. *Black Ballots: Voting Rights in the South, 1944- 1969*. New York: Columbia University Press, 1976.

_____. *In Pursuit of Power: Southern Blacks and Electoral Politics, 1965-1982*. New York: Columbia University Press, 1985.

McKissick, Floyd B. *Three-fifths of a Man*. New York: Macmillan, 1969.

Marable, Manning. *Beyond Black and White: Transforming African- American Politics*. New York: Verso, 1995.

_____. *Race, Reform, and Rebellion: The Second Reconstruction in Black America, 1945-1991*. Jackson: University Press of Mississippi, 1991.

Merelman, Richard M. *Representing Black Culture: Racial Conflict and Cultural Politics in the United States*. New York: Routledge, 1995.

Norton, Philip. *Black Nationalism in America*. Hull, Humberside, England: Department of Politics, University of Hull, 1983.

Ogbar, Jeffrey O. G. *Black Power: Radical Politics and African American Identity*. Baltimore: Johns Hopkins University Press, 2004.

Orfield, Gary, and Carol Ashkinaze. *The Closing Door: Conservative Policy and Black Opportunity*. Chicago: University of Chicago Press, 1991.

Perkins, Joseph, ed. *A Conservative Agenda for Black Americans*. Washington, D.C.: Heritage Foundation, 1990.

Persons, Georgia A., ed. *Dilemmas of Black Politics: Issues of Leadership and Strategy*. New York: HarperCollins, 1993.

Reed, Adolph L. *The Jesse Jackson Phenomenon: The Crisis of Purpose in Afro-American Politics*. New Haven, Conn.: Yale University Press, 1986.

Singh, Robert. *The Farrakhan Phenomenon: Race, Reaction, and the Paranoid Style in American Politics*. Washington, D.C.: Georgetown University Press, 1997.

Smith, T. Alexander, and Lenahan O'Connell. *Black Anxiety, White Guilt, and the Politics of Status Frustration*. Westport, Conn.: Praeger, 1997.

Sonenshein, Raphael J. *Politics in Black and White: Race and Power in Los Angeles*. Princeton, N.J.: Princeton University Press, 1993.

Swain, Carol M. *Black Faces, Black Interests: The Representation of African Americans in Congress*. Cambridge, Mass.: Harvard University Press, 1993.

Tate, Katherine. *From Protest to Politics: The New Black Voters in American Elections*. Cambridge, Mass.: Harvard University Press, 1994.

Walton, Hanes, Jr. *Black Politics*. Philadelphia: J. B. Lippincott, 1972.

RELIGION AND THE BLACK CHURCH

Allen, Richard. *The Life, Experience, and Gospel Labors of the Right Reverent Richard Allen*. 1833. Reprint. Nashville, Tenn.: Abingdon Press, 1983.

Angell, Stephen W., ed., and Anthony B. Pinn. *Social Protest Thought in the African Methodist Episcopal Church, 1862-1939*.

Knoxville: University of Tennessee Press, 2000.

Campbell, James T. *Songs of Zion: The African Methodist Episcopal Church in the United States and South Africa*. New York: Oxford University Press, 1995.

Chireau, Yvonne, and Nathaniel Deutsch, eds. *Black Zion: African American Religious Encounters with Judaism*. New York: Oxford University Press, 2000.

Cone, James H. *Black Theology and Black Power*. New York: Seabury Press, 1969.

_____. *A Black Theology of Liberation*. 20th anniversary ed. Maryknoll, N.Y.: Orbis Books, 1990.

Dodson, Jualynne E. *Engendering Church: Women, Power, and the AME Church*. Lanham, Md.: Rowman & Littlefield, 2002.

Evans, James H., Jr. *Spiritual Empowerment in Afro-American Literature*. Lewiston, N.Y.: Edwin Mellen, 1987.

Findlay, James F., Jr. *Church People in the Struggle: The National Council of Churches and the Black Freedom Movement, 1950-1970*.

New York: Oxford University Press, 1993.

Fitts, LeRoy. *A History of Black Baptists*. Nashville, Tenn.: Broadman Press, 1985.

Frazier, E. Franklin, and C. Eric Lincoln. *The Negro Church in America: The Black Church Since Frazier*. New York: Schocken Books, 1974.

George, Carol V. R. *Segregated Sabbaths: Richard Allen and the Rise of Independent Black Churches, 1760-1840*. New York: Oxford University Press, 1973.

Harvey, Paul. *Redeeming the South: Religious Cultures and Racial Identities Among Southern Baptists, 1865-1925*. New York: Oxford University Press, 1997.

Lee, Martha F. *The Nation of Islam: An American Millenarian Movement*. Lewiston, N.Y.: Edwin Mellen Press, 1988.

Lincoln, C. Eric. *The Black Muslims in America*. Rev. ed. Boston: Beacon Press, 1973.

Lincoln, C. Eric, and Lawrence H. Mamiya. *The Black Church in the African-American Experience*. Durham, N.C.: Duke University Press, 1990.

Little, Lawrence S. *Disciples of Liberty: The African Methodist Episcopal Church in the Age of Imperialism, 1884-1916*. Knoxville: University of Tennessee Press, 2000.

Luker, Ralph E. *The Social Gospel in Black and White: American Racial Reform, 1885-1912*. Chapel Hill: University of North Carolina Press, 1991.

Marsh, Clifton E. *From Black Muslims to Muslims: The Transition from Separatism to Islam, 1930-1980*. Metuchen, N.J.: Scarecrow Press, 1984.

Mitchell, Henry H. *Black Church Beginnings: The Long-Hidden Realities of the First Years*. Grand Rapids, Mich.: W. B. Eerdmans, 2004.

Muhammad, Elijah. *The Supreme Wisdom*. 2 vols. Brooklyn: Temple of Islam, 1957.

Mukenge, Ida Rousseau. *The Black Church in Urban America*. Lanham, Md.: University Press of America, 1983.

Nelson, Timothy J. *Every Time I Feel the Spirit: Religious Experience and Ritual in an African American Church*. New York: New York University Press, 2005.

Paris, Peter J. *The Social Teaching of the Black Churches*. Philadelphia: Fortress Press, 1985.

Phillips, C. H. *The History of the Colored Methodist Episcopal Church in America*. 1898. Reprint. New York: Arno Press, 1972.

Pinn, Anthony B. *The Black Church in the Post-Civil Rights Era*. Maryknoll, N.Y.: Orbis Books, 2002.

Sernett, Milton C. *Afro-American Religious History: A Documentary Witness*. Durham, N.C.: Duke University Press, 1985.

Seymour, Robert E., Jr. *"Whites Only": A Pastor's Retrospective on Signs of the New South*. Valley Forge, Pa.: Judson Press, 1991.

Smith, Theophus H. *Conjuring Culture: Biblical Formations of Black America*. New York: Oxford University Press, 1994.

Turner, Richard Brent. *Islam in the African American Experience*. Bloomington: Indiana University Press, 1997.

Wesley, Charles. *Richard Allen: Apostle of Freedom*. Washington, D.C.: Associated Publishers, 1935.

White, Vibert L., Jr. *Inside the Nation of Islam: A Historical and Personal Testimony by a Black Muslim*. Gainesville: University Press of Florida, 2001.

Williams, Juan, and Quinton Dixie. *This Far by Faith: Stories from the African-American Religious Experience*. New York: William Morrow, 2003.

Wilmore, Gayraud S., ed. *African American Religious Studies: An Interdisciplinary Anthology*. Durham, N.C.: Duke University Press, 1989.

_____. *Black Religion and Black Radicalism*. 3d ed. Rev. and enlarged. Maryknoll, N.Y.: Orbis Books, 1998.

SLAVERY

Abbott, Richard H. *Cotton and Capital: Boston Businessmen and Antislavery Reform, 1854-1868*. Amherst: University of Massachusetts Press, 1991.

Angle, Paul M., ed. *Created Equal? The Complete Lincoln-Douglas Debates of 1858*. Chicago: University of Chicago Press, 1958.

Aptheker, Herbert. *American Negro Slave Revolts*. 1943. Rev. ed. New York: Columbia University Press, 1969.

Ball, Edward. *Slaves in the Family*. New York: Farrar, Straus & Giroux, 1998.

Barber, John Warner. *A History of the Amistad Captives*. New York: Arno Press, 1969.

Barnes, Gilbert Hobbs. *The Antislavery Impulse: 1830-1844*. New York: Harcourt, Brace & World, 1964.

Bender, Thomas, ed. *The Antislavery Debate: Capitalism and Abolitionism as a Problem in Historical Interpretation*. Berkeley: University of California Press, 1992.

Berlin, Ira. *Many Thousands Gone: The First Two Centuries of Slavery in North America*. Cambridge, Mass.: Belknap Press, 1998.

Berlin, Ira, et al. *Slaves No More: Three Essays on Emancipation and the Civil War*. Cambridge, England: Cambridge University Press, 1992.

Blackburn, Robin. *The Overthrow of Colonial Slavery, 1776-1848.*
New York: Verso, 1988.

Blassingame, John W. *The Slave Community: Plantation Life in the Antebellum South.* New York: Oxford University Press, 1972.

Blassingame, John W., and John R. McKivigan, eds. *The Frederick Douglass Papers.* Series 1, *Speeches, Debates, and Interviews.* Vol. 3, *1855-1863.* New Haven, Conn.: Yale University Press, 1991.

Blight, David W., ed. *Passages to Freedom: The Underground Railroad in History and Memory.* Washington, D.C.: Smithsonian Books in association with the National Underground Railroad Freedom Center, Cincinnati, Ohio, 2004.

Bontemps, Arna, ed. *Great Slave Narratives.* Boston: Beacon Press, 1969.

Boskin, Joseph. *Into Slavery: Racial Decisions in the Virginia Colony.* Philadelphia: J. B. Lippincott, 1976.

Boyer, Richard O. *The Legend of John Brown: A Biography and a History.* New York: Alfred A. Knopf, 1972.

Buckmaster, Henrietta. *Let My People Go: The Story of the Underground Railroad and the Growth of the Abolition Movement.* Boston: Beacon Press, 1941.

Campbell, Stanley. *The Slave Catchers: Enforcement of the Fugitive Slave Law, 1850-1860.* Chapel Hill: University of North Carolina Press, 1970.

Catterall, Helen T., ed. *Judicial Cases Concerning American Slavery and the Negro.* 5 vols. New York: Octagon Books, 1968.

Curtin, Philip D. *The Atlantic Slave Trade.* Madison: University of Wisconsin Press, 1969.

Daniel, Pete. *The Shadow of Slavery: Peonage in the South, 1901-1969.* Urbana: University of Illinois Press, 1972.

Davis, David Brion. *The Problem of Slavery in the Age of Revolution, 1770-1823.* Ithaca, N.Y.: Cornell University Press, 1975.

_____. *The Problem of Slavery in Western Culture.* Ithaca, N.Y.: Cornell University Press, 1966.

_____. *Slavery and Human Progress.* New York: Oxford University Press, 1984.

Duberman, Martin, ed. *The Antislavery Vanguard: New Essays on the Abolitionists.* Princeton, N.J.: Princeton University Press, 1965.

Elkins, Stanley M. *Slavery: A Problem in American Institutional and Intellectual Life.* Chicago: University of Chicago Press, 1959.

Eltis, David, and James Walvin, eds. *The Abolition of the Atlantic Slave Trade: Origins and Effects in Europe, Africa, and the Americas.* Madison: University of Wisconsin Press, 1981.

Faust, Drew Glipin. *The Ideology of Slavery: Proslavery Thought in the Antebellum South, 1830-1860.* Baton Rouge: Louisiana State University Press, 1981.

Filler, Louis. *The Crusade Against Slavery, 1830-1860.* New York: Harper & Row, 1960.

Finkelman, Paul, ed. *Slavery and the Founders: Race and Liberty in the Age of Jefferson.* Armonk, N.Y.: M. E. Sharpe, 1996.

Finley, Moses I. *Ancient Slavery and Modern Ideology.* New York: Viking Press, 1980.

Fogel, Robert. *Without Consent or Contract: The Rise and Fall of American Slavery.* New York: W. W. Norton, 1989.

Franklin, Raymond S. *Shadows of Race and Class.* Minneapolis: University of Minnesota Press, 1991.

Friedman, Lawrence J. *Gregarious Saints: Self and Community in American Abolitionism, 1830-1870.* New York: Cambridge University Press, 1982.

Frost, J. William, ed. *The Quaker Origins of Antislavery.* Norwood, Pa.: Norwood Editions, 1980.

Gara, Larry. *The Liberty Line: The Legend of the Underground Railroad.* Lexington: University of Kentucky Press, 1961.

Genovese, Eugene D. *Roll, Jordan, Roll: The World the Slaves Made.* New York: Pantheon Books, 1974.

_____. *The Slaveholders' Dilemma: Freedom and Progress in Southern Conservative Thought, 1820-1860.* Columbia: University of South Carolina Press, 1992.

Giddings, Joshua R. *The Exiles of Florida: Or, The Crimes Committed by Our Government Against the Maroons Who Fled from South Carolina and Other Slave States, Seeking Protection Under Spanish Laws.* 1858. Reprint. Gainesville: University of Florida Press, 1964.

Goldwin, Robert A., and Art Kaufman. *Slavery and Its Consequences: The Constitution, Equality, and Race.* Washington, D.C.: American Enterprise Institute Press, 1988.

Goodheart, Lawrence, Richard D. Brown, and Stephen Rabe, eds. *Slavery in American Society.* 3d ed. Lexington, Mass.: Heath, 1993.

Goodman, Paul. *Of One Blood: Abolitionism and the Origins of Racial Equality.* Berkeley: University of California Press, 1998.

Gordon-Reed, Annette, et al. *Slavery and the American South: Essays and Commentaries*. Edited by Winthrop D. Jordan. Jackson: University Press of Mississippi, 2003.

Gutman, Herbert. *The Black Family in Slavery and Freedom, 1750-1925*. New York: Pantheon, 1976.

Hagedorn, Ann. *Beyond the River: The Untold Story of the Heroes of the Underground Railroad*. New York: Simon & Schuster, 2002.

Harris, Marvin. *Patterns of Race Relations in America*. New York: Walker, 1964.

Harrold, Stanley. *The Rise of Aggressive Abolitionism: Addresses to the Slaves*. Lexington: University Press of Kentucky, 2004.

Hoetink, H. *Slavery and Race Relations in the Americas: Notes on Their Nature and Nexus*. New York: Harper & Row, 1973.

Holzer, Harold, ed. *The Lincoln-Douglas Debates: The First Complete, Unexpurgated Text*. New York: HarperCollins, 1993.

Horowitz, David. *Uncivil Wars: The Controversy over Reparations for Slavery*. San Francisco: Encounter Books, 2002.

Horton, James Oliver, and Lois E. Horton. *Slavery and the Making of America*. New York: Oxford University Press, 2005.

Howard, Warren S. *American Slavers and the Federal Law: 1837-1862*. Berkeley: University of California Press, 1963.

Huggins, Nathan Irvin. *Slave and Citizen: The Life of Frederick Douglass*. Boston: Little, Brown, 1980.

James, Sydney V. *A People Among Peoples: Quaker Benevolence in Eighteenth Century America*. Cambridge, Mass.: Harvard University Press, 1963.

Jeffrey, Julie Roy. *The Great Silent Army of Abolitionism: Ordinary Women in the Antislavery Movement*. Chapel Hill: University of North Carolina Press, 1998.

Jenkins, William S. *Pro-Slavery Thought in the Old South*. Chapel Hill: University of North Carolina Press, 1935.

Johnson, Walter. *Soul by Soul: Life Inside the Antebellum Slave Market*. Cambridge, Mass.: Harvard University Press, 1999.

Kolchin, Peter. *American Slavery: 1619-1877*. New York: Hill & Wang, 1993.

Kraditor, Aileen S. *Means and Ends in American Abolitionism: Garrison and His Critics on Strategy and Tactics, 1834-1850*. New York: Vintage Books, 1970.

Kraut, Alan M., ed. *Crusaders and Compromisers: Essays on the Relationship of the Antislavery Struggle to the Antebellum Party System*. Westport, Conn.: Greenwood Press, 1983.

Levine, Alan J. *Race Relations Within Western Expansion*. Westport, Conn.: Praeger, 1996.

Litwack, Leon F. *Been in the Storm So Long: The Aftermath of Slavery*. New York: Alfred A. Knopf, 1979.

_____. *North of Slavery: The Negro in the Free States: 1790-1860*. Chicago: University of Chicago Press, 1961.

McGary, Howard, and Bill E. Lawson. *Between Slavery and Freedom: Philosophy and American Slavery*. Bloomington: Indiana University Press, 1992.

McKivigan, John R. *The War Against Proslavery Religion: Abolitionism and the Northern Churches, 1830-1865*. Ithaca, N.Y.: Cornell University Press, 1984.

MacLeod, Duncan J. *Slavery, Race, and the American Revolution*. London: Cambridge University Press, 1974.

McManus, Edgar J. *A History of Negro Slavery in New York*. Syracuse, N.Y.: Syracuse University Press, 1966.

Martin, Christopher. *The "Amistad" Affair*. New York: Abelard-Schuman, 1970.

Martin, Waldo E. *The Mind of Frederick Douglass*. Chapel Hill: University of North Carolina Press, 1984.

Mayer, Henry. *All on Fire: William Lloyd Garrison and the Abolition of Slavery*. New York: St. Martin's Press, 1998.

Melish, Joanne Pope. *Disowning Slavery: Gradual Emancipation and "Race" in New England, 1780-1860*. Ithaca, N.Y.: Cornell University Press, 1998.

Meltzer, Milton, ed. *Frederick Douglass, in His Own Words*. San Diego, Calif.: Harcourt, Brace, 1995.

Merrill, Walter M. *Against Wind and Tide: A Biography of William Lloyd Garrison*. Cambridge, Mass.: Harvard University Press, 1963.

Morgan, Edmund S. *American Slavery, American Freedom: The Ordeal of Colonial Virginia*. New York: W. W. Norton, 1975.

Morris, Thomas D. *Free Men All: The Personal Liberty Laws of the North, 1780-1861*. Baltimore: Johns Hopkins University Press, 1974.

Mullin, Michael. *Africa in America: Slave Acculturation and Resistance in the American South and the British Caribbean, 1736-1831*. Urbana: University of Illinois Press, 1992.

Newman, Richard S. *The Transformation of American Abolitionism: Fighting Slavery in the Early Republic*. Chapel Hill: University of North Carolina Press, 2002.

Nye, Russel B. *William Lloyd Garrison and the Humanitarian Reformers*. Boston: Little, Brown, 1955.

Oakes, James. *The Ruling Race: A History of American Slaveholders*. New York: Alfred A. Knopf, 1982.

————. *Slavery and Freedom: An Interpretation of the Old South*. New York: Alfred A. Knopf, 1990.

Owen, Robert Dale. *The Wrong of Slavery, the Right of Emancipation, and the Future of the African Race in the United States*. Philadelphia: J. B. Lippincott, 1864.

Owens, William A. *Black Mutiny: The Revolt on the Schooner "Amistad."* Philadelphia: Pilgrim Press, 1968.

Patterson, Orlando. *Slavery and Social Death: A Comparative Study*. Cambridge, Mass.: Harvard University Press, 1982.

————. *The Sociology of Slavery*. Rutherford, N.J.: Fairleigh Dickinson University Press, 1975.

Perry, Lewis, and Michael Fellman, eds. *Antislavery Reconsidered: New Perspectives on the Abolitionists*. Baton Rouge: Louisiana State University Press, 1979.

Peterson, Merrill D. *John Brown: The Legend Revisited*. Charlottesville: University of Virginia Press, 2002.

Phillips, Ulrich B. *American Negro Slavery*. Baton Rouge: Louisiana State University Press, 1966.

Phillips, William D. *Slavery from Roman Times to the Early Transatlantic Trade*. Minneapolis: University of Minnesota Press, 1985.

Quarles, Benjamin. *Black Abolitionists*. New York: Oxford University Press, 1969.

Rawley, James A. *The Transatlantic Slave Trade: A History*. New York: W. W. Norton, 1981.

Reynolds, David S. *John Brown, Abolitionist: The Man Who Killed Slavery, Sparked the Civil War, and Seeded Civil Rights*. New York: Alfred A. Knopf, 2005.

Richards, Leonard L. *The Slave Power: The Free North and Southern Domination, 1780-1860*. Baton Rouge: Louisiana State University Press, 2000.

Rogers, William B. *"We Are All Together Now": Frederick Douglass, William Lloyd Garrison, and the Prophetic Tradition*. New York: Garland, 1995.

Schwartz, Philip J. *Twice Condemned: Slaves and the Criminal Laws of Virginia, 1705-1865*. Baton Rouge: Louisiana State University Press, 1988.

Shaw, Robert B. *A Legal History of Slavery in the United States*. Potsdam, N.Y.: Northern Press, 1991.

Siebert, Wilbur H. *The Underground Railroad from Slavery to Freedom*. 1898. Reprint. New York: Arno Press, 1968.

Smith, John D. *Black Slavery in the Americas: An Interdisciplinary Bibliography, 1865-1980*. 2 vols. Westport, Conn.: Greenwood Press, 1982.

Sorin, Gerald. *Abolitionism: A New Perspective*. New York: Praeger, 1972.

Stampp, Kenneth M. *The Peculiar Institution: Slavery in the Ante- Bellum South*. New York: Alfred A. Knopf, 1956.

Stewart, James Brewer. *Holy Warriors: The Abolitionists and American Slavery*. New York: Hill & Wang, 1976.

————. *William Lloyd Garrison and the Challenge of Emancipation*. Arlington Heights, Ill.: Harlan Davidson, 1992.

Still, William. *The Underground Railroad*. 1872. Reprint. Chicago: Johnson, 1972.

Stuckey, Sterling. *Slave Culture*. New York: Oxford University Press, 1987.

Styron, William. *Confessions of Nat Turner*. New York: Random House, 1967.

Thomas, John L. *The Liberator: William Lloyd Garrison, a Biography*. Boston: Little, Brown, 1963.

Tise, Larry E. *Proslavery: A History of the Defense of Slavery in America, 1701-1840*. Athens: University of Georgia Press, 1987.

Tushnet, Mark V. *The American Law of Slavery, 1810-1860: Considerations of Humanity and Interest*. Princeton, N.J.: Princeton University Press, 1981.

Washington, Booker T. *Up from Slavery*. 1901. Reprint. New York: Gramercy Books, 1993.

Watson, Alan. *Slave Law in the Americas*. Athens: University of Georgia Press, 1989.

White, Shane. *Somewhat More Independent: The End of Slavery in New York City, 1770-1810*. Athens: University of Georgia Press, 1991.

Wilson, Carol. *Freedom at Risk: The Kidnapping of Free Blacks in America, 1780-1865*. Lexington: University Press of Kentucky, 1994.

Winbush, Raymond A., ed. *Should America Pay? Slavery and the Raging Debate on Reparations*. New York: Amistad, 2003.

Woodward, C. Vann. *American Counterpoint: Slavery and Racism in the North-South Dialogue*. Boston: Little, Brown, 1971.

Zilversmit, Arthur. *The First Emancipation: The Abolition of Slavery in the North*. Chicago: University of Chicago Press, 1967.

THE SOUTH AND SEGREGATION

Baer, Hans A., and Yvonne Jones, eds. *African Americans in the South: Issues of Race, Class, and Gender*. Athens: University of Georgia Press, 1992.

Bartley, Numan V. *The New South: 1945-1980*. Baton Rouge: Louisiana State University Press, 1995.

Bayor, Ronald H. *Race and the Shaping of Twentieth-Century Atlanta*. Chapel Hill: University of North Carolina Press, 1996.

Clinton, Catherine. *The Plantation Mistress: Woman's World in the Old South*. New York: Pantheon Books, 1982.

Davis, Allison, Burleigh B. Gardner, and Mary R. Gardner. *Deep South: A Social Anthropological Study of Caste and Class*. Chicago: University of Chicago Press, 1941.

Dollard, John. *Caste and Class in a Southern Town*. New Haven, Conn.: Yale University Press, 1947.

Fossett, Mark A., and Therese Siebert. *Long Time Coming: Racial Inequality in the Nonmetropolitan South, 1940-1990*. Boulder, Colo.: Westview Press, 1997.

Fox-Genovese, Elizabeth. *Within the Plantation Household: Black and White Women of the Old South*. Chapel Hill: University of North Carolina Press, 1988.

Goldfield, David R. *Black, White, and Southern: Race Relations in Southern Culture, 1940 to the Present*. Baton Rouge: Louisiana State University Press, 1990.

_____. *Region, Race, and Cities: Interpreting the Urban South*. Baton Rouge: Louisiana State University Press, 1997.

Hale, Grace Elizabeth. *Making Whiteness: The Culture of Segregation in the South, 1890-1940*. New York: Pantheon, 1998.

McLaurin, Melton A. *Separate Pasts: Growing Up White in the Segregated South*. Athens: University of Georgia Press, 1987.

McMillen, Neil R. *Dark Journey: Black Mississippians in the Age of Jim Crow*. Urbana: University of Illinois Press, 1990.

Newby, I. A. *Jim Crow's Defense*. Baton Rouge: Louisiana State University Press, 1965.

Odum, Howard W. *Race and Rumors of Race: The American South in the Early Forties*. Baltimore: Johns Hopkins University Press, 1997.

Packard, Jerrold M. *American Nightmare: The History of Jim Crow*. New York: St. Martin's Press, 2002.

Perman, Michael. *Struggle for Mastery: Disfranchisement in the South, 1888-1908*. Chapel Hill: University of North Carolina Press, 2001.

Stokes, Melvyn, and Rick Halpern, eds. *Race and Class in the American South Since 1890*. Providence, R.I.: Berg, 1994.

Williamson, Joel. *A Rage for Order: Black-White Relations in the American South Since Emancipation*. New York: Oxford University Press, 1986.

Wilson, Theodore B. *The Black Codes of the South*. Tuscaloosa: University of Alabama Press, 1965.

Woods, Jeff. *Black Struggle, Red Scare: Segregation and Anti-communism in the South, 1948-1968*. Baton Rouge: Louisiana State University Press, 2003.

Woodward, C. Vann. *The Strange Career of Jim Crow*. Afterword by William S. McFeely. New York: Oxford University Press, 2002.

Category Index

SUBJECT INDEX

A

Aaron, Hank, 568–570
Abbott, Robert S., 23, 283
Abelman v. Booth, 76
Abernathy, Ralph David, 402–404, 512
Abolitionist Movement, 71–72, 160
Abrahams, Peter, 295
"Act for Gradual Abolition of Slavery," 109
Adams, John Quincy, 142
Adams, Samuel, 111
Adarand Constructors v. Peña, 645
Affirmative action, 489–491
Affirmative Discrimination (Glazer), 36
African American Baptist Church, 105–107
African American churches, bombings of, 420–422
The African American Education Data Book, 30
African-American Holiness Pentecostal Movement, 246–248
The African Intelligencer, 174
African Liberation Day, 446
African Methodist Episcopal (AME) Church, 5
Afrocentrism, 622
Agricultural Adjustment Act (AAA), 8
Agriculture
    black farmers after slavery, 7–8
    decline of African American, 9
    federal government and, 9
    Great Depression and, 8–9
    Great Migration, 8
Aiello, Danny, 625

Aiken, George L., 78
Ailey, Alvin, 410–412
"Ain't I a Woman?", 157
Akron Woman's Rights Convention, 155–158
Albany Movement, 435–436
Albemarle Paper Company v. Moody, 573
Alcis, Carlos, 683
Alexander, Will, 45
Alexander Nevsky, 288
Alexander v. Holmes County Board of Education, 550
Ali, Muhammad, 12, 78, 459–460, 571–573. *See also* Clay, Cassius
Alien Act, 292
Allen, Raymond, 682
Allen, Richard, 114–115, 164
Allen, Thomas, 685
Allen, Walter, 79
Allen, Wendell, 682
All in the Family, 546–548
The All-Negro Hour, 46
All-volunteer force (AVF), 48–49
Alpha Kappa Alpha, 271
Alpha Phi Alpha, 271
"Alvin Ailey and Company," 410–412
American Anti-Slavery Society (AASS), 125, 135–138
The American Baptist, 253
American Broadcasting Company (ABC), 47
American Civil Liberties Union (ACLU), 291–293, 504
American Colonization Society (ACS), 130
American Indian Movement (AIM), 54

American Negro Labor Congress (ANLC), 305–306
American Psychological Association, 386
American Revolution, 104, 110
An American Tragedy (Dreiser), 15
Ames, Jessie Daniel, 45
AME Zion Book Concern, 45–46
AME Zion Church, 5
Amistad Slave Revolt, 140–142
Amnesty International, 454
Amos, 46
Anderson, Al, 575
Anderson, James Craig, 682
Anderson, Marian, 332–335
Anderson, Talmadge, 32
Anderson, Tanisha, 684
Annunzio, Frank, 589
Antelope, 141
Anti-lynching movement, 254
Anti-Slavery Bugle, 156
Antislavery Movement, 64–65
An Appeal to Caesar (Tourgée), 257
An Appeal to the Christian Women of the South (Grimké), 71
An Appeal to the Women of the Nominally Free States (Grimké), 71
Arafat, Yasser, 42
Are You Experienced?, 500–502
Arkwright, Sir Richard, 122
Armstrong, Lillian Hardin, 307
Armstrong, Louis, 281, 295, 307–309, 314
Armstrong, Samuel C., 29–30
Asbury, Francis, 117
Ashe, Arthur, 12
Ashley, Alonzo, 682